INDEX VERBORUM VALERIANUS

IOWA STUDIES IN CLASSICAL PHILOLOGY

Roy C. Flickinger, Editor
State University of Iowa

INDEX VERBORUM VALERIANUS

By
WILLIAM H. SCHULTE, M.A.
Professor of Latin and Greek
Columbia College

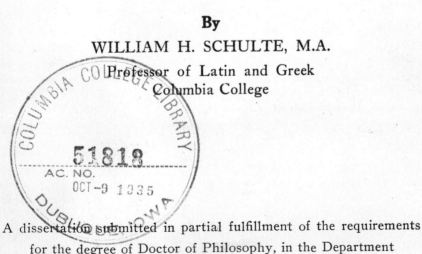
A dissertation submitted in partial fulfillment of the requirements
for the degree of Doctor of Philosophy, in the Department
of Classical Languages, in the Graduate College
of the State University of Iowa
June, 1931

Printed in the United States of America

by

THE MENNONITE PRESS

Scottdale, Pennsylvania

1935

Copies at $2.50 each may be obtained by addressing the author,

c/o Columbia College, Dubuque, Iowa

PARENTIBUS MEIS

INTRODUCTION

The present work is an *Index Verborum* to the poem of C. Valerius Flaccus.

An *Index Verborum* to an author lists partially in alphabetical, partially in formal order every word that is used by him in his literary work or works. It differs from the *Lexicon* which seeks to establish the specific meanings of words in their various appearances in an author. A *Concordance* lists alphabetically the words which appear in an author's work or works and cites the passages in which they occur.

The preparation of an *Index Verborum* or of a *Lexicon* supposes the understanding of an author and of his thought. The *Lexicon* cannot establish the definite meaning of a word in a certain line or paragraph unless the compiler of the *Lexicon* has clearly understood the meaning of the author. A simple illustration is the word *aequor*. In Valerius Flaccus VI, 30 the meaning of *aequor* is not "sea," but it signifies rather the "open field." Similarly the compiler of an *Index Verborum* must appreciate his author's thought in order to determine definitively a noun-case or verb-tense, e. g. in instances of the dative-ablative type where two analyses are possible. In Valerius Flaccus II, 16,

> *Metus ecce deum damnataque bello*
> *Pallene,*

deum is genitive (not accusative), and *bello* is either a dative or an ablative. Langen[1] in his commentary on this passage calls it preferably a dative, so that the passage means *destinata bello*. However, the meaning would rather seem to be that Pallene is condemned by the gods "on account of" the war which they fought with the giants in this place.

An *Index Verborum* is not only an aid to the study of an author for the purpose of deciding upon an intended meaning. It also puts at the disposal of others material for analysis of an author's peculiarities of word-use, syntax, idioms, etc. If an *Index Verborum* existed for every writer of Latin Literature it would be a comparatively simple matter to make a study of the behavior of a particular word, e. g. *cedere*, or of a particular construction, e. g. causal *quod*. A word for word comparison of this *Index* with those

---

[1] P. Langen, *C. Valeri Flacci Setini Balbi Argonauticon Libri Octo*: Berlin, S. Calvary and Co. (1896-7).

of Wetmore and Mooney[2] will reveal some rather interesting similarities as well as striking differences between the vocabularies and syntax of three Roman writers of Epic.

Of all the writers of antiquity only Quintilian in his *Institutio Oratoria* (x, 1, 90) mentions Valerius Flaccus. He says: *Multum in Valerio Flacco nuper amisimus*. There was no more known of this Roman writer of epic until Poggio in 1417 discovered a manuscript of his work at St. Gall.[3]

The manuscript tradition of the *Argonautica* of Valerius Flaccus is ably discussed by Kramer[4] in his Introduction to the Teubner text. The building of the *Argonautica* text is by no means complete. Convincing reasons for this attitude are adduced by Professor Walter C. Summers in his review of Kramer[5] and also by Professor B. L. Ullman.[6]

The commentaries on our author's work average, when we consider those that are of some length, about one per century in the last three hundred years. Pieter Burman[7] in a colossal work with the *notae variorum*, Joannes Wagner[8] in a clear effort at thought paraphrase, and P. Langen (*op. cit.*) in an attempt to clear away still-existent difficulties, are of invaluable aid in arriving at a fair understanding of the Argonautic epic of Valerius Flaccus.

Only one book of the *Argonautica* had been done into English before 1934. Noble[9] translated the first book into English verse so well that one regrets that he was unable to complete the translation of the remaining seven books. Blomfield[10] in scholarly fashion has given us a prose translation with ample notes. At times he

---

2 Monroe Nichols Wetmore, *Index Verborum Vergilianus*[2]: New Haven, Yale University Press (1930) ; and George W. Mooney, *Index to the 'Pharsalia' of Lucan*: Dublin, Hodges, Figgis and Co. (1927).

3 Cf. Walter C. Summers, *A Study of the Argonautica of Valerius Flaccus*: Cambridge, Deighton, Bell and Co. (1894), 1.

4 Otto Kramer, *C. Valeri Flacci Setini Balbi Argonauticon Libri Octo*: Leipzig, B. G. Teubner (1913).

5 Cf. *Class. Rev.* xxviii (1914), 19f.

6 Cf. B. L. Ullman, "Valerius Flaccus in the Mediaeval *Florilegia*," *Class. Phil.* xxvi (1931), 21-30.

7 Petrus Burmannus, *C. Valerii Flacci Setini Balbi Argonauticon Libri Octo* (*cum Notis*) : Leyden, Samuel Luchtmans (1724).

8 Ioannes Augustinus Wagner, *C. Valerii Flacci Setini Balbi Argonauticon Libri VIII*: Göttigen, Heinrich Dieterich (1805).

9 T. Noble, *Blackheath and Other Poems*: London, J. B. Courthope (1808).

10 H. G. Blomfield, *The Argonautica of Gaius Valerius Flaccus Setincs Balbus Book I, Translated into English Prose with Introduction and Notes*: Oxford, B. H. Blackwell (1916).

departs rather freely from the traditional interpretation of certain passages. Professor Mozley's is the latest translation and includes the entire work of Valerius Flaccus.[11] The artistic touch of one who has grasped and appreciated the letter and the spirit of his author is apparent in every line of this discerning translation.

There has been no complete *Index Verborum* to Valerius Flaccus. In his review of Mooney's *Index to the 'Pharsalia' of Lucan* in *Class. Rev.* XLII (1928), 84f W. B. Anderson says that "the student of post-Augustan Epic will wish that someone   .   .   . might be incited to do the same [i. e. compile an *Index Verborum*] for Valerius Flaccus   .   .   .   ." Burman in his edition has an *Index Verborum et Locutionum* which is distressingly incomplete and frequently inaccurate. Faider[12] says:

> Les editions de Lamp. Alardus, Leipzig, 1630, et de Jo. Ant. Vulpius, Padoue, 1720, contiennent des *indices* assez developpés. Pas d' edition *in usum Delphini*.
> C. Valerii Flacci Setini Balbi Argonauticon libri octo   .   .   . curante Petro Burmann, Leyde, Luchtmans, 1724, in 4°.—Index p. 760. C. Valerii Flacci Setini Balbi Argonauticon libros octo   .   .   . edidit N. E. Lemaire. Paris, Didot, 1824-1825, 2 vol. in 8° *Bibl. cl. L.—Index*: t. II. pp. 419-600.

Although Faider's *Repertoire* was published as late as 1926, he fails to mention the *Index Nominum* of Kramer and of Langen at the end of their respective texts.

In his text of Valerius Flaccus VIII, 161 Langen reads:
   Ex quo Thessalici subierunt   .   .   .   .
Kramer reads the same line thus:
   Ex quo Thessalici subierunt Colchida reges.

It seems rather strange that this occurrence of *Colchida* was omitted in Kramer's *Index Nominum* which in all other instances is very complete. Needless to say, Langen, who published the text some seventeen years before Kramer's, did not list the word, since it does not occur in his text. But why did Kramer omit it?

In this *Index* I have followed the edition of Kramer as the basic text. His is the latest attempt to give us the best reading. But besides Kramer I have used the texts of Langen, Giarratano, and

---

11 J. H. Mozley, *Valerius Flaccus with an English Translation* (Loeb Classical Library) : Cambridge, Mass., Harvard University Press (1934).

12 Paul Faider, *Repertoire des Index et Lexiques d'Auteurs Latins*: Paris, Societé d'Edition "Les Belles Lettres" (1926), s. v. "Valerius Flaccus."

Bury.[13] Whenever a reading varied between these editors this fact is indicated. The initials of the various editors identify their readings. Thus, e. g., *s. v.* "a" in the *Index* we find: 4. 242 (K;BG o; L e). This means that in Book IV, vs. 242, K(ramer) reads *a*; in the same book and vs. B(ury) and G(iarratano) read *o*, whereas the reading of L(angen) is *e*. The same information pertaining to this textual variation is also noted in the Index *s. v.* "o" and "e." When no parenthesis reveals any variation of text, the four editors are in agreement.

Differences of spelling in words as *penna (pinna), urgeo (urgueo)*, etc. have not been noted as they appeared to be but peculiarities of editors, and not real textual variants.

The forms are arranged under each word in paradigm order without identification unless there is need for it. In those declensions where either vocative and ablative, or accusative and vocative are identical in spelling, unless the vocative is clearly indicated, the form is to be understood as ablative or accusative respectively. In such instances where a form is doubtful, e. g. where a noun may be analyzed as either dative or ablative, it is given under both with a cross-reference indication.

The advisability of compiling an *Index Verborum* to Valerius Flaccus was suggested to me by Dr. Roy C. Flickinger of the University of Iowa. I take this opportunity to express to him my sincere gratitude for his many helpful suggestions in the course of its preparation.

I wish also to express my gratitude and appreciation to my former teachers, especially to Dr. B. L. Ullman of the University of Chicago and to Professor F. H. Potter of the State University of Iowa.

---

[13] Caesare Giarratano, *C. Valeri Flacci Balbi Setini Argonauticon Libri Octo*: Milan, Remo Sandros (1904); and J. B. Bury, *C. Valeri Flacci Balbi Setini Argonauticon Libri Octo*: London, G. Bell and Sons (1905).

INDEX VERBORUM VALERIANUS

a (29)
1. 285, 365, 372, 532, 579; 2. 255, 417, 423, 427, 515, 530; 3. 100, 229, 324; 4. 242 (K; BG o; L e), 349 (B; KG L om.), 398; 5. 152, 350, 445; 6. 64, 369; 7. 259 (a superis KG; BL Hesperiis), 270, 604, 621, 647; 8. 289, 327.

a (ah)
a 1. 447; 6.498,
ah 7. 161 (L; KBG ac); 8. 164 (aliena ah L; KBG alieno).

ab (109)
1. 16, 22, 35, 290, 314, 387, 394, 399, 404, 419, 456, 481, 538, 549, 575, 597, 598, 657, 700, 732; 2. 3, 22, 73, 185, 304, 318, 592; 3. 36, 48 (KL; BG ad), 54, 125, 130, 204, 213, 259, 363, 469, 532, 666; 4. 22, 44, 120, 159, 198, 203, 381, 417, 429, 483, 589, 669; 5. 20, 36, 91, 140, 151, 173, 242, 326, 359, 487, 527, 565, 618; 6. 28, 79, 114, 163, 164, 204, 209, 261, 318, 344, 389, 480, 553, 565, 608, 632, 634, 690, 740; 7. 1, 88, 102, 164, 169, 330, 376, 462, 484, 558 (BL; KG in), 560, 610; 8. 70, 76, 79, 82 (ab arbore KG; BL corpore), 125, 129, 177, 228, 299, 309, 317, 366, 374, 428.

Abaris
Abarim 3. 152.

Abas
Abas 1. 453.

abdo
abdita (nom. f.) 2. 641 (L; KBG ardua),
abdita (acc.) 4. 479.

abduco
abduxerat 5. 159,
abducere 6. 298; 7. 49; 8. 156,
abducta (nom. n.) 5. 162,
abductis (abl. m.) 4. 677.

abeo
abis 4. 387; 8. 145,
abit 2. 135; 4. 203, 528; 6. 654, 705; 8. 329 (KGL; B adest),
abeunt 6. 147,
abibo 7. 429, 486 (K; BGL obibo),
abiit 6. 612; 8. 366,
abiere 4. 633,
abiret 6. 581,
abito 7. 20,
abire 7. 424.

abicio
abiecti (gen. m.) 4. 654.

abies
abies 3. 165; 6. 197, 236,
abietibus (dat.) 7. 405.

abigo
abigis 5. 627,
abactam 8. 51.

abitus
abitus (acc.) 3. 223 (G; K habitus; B auctus; L aestus).

abluo
abluit 5. 76,
abluit 8. 239.

abnego
abnegat 5. 668,
abneget 3. 695.

abnuo
abnuit 3. 678,
abnuit 1. 521.

aboleo
abolete 3. 449.

abripio
abripit 4. 144,
abripiam 1. 154 (vid. subi.),
abripiam 1. 154 (vid. ind.).

abrumpo
abrumpit 7. 388,
abrumpere 3. 250; 6. 310,
abruptus 6. 84,
abrupta (abl.) 8. 330,
abruptis (abl.) 4. 413,
abruptis (f.) 2. 615.

abscedo
abscedunt 4. 636,
abscessit 8. 374,
abscessere 7. 653,
abscedat 4. 37.

abscessus
abscessu (abl.) 3. 9.

abscido
abscisa 1. 827 (BGL; K abscissa),
abscisum (acc. n.) 7. 324; 8. 314.

abscindo
abscidit 1. 489; 2. 161, 529, 618,
abscissa (nom. f.) 1. 827 (K; BGL abscisa).

absens vid. absum.

absisto
absistunt 4. 404,
absistite 3. 451.

abstineo
abstineant 6. 23.

absum
abest 2. 24,
aberis 7. 478,
absit 5. 324,
afore 3. 629,
absens (n.) 1. 272,
absentis (n.) 4. 188,
absenti (m.) 7. 197,
absentem (m.) 3. 589; 7. 315,
absentibus (dat. m.) 7. 466.

absumo
absumis 4. 25,
absumere 6. 5,

Acheron
Acheron 4. 595,
Acheronte 4. 73.
Acherusis
Acherusidos 5. 73.
Achilles
Achilli 1. 408,
Achillen 1. 133, 256.
Achivus
1. subst. m.
Achivi (gen.) 8. 347,
Achivum (gen.) 3. 86,
Achivis 6. 544,
Achivos 5. 434; 6. 10, 734,
Achivis 4. 737; 5. 552,
2. adi.
Achivae (gen.) 6. 606,
Achivo (dat. m.) 6. 450.
acies
acies 6. 66, 279, 424,
aciem 3. 55, 126, 220, 502, 572; 5. 285,
617; 6. 72,
acies (acc.) 2. 657; 3. 300, 539; 4. 237,
756; 5. 77, 607; 6. 2, 372, 758.
acinaces
acinace 6. 701.
aclys (aclis)
aclis 7. 560 (K; B ales; GL axis),
aclyde 6. 99.
acriter
acrius 2. 457; 5. 101 (L; KBG altius).
acta
acta (abl.) 5. 96.
Actaeus
Actaeus 2. 68,
Actaei 6. 217,
Actaeae (gen.) 4. 465,
Actaeis (abl. f.) 1. 394.
Actor
Actora 1. 146.
Actorides
Actorides 1. 407.
actum vid. ago.
actus
actum 3. 519 (K; BGL astum),
actu 4. 43,
actus (acc.) 2. 5; 4. 163; 5. 507.
acuo
acuunt 2. 172,
acuat 1. 761.
acus
acu (abl.) 2. 411; 6. 526.
ad (173)
1. 80, 93, 120, 165, 183, 238, 257, 270,
321, 330, 379, 521, 537, 552, 561, 576,
614, 654, 689, 690, 716, 726, 738, 802;
2. 57, 136 (BGL; K qua), 162, 173, 235,
254, 326, 332, 366, 369, 464 (ad primos
KBG; L adsiduo), 574, 575, 634, 637;
3. 8, 24, 48 (BG; KL ab), 49 (ad medias
KBG; L media), 58, 101, 264, 267, 282,
311, 343, 360, 372, 385, 398, 421, 435,
437, 452, 518, 526, 553, 557, 561, 594,
595, 607, 616, 641, 656, 662, 701; 4. 58,
73, 152, 157, 171, 227, 229, 259, 353, 397,

434, 465, 473, 512, 532, 539, 555, 561,
586, 606, 616, 628, 696, 705, 712, 741;
5. 16, 66, 88, 117, 128, 193, 219, 255, 300,
313, 325, 331, 381, 387, 397, 403, 417,
420, 449, 464, 510, 563, 622, 674, 695;
6. 12, 80, 108, 180, 218, 274, 374, 406,
429, 441 (ad fremitus L; KB adfatus;
G adflatus), 478, 490, 498, 608, 641, 651,
667, 686, 696; 7. 17, 79, 98, 130, 134, 179,
259, 264 (L; KBG et), 268, 350, 448,
488, 496, 497, 562, 587 (adque KG; BL
atque), 614, 623, 625; 8. 110, 113, 130,
134, 140 (ad hanc B; KGL adhuc),
180, 213, 216, 243, 273, 277, 421, 438.
Vid. usque.
adamas
adamante 3. 225.
adcelero
adcelerat 1. 542; 2. 204,
adcelerate 8. 265,
adcelerare 5. 556.
adcingo vid. accingo.
adclinis
adclinis 1. 147,
adclinis (nom. f.) 3. 533,
adclinem (m.) 2. 92.
adcresco
adcrescere 1. 178.
adcubo
adcubat 2. 193.
adcumulo
adcumulant 4. 340.
addo
addit 3. 203,
addunt 1. 825; 2. 236,
addidit 3. 13, 429; 5. 113; 7. 546 (-que
addidit KBG; L concidit); 8. 19,
addat 4. 720; 6. 181,
adde 2. 59, 156,
additur 3. 388; 5. 544 (L; KBG additus),
addimur 5. 285,
additus 1. 271; 5. 544 (KBG; L additur),
addita (nom. f.) 4. 417,
addita (acc.) 5. 84.
adduco
adducere 6. 133,
adductis (abl. f.) 6. 271.
adedo
adesi (n.) 2. 30,
adeso (abl. n.) 7. 359.
adeo
adit 2. 98; 6. 163 (B; KGL agit), 166
(KGL; B agit),
adeunt 8. 244,
adeas 8. 283,
adirem 3. 307,
adirent 5. 408,
adi 5. 502,
adire 5. 481,
aditure 1. 320.
adeo (11)
adeo 2. 61 (KBG; L dei), 225, 641; 3.
70; 4. 64, 239; 5. 40, 395 (KGL; B

ideo); 8. 102, 344,
usque adeo 4. 120.
adfatus
  adfatus (nom. pl.) 6. 473,
  adfatus 1. 299; 6. 441 (KB; G adflatus;
  L ad fremitus).
adfero
  attulit 3. 172,
  attulerat 5. 157,
  adferat 2. 660,
  attulerit 3. 575,
  adferte 1. 243.
adficio
  adficit 3. 579.
adfigo
  adfixam 8. 233.
adflatus
  adflatus (acc.) 6. 441 (G; KB adfatus;
  L ad fremitus).
adfligo
  adflicta (abl.) 4. 612.
adflo
  adflavit 3. 213; 6. 183,
  adflarat 7. 489.
adfor
  adfata est 5. 352,
  adfari 6. 16.
adfremo
  adfremit 1. 528.
adglomero
  adglomerat 2. 197,
  adglomerant 2. 171; 3. 87,
  adglomerare 2. 499.
adgnosco (agnosco)
  adgnoscit 6. 759,
  agnoscit 1. 485; 3. 275; 4. 533 **bis**; 6.
  578; 7. 146; 8. 372,
  adgnoscunt 4. 523; 8. 294,
  agnoscunt 7. 445,
  adgnoscent 5. 201,
  agnovit 3. 171, 288,
  agnoscere 7. 64,
  agnoscitur 1. 144,
  agnita (voc. f.) 4. 437.
adgredior
  adgreditur 6. 459, 587,
  adgressa es 7. 172,
  adgressae (nom.) 5. 658.
adhibeo
  adhibe 3. 412 (KG; BL adhibere),
  adhibere 3. 412 (BL; KG adhibe).
adhuc (29)
  1. 327, 692, 776, 808; 2. 4, 22; 3. 262,
  278, 724; 4. 540; 5. 24, 86, 300; 6. 141,
  177, 255, 309, 626; 7. 73, 106, 192, 262,
  375; 8. 27, 114, 126, 140 (KGL; B ad
  hanc), 205, 429.
adiaceo
  adiacet 1. 452; 2. 192.
adicio
  adicias 7. 508,
  adice 8. 41.
adigo
  adacto (abl. m.) 6. 307,
  adacto 6. 273,

adactis (abl.) 3. 164,
adactis (f.) 6. 183.
adimo
  adimam (ind.) 5. 655,
  ademptus 6. 282,
  adempti 3. 649; 4. 315,
  ademptae (gen.) 3. 737.
aditus
  aditus (acc.) 1. 595; 2. 220; 5. 396.
adiungo
  adiungit 4. 367,
  adiungier 2. 421,
  adiunctas 1. 524 (L; KBG et iunctas).
adiuvo
  adiuta 2. 528,
  adiutum (acc. n.) 6. 540,
  adiutae 3. 564.
adlabor
  adlapsa (nom. f.) 3. 43.
adlevo
  adlevat 3. 339.
adloquium
  adloquio 2. 354,
  adloquio 7. 289,
  adloquiis 5. 406 (vid. abl.),
  adloquiis 1. 251; 5. 406 (vid. dat.);
  7. 374.
adloquor
  adloquitur 3. 492.
adludo
  adludit 6. 665.
Admetus
  Admete 1. 445.
admiror
  admirans (f.) 4. 142.
admitto
  admittere 2. 399,
  admissis (abl. f.) 6. 303.
Admon
  Admon 3. 167 (BL; K Hidmon; G Idmon).
admoneo
  admonet 5. 12, 406, 465; 7. 27,
  admonuit 3. 147,
  admonita (abl.) 4. 349.
admoveo
  admoverit (ind.) 3. 502,
  admota (abl.) 5. 241,
  admotis (abl. m.) 5. 50.
adnuo
  adnuit 2. 577; 8. 232 (K; BGL adsunt),
  adnuet 5. 320,
  adnuit 2. 94,
  adnue 1. 41; 2. 294, 489; 5. 199; 6. 461;
  7. 497,
  adnuitur 5. 258.
adoleo
  adolentur 3. 443.
adoreus
  adorea (acc.) 2. 448.
adorior
  adortus 1. 694,
  adorta (nom.) 4. 360,
  adorti (nom.) 4. 541,
  subst. m. adortis (dat.) 2. 375.

advoco
    advocat 6. 287; 7. 186 (L; KBG aspicit); 8. 62 (B; KGL ac vocat),
    advocet 1. 73.
advolo
    advolat 1. 108, 163; 2. 124; 3. 72; 4. 300; 6. 342, 370, 655; 7. 265, 618.
adytum
    adytis 5. 404,
    adytis 1. 62; 2. 437; 8. 241.
Aea
    Aea (nom.) 1. 742; 5. 51; 6. 96.
Aea
    Aean 5. 425.
Aeacides
    Aeacides 1. 139; 2. 511; 3. 693, 715, 722; 6. 348,
    Aeacide (voc.) 1. 405; 2. 427,
    Aeacidae 4. 223,
    Aeacidum 5. 573.
Aeaeus
    Aeaei (m.) 5. 547,
    Aeaeum (m.) 6. 189,
    Aeaeo (m.) 1. 451,
    Aeaea (abl.) 5. 620,
    Aeaeis (f.) 5. 277,
    Aeaeos 7. 281,
    Aeaea 7. 191,
    Aeaeis (f.) 7. 119.
aedes
    aedibus (abl.) 1. 724.
aestivus
    aestiva (abl.) 8. 28.
Aeetes
    Aeetes 1. 43; 3. 495; 5. 285, 553, 589, 599; 6. 13, 438 (L; KBG ante diem); 7. 640; 8. 138,
    Aeetae 4. 14; 6. 22,
    Aeetae 5. 289, 401,
    Aeeten 2. 379; 5. 317, 393, 685; 6. 436 (B; KGL haec etenim),
    Aeeta 7. 89; 8. 11, 350.
Aeetis
    Aeetida 6. 481; 7. 445; 8. 233.
Aeetius
    Aeetius 8. 379,
    Aeetia (nom. f.) 6. 267, 542; 7. 565,
    Aeetia (acc.) 6. 691.
Aegaeus
    Aegaei (n.) 1. 160; 2. 383,
    Aegaea (acc.) 1. 561,
    subst. n. Aegaeo (abl.) 2. 366.
aeger
    aeger 1. 777; 3. 571; 7. 514,
    aegra 3. 365, 738 (L; KBG terga); 4. 46, 379; 6. 719, 753; 7. 5, 125,
    aegram 3. 395,
    aegro 2. 93,
    aegro 5. 131, 264,
    aegri 3. 283,
    aegra 3. 74; 5. 145; 8. 163,
    aegros 4. 276,
    aegra 6. 623,
    aegris (m.) 3. 357.

aegis
    aegida 4. 521; 5. 287; 6. 396,
    aegide 2. 97; 4. 670; 5. 652; 6. 174.
aegisonus
    aegisono (abl. n.) 3. 88.
Aegon
    Aegon 1. 629; 4. 715.
Aemathia
    Aemathiae (gen.) 2. 640.
aemulus
    aemulus 1. 665,
    aemula (nom. f.) 5. 86.
Aeneadae
    Aeneadum 2. 573.
Aenidae
    Aenidae 3. 4.
aenus
    aena (acc.) 7. 596,
    subst. n. aeni 5. 512,
    aeno (abl.) 8. 254.
Aeolia
    Aeoliae (gen.) 6. 354,
    Aeoliam 1. 576.
Aeolides
    Aeoliden 1. 286,
    Aeolidae 5. 461.
Aeolius
    Aeolii 6. 542,
    Aeoliae (gen.) 1. 654 (BGL; K Aeoliam); 6. 548; 7. 54,
    Aeolium (n.) 1. 770,
    Aeolio (n.) 7. 517; 8. 79,
    Aeolios 2. 594.
Aeolius
    Aeoliam 1. 654 (K; BGL Aeoliae).
Aeolus
    Aeolus 1. 417, 587, 751; 5. 477,
    Aeole 1. 598.
aequalis
    aequali (abl. f.) 4. 615; 5. 342; 7. 181,
    aequales (f.) 8. 142,
    aequales (f.) 6. 497.
aeque
    3. 201, 599, 674, 703 (L; KB atque; G satque); 6. 241.
aequo
    aequat 6. 95; 7. 620,
    aequantes (nom. m.) 6. 160,
    aequata (nom. f.) 4. 731,
    aequatum (n.) 2. 6 (vid. acc.),
    aequatum (n.) 2. 6 (vid. nom.).
aequor
    aequor 1. 324; 2. 513 (vid. acc.), 597; 3. 732; 4. 688,
    aequoris 2. 232; 5. 78; 8. 3,
    aequor 1. 363, 414, 537; 2. 375, 380, 513 (vid. nom.); 3. 621; 4. 270, 541, 588, 696; 5. 134 (in aequor L; KBG sanguine), 179, 511; 8. 201,
    aequore 1. 284, 306, 342, 579, 630, 654 (KL; BG aequora), 815 (G; KBL aequora); 2. 37, 63, 112, 295, 323; 3. 500 (KBG; L aethere), 726; 4. 56, 280, 566, 657, 666, 729; 5. 167, 543; 6. 88, 163, 328, 569, 592; 7. 38, 648; 8. 144, 265,

aequora 1. 641; 2. 405; 3. 32, 351, 661;
4. 721; 6. 412; 7. 581,
aequora 1. 131, 293, 303, 382, 526, 600,
608, 654 (BG; KL aequore), 815
(KBL; G aequore); 2. 12, 187, 319,
586, 592, 608, 631; 3. 107, 277, 388, 472,
605; 4. 110, 345, 488, 510; 5. 45, 59, 228,
619, 669; 6. 30, 105, 239, 390; 7. 56, 92,
113, 469, 474, 548, 553; 8. 50, 140, 307,
327.
aequoreus
aequorei (n.) 5. 91,
aequoreo 1. 193,
aequoreo 4. 750,
aequoream 2. 127,
aequoreo (m.) 4. 249,
aequoreos 1. 138, 212, 483,
aequoreas 3. 421.
aequus
aequa 6. 98,
aequae (gen.) 4. 151,
aequom (m.) 4. 621,
aequum (n.) 1. 435,
aequo 3. 675,
aequo 2. 606,
aequos 8. 320,
aequis 1. 795; 2. 505; 4. 1,
aequis (f.) 5. 284,
subst. n. aequi 5. 406,
aequis (abl.) 3. 648,
aequissima (nom. f.) 4. 113.
aer
aer 1. 497; 2. 333, 524,
aera 1. 233; 7. 376,
aere 5. 400; 6. 261.
aeratus
aeratam 6. 88,
aeratis (abl. f.) 1. 339.
aereus
aerii (gen. m.) 1. 67.
aeripes
aeripides (acc. m.) 7. 545.
aerisonus
aerisono (abl.) 3. 28,
aerisona (abl.) 1. 704.
aerius
aerii (m.) 2. 553,
aeriam 8. 113.
aes
aeris 2. 389; 6. 141,
aere 1. 688; 3. 63 (incitat aere B; KGL
inde ciere); 6. 198, 525,
aera 2. 260,
aera 2. 266; 5. 78; 6. 342.
Aesepius
Aesepia (acc.) 3. 420.
Aeson
Aeson 1. 144, 296, 335, 756, 767, 825;
7. 494,
Aesonis 4. 549,
Aesona 1. 72, 152, 734; 5. 48,
Aesona 1. 149.
Aesonides
Aesonides 1. 161, 194, 474, 488; 2. 334,
346, 385, 659; 3. 339, 369; 4. 675, 755;

5. 4, 35, 543, 577, 587, 636; 6. 655; 7.
530, 587, 594, 645; 8. 118, 166, 197, 244,
353,
Aesonidae 7. 464,
Aesonidae 3. 8; 6. 429,
Aesoniden 1. 98; 4. 738; 5. 302, 571; 6.
173, 592, 684, 736; 7. 165, 409, 476, 490,
541, 639; 8. 387, 414,
Aesonide (voc.) 1. 226; 2. 380; 8. 105,
155, 178, 192, 442.
Aesonius
Aesonius 1. 241,
Aesonii 3. 240; 7. 178 (KGL; B Haemonii),
Aesoniae (gen.) 3. 285; 6. 653 (KGL;
B Haemoniae),
Aesonium 1. 32; 4. 8; 7. 188,
Aesoniam 1. 660,
Aesonium 5. 294; 6. 579, 687,
Aesonias 7. 17 (KGL; B Haemonias).
aestuo
aestuat 7. 294.
aestus
aestus (nom.) 2. 614,
aestu (abl.) 1. 291; 3. 365, 676; 4. 132;
7. 647,
aestus 7. 195, 242,
aestus 3. 223 (L; K habitus; B auctus;
G abitus), 506 (KBG; L astus), 572;
5. 302.
aetas
aetas 2. 325; 5. 314; 6. 62, 115,
aetate 6. 444.
aeternus
aeterni (n.) 5. 409,
aeternum (n.) 2. 358,
aeterno 6. 38,
aeterna (abl.) 7. 282,
aeterna (acc.) 1. 846,
adv. aeternum 1. 832 (KG; BL infernum); 4. 151, 708.
Aethalides
Aethalides 1. 437.
aether
aether 1. 307, 616; 2. 42; 3. 348, 467,
aetheris 2. 119; 3. 226; 4. 179,
aethera 1. 91, 466, 580; 2. 20, 241; 5.
565; 6. 165,
aethere 1. 82, 591; 2. 36, 415; 3. 43, 54,
130, 500 (L; KBG aequore); 4. 355,
377, 407, 682; 5. 182; 8. 73, 318.
aetherius
aetheriae (gen.) 2. 84; 4. 67,
aetherias 2. 444; 5. 163.
aethra
aethra (abl.) 1. 156; 6. 748.
Aetna
Aetna 4. 287 (KG; BL ipse),
Aetnam 2. 29,
Vid. Aetne.
Aetnaeus
Aetnaei (gen. m.) 2. 420,
Aetnaeis (abl. n.) 4. 104.

Aetne
　Aetne (nom.) 2. 95,
　Vid. Aetna.
aevum
　aevi 1. 760, 771 (K; BGL aevum); 2.
　618; 3. 688; 5. 3, 225, 357; 6. 122, 649;
　7. 361,
　aevum 1. 286, 771 (BGL; K aevi),
　aevo 1. 474; 4. 426; 6. 636; 7. 338.
Africus
　Africus 2. 506.
Agenor
　Agenore 4. 444.
Agenoreus
　Agenoreis (abl. n.) 4. 522.
Agenorides
　Agenoride (voc.) 4. 582.
ager
　ager 2. 73; 3. 167; 5. 372; 6. 168, 186;
　8. 122,
　agri 2. 635,
　agri 2. 476; 3. 218,
　agris 5. 421,
　agros 1. 665; 3. 222, 254; 6. 336, 426,
　443; 7. 68,
　agris 4. 392; 6. 405; 7. 544, 558, 609.
agger
　agger 5. 641,
　aggere 3. 337; 5. 91, 186; 6. 149,
　aggeribus (abl.) 3. 281.
aggero
　aggeritur 5. 62.
agito
　agitet 1. 802,
　agitent 2. 164,
　agitari 6. 448.
agmen
　agmen (acc.) 3. 229; 6. 751,
　agmine 2. 530; 3. 91, 110, 259, 265, 450,
　522, 619; 4. 721; 5. 353, 560; 6. 111, 389,
　452; 7. 559; 8. 332,
　agmina 2. 412; 4. 279; 6. 403; 7. 642,
　agminibus 6. 544,
　agmina 1. 520; 2. 130, 227; 3. 162, 222,
　315, 434, 497, 505, 670 (GL; KB teg-
　mina); 4. 528; 5. 437, 469; 6. 70, 114,
　183, 228, 300, 410, 522, 610, 697; 7. 148,
　615, 624; 8. 430.
agna
　agna 3. 706,
　agnam 1. 157.
agnosco vid. adgnosco.
ago
　agit 1. 689, 841; 2. 122, 215, 362, 632;
　3. 8, 393; 4. 87, 263, 302, 410; 5. 15; 6.
　88, 163 (KGL; B adit), 166 (B; KGL
　adit), 569, 706; 7. 143, 603, 638; 8. 131,
　333,
　agimus 2. 114,
　agunt 5. 664; 6. 121,
　agit 3. 685; 4. 382; 6. 603; 7. 36, 218,
　egere 3. 441; 5. 479,
　agat 1. 71; 2. 352; 4. 607; 5. 527, 531;
　7. 309; 8. 370,
　age 1. 306; 2. 127, 565, 612; 3. 212, 311,

416; 4. 35, 471; 5. 538, 635; 6. 33, 213,
516; 7. 48, 467; 8. 41, 64, 74, 111, 191,
　agite 2. 55; 3. 523; 6. 29, 285; 7. 93,
　agens 3. 40; 4. 111; 6. 633; 7. 151,
　agens (f.) 1. 783; 3. 431; 6. 591,
　agentes (acc. m.) 5. 46,
　acturus 1. 371,
　agor 2. 602; 6. 331 (B; KGL amor),
　agitur 2. 77; 3. 114; 6. 667,
　agi 2. 179; 6. 610,
　acta 4. 106; 8. 35,
　actum 5. 299,
　acti (n.) 3. 627,
　actum 7. 138,
　actam 2. 603,
　acti 2. 236 (B; KGL atris); 3. 186, 219,
　actae 2. 247; 4. 563,
　acta (nom.) 3. 355,
　actis (abl. m.) 3. 67; 6. 522 (L; K altis;
　BG atris),
　subst. n. acti 5. 673,
　actis 2. 378; 3. 423, 678, 694; 5. 542
　(vid. abl.),
　actis 1. 40, 376 (KG; BL annis); 5.
　542 (vid. dat.); 6. 128.
agrestis
　subst. m. agrestum 1. 684; 2. 461.
agricola
　agricolis (dat.) 3. 578.
ahenus
　subst. n. ahenis (abl.) 4. 686 (B; KGL
　harenis).
aio
　ait 1. 164, 175, 194, 266, 348, 598, 651,
　713, 763; 2. 66, 250, 257, 322, 336, 380,
　419, 425, 468, 574, 663; 3. 144, 169, 373,
　377, 521, 545; 4. 79, 140, 145, 161, 191,
　313, 335, 387, 437, 474, 485, 675, 758;
　5. 57, 129, 213, 283, 293, 314, 359, 363,
　404, 582, 587, 600, 652; 6. 269, 292, 461,
　475, 540, 547, 592, 648; 7. 89, 128, 138,
　257, 266, 287, 331, 339, 413, 431, 490,
　531; 8. 44, 54, 59, 111, 178, 195.
ala
　ala (abl.) 7. 398 (BGL; K alis),
　alae 4. 498,
　alas 1. 611; 4. 502; 6. 56, 160, 218, 264;
　7. 546 (K; BG ausa; L illa),
　alis 1. 577, 705; 2. 97, 579; 4. 49, 453,
　527; 6. 494, 527; 7. 398 (K; BGL ala).
alacer
　alacrem (m.) 4. 81,
　alacres (nom. m.) 3. 462.
Alani
　Alanis 6. 656,
　Alanos 6. 42.
Alazon
　Alazona 6. 101.
Alba
　Alba (abl.) 2. 304.
Albanus
　1. subst.
　Albanus 6. 271,
　2. adi.

Albani (m.) 5. 258; 6. 194,
Albano (dat. m.) 6. 44; 8. 153,
Albana (abl.) 3. 497,
Albanis (abl. f.) 5. 459.
albeo
albet 2. 73; 3. 167,
albentes (acc. f.) 6. 99.
albesco
albescere 3. 258.
albus
alba 1. 385,
alba (abl.) 5. 10,
alba (nom.) 6. 492.
Alcides
Alcides 1. 35, 354; 2. 451, 462, 521, 533,
543; 3. 475, 550, 586; 4. 78, 701; 5. 90,
Alcidae 4. 247,
Alcidae 8. 230,
Alciden 3. 65, 580, 644, 662, 701, 724;
4. 62; 5. 156, 172, 488, 574.
Alcimede
Alcimede 1. 297, 335, 731,
Alcimedes 1. 317.
ales
subst. m. ales 4. 72, 385; 7. 560 (B; K
aclis; GL axis),
alitibus (abl.) 1. 361,
subst. f. alitis 5. 176.
alga
alga (abl.) 1. 252.
alias
haud alias 7. 525.
alibi
4. 714.
alienus
alienae 6. 23,
alieni 6. 474,
alieno (abl. m.) 8. 164 (KBG; L aliena
ah),
aliena (nom.) 8. 164 (aliena ah L; KBG
alieno),
subst. n. aliena (acc.) 5. 508.
aliger
aligeri (nom.) 7. 120,
aligerum (gen. m.) 7. 171,
aligeris (abl. m.) 1. 224; 5. 453.
alipes
alipedi (abl. m.) 5. 611,
alipedum (m.) 5. 183,
subst. m. alipedem 6. 208.
aliquis
aliquem 8. 384,
aliquam 5. 473, 661; 7. 413, 452,
subst. aliquid (acc.) 2. 184; 8. 440, 467,
aliquae 5. 670 (B; K aliqua et; G aliqua; L que vae),
aliqua (acc.) 5. 670 (aliqua et K; B
aliquae; G aliqua; L que vae).
aliter (12)
aliter 7. 58,
haut aliter 1. 489; 4. 50,
ac velut . . . haud aliter 2. 47,
ceu . . . haud aliter 7. 305,
non aliter 3. 737; 4. 236,

non aliter quam si 5. 408,
non aliter . . . quam si 4. 368,
qualis ubi . . . haut aliter 7. 114,
qualis . . . haud aliter 7. 380,
qualem . . . haut aliter 5. 25,
Vid. haud.
alius
   I. alius
alius 3. 345; 8. 399, 433,
alium 2. 382, 628; 4. 62; 5. 493; 6. 324;
7. 92,
aliud 1. 354; 2. 209; 8. 191, 365,
alio 3. 568 (KBG; L alia); 4. 575; 6.
757; 7. 35, 257,
alia 1. 140; 3. 314, 568 (L; KBG alio);
6. 265; 8. 236,
alio 2. 361,
alii 2. 347; 8. 281,
aliae 1. 607; 4. 126; 6. 123; 8. 141,
aliis 1. 323,
aliis (f.) 8. 362 (BG; KL altis),
alios 1. 402; 5. 5, 217, 291, 308 (KBG;
L altos), 396; 7. 263, 448; 8. 200,
alias 1. 556; 6. 445; 7. 448; 8. 429,
alia 5. 291; 7. 92,
aliis 2. 151 (KGL; B tales); 8. 102,
aliis (f.) 1. 405; 4. 219,
subst. alium 3. 644; 7. 596,
aliam 6. 451,
aliud 1. 326; 8. 316,
alii 1. 636; 3. 72, 472; 5. 463,
aliis (m.) 6. 644,
alios 5. 26, 103; 7. 44,
   II. alius . . . alius
aliis . . . aliis (dat. m.) 6. 416,
subst. alii . . . alii (nom.) 8. 301,
aliae . . . aliae 2. 235,
hi . . . alii 1. 313,
hos . . . alios 6. 578,
altera . . . aliam 1. 834,
pars . . . pars . . . alius 2. 449,
Vid. haud, non, quam.
allevo
allevat 8. 212.
alligo
alligat 1. 48; 5. 428; 6. 443; 7. 244 (L;
KBG arida).
alluo
alluit (perf.) 4. 132.
Almo
Almo 8. 239.
almus
alma 1. 311; 2. 102,
almae (gen.) 1. 850 (KBL; G clarae),
almum (n.) 5. 310,
alma (voc. f.) 5. 550.
alnus
alnus 1. 637,
alnum 1. 203,
alno 2. 300; 3. 536.
alo
alit 4. 361; 6. 146, 660; 7. 359 (KBL;
G edit),
alat 2. 644,
subst. m. alentem 6. 713.

Aloidae
Aloidae 5. 651.
Alpes
Alpes (nom.) 6. 393.
Alpheos
Alpheos 8. 91.
altare
altaria (acc.) 1. 90; 4. 152.
alte
alte 3. 131, 437,
altius 5. 101 (KBG; L acrius); 8. 258.
alter
alter 4. 595; 5. 276,
altera (nom. f.) 1. 582, 771; 5. 1; 6. 419;
8. 183, 463,
subst. alter 1. 191,
altera . . . aliam 1. 832,
Vid. non, quam.
alternus
alternus 4. 266; 6. 185, 231,
alternae (nom.) 6. 185, 363,
alternos 2. 93,
alternis (n.) 5. 671.
altrix
altricem 6. 325.
altus
altus 2. 304; 5. 413; 8. 309,
alta 3. 206, 731; 4. 16; 5. 107, 334; 6. 14,
687; 8. 286 (vox alta L; KB vexilla; G
vox illa),
alti 1. 16 (L; KBG omni), 662; 3. 501,
altae (gen.) 2. 288,
alto (n.) 4. 414 (vid. abl.),
altum (n.) 5. 95, 318,
alto 1. 700; 7. 88,
alta 1. 314, 404; 2. 462; 3. 201, 275; 5.
304; 6. 209; 8. 177,
alto 1. 597; 4. 414 (vid. dat.); 5. 268,
altae 8. 88,
alta 1. 728,
altis (f.) 8. 362 (KL; BG aliis),
altos 5. 308 (L; KBG alios),
altas 7. 394,
alta 2. 459, 548; 7. 473,
altis 3. 58; 4. 202; 6. 28, 456, 495, 522
(K; BG atris; L actis),
altis 1. 724; 2. 190; 8. 367,
altis 5. 151; 6. 421,
subst. n. altum (acc.) 1. 271, 765; 2. 15,
26, 74; 4. 561, 569,
alto 2. 22, 506; 3. 213, 429; 4. 268, 483;
5. 173, 522,
alta 3. 2; 4. 405,
alta 1. 136 (K; BGL antra), 160; 2. 2;
4. 7, 505; 5. 126; 7. 129,
altior 1. 353,
altior 5. 346; 6. 238 (KG; BL tardior),
altissima (nom. f.) 6. 180.
alumna
alumnam 5. 358.
alumnus
alumnus 6. 222,
alumnum 1. 422; 3. 160; 8. 94,
alumni 4. 223,
alumnos 5. 573; 8. 219.

Amanus
Amano (abl.) 1. 493.
amarus
amari (gen. m.) 4. 721,
amaris (abl. n.) 2. 385.
Amastris
Amastrin 6. 554.
Amastrus
Amastrum 3. 145.
Amazon
Amazon 5. 89.
Amazonis
Amazonidum 4. 602.
ambages
ambage 1. 227,
Ambenus
Ambenus 6. 85.
Ambenus
Ambenus 6. 251.
ambiguus
ambiguum (m.) 2. 318,
ambigua (nom.) 5. 301.
ambio
ambit 3. 189; 5. 631; 7. 256,
ambitum (m.) 5. 621.
ambo
ambae (nom.) 4. 300,
amborum (m.) 5. 688,
ambobus (m.) 1. 36,
ambas 8. 140,
subst. ambo 4. 279; 6. 128 (ambo animis KBG; L unanimes), 128; 7. 404,
653 bis,
ambae 8. 168,
amborum (m.) 1. 432, 530, 572; 8. 345,
ambobus (dat. m.) 5. 477.
Ambrosius
Ambrosium 3. 138.
amburo
ambusta (acc.) 4. 70.
amens
amens 2. 180; 3. 226, 576; 4. 50; 7. 631,
amens (f.) 1. 111.
amicitia
amicitiam 3. 205.
amictus
amictu (abl.) 1. 659; 3. 470; 6. 745.
amicus
amico (m.) 3. 42,
amicum (n.) 3. 171,
amico (n.) 2. 450,
amicos 3. 289; 5. 577,
subst. m. amici 3. 563; 4. 136,
amice 3. 296.
amitto
amissas 4. 448.
amnigena
amnigenam 5. 584.
Amnis
Amnes (nom.) 1. 106; 2. 537.
amnis
amnis 5. 103, 122, 134; 8. 210,
amnis 8. 190,
amnem 2. 595; 3. 101; 4. 195, 616, 705;
5. 191, 397, 420, 430; 6. 319, 635,

anhelus
anhelo (abl. m.) 2. 278,
anhelo 2. 233 (BL; KG anhela),
anheli 4. 699,
anhelae 4. 514,
anhela 2. 233 (KG; BL anhelo),
anhelis (m.) 1. 186,
anhelos 6. 240,
anhelis (m.) 2. 75.
anima
animam 1. 749; 2. 483; 4. 436, 443; 6.
289, 560; 7. 286, 441,
animae 1. 151, 237, 544; 3. 84; 8. 274,
animas 1. 676; 3. 382, 449 (G; KL minas; B animos); 7. 274; 8. 389.
animo
subst. n. animantibus (abl.) 7. 227.
animus
animus 1. 166; 4. 193,
animi 1. 79,
animo 1. 26; 4. 577; 6. 439; 7. 244,
animum 1. 41, 321; 2. 264; 3. 615; 4.
539; 6. 580; 7. 173,
animo 5. 610,
animi 1. 55, 603, 702; 3. 468; 4. 673;
6. 417; 7. 383,
animis 1. 271 (L; KG mero; B viae);
3. 519; 4. 621, 744,
animos 1. 76, 182, 243, 336, 540, 772;
3. 17, 449 (B; KL minas; G animas),
547; 4. 125, 593, 651 (G; KBL Amyci);
5. 322, 390; 6. 17, 279, 284; 7. 293,
animis 3. 703; 5. 649; 6. 128 (ambo animis KBG; L unanimes), 630.
annosus
annosi (gen. m.) 4. 321.
annus
annus 3. 454; 6. 167,
annum 1. 843; 5. 423; 6. 324,
anni 3. 179,
annos 3. 242, 356, 401; 7. 295, 480; 8.
118, 409,
annis 1. 22, 53, 376 (BL; KG actis),
505, 810 (L; KBG armis); 3. 316; 5.
384, 457; 6. 571; 7. 62.
annuus
annua (nom. f.) 3. 361; 7. 635.
ante (adv.) (23)
1. 322, 783; 3. 39; 4. 30, 205, 475 (KBG;
L parce), 492; 5. 222 **bis**, 260, 448, 496;
6. 197, 262, 283, 582, 664; 7. 33 (ante
petit K; B ante rapit; G ante aperit;
L antevenit), 55, 248, 324, 621; 8. 8
(KBG; L ungue),
Vid. antequam.
ante (praepos.) (24)
1. 458, 623, 771; 2. 140; 3. 167, 621, 691;
4. 61, 237, 644; 5. 26, 103; 6. 72, 438
(ante diem KBG; L Aeetes), 717 **bis**,
723; 7. 11, 44, 62, 126, 263, 396; 8. 293.
anteeo
anteire 1. 31.
antemna
antemna (nom.) 1. 623.

antequam
ante . . . quam (c. ind. perf.) 1. 85;
7. 220.
antevenio
antevenit (prs.) 7. 33 (L; K ante petit;
B ante rapit; G ante aperit).
antiquus
antiqua 2. 394,
antiqui 8. 8 (perantiqui BGL; K peranti),
antiquae (gen.) 5. 528.
antrum
antro (abl.) 1. 407; 2. 337; 3. 636; 4.
651; 5. 209; 8. 256, 315,
antra 3. 49; 4. 92, 356,
antris 2. 624,
antra 1. 136 (BGL; K alta), 576, 582;
2. 335; 3. 299, 728; 4. 200,
antris 1. 417; 2. 318; 4. 104; 5. 140, 618;
6. 79, 565; 7. 647; 8. 125.
anxius
anxius 1. 401; 2. 300, 413,
anxia 1. 684, 731; 3. 256; 4. 7; 5. 50;
8. 384,
anxia (voc. f.) 2. 113.
Anxur
Anxur 6. 68.
Aeonius
Aeonias 1. 379,
Aeoniis (m.) 8. 447.
aper
aper 3. 634.
aperio
aperit 2. 218; 3. 371; 6. 432, 552; 7. 33
(ante aperit G; K ante petit; B ante
rapit; L antevenit),
aperimus 1. 169,
aperite 7. 548,
aperire 6. 459,
aperti 1. 735 (K; BGL operti),
aperti 1. 7,
aperto (abl. n.) 3. 154; 4. 678; 7. 360,
541 (BGL; K apertis),
apertis (abl. f.) 4. 710; 7. 114,
apertis 2. 566; 7. 541 (K; BGL aperto).
apex
apex 3. 189; 4. 508.
Apidanus
Apidani 1. 357.
apis
apes (acc.) 1. 395.
Apollo
Apollo 1. 234, 567; 2. 492; 4. 61, 445;
5. 17, 112, 693.
appareo
apparent 4. 412; 5. 440,
apparuit 3. 137; 4. 177; 5. 227; 7. 606;
8. 128.
apparo
apparat 5. 285, 448,
apparet 3. 586; 4. 55.
appello
appellat 4. 537.
appello vid. adpello.

Apres
Aprem 6. 638.
apricus
aprica 1. 844,
aprici (gen. m.) 3. 361.
apto
aptat 2. 544; 6. 669,
aptans (m.) 8. 126.
aptus
apta (nom. f.) 5. 609.
apud
3. 570; 6. 165.
aqua
aquae (gen.) 1. 502 (aquaeque KB;
GL quaeque),
aqua 6. 329; 8. 330,
aquarum 1. 188,
aquis 2. 8; 6. 294,
aquas 2. 590; 4. 595, 600, 687, 716; 5.
177,
aquae 5. 80,
aquis 1. 657; 2. 79, 320, 532, 614; 3. 560;
4. 48; 5. 307; 6. 711; 8. 187, 291, 368.
aquila
aquilis (abl.) 6. 404.
Aquilo
Aquilone 4. 432.
Aquilonius
Aquilonia (nom. f.) 4. 462, 501.
aquilonius
aquilonia (nom. f.) 6. 715.
Aquites
Aquites 6. 295.
ara
ara 2. 99, 331,
arae (dat.) 2. 302; 5. 10,
arae 1. 142; 2. 598; 5. 206, 479,
aris 3. 456; 4. 186,
aras 1. 28, 42, 188, 279, 379, 521, 677,
755; 2. 625; 3. 426; 5. 193, 403, 449; 8.
224, 243,
aris 6. 440.
Arabes
Arabas 6. 139.
aratrum
aratri 1. 103; 7. 555,
aratro (dat.) 7. 602.
arbiter
arbiter 1. 558.
arbitrium
arbitrio (abl.) 4. 383.
arbor
arbor 2. 46; 3. 353; 7. 379, 527; 8. 119,
289,
arboris 8. 110,
arbore 1. 399, 496; 5. 203; 7. 519; 8. 82
(ab arbore KG; BL corpore),
arboribus (abl.) 4. 178.
arbustum
arbusta (acc.) 3. 102.
Arcadius
Arcadio (abl. m.) 4. 384,
Arcadio 1. 108, 481.

arcanus
arcana 2. 432,
arcanum 1. 808; 2. 598,
arcani (n.) 3. 419,
arcana 3. 322,
arcano 4. 15,
arcanis (n.) 2. 624,
arcanis (n.) 6. 477.
Arcas
Arcas (m.) 7. 543,
Arcados (f.) 5. 205,
subst. m. Arcas 1. 36; 5. 370.
arceo
arcet 2. 118, 368 (BGL; K arcens);
4. 74,
arcuit 4. 317,
arcens (m.) 2. 368 (K; BGL arcet),
arcentibus (abl. m.) 1. 360.
Arctos
Arcto (abl.) 1. 419; 6. 632 (B; KGL
arcu),
Arctos (acc.) 5. 46.
arctos
arctos 6. 147,
arcton 4. 210; 5. 272,
arcto 5. 317; 6. 140,
arctos 3. 359; 5. 155; 6. 40, 612.
Arctous
Arctoo (abl. m.) 3. 499,
Arctois (abl. n.) 6. 295.
arctous
arctoa (acc.) 5. 619,
arctois (n.) 6. 330.
arcus
arcus (nom.) 1. 656; 3. 523; 4. 524
(BGL; K arquos); 6. 124,
arquos 4. 524 (K; BGL arcus),
arcum 1. 401; 2. 521; 4. 95, 728,
arcu 1. 446; 3. 133, 591; 5. 579; 6. 632
(KGL; B Arctoo), 707,
arcus (acc.) 1. 109; 3. 161; 6. 686.
ardeo
ardet 1. 69 (K; GL creditus; B creditur); 6. 1, 526; 8. 159,
ardent 5. 85,
arsere 2. 476,
arserit (subi.) 5. 139; 6. 46,
ardere 1. 226,
ardens 1. 701; 2. 3; 3. 583; 5. 670; 6.
293, 364,
ardens (f.) 2. 175,
ardentis (m.) 1. 458 (vid. acc. f.); 7.
561; 8. 335,
ardenti (m.) 8. 116,
ardenti (n.) 1. 400,
ardentem (m.) 1. 346,
ardenti (f.) 1. 146; 4. 3,
ardenti 1. 488; 3. 429; 5. 230,
ardentes (nom. m.) 7. 63,
ardentes (m.) 6. 42; 7. 110; 8. 437, 450,
ardentis (f.) 1. 458 (vid. gen. m.),
ardentes (acc. f.) 3. 340; 6. 601; 7. 566;
8. 87,
ardentia 7. 587,
ardentibus 6. 658,

arrigo
arrectae (nom.) 2. 186,
arrectas 2. 213 (KBG; L arrectis),
arrectis (f.) 2. 213 (L; KBG arrectas).

Aron
Aron 5. 590; 6. 524, 536.

arquipotens
arquipotens (m.) 5. 17.

arquos vid. arcus.

aripio
arripit 7. 476; 8. 299,
arripe 4. 623,
arrepto (abl. n.) 6. 357,
adreptis (abl. n.) 8. 311.

ars
ars 2. 61 (arsque B; KGL atque),
arte 1. 67; 2. 53, 148, 465; 3. 206, 504;
4. 272, 554; 5. 7, 433; 6. 155; 7. 482;
8. 353,
artes 6. 152; 7. 506,
artes 2. 284; 6. 438; 7. 317, 625,
artibus 6. 241.

Arsinoe
Arsinoen 5. 422.

artifex
artificis (f.) 6. 465,
subst. m. artificum 4. 287.

artus
arto (abl. m.) 6. 361,
arta (abl.) 1. 757,
artis (abl. f.) 5. 324,
subst. n. arto (abl.) 6. 346.

artus
artu (dat.) 4. 310,
artus 4. 192, 376; 5. 561; 6. 413,
artus 1. 48, 219, 749; 2. 253, 268; 3. 263,
289, 310, 556; 4. 245, 276, 552; 5. 170,
333; 6. 480, 670; 7. 141, 244 (L; K om.;
B lingua; G febris), 369, 463; 8. 123.

arvum
arvi 1. 683,
arvo (abl.) 6. 553 (BGL; K auso),
arva 3. 404,
arvorum 1. 103,
arvis 3. 94,
arva 1. 511, 513; 2. 616, 631; 3. 86, 306,
662; 4. 320, 601; 5. 501; 7. 608,
arvis 1. 445, 751; 3. 729; 4. 611; 6. 170,
295 (B; KGL armis), 330, 508; 7. 206.

arx
arcem 2. 306,
arce 1. 498, 575, 598; 3. 469; 4. 261, 417;
5. 304; 7. 85,
arces (acc.) 2. 94, 444; 3. 481; 4. 73;
5. 163, 409, 646; 7. 193, 562; 8. 446,
arcibus 3. 565.

ascendo
ascenderit (ind.) 3. 411 (BGL; K ac-
cenderit),
ascendere 6. 45.

Asia
Asiae 4. 210,
Asiae 6. 334,
Asiam 1. 542, 554; 2. 614; 4. 728; 7. 43;
8. 396.

asilus
asilo (abl.) 3. 581.

aspecto
aspectans (m.) 4. 704.

aspectus
aspectu (abl.) 1. 637; 7. 551.

asper
asper 3. 21, 271; 4. 222; 5. 578,
aspera (nom.) 2. 405; 3. 362, 706; 6.
590,
aspera (nom.) 4. 254,
aspera 1. 200, 420 (celer aspera KG;
BL caelataque); 3. 141, 642; 5. 488;
7. 242,
subst. n. aspera (acc.) 5. 157,
subst. n. asperrima (acc.) 1. 725.

asperno
aspernandus 4. 163.

aspero
asperat 2. 435; 5. 368.

aspicio
aspicio 1. 49, 211, 224,
aspicis 6. 324, 595; 8. 61,
aspicit 2. 591; 4. 536; 5. 96, 620; 7. 186
(KBG; L advocat), 431,
aspiciunt 1. 687,
aspice 4. 250.

aspis
aspide 4. 418.

Assyrius
Assyrios 5. 109.

ast (19)
1. 834; 2. 239; 3. 115, 188, 227, 326, 670
(G; K et; BL en); 4. 407, 568; 5. 371,
407, 548, 645 (suus ast G; K lucis; B
suus at si; L suus atque); 6. 95, 197,
333, 503; 8. 255, 363.

Asterion
Asterion 1. 355.

asto vid. adsto.

Astraea
Astraea (nom.) 2. 363.

astrifer
astriferas 6. 752.

astrum
astrum (acc.) 2. 357 (L; KBG astro),
astro 1. 481; 2. 357 (KBG; L astrum);
5. 227, 366,
astra 2. 42; 3. 211; 4. 36,
astris 2. 491; 8. 68,
astra 1. 466, 563; 3. 67, 378; 4. 237, 489;
8. 330,
astris 2. 171; 3. 83; 4. 90; 5. 566; 8. 454.

astus
astus (gen.) 5. 541,
astum 3. 519 (BGL; K actum),
astu 1. 492; 2. 555,
astus (acc.) 3. 506 (L; KBG aestus);
4. 365; 5. 222.

at (79)
at 1. 96, 103, 158, 184, 264, 376, 433, 452,
457 (K; BGL et), 462, 608, 693; 2. 437;
3. 39 (at qui BL; KG atque), 69, 74,
103 (K; BGL et), 113, 182, 231, 292,
391, 506, 598, 628 (KB; GL et), 637,

667, 668; 4. 6, 85, 181 (KL; BG ut),
199, 249, 324, 392 (B; KGL et); 5. 4,
228, 280, 297, 363 (KGL; B et), 412,
431, 645 (suus at si B; K lucis; G suus
ast; L suus atque); 6. 1, 173, 211, 214
(BL; KG et), 234, 484, 565, 572, 602
(KGL; B ac), 621, 657, 665, 683, 699,
721; 7. 26, 86 (BGL; K et), 103, 110
(BGL; K et), 139, 234, 515 (B; KGL
ac), 556; 8. 1, 35, 312, 357, 385, 427 (L;
KBG an),
at contra 6. 472,
at non 3. 362; 6. 529,
at tamen 7. 285 (K; B ac tamen; GL
ut tamen),
at vero 3. 280; 6. 345; 7. 616.

atavus
atavos 1. 737; 2. 343.

ater
ater 5. 430,
atra 5. 41,
atro (abl. m.) 1. 81; 4. 676; 6. 415, 708,
745; 7. 572,
atra 3. 406; 5. 94,
atro 3. 500,
atrae 2. 205,
atras 3. 96,
atris (m.) 2. 236 (KGL; B acti); 4.
457; 5. 176; 6. 522 (BG; K altis; L
actis).

Athamas
Athamanta 1. 280.

Athos
Athos 2. 201; 4. 322,
Athon 1. 664; 2. 76.

Atlans
Atlans 2. 620; 5. 410,
Atlantis 1. 841.

Atlantis
Atlantidis 2. 72 (KGL; B Pallantidos).

atque (176)
1. 25, 52, 72, 106, 344, 346, 536, 562, 636,
639, 679, 742, 760, 773, 801, 838; 2. 61
(KGL; B arsque), 117, 126, 168, 334,
374, 399, 500, 555, 627, 655; 3. 39 (KG;
BL at qui), 219, 289, 340, 366, 387, 388,
430, 448, 472, 478, 498, 500, 504, 666, 703
(KB; G satque; L aeque); 4. 1, 58, 65,
81, 128, 151, 154, 165, 189, 213 (BGL;
K haec), 255, 295, 402, 410, 416, 435,
497, 506, 510, 512, 554, 593, 624, 727,
734, 742, 747; 5. 20, 93, 135, 176, 190,
194, 210, 309, 382, 390, 396, 504, 509,
518, 521, 529 (L; KBG aut), 589, 602,
607, 611, 645 (suus atque L; K lucis;
B suus at si; G suus ast); 6. 13, 46, 170,
206, 238, 252, 264, 272, 284, 300 (BG;
KL utque), 304, 310, 369, 385, 391, 425,
463, 478, 481, 545, 577, 599, 603, 625,
630, 691, 717, 758; 7. 30, 49, 65, 109, 118,
140, 150, 162, 164, 170, 202, 240 (atque
illum KL; B ac vanum; G atque tuum),
253, 258, 265, 275, 318 (KBG; L et),
321, 345, 383, 398, 425, 465, 471, 473,
481, 492, 500, 509, 527, 572, 587 (BL;

KG adque), 589, 601, 618, 643; 8. 9, 54,
86, 89, 105, 131, 141, 164, 204, 264, 276,
285 (KL; BG itque), 300, 328, 353, 382,
384, 396, 399, 426, 440.

Atracius
Atracia (abl.) 1. 141,
Atracio 6. 447.

atrium
atria (nom.) 7. 31.

atrox
atrox 1. 700; 6. 644,
atrox (f.) 6. 662.

attamen
2. 151 (GL; KB ac tamen).

attollo
attollit 2. 9; 4. 435,
attolle 7. 258,
attollere 4. 326; 5. 85,
attollens 1. 336,
attollens (f.) 7. 436.

attonitus
attonitus 3. 178,
attoniti (m.) 7. 564,
attonitum 2. 193,
attonitam 6. 590,
attonito 8. 21,
attonita 8. 132,
attonito 3. 259; 5. 373,
attoniti 2. 454; 5. 16; 7. 404,
attonitos 3. 532; 6. 534; 7. 101, 191, 635,
attonitas 3. 209.

Auchates
Auchates 6. 132.

Auchus
Auchus 6. 60,
Auchi 6. 619.

auctor
auctor 2. 251; 3. 622; 4. 560; 5. 477.

auctus
auctus (acc.) 3. 223 (B; K habitus; G
abitus; L aestus).

audacia
audacia (nom.) 2. 264.

audax
audax (m.) 6. 423; 7. 573,
audacem (m.) 5. 497,
audaci (f.) 7. 512.

audenter
audentius 6. 681.

audeo
audet 2. 435, 283; 4. 47; 6. 662,
audeat 4. 156; 7. 80, 164, 183,
ausim 6. 626,
audentem (f.) 2. 121 (KBG; L auditam); 4. 382,
audentior (f.) 4. 284,
ausus 2. 109; 3. 160, 183, 613 (vid. ausus) (KBG; L ultro); 8. 221,
ausa 1. 3, 541; 7. 8,
ausum (m.) 4. 234,
ausi 3. 394; 5. 467; 7. 18,
ausae 2. 398,
ausas 3. 231,
subst. n. ausi 2. 280; 4. 295,
auso (abl.) 6. 553 (K; BGL arvo),

ausis 4. 652; 5. 627, 661,
ausa 4. 569; 5. 523; 7. 546 (BG; K alas;
L illa),
ausis 1. 211; 2. 242; 4. 317, 669; 5. 269,
313.
audio
audis 1. 42 (K; BGL audisti),
audit 2. 166; 3. 237; 5. 132, 356, 405,
574; 6. 101,
audiet 3. 544,
audisti 1. 42 (BGL; K audis),
audiit 7. 509,
audiere 7. 630 (L; KBG videre),
audierat 2. 571,
audi 7. 257,
audire 1. 172; 2. 372; 8. 419,
auditur 5. 141,
audiri 5. 169,
auditus 4. 73; 6. 292,
audita 6. 32,
auditam 2. 121 (L; KBG audentem),
auditi 4. 641,
auditae 4. 21; 7. 308,
audita 1. 341,
auditas 2. 321; 4. 207,
auditis (m.) 4. 737.
aufero
aufert 1. 640; 2. 543; 3. 56; 6. 489,
abstulit 1. 497; 2. 27; 3. 266, 636; 4. 131;
5. 94; 6. 190, 284; 7. 563,
abstulerint 2. 245,
abstulerint 1. 644,
auferre 8. 65,
aufertur 3. 542, 551,
ablatam 6. 682.
augeo
auget 2. 45, 199; 3. 207; 6. 279,
augent 6. 521,
auxit 6. 532,
auxerat 2. 38, 493; 4. 552,
augeat 4. 173,
auxisse 3. 569.
augur
augur 1. 234,
auguris 5. 10.
augurium
augurium (acc.) 1. 161,
augurio 6. 729,
auguriis (abl.) 2. 486; 5. 259.
auguro
auguret 3. 356.
aula
aula 1. 828; 2. 349,
aula 6. 47; 7. 102, 301; 8. 166.
Aulon
Aulon 1. 389.
aura
aura 3. 34; 5. 564; 8. 175,
aura 4. 615; 5. 588,
aurae 2. 585; 4. 21, 344,
auras 1. 159, 208, 224; 2. 200; 3. 196,
350; 4. 217, 302; 5. 176, 453; 6. 113, 561;
7. 157, 528; 8. 143, 247,
auris 4. 580 (KBG; L aures), 722; 7.
259 (KBG; L oris).

aureus
aureus 1. 281; 6. 27; 8. 128,
aurea (nom.) 5. 566; 7. 30,
aureo (abl. n.) 2. 103 (B; KGL auro),
aurea 5. 200,
aurea 1. 453; 2. 589, 653; 5. 433, 553; 7.
167; 8. 42, 131,
aureis (n.) 6. 71.
auricomus
auricomis (abl. f.) 4. 92.
aurifer
auriferum (acc. n.) 5. 637.
auriga
auriga (nom.) 3. 52.
auriger
aurigerae (gen.) 8. 110.
auris
aurem 7. 268,
aure 2. 44,
aures 4. 309,
auribus 1. 334 (vid. abl.),
aures 2. 125, 388, 452; 4. 580 (L; KBG
auris), 664; 7. 98, 296, 419; 8. 134,
auribus 1. 334 (vid. dat.).
auro
auratae (gen.) 5. 490; 8. 203,
aurata 3. 431,
aurato 5. 209,
auratos 6. 57,
auratis (m.) 1. 273,
auratis (n.) 1. 89.
Aurora
Aurora 1. 283; 4. 423; 5. 559,
Auroram 2. 261.
aurum
aurum (acc.) 6. 670,
auro 1. 148, 290, 338, 430, 661, 805; 2. 58
(KB; GL Euro), 103 (KGL; B aureo),
472, 651; 3. 11, 340; 5. 139, 242, 369;
6. 226, 378, 692, 710; 7. 54; 8. 79, 258.
Ausonia
Ausoniam 7. 86.
Ausonius
Ausonii (gen. m.) 7. 232.
auster
auster 2. 15; 3. 652; 6. 665; 7. 406,
austri (gen.) 7. 561,
austris 2. 52,
austros 1. 97; 5. 521,
austris 3. 341, 598, 700.
ausus
ausus (acc.) 3. 613 (vid. audeo).
aut (112)
aut 1. 18, 68, 166, 187, 199, 471, 582,
647, 811, 837; 2. 96, 103 (GL; K eadem;
B ea cum), 143, 181, 232, 353, 467, 495;
3. 55, 75, 161, 174, 201, 319, 327, 373,
376, 559, 636, 735; 4. 103, 124, 228, 230,
280, 365, 378, 399, 445, 600, 697, 731;
5. 93, 164, 344, 453, 529 (KG; BL ac),
529 (KBG; L atque), 559, 658; 6. 22,
148, 165, 201, 383, 471, 677, 720; 7. 17,
40, 41, 57 (KB; GL haut), 182, 331,
405, 421, 424, 562, 569, 621, 642, 647;
8. 90, 115, 156, 166 (B; KGL ut), 168,

229, 242, 266 (KGL; B haut), 272, 350,
364 (KBL; G quantum), 443,
aut . . . aut 1. 664; 4. 448, 585, 726;
5. 41, 307, 501, 529 (vid. aut supra);
6. 285, 326, 585; 7. 116, 452, 622.

autem (20)
1. 686; 2. 587; 3. 257 (K; BGL levi),
262; 4. 291; 5. 128, 171, 399, 576, 599,
605, 618; 6. 248, 273, 575; 7. 32, 131;
8. 32, 224, 287.

Autolycus
Autolycum 5. 114.

autumnus
autumni 6. 607 (KGL; B autumno),
autumno (abl.) 5. 368; 6. 607 (B; KGL
autumni).

auxilium
auxilium (acc.) 4. 568; 5. 555,
auxilio 5. 633; 7. 275,
auxiliis 1. 119 (vid. abl.),
auxilia 3. 563; 6. 732; 7. 326,
auxiliis 1. 119 (vid. dat.); 4. 619.

aveho
avehit 1. 783,
avecti (gen. m.) 1. 328.

avello
avellere 1. 304; 7. 48,
avelli 5. 29.

avena
avena (abl.) 4. 386.

aveo
avet 1. 100, 199 (L; KBG tamen); 2.
103 (tunc avet L; K tantum; B iam
tum; G iam tumet),
avens 1. 485 (KBG; L ovans),
avens (f.) 2. 124.

Avernus
1. subst.
Averni 2. 602; 4. 493, 700,
Averno (abl.) 5. 347,
2. adi.
Averna (nom. f.) 6. 158.

averto
averterit (subi.) 6. 17,
avertere 3. 491; 4. 128; 5. 629,
averti 7. 391,
aversa 6. 463 (BG; KL adversa),
averso (m.) 4. 307,
averso (m.) 4. 332,
aversis (dat. f.) 1. 518 (KB; GL ad-
versis).

avide
1. 818.

avidus
avidus 3. 557; 4. 297,
avidos 1. 183; 5. 85,
avidas 3. 562.

avis
avem 6. 261,
aves (acc.) 2. 75,
avibus 3. 360.

avius
avia (nom. n.) 4. 286,
subst. n. avia (acc.) 2. 459; 3. 545, 597;
5. 475; 6. 441.

avus
avi 6. 442, 518; 8. 460,
avo (abl.) 5. 458,
avorum 1. 476; 3. 344,
avis 6. 125,
avos 6. 110.

axis
axis (nom.) 1. 670; 3. 731; 7. 560 (GL;
K aclis; B ales),
axem 5. 431,
axe 2. 65; 5. 205, 517; 7. 457,
axes 6. 409,
axes 6. 387; 7. 278.

bacchor
bacchatus 6. 634,
bacchata (acc.) 3. 20.

Bacchus
Bacchus 2. 348; 3. 538; 5. 75; 7. 301;
8. 447,
Bacchi 2. 254, 623; 4. 533; 5. 192, 215,
Bacchum 2. 272; 3. 5; 4. 237; 5. 497;
6. 137,
Bacche 2. 275,
Baccho 1. 260; 2. 70.

baculum
baculo (abl.) 4. 434.

Balloniti
Balloniti 6. 161.

balteus
balteus 3. 190; 4. 95; 5. 139, 578.

barathrum
barathri 2. 86, 192.

barba
barbam 3. 168,
barba 5. 595.

barbaricus
barbaricae (gen.) 6. 702; 8. 460,
barbarico (abl.) 8. 69,
barbarica 6. 526,
barbarici 6. 187,
barbaricae 6. 90,
barbaricas 3. 494.

barbarus
barbarus 1. 517; 2. 241; 5. 425; 6. 556,
barbara (nom. f.) 1. 451; 2. 111, 150;
3. 231; 8. 292,
barbara (acc.) 3. 643,
subst. barbarus 5. 522,
barbara (voc. f.) 8. 148, 251.

Barisas
Barisanta 6. 557.

Batarnae
Batarnas 6. 96.

beatus
beatior (m.) 5. 383; 6. 47.

Bebrycia
Bebrycia 4. 762,
Bebryciae (gen.) 4. 743; 5. 502.

Bebrycius
Bebrycii (n.) 4. 99,
Bebrycium (n.) 4. 220,
Bebrycio 6. 344,
Bebrycio 4. 442,
Bebryciis (abl. f.) 4. 590,
Bebryciis 4. 739.

Bebryx
Bebryx 4. 157, 261, 290,
Bebrycis 2. 648,
Bebrycas 4. 315.
bellator
bellator 2. 386; 6. 559,
bellatoris 5. 585.
bellatrix
bellatrix 7. 612.
belliger
belligeros 5. 617.
Bellipotens
subst. m. Bellipotens 1. 529.
bello
bellabimus 6. 373,
bellare 6. 338.
Bellona
Bellona 2. 228; 3. 60; 7. 636,
Bellona (voc.) 1. 546.
bellum
bellum 3. 498,
belli 1. 54; 2. 114, 139, 179; 3. 48, 253
(KGL; B leti); 5. 132, 143, 307, 495,
532, 539, 598 (KGL; B Phoebi); 6. 6,
20, 104, 301, 312, 514, 545, 576, 677, 739,
753; 8. 385,
bello 2. 16 (vid. abl.); 5. 679; 7. 627; 8.
384,
bellum 5. 681; 8. 394,
bello 2. 16 (vid. dat.), 549; 4. 752; 5.
554; 7. 47, 609; 8. 138,
bella 3. 296; 5. 460, 545; 8. 427,
bellorum 2. 654,
bellis 3. 183 (vid. abl.),
bella 1. 33, 268, 322, 552, 564, 770; 2.
129; 3. 30, 122 (L; KBG tela), 511
(bellave BG; K belua; L proelia); 5.
218, 419, 665; 6. 35, 535, 728,
bellis 1. 100, 540, 789; 2. 419; 3. 183
(vid. dat.), 451; 4. 9; 5. 655; 6. 134.
belua
belua (nom.) 2. 479, 535 (GL; K donec; B pistris); 3. 511 (?) (K; BG bellave; L proelia).
benignus
benigno (abl.) 5. 113,
benigna (abl.) 3. 174; 4. 554.
Bessi
Bessi 2. 231.
bibulus
bibulas 1. 289.
bidens
subst. bidentes (acc. f.) 3. 431.
Bienor
Bienor 3. 112.
bifidus
bifidum (acc. n.) 1. 570.
biformis
biformes (acc. m.) 1. 669.
biga
bigis 3. 211 (vid. abl.),
bigas 2. 295,
bigis 2. 261; 3. 211 (vid. dat.).

biiugis
subst. m. biiuges 6. 413,
biiuges 2. 566.
biiugus
biiugis (abl. m.) 7. 218.
bini
bini 5. 39,
bina 3. 413.
bipennis
subst. f. bipenni (abl.) 1. 122, 192; 4.
337.
bipes
bipedum (m.) 2. 508.
biremis
subst. f. biremes (nom.) 8. 427.
bis (9)
1. 392, 429, 430; 2. 570; 3. 364; 4. 659,
660; 7. 537 (KB; G vix; L mihi), 583.
Bisaltae
Bisaltae 6. 48.
bissenus
bisseno (abl. n.) 4. 93.
Bistones
Bistonas 1. 726; 3. 83.
Bistonia
Bistoniae (gen.) 3. 160.
Bithynus
Bithyno (abl. n.) 3. 6.
bitumen
bitumine 3. 124.
blandus
blandus 1. 187,
blanda 3. 534,
blandae (dat.) 6. 668,
blando (abl.) 2. 451,
blanda 8. 63,
blando 8. 36,
blandos 2. 354; 3. 507; 4. 353; 5. 110,
blanda 2. 417; 6. 465,
blandis (n.) 7. 373,
blandior (f.) 7. 123.
Boebeis
Boebeide 1. 449.
Boebeius
Boebeia (nom. f.) 3. 543.
Boeotius
Boeotia (nom. f.) 5. 80.
bonus
bonus 1. 438,
bona (voc. f.) 1. 327,
melior 1. 424; 3. 112; 5. 489; 7. 115,
melior 4. 158; 6. 514; 8. 15,
melioris (f.) 2. 369, 573,
melius 1. 732,
meliore (n.) 2. 152,
meliora 1. 675,
meliora 5. 494,
melioribus (m.) 6. 676,
subst. n. meliora 5. 458,
meliora 7. 225,
optimus 1. 143,
optima 4. 452,
optime 4. 65; 8. 441,
optima (nom.) 2. 263,

subst. n. optume 1. 175,
optime 3. 318.
Bootes
Bootes 2. 68; 7. 457 (BL; KG Booten),
Booten 7. 457 (KG; BL Bootes).
Boreas
Boreas 1. 575, 597; 2. 515; 6. 164,
Boreae 4. 630; 7. 563,
Boreae 4. 722,
Borean 1. 604.
bos
bos 6. 537,
bovis 2, 387 (B; KG brevis; L resti);
4. 395; 6. 358,
bovem 1. 190; 4. 362,
boum 6. 559.
Bosporos
Bosporos 4. 345,
Bosporon 4. 419.
bracae
bracae 6. 227,
bracis (abl.) 5. 424.
bracchium
bracchia 4. 182; 8. 114,
bracchia 1. 126, 258, 421; 4. 210, 263,
280, 303; 6. 326, 620.
brevis
brevis 2. 387 (KG; B bovis; L resti),
524,
brevis (nom.) 3. 194; 4. 572; 6. 493,
breve (acc.) 8. 249,
breves (acc. m.) 3. 379,
brevibus 6. 571,
brevibus (f.) 2. 614; 7. 377,
brevior (f.) 6. 98,
breviore 1. 460,
breviore (f.) 5. 414,
brevioribus (abl. f.) 1. 705,
brevissima (nom. n.) 7. 332.
Brontes
Bronten 3. 152.
bruma
brumae (gen.) 5. 196 (KL; BG placidus),
bruma 4. 723; 5. 602.
bustum
busti 5. 91,
busta (acc.) 2. 10.
Butes
Butes 1. 394.
buxus
buxus 3. 231,
buxo 2. 583,
buxum 1. 319.
Byces
Bycen 6. 68.
Byzeres
Byzeres (nom.) 5. 152.
cacumen
cacumina (acc.) 2. 542; 6. 664.
cadaver
cadavera (acc.) 3. 143.
Cadmeius
Cadmeia (nom. f.) 7. 282.

Cadmeus
Cadmei (gen. m.) 6. 437; 7. 76.
Cadmus
Cadmi 6. 137.
cado
cadit 2. 63; 3. 40; 6. 194, 221, 508, 718,
753; 8. 34, 189,
cadunt 3. 53; 6. 259,
cadet 6. 214 (BGL; K cadat),
cadent 6. 627,
cecidit 2. 54; 4. 308 (BG; KL cedit);
7. 423,
ceciderunt 1. 300,
cecidere 1. 238, 623; 4. 301, 673 (BG;
KL rediere); 6. 282, 627; 8. 88,
cadat 1. 812; 6. 39, 214 (K; BGL
cadet); 7. 132,
caderet 3. 353,
cecidisset 8. 317,
cadens (m.) 3. 171,
cadentis (m.) 6. 655,
cadentem (m.) 1. 355,
subst. m. cadentum 2. 210; 3. 206; 6.
723.
caecus
caecus 4. 652 (caecus erat L; KG perculerat; B nuper erat); 6. 454,
caeca 3. 151,
caecae (gen.) 7. 380,
caeco (abl.) 2. 461,
caeca 3. 79; 5. 663; 6. 422,
caeco 3. 110,
caecae 7. 402,
caecis (n.) 2. 630,
caecis (abl. m.) 7. 147.
caedes
caedis 3. 274,
caede 1. 225; 2. 274; 5. 340, 454, 545;
6. 415, 615; 7. 150,
caedibus (abl.) 6. 184, 546 (B; KGL
laudibus).
caedo
caedunt 4. 337; 5. 9,
caesi (m.) 3. 266; 4. 136,
caeso (m.) 6. 213,
caeso (abl.) 6. 551,
caesa (abl.) 7. 55,
caesas 3. 268 (L; KBG socias),
subst. m. caesorum 3. 363; 4. 258,
caesis (dat.) 3. 312, 366, 409.
caelamen
caelamina (acc.) 2. 626 (B; KGL
velamina).
caelestis
caelestes (acc. f.) 8. 230,
caelestia 8. 334,
caelestibus (n.) 6. 485.
caelicola
caelicolae (nom.) 5. 472,
caelicolum 2. 83,
caelicolis (dat.) 5. 111.
caelo
caelarat 5. 434,
caelata (acc.) 1. 402, 420 (BL; KG
celer aspera); 5. 6; 6. 53.

caelum
caelum 2. 55, 494, 627,
caeli 1. 168, 565, 765; 2. 88; 3. 481; 4. 28; 5. 53; 7. 479,
caelo 1. 668; 2. 18, 407; 3. 382; 4. 35, 692,
caelum 1. 418, 655; 6. 315, 562, 726,
caelo 1. 305, 483, 617; 2. 475, 517; 3. 277 (KBG; L campo); 558; 4. 35, 415; 5. 295, 371, 626; 6. 159, 466, 528.
caeruleus
caerulei 7. 378, 563,
caerulei 8. 3,
caeruleum 1. 82,
caeruleum 1. 642,
caeruleo 3. 400,
caeruleo 3. 91,
caeruleae 1. 220, 776,
caeruleas 6. 302,
caeruleis 7. 535,
caeruleis (f.) 1. 189.
caerulus
caerulus 1. 652; 3. 189,
caerula (acc.) 6. 563,
subst. n. caerula (acc.) 1. 460, 561.
caesaries
caesaries 6. 227.
caespes
caespite 5. 61.
caestus
caestu 4. 182,
caestu 4. 160, 298, 332,
caestus 4. 214, 754,
caestus 4. 148, 209, 251, 275,
caestibus 1. 390; 4. 113.
Caicus
Caico 6. 688,
Caice 6. 688.
Calaber
Calabri (n.) 1. 683,
Calabris (abl. n.) 3. 582, 729.
Calais
Calais 3. 692; 4. 465; 6. 557.
calco
calcat 8. 113,
calcare 7. 536 (L; KBG calcantem),
calcantem (m.) 7. 536 (KBG; L calcare).
Caledonius
Caledonius 1. 8.
caleo
calet 2. 331,
calent 3. 216,
calentia (acc.) 8. 260.
calidus
calidis (abl. m.) 5. 372.
caligo
caligine 4. 596; 6. 577.
Callichorus
Callichoron 5. 75.
callidus
callida (nom. f.) 7. 375 (BL; KG pallida).

callis
calle 3. 568,
calles (acc.) 5. 394.
calor
calor 1. 271; 3. 680.
Calpe
Calpen 1. 588.
Calydon
Calydonis 4. 223,
Calydonos 5. 573,
Calydona 3. 658,
Calydone 3. 646.
Campesus
Campesus 5. 593; 6. 243.
campus
campus 2. 10, 46; 4. 361; 5. 307; 7. 63,
campi 3. 151; 4. 267; 5. 327,
campo (abl.) 3. 277 (L; KBG caelo); 4. 726; 5. 549; 6. 588; 7. 75,
campi 1. 444; 3. 148; 6. 721,
campis 6. 600,
campos 1. 84, 834; 4. 116, 596; 5. 610; 6. 511; 7. 281, 607; 8. 121,
campis 2. 129; 3. 438; 5. 221; 6. 27, 235, 428, 631; 7. 613.
candeo
candentis (n.) 6. 225,
candenti (abl. f.) 3. 432,
candentes (acc. m.) 2. 487; 4. 380,
candentia 2. 447,
candentibus (f.) 4. 97,
candentior (m.) 3. 481.
candesco
candescere 7. 22.
candidus
candidus 6. 61,
candida (nom. f.) 3. 559; 5. 70; 8. 247,
candida (acc.) 1. 381.
candor
candor 3. 179,
candore 6. 206.
caneo
canebant 3. 32,
canentis (n.) 6. 122.
canis
canis (nom.) 3. 228; 6. 607; 7. 125,
canum 1. 159; 3. 335; 6. 107, 313,
canes 6. 647.
canistrum
canistris (dat.) 1. 254.
canities
canitiem 6. 306.
canna
canna (abl.) 2. 108.
cano
canit 1. 234; 4. 351, 553,
canimus 1. 1,
canunt 1. 28, 105; 6. 94,
canebat 8. 397,
canens 3. 68; 5. 43, 224,
canens (f.) 2. 274; 3. 303,
canenti (m.) 1. 11, 238,
canentem 2. 218; 6. 116,
canentem 2. 117.

canor
  canor 6. 165.
Canthus
  Canthus 1. 166, 451; 7. 422,
  Canthi 3. 192; 6. 350,
  Canthum 6. 364, 368 bis,
  Canthe 6. 317, 346.
cantus
  cantus (nom.) 5. 443,
  cantu (abl.) 1. 62; 3. 158, 448; 4. 388
  (G; KL om.; B centum); 7. 184; 8. 85,
  152,
  cantus 8. 354,
  cantus 4. 387 (KBL; G custos); 5. 217;
  7. 492,
  cantibus 4. 390; 6. 448; 7. 488, 574.
canus
  canis (abl. f.) 2. 287; 5. 306,
  subst. m. canis (abl.) 1. 711.
capax
  capax (f.) 1. 111.
capesso
  capessit 4. 548; 6. 108,
  capessunt 4. 316, 344; 5. 407; 6. 503,
  capessat 1. 74, 759, 768; 8. 370,
  capessere 1. 540; 2. 224.
Caphereus
  Caphereu 1. 371.
capillus
  capillo (abl.) 1. 378,
  capillis (dat.) 5. 592.
capio
  capit 1. 660; 3. 14,
  capient 3. 698,
  cape 7. 446,
  captus 2. 43; 6. 51,
  capta 4. 269,
  capti (n.) 2. 493,
  captum (m.) 1. 717,
  capta 3. 569,
  capto 8. 178,
  captos 2. 131,
  captas 7. 29,
  capta 4. 109, 236; 6. 320,
  subst. captae (dat.) 2. 146.
captivus
  captiva (nom. f.) 6. 501,
  captiva (acc.) 3. 25; 6. 216,
  subst. captiva (nom. f.) 8. 417.
capto
  captaret 1. 448.
caput
  caput 3. 510; 8. 89,
  capitis 6. 379,
  capiti 8. 126,
  caput 1. 52, 148, 203, 267, 528, 613, 642;
  2. 254; 3. 480; 4. 24, 91, 272, 333, 401,
  561; 5. 11, 18, 97, 294, 486, 526; 6. 179,
  235, 579, 619, 651, 687, 707, 746; 7. 94,
  599; 8. 92, 110, 346,
  caput 2. 404,
  capitum 4. 183.
Carambis
  Carambis 5. 107,
  Carambin 4. 599; 8. 214.

carbasus
  carbasus 2. 597; 4. 615,
  carbasa 6. 225,
  carbasa 1. 8, 575, 607; 4. 422; 5. 424.
carcer
  carcere 1. 602, 610; 3. 499 (BG; KL
  cardine).
carchesium
  carchesia (acc.) 1. 193; 2. 655.
cardo
  cardine 1. 827; 3. 499 (KL; BG carcere); 5. 19; 7. 322.
careo
  carent 6. 751,
  caruisse 6. 314,
  carens (m.) 6. 382.
Caresus
  Caresus 6. 192.
carina
  carinae 1. 117, 301; 2. 636; 4. 647; 5. 14,
  150; 7. 326; 8. 417,
  carinae 1. 154, 487; 8. 40,
  carinam 2. 50,
  carina 3. 724; 5. 106, 472, 628; 6. 318;
  7. 129,
  carinae 1. 644; 6. 666; 7. 220,
  carinis (dat.) 1. 17.
Carmeius
  Carmeius 5. 582.
carmen
  carminis 7. 590 (KG; BL cornibus),
  carmen 1. 783; 4. 87, 386 (KBG; L
  carmina),
  carmine 1. 471; 2. 244; 4. 343; 5. 439;
  6. 275; 8. 342, 351,
  carmina 1. 845,
  carmina 1. 738; 3. 408; 4. 386 (L; KBG
  carmen); 5. 98; 7. 353, 463; 8. 69.
carpo
  carpit 2. 44,
  carpunt 3. 393,
  carpsit 4. 379; 8. 8,
  carpere 1. 178; 5. 48,
  carpitur 3. 365,
  carpere (fut.) 7. 533 (B; KG mihi care;
  L carpende),
  carpende 7. 533 (L; KG mihi care; B
  carpere).
carus
  carus 1. 724; 8. 213, 316,
  cara 1. 812; 2. 95; 5. 614; 7. 336,
  cari 4. 37; 8. 92,
  carae 5. 88; 6. 126; 7. 117,
  caro 1. 408; 2. 408; 3. 491; 6. 570,
  carae 4. 362; 5. 345,
  carum 1. 93,
  caram 1. 171; 5. 47; 7. 137,
  carum 4. 24; 8. 346,
  care 2. 293; 4. 53; 7. 533 (mihi care
  KG; B carpere; L carpende),
  cara 7. 347,
  cara 1. 259,
  caro 3. 287,
  caris (m.) 3. 4; 6. 286,
  caros 7. 145,

caras 2. 132; 5. 57,
cara 2. 220; 5. 36, 645 (K; BGL clara),
subst. m. care 2. 603,
carior (m.) 8. 12,
carius (voc.) 2. 404.
Caspiadae
Caspiadae 6. 107.
Caspius
Caspius 6. 189.
Caspius
Caspia (acc.) 5. 124.
cassis
cassis 1. 386; 3. 53, 197 (KG; BL cuspis),
cassidis 6. 199,
casside 3. 197 (BL; KG cuspide); 6. 760; 7. 617.
cassus
cassus 6. 561,
cassi 7. 59,
cassae (gen.) 4. 423,
cassa (abl.) 6. 556.
castellum
castella (nom.) 3. 739.
castigo
castigat 6. 660,
castiganda (nom. n.) 3. 370.
Castor
Castor 1. 425; 3. 187, 189, 668; 4. 333; 6. 204, 239,
Castora 4. 226; 5. 546, 549,
Castore 2. 427; 3. 330, 723.
castra
castra 4. 617; 5. 396,
castra 2. 448; 5. 681; 6. 2,
castris 5. 537; 6. 8.
castus
castus 3. 424,
castum (acc. n.) 2. 137,
casta (abl.) 1. 6, 839,
castos 5. 239,
castis (m.) 5. 335.
casus
casus 1. 670; 3. 574; 4. 483,
casus 1. 763; 4. 592,
casu (abl.) 3. 683; 5. 113; 7. 9, 164, 289,
casus (acc.) 1. 153, 321, 398; 2. 2, 151, 351, 654; 3. 318, 517; 4. 349; 5. 215, 475; 7. 201a, 448,
casibus 3. 122; 4. 447; 7. 443.
cateia
cateias 6. 83.
catena
catena (abl.) 6. 233,
catenae 2. 100; 7. 370,
catenas 3. 225.
caterva
catervae (gen.) 5. 377,
caterva 5. 342; 7. 181,
catervas 4. 603; 5. 137; 6. 497,
catervis 3. 20 (B; KGL lacertis); 8. 27.
catulus
catulos 6. 347,
catulis 1. 493.

Caucaseus
Caucaseum (m.) 4. 63; 7. 357,
Caucaseae 4. 72; 5. 381; 7. 565,
Caucaseis (abl.) 5. 253,
Caucaseis (f.) 7. 190.
Caucasus
Caucasus 5. 155, 161, 518; 6. 612; 7. 55.
Caucasus
Caucasus 6. 641.
cauda
cauda (nom.) 2. 502.
causa
causa 1. 648; 7. 16, 38, 223,
causam 2. 239; 7. 8 (B; KGL paulum),
causa (voc.) 8. 39,
causas 2. 335; 3. 15, 377.
cautes
cautes 4. 671,
cautes 1. 630; 7. 41,
cautis (acc.) 1. 59 (BL; K certus; G certas),
cautes (acc.) 4. 564, 587, 659,
cautibus 2. 449.
cavea
caveae (gen.) 4. 228.
caveo
cavere 6. 417 (cura cavere G; KB om.; L in peste revinctos),
cavens (f.) 7. 295.
cavus
cava 1. 687; 4. 384,
cava (abl.) 4. 259; 6. 760,
cava (acc.) 4. 83.
ce (ci)
ci 1. 151, 630; 7. 417.
Cecropius
Cecropiae (gen.) 1. 468.
Cecrops
Cecropis 5. 646.
cedo
cedo 7. 349,
cedit 4. 308 (KL; BG cecidit); 8. 335,
cedunt 3. 210; 4. 89,
cedam 5. 670 (cedam tibi L; KBG nequeat sic),
cessit 5. 67; 7. 175, 462, 614; 8. 368,
cesserunt 4. 714,
cessere 1. 216; 2. 71; 3. 196; 4. 483,
cesserat 4. 672,
cedam 1. 347,
cederet 1. 514,
cesserit 6. 392,
cede 8. 102, 436,
cedere 6. 363; 7. 58, 95, 425,
cessisse 3. 221,
cedens 4. 722,
cedens (f.) 4. 373, 677,
cedentis (gen. m.) 3. 199,
cedentibus (abl. n.) 4. 485,
cessuram 7. 319.
Celaeneus
Celaeneus 3. 406.
Celaeno
Celaeno 4. 453, 499.

celebro
  celebro 8. 279,
  celebrantem (m.) 1. 423.
celer
  celer 1. 355, 420 (celer aspera KG; BL
  caelataque); 4. 734, 6. 161,
  celerem 1. 442 (KG; BL cinerem); 3.
  545,
  celerem 4. 390,
  celeri 1. 91,
  celeri 2. 604; 4. 291,
  celeri 3. 185,
  celeres 4. 316; 5. 117,
  celeres (nom. f.) 4. 574.
celero
  celeras 4. 240 (B; KGL celera),
  celeravit 3. 251,
  celera 4. 240 (KGL; B celeras),
  celerans (m.) 4. 385,
  celeranda (acc.) 4. 80.
cella
  cellas 1. 396.
celsus
  celsi 3. 695; 4. 75; 6. 72,
  celsi 2. 514, 626,
  celso (abl.) 1. 312,
  celsa 5. 9, 214,
  celso 3. 339,
  celsis (f.) 1. 719,
  celsa (acc.) 1. 455,
  celsis 3. 462 (GL; K raptis; B summis), 652; 6. 681,
  celsis 3. 351,
  celsis 4. 405,
  celsior 1. 496; 2. 547,
  celsior 6. 76.
Centores
  Centoras 6. 151.
centum
  centum (nom. m.) 2. 652,
  centum (acc. m.) 6. 559,
  centum (n.) 1. 15 (L; K gentis; BG
  genti); 4. 388 (B; KL om.; G cantu);
  6. 559,
  centum (f.) 6. 397.
centumgeminus
  centumgeminae (gen.) 6. 118.
Cepheus
  Cepheus 1. 375.
cera
  cera (abl.) 1. 480,
  cerae 1. 128.
Ceramnus
  Ceramni 6. 550.
Ceraunia
  Ceraunia (acc.) 3. 465,
cerebrum
  cerebro (abl.) 3. 166; 4. 153.
Ceres
  Ceres 1. 578; 5. 216,
  Cereris 1. 69; 2. 69; 4. 532,
  Cererem 1. 254; 3. 5.
cerno
  cerno 1. 226, 236; 2. 155, 643; 4. 619;
  5. 360; 7. 41, 92, 249, 260,

cernis 5. 283; 6. 592; 7. 239,
cernit 1. 121; 2. 464; 4. 56, 143; 8. 321,
cernimus 4. 466,
cernunt 1. 502; 3. 75, 215,
cernam 4. 10,
cernes 1. 553,
cernat 1. 806,
cernant 2. 227,
cerneret 8. 452,
cerne 5. 585, 667,
cernere 3. 687; 6. 487, 519,
cernens 3. 66; 5. 35,
cernens (f.) 6. 429,
cernitur 1. 583; 5. 155, 439,
cernimur 5. 476,
cerni 5. 400.
certamen
  certamine 3. 717; 4. 116, 212,
  certamina (acc.) 3. 470, 475; 6. 576.
certatim
  2. 77; 3. 333; 4. 325; 6. 427.
certe (7)
  4. 588, 651; 5. 320; 7. 10, 385; 8. 168, 422.
certo
  certat 3. 555, 597,
  certant 3. 92; 4. 566; 5. 644,
  certasse 6. 314,
  certante (f.) 5. 346,
  certantibus (abl. m.) 2. 476; 4. 270.
certus
  certus 1. 59 (K; BL cautis; G certas),
  366, 436, 560; 2. 57,
  certa 2. 317, 455; 3. 599; 4. 47, 730, 744;
  8. 316,
  certi 2. 66,
  certi 5. 311,
  certam 4. 433; 5. 70,
  certa 6. 547,
  certo 3. 239; 4. 140,
  certa 4. 709,
  certo 5. 211, 353; 8. 190,
  certi 2. 457,
  certas 1. 59 (G; K certus; BL cautis),
  certa 3. 134,
  certis (f.) 1. 233,
  certior 1. 191; 3. 622,
  certior 1. 18.
ceruchi
  ceruchos 1. 469.
cerva
  cerva 3. 634,
  cervae (gen.) 6. 70.
cervix
  cervix 2. 502; 4. 310; 6. 199; 8. 89,
  cervice 1. 259, 349; 2. 426; 3. 141, 334;
  4. 266; 6. 700.
cervus
  cervum 3. 545,
  cervos 6. 420, 568.
Cessaeus (K; Cissaeus G; Cossaeus BL)
  Cessaeae (nom.) 6. 130.
cesso
  cessat 4. 414,
  cessantem (m.) 1. 443,
  cessante (m.) 3. 483.

ceterus
cetera (nom. f.) 1. 354; 3. 668; 4. 692;
6. 484; 8. 15, 310,
subst. n. cetera 3. 281, 443,
cetera 1. 267, 696; 2. 179; 5. 630; 7. 170,
222, 225.
cetus
cete 2. 317 (?) (BG; K taetae; L taete).
ceu (30)
1. c. sing. verbis.
ceu 2. 630; 3. 101; 4. 152, 401, 452, 531,
550; 5. 543; 6. 587; 8. 90,
2. c. ind.
ceu 3. 83, 558 (L; KBG sic), 577; 5.
521; 6. 346; 8. 63, 230 (L; KBG seu),
ceu . . . cum 3. 465; 4. 44, 280; 7. 301,
ceu . . . tali 3. 581,
ceu . . . ubi 3. 264,
3. c. subi.
ceu 3. 281, 654; 4. 564 (KL; BG cum);
5. 163, 191, 353, 580.
Vid. aliter, haud, sic.
Chalcidicus
Chalcidicas 1. 454.
Chalciope
Chalciopes 7. 156,
Chalciopen 6. 479.
Chalybes
Chalybum 4. 611; 5. 141.
chalybs
chalybs 1. 593; 5. 168, 540; 6. 342.
Chaonius
Chaonii (m.) 1. 303,
Chaonio (abl. m.) 8. 461.
Chaos
Chaos (nom.) 1. 830.
chaos
chaos (acc.) 2. 86; 4. 123; 5. 95; 7. 402.
chelys
chelyn 1. 139.
Chiron
Chiron 1. 139, 255,
Chironis 1. 407,
Chiron 1. 267.
chlamys
chlamys 3. 118; 5. 588; 6. 226, 526, 708,
chlamydem 2. 409; 5. 512.
Choaspes
Choaspen 5. 584.
Choatrae
Choatras 6. 151.
chorus
chorus 2; 259 (KBG; L tholus), 537;
5. 565, 693,
chori (nom.) 1. 844,
choros 2. 188, 282; 5. 239, 344.
ci vid. ce.
cieo
ciet 1. 751; 2. 304; 7. 578,
ciebat 8. 69,
ciere 1. 754; 3. 63 (inde ciere KGL; B
incitat aere),
ciens 1. 803; 3. 156; 4. 549,
ciens (f.) 7. 313,
cientem (m.) 3. 562.

Cimmerii
Cimmerium 3. 399.
Cimmerius
Cimmerias 6. 61.
cingo
cingit 2. 554,
cingent 1. 90,
cinxere 4. 102; 6. 68,
cingentibus (abl. f.) 4. 92 (KG; BL
urgentibus),
cingitur 5. 566; 6. 477; 7. 355; 8. 377
(B; KGL scinditur),
cincta 4. 418 (KGL; B vincta),
cinctum (m.) 6. 135.
cingulum
cingula 7. 174,
cingula 3. 142, 342, 526; 6. 471.
cinis
cinis 4. 509; 7. 206,
cineri 2. 600; 3. 357; 5. 97,
cinerem 1. 442 (BL; KG celerem);
5. 62.
circa (adv.)
3. 283; 8. 2,
circa (praepos.)
4. 759; 6. 173.
Circaeus
Circaei (gen. m.) 5. 327,
Circaeos 6. 426,
Circaeis (m.) 7. 544.
Circe
Circe 6. 445,
Circen 7. 120, 212,
Circe (voc.) 7. 217, 347.
circueo
circuit 7. 114.
circum (adv.) (16)
1. 690, 714; 2. 17, 40, 266, 348, 412; 3.
418, 426; 4. 488, 640; 5. 337, 694; 7. 168,
305; 8. 93.
circum (praepos.)
1. 223; 6. 66, 302, 746; 7. 526.
circumdo
circumdata (nom. f.) 8. 33.
circumfero
circumfert 6. 349; 7. 123.
circumfluo
circumfluat 2. 645.
circumfluus
circumflua (nom. f.) 5. 442.
circumfundo
circumfusa (nom. f.) 1. 384.
circumspicio
circumspicit 1. 756, 767; 6. 438,
circumspice 5. 355.
circumvenio
circumvenit (prs.) 1. 400; 3. 118.
Cissaeus vid. Cessaeus.
cista
cistam 7. 333 (B; KGL qua non),
cistas 2. 267,
cistis 8. 17.
cithara
citharae (gen.) 5. 693,
cithara 3. 158.

Cithaeron
  Cithaeron 5. 81.
cito
  citatarum 3. 527,
  citato (abl. n.) 6. 198.
citus
  citus 1. 159, 749; 4. 382; 5. 622; 6. 218;
  7. 179,
  cita 3. 197,
  citum (m.) 2. 449,
  cita (abl.) 5. 106,
  citis (abl. f.) 3. 498.
clades
  cladem 4. 173; 6. 725,
  clade 5. 419; 8. 375.
clam
  4. 136.
clamo
  clamat 8. 145,
  clamantem 1. 256; 5. 441,
  clamantem 4. 411,
  clamantia (acc.) 1. 292.
clamor
  clamor 1. 186, 681; 2. 112, 240, 389;
  3. 58, 84; 7. 629; 8. 129,
  clamorem 8. 295,
  clamore 1. 158, 752; 2. 391, 461; 3. 95,
  128, 350; 4. 502, 516, 575; 5. 28; 8. 172,
  263, 326,
  clamoribus (abl.) 1. 646; 2. 539; 4. 72;
  6. 521, 751.
clango
  clangente (f.) 3. 349.
clangor
  clangor 7. 611,
  clangore 4. 579.
Clanis
  Clanis (nom.) 1. 146.
clareo
  claret 1. 671 (K; BG stare et; L stare).
claresco
  clarescant 7. 31.
Clarius
  Clarii (gen. m.) 3. 299.
clarus
  clarus 3. 537; 8. 26,
  clara 6. 181,
  clari 1. 452; 6. 222,
  clarae (gen.) 1. 416, 850 (G; KBL
  almae); 4. 82,
  clarum (m.) 7. 84,
  claro (m.) 4. 348; 8. 152,
  claros 5. 507,
  clara 1. 495; 5. 645 (BGL; K cara),
  clarior (f.) 6. 146.
classis
  classem 1. 720; 8. 324,
  classe 1. 551; 8. 261, 380,
  classes (acc.) 1. 800.
claudo
  claudit 1. 395,
  claudat 1. 803,
  clausus 1. 602,
  clausa 1. 703,
  clausum 4. 688,

clausae (gen.) 2. 338,
clausum (m.) 2. 568,
clausos 8. 371, 387,
clausis (n.) 1. 417; 5. 140.
claustrum
  claustra 1. 557; 3. 53,
  claustra 1. 595; 5. 77, 124,
  claustris 5. 604; 6. 106; 7. 570.
clava
  clavae (gen.) 1. 111,
  clavam 3. 168,
  clava 3. 162.
clavus
  clavi 2. 430,
  clavo (abl.) 3. 40.
clemens
  clementi (abl. m.) 6. 747.
Cleonaeus
  Cleonaeo (abl. m.) 1. 34.
Cleopatra
  Cleopatra (nom.) 4. 464.
Clio
  Clio (voc.) 3. 15.
clipeus
  clipei 3. 199; 6. 367, 517,
  clipeo 7. 585,
  clipeum 6. 551, 654; 7. 465,
  clipeo 8. 310,
  clipei 3. 76,
  clipeos 8. 301.
Clite
  Clite (nom.) 3. 11, 314.
clivus
  clivos 5. 484 (KBL; G divos).
cludo
  cluseris (subi.) 7. 230 (B; KGL cluserit),
  cluserit 7. 230 (KGL; B cluseris),
  clusus 1. 34,
  clusos 1. 239.
Clymenus
  Clymenus 1. 369.
Coastes
  Coastes 6. 155.
Codrus
  Codri 2. 136.
Cocytius
  Cocytia (nom. f.) 4. 495.
Coelaletae
  Coelaletae 6. 81.
coeo
  coit 1. 684; 2. 460; 3. 253, 579; 8. 137,
  coeunt 5. 635,
  coiere 6. 9 (BGL; K que coire), 232
  (BGL; K que coire); 8. 120,
  coire 6. 9 (que coire K; BGL coiere),
  232 (que coire K; BGL coiere); 8. 284
  (que coire BG; KL coiisse), 429,
  coiisse 8. 284 (KL; BG que coire).
coepi
  coepistis 5. 676,
  coeperat 1. 285; 4. 677; 5. 178, 670; 7.
  390, 451,
  coeptis (abl. f.) 2. 349,

subst. n. coepti 2. 525,
  coepto (abl.) 3. 513 (L; KBG ponto),
  caeptis 1. 165, 242; 2. 264, 596; 3. 416;
  6. 287,
  coepta 1. 499; 3. 503; 7. 183,
  coeptis 2. 368.
coeptum vid. coepi.
coerceo
  coercet 4. 683; 5. 672.
coetus
  coetu (abl.) 1. 121; 3. 629; 5. 312,
  coetus (acc.) 3. 413.
Coeus
  Coeus 3. 224.
cogito
  cogitat 8. 404,
  cogitet 8. 242.
cognatus
  cognati (gen. m.) 5. 186; 6. 593; 7. 14,
  cognatis (m.) 6. 544,
  cognatas 5. 538.
cognomen
  cognomen (nom.) 6. 642.
cognosco
  cognoscit 6. 266,
  cognovit 6. 210,
  cognoscere 1. 168; 2. 2; 8. 416,
  cognita est 3. 397,
  cognita (nom. f.) 4. 577; 5. 354,
  cognita (voc.) 2. 639,
  cognita (nom.) 1. 789.
cogo
  cogit 2. 505; 4. 144; 7. 112, 595,
  cogam (ind.) 7. 185,
  cogat 8. 388,
  cogere 1. 438,
  cogar (subi.) 7. 202, 239,
  cogi 1. 65,
  coactum (nom.) 2. 465; 8. 88,
  coacto (abl. m.) 4. 687,
  coacta (acc.) 3. 496.
cohibeo
  cohibens (f.) 4. 359.
cohors
  cohors 1. 593, 703; 6. 112,
  cohortes (acc.) 7. 637.
Colaxes
  Colaxes 6. 48, 621, 646.
Colchi
  Colchi 3. 698; 4. 706; 5. 440; 6. 190, 242,
  Colchorum 6. 417,
  Colchis 3. 681; 5. 451, 633; 6. 742; 8. 156,
  320, 326,
  Colchos 1. 66, 201, 327, 391, 743; 3. 82;
  4. 618; 5. 178, 283, 421; 6. 30, 389, 530,
  691; 7. 231; 8. 313, 328 (L; KBG
  Minyas),
  Colchi 8. 264,
  Colchis 5. 50.
Colchis
  Colchis 5. 349; 7. 181, 389, 584, 596;
  8. 68, 70, 83, 338,
  Colchidos 7. 369, 625,
  Colchida 6. 468; 7. 153, 190, 575; 8. 2.

Colchis
  1. subst.
  Colchidos 2. 423; 5. 202,
  Colchida 1. 52; 5. 505; 8. 161 (K; BG
  litora; L om.),
  2. adi.
  Colchidos 5. 418,
  Colchides (nom.) 8. 142.
colligo
  colligit 2. 354; 7. 88, 335,
  collegerat 6. 57,
  collectas 1. 433.
collis
  colle 3. 7,
  collibus (abl.) 2. 537; 7. 391.
colloquium
  colloquiis (dat.) 3. 293.
collum
  collo (dat.) 6. 669; 7. 618,
  colla (acc.) 1. 90, 192, 378; 2. 425, 533,
  547; 3. 331; 6. 365; 8. 124.
colo
  colit 1. 44,
  colunt 4. 103; 6. 405,
  colimur 5. 642,
  culta est 5. 591,
  culta (nom. f.) 1. 838.
colonus
  colono (dat.) 7. 549,
  coloni 2. 461,
  colonis (dat.) 4. 597; 6. 334.
color
  color 8. 163,
  colores 2. 467,
  colores 6. 492.
coluber
  colubris (abl.) 6. 175.
columba
  columbae (gen.) 8. 32.
columen
  columen (acc.) 1. 117.
columna
  columnae (nom.) 6. 91.
colus
  colus (gen.) 2. 148,
  colus (acc.) 6. 445, 645.
coma
  coma 3. 50; 5. 588, 591,
  comam 1. 208; 2. 265,
  comae 3. 54, 560; 6. 709,
  comarum 1. 229,
  comis 3. 436; 8. 238,
  comas 2. 213 (KBG; L comis); 3. 315,
  716; 4. 418; 6. 664,
  comis 1. 777; 2. 26, 213 (L; KBG
  comas).
comes
  comes 1. 95; 705; 2. 420, 451; 3. 387,
  678; 4. 163, 468, 701; 5. 187, 403; 6. 71;
  7. 202; 8. 55,
  comitis 3. 579, 734; 4. 37,
  comiti 1. 119; 3. 688; 5. 6,
  comitem 1. 763; 3. 195, 662, 694; 5. 90;
  6. 213,
  comite 4. 6,

comitum 4. 591; 5. 40, 128, 346; 6. 161;
7. 121, 265; 8. 27, 390, 431, 436,
comites 5. 113.
Cometes
Cometes 1. 356.
cometes
cometae (nom.) 6. 608.
comitatus
comitatus (nom. s.) 6. 113.
comitor
comitatur 6. 524,
comitentur 5. 325,
comitantem (m.) 6. 558,
comitante (f.) 5. 342,
comitanda (nom. f.) 5. 292.
commemoro
commemorant 5. 181.
commendo
commendat 5. 62.
commercium
commercia (acc.) 1. 246.
comminiscor
commenta (nom. f.) 1. 599.
comminus (12)
1. 232, 263, 366; 3. 104, 635; 4. 324,
563, 682; 5. 582; 6. 347, 356, 518.
committo
committunt 3. 190,
commisit 6. 31,
committat 8. 396,
committere 1. 413,
committitur 4. 310,
commissa (nom. f.) 6. 491.
commoveo
commovet 2. 33,
commovit 4. 486,
commoverat 5. 71,
commotus 4. 76,
commotis (abl. m.) 7. 195.
communis
commune 8. 167,
communem (m.) 7. 227,
communes (acc. m.) 4. 761; 7. 228.
como
comanti (abl. n.) 3. 136, 402,
comantem 5. 594,
comantem 8. 122,
comantes (acc. m.) 5. 366,
comantes 1. 429,
subst. comatos 7. 636.
como
comptis (dat. m.) 5. 592.
compello
compellat 2. 402, 591; 7. 451.
compendium
compendia (acc.) 1. 484.
compesco
compescuit 1. 338,
compesce 1. 606; 6. 306,
compescere 6. 153; 7. 185.
complector
complecteris (prs.) 1. 195,
complexus 3. 289,
complexa (nom. f.) 5. 109; 8. 7,
complexa (acc.) 5. 230.

compleo
complerunt 3. 261,
compleverat 5. 225,
complerat 6. 621,
complentur 8. 138.
compono
componunt 3. 279,
componam (ind.) 7. 208,
componere 1. 321; 5. 295; 6. 326; 7.
247; 8. 394.
comprehendo
comprehensa (acc.) 3. 609.
compresso
compressans (m.) 1. 491 (K; BGL
compressus).
comprimo
compressus 1. 491 (BGL; K compressans),
compressa (acc.) 3. 106, 331.
conamen
conamina (acc.) 4. 40.
concavus
concava (acc.) 4. 594.
concedo
concedit 3. 616,
concedere 1. 554.
concentus
concentus (nom. s.) 6. 166.
concido
concidit (perf.) 4. 123; 7. 546 (L; KBG
que addidit),
conciderit (subi.) 3. 203.
concieo
concierit (subi.) 6. 35,
concitus 1. 211, 291, 577,
concita (nom. f.) 2. 460,
concita (nom. f.) 6. 705,
concita (acc.) 5. 576,
concita (acc.) 1. 3; 3. 556; 4. 672.
concilio
conciliat 3. 496; 4. 29,
conciliet 1. 794.
concilium
concilium (acc.) 1. 213; 2. 313,
conciliis (abl.) 1. 789 (KBG; L consiliis).
concipio
concipit 1. 748; 3. 227; 5. 521.
concito
concitat 3. 583; 6. 264, 341.
conclamo
conclamat 3. 259; 6. 29,
conclamant 4. 292, 693.
concolor
concolor (m.) 1. 611.
concordia
concordia (nom.) 3. 464.
concors
concordes (acc. m.) 6. 407,
concordia 8. 248.
concresco
concrescere 4. 723,
concretos 3. 286.

concurro
concurrunt 1. 630; 6. 242, 409,
concurrere 1. 59; 2. 660; 3. 18, 512; 4. 155, 562; 6. 25, 177; 8. 196.

concutio
concutit 7. 590,
concute 6. 476,
concutiens (m.) 2. 530; 6. 7; 8. 263,
concusso (abl.) 1. 340,
concussa 6. 650,
concussi 3. 348.

condensus
condensae (nom.) 2. 172.

condo
condit 1. 148; 2. 320,
condunt 4. 636; 5. 106,
condebat 2. 443,
condidit 3. 636, 731; 4. 676; 5. 90,
condere (fut.) 1. 680,
condere 7. 390,
condi 7. 298,
conditus 2. 64; 5. 88,
condita (nom. f.) 5. 198,
condita (nom.) 1. 531,
condita 8. 17.

conduco
conducere 1. 480.

conecto
conectit 4. 334.

confercio
confertae (gen.) 3. 274 (KGL; B consortis).

confero
contulit 1. 359,
conferre 2. 222; 3. 309,
conlatis (abl. m.) 6. 270.

conficio
confecta (nom. f.) 6. 384.

confido
confidere 1. 176; 6. 625.

confingo
confingis 2. 130 (L; KBG cum fingis).

confinis
confinibus (abl. f.) 2. 632,
subst. n. confine (acc.) 6. 374,
confinia (acc.) 2. 634; 4. 574; 8. 180.

confodio
confodiunt 6. 419.

confragus
subst. n. confraga (acc.) 3. 582.

confundo
confundere 5. 580,
confusa (acc.) 1. 79.

congelo
congelat 3. 578.

congemino
congeminat 2. 201, 535,
congeminant 4. 71; 6. 513,
congeminans (f.) 6. 379.

congemo
congemuere 5. 12.

congeries
congeries 3. 98,
congeriem 6. 511.

congero
congerit 4. 306, 717; 6. 630.

congressus
congressu (abl.) 6. 322.

congruo
congruit (prs.) 6. 59,
congruerat 2. 307.

conicio
coniciunt 6. 271,
coniectis (dat. f.) 6. 381.

conitor
conisus 3. 193.

coniugium
coniugii 8. 206, 227,
coniugio 3. 535; 8. 279,
coniugio 1. 523; 8. 300,
coniugiis 8. 393,
coniugia 2. 173.

coniungo
coniungere 4. 176; 6. 450, 732; 7. 344.

coniunx
coniunx 1. 729, 734, 762; 2. 144, 191, 208, 229, 237, 427; 3. 10, 114, 276, 316, 323; 4. 684; 5. 446, 647; 6. 44, 82, 688; 7. 199, 232, 236, 486; 8. 23,
coniugis 1. 86, 116; 2. 99; 6. 274, 585,
coniunx 2. 113; 5. 677; 7. 497; 8. 419,
coniuge 1. 138, 403; 2. 183, 226, 551; 8. 243.

conlabor
conlabitur 7. 152,
conlapsa 7. 251,
conlapsam 1. 348.

conluceo
conlucent 3. 351.

conluvies
conluvie 4. 497.

conor
conanti (dat. m.) 1. 156 (BGL; K cunctanti),
conantem (f.) 4. 372,
conante (m.) 5. 338,
conata (nom. f.) 7. 118.

conscendo
conscenderat 2. 444,
conscendere 1. 410 (KBG; L escendere).

conscius
conscius 2. 280; 4. 295; 5. 3 (L; KBG inscius),
conscia (nom.) 1. 5, 526; 3. 211, 301, 584; 8. 401,
conscia (nom.) 4. 356,
conscia 2. 254, 410; 3. 262.

consero
conseruere 3. 123,
conserat 3. 31,
consere 6. 539,
conseritur 6. 353,
conserta (acc.) 2. 616,
consertis (abl. n.) 6. 182.

consido
considunt 2. 442,
consedit 1. 4,
consideret 8. 166,

consederit 7. 119,
considere 3. 459; 4. 511; \5. 234.
consilium
consilia 7. 349; 8. 384,
consiliis 6. 14; 7. 70,
consilia 4. 480; 5. 281; 6. 432; 8. 436,
consiliis 1. 789 (L; KBG conciliis);
3. 504.
consisto
consistit 8. 133,
constitit 1. 127; 2. 462, 588; 6. 209 (KB;
G contigit; L insilit); 8. 311,
constiterat 5. 275.
consono
consonat 5. 160.
consors
consortis (f.) 3. 274 (B; KGL confertae),
consortem (f.) 3. 489.
consortium
consortia (acc.) 3. 677.
conspicio
conspicit 6. 579; 8. 57,
conspiciunt 1. 823,
conspexit 1. 786,
conspicienda (nom. n.) 1. 261,
conspecta (nom. f.) 8. 210,
conspecta (nom.) 6. 296.
conspicuus
conspicuus 1. 253.
constituo
constituit (prs.) 3. 92; 4. 153.
constringo
constringit 3. 80,
constrictos 6. 422.
consuesco
consuetis (dat. n.) 4. 449.
consulo
consulit 3. 38,
consulite 3. 624; 4. 154.
consultum
consulta (acc.) 1. 241; 8. 418.
consumo
consumere 1. 831.
consurgo
consurgit 1. 362, 387; 7. 88,
consurgere 1. 75, 499, 625, 673; 2. 478,
consurgens (m.) 5. 91, 155.
contego
contegat 1. 814; 5. 58,
contectus 1. 279,
contecta (nom. f.) 4. 178.
contendo
contendere 3. 452, 548,
contenta (nom. f.) 3. 136,
contenta (nom.) 4. 748.
contentus
contenta (nom. f.) 7. 354; 8. 453,
contenti (nom.) 8. 178.
conterreo
conterret 7. 515,
conterrita (nom. f.) 7. 397; 8. 22.
contexo
contexere 2. 108,
contextis (abl. m.) 3.90.

conticeo
conticuit 3. 302.
conticesco
conticuit 1. 59,
conticuere 1. 295; 3. 732,
conticuisse 2. 263; 7. 432.
contingo
contigit 1. 817; 3. 587; 6. 209 (G; KB
constitit; L insilit), 677; 7. 5,
contigimus 5. 506,
contigeras 6. 320,
contingat 7. 537,
contingere 1. 377; 4. 620; 7. 173.
continuo (8)
1. 576; 3. 254, 459, 581; 4. 261; 6. 184;
7. 174, 184.
continuus
continuam 4. 319.
contollo
contollit 8. 446 (L; KBG cum tollit).
contorqueo
contorquens (m.) 1. 455,
contorto (abl. m.) 1. 609.
contra (adv.) (52)
contra 1. 137, 228, 387 (L; KBG etiam),
529, 539, 762, 806, 834; 2. 98, 224, 550;
3. 13, 155, 495; 4. 112, 137, 194, 209,
409, 689; 5. 26, 171, 263, 442, 511, 541,
581, 599, 672; 6. 178, 248, 307, 362, 363,
488, 512, 590; 7. 237, 307 **bis**, 328, 388,
477, 506, 543, 556, 630; 8. 45, 62 (KGL;
B quoniam), 83, 372,
at contra 6. 472.
contra (praepos.) (11)
1. 151, 663; 3. 644, 706; 4. 94, 165; 6.
216, 348, 373; 7. 362, 371.
contraho
contrahit 3. 728; 7. 369.
contrecto
contrectat 6. 669.
contremo
contremuit 7. 80.
contristo
contristat 3. 427; 6. 622.
contundo
contundere 1. 424.
contus
conti 6. 72, 162,
conto 6. 256 (vid. abl.),
conto 6. 256 (vid. dat.).
conubium
conubia (acc.) 8. 277, 421.
conus
conus 3. 51,
coni 6. 604,
cono (abl.) 1. 386.
convallis
convallibus (abl.) 2. 515.
convello
convellens (m.) 5. 158.
convenio
conveniunt 5. 467.
converto
converte 4. 539,
convertere 7. 625,

conversus 3. 343; 5. 128,
conversa (nom.) 1. 618; 7. 160, 470,
conversae (nom.) 7. 634,
conversas 6. 698,
conversa 3. 256.
convivium
convivia (acc.) 2. 341; 4. 760; 5. 570.
copia
copia (nom.) 1. 102; 6. 337.
coquo
coquitur 2. 333.
cor
corde 1. 734; 2. 568; 5. 132, 264, 654; 6. 2,
corda 1. 316; 2. 647; 3. 75, 94, 237, 375, 722,
corda 1. 799; 2. 187; 3. 693; 4. 158; 5. 290.
Coralli
Coralli 6. 89.
corniger
corniger 2. 482.
cornipes
subst. m. cornipedes (acc.) 2. 488.
cornu
cornu (abl.) 1. 624; 2. 56; 4. 685; 5. 153, 485; 6. 92; 7. 592; 8. 72, 186,
cornua 1. 36; 2. 271; 3. 266; 7. 611,
cornua 1. 312, 726, 776, 787; 3. 238; 4. 96, 361; 5. 79; 6. 376; 7. 302, 588; 8. 294,
cornibus 1. 89, 106, 282; 3. 546; 4. 406; 6. 71, 160, 421, 532; 7. 590 (BL; KG carminis); 8. 29.
cornus
cornum 3. 156.
corona
coronae (gen.) 5. 447,
coronam 8. 235,
corona 4. 336.
corono
coronatae (gen.) 1. 301.
corpus
corpus 4. 41,
corpus 7. 285; 8. 108, 347, 349,
corpore 6. 52, 351 (KGL; B pectore), 352, 357; 8. 82 (BL; KG ab arbore),
corpora 4. 183 (L; KBG ossaque), 283; 6. 185,
corpora 2. 70 (BGL; K pectora), 221, 324, 484, 653; 3. 333; 4. 108; 5. 36, 611; 6. 522, 559.
corripio
corripit 1. 132; 4. 654; 6. 277, 292; 7. 148, 460; 8. 117,
corripiunt 5. 328,
corripuit 6. 284,
corripe 3. 501,
correpta 5. 450; 6. 263,
correpto (abl. m.) 6. 189.
cortex
corticis 6.97.
cortina
cortina (nom.) 1. 6.

corusco
coruscat 1. 703; 5. 304,
coruscet 2. 228,
coruscanti (abl. f.) 4. 670.
coruscus
coruscus 3. 129; 6. 517,
corusci 7. 567,
corusci 6. 55,
coruscum 1. 486,
coruscum 1. 805,
corusco (m.) 5. 182,
coruscae 1. 622,
coruscis (abl. f.) 3. 458.
corymbus
corymbis 4. 691,
corymbis 1. 273; 8. 194.
Corythus
Corythi 3. 99.
Cossaeus vid. Cessaeus
cothurnus
cothurno (dat.) 1. 384.
Cotys
Cotys 3. 112.
cras
5. 607 **bis**; 7. 441 (K; BGL pars).
crastinus
crastinus 7. 97,
crastina (nom. f.) 2. 566; 8. 180.
crater
cratera 1. 337; 4. 343; 5. 615, 694,
cratere 5. 571,
crateres (nom.) 1. 142.
crates
cratem 2. 109; 3. 199.
creatrix
creatrix 5. 142.
creber
crebra 8. 334,
crebro (abl. m.) 4. 285; 5. 310,
crebros 4. 306,
crebra 2. 23,
crebris (m.) 3. 338,
crebrior (m.) 5. 550.
crebresco
crebrescit 3. 210 (KBG; L crudescit).
credo
credo 4. 206, 476, 653; 5. 379; 7. 445,
credis 6. 675; 7. 491; 8. 147,
credit 3. 223, 549, 569; 7. 151,
credam 1. 332,
credidit 8. 437,
credideras 8. 315,
credat 5. 171,
credamus 7. 52,
credideris 1. 176,
crede 3. 542, 689; 4. 125, 603; 5. 510; 7. 228, 449, 478, 520; 8. 12,
credite 2. 322; 3. 82; 4. 477,
credere 1. 84; 2. 292; 4. 622; 6. 51, 661,
creditur 1. 69 (B; K ardet ut; GL creditus); 5. 103,
creditus 1. 69 (GL; K ardet ut; B creditur); 5. 357,
credita (nom. f.) 2. 345; 4. 150,
credita (acc.) 6. 215.

Cremedon
Cremedonis 6. 194.
cremo
cremari 5. 33,
cremandis (dat. m.) 5. 275.
Crenaeus
Crenaee 3. 178.
creo
creavit 5. 657 (BG; KL crearit),
crearit (subi.) 5. 657 (KL; BG creavit),
creantia (acc.) 5. 484 (G; K gravantia;
B armantia; L ornantia),
creari 7. 612,
subst. m. creatis (dat.) 4. 432.
crepido
crepidine 4. 44.
cresco
crescit 5. 31,
crescunt 7. 308,
crevit 6. 262,
crescere 1. 502,
cretus 4. 444.
Cretheius
Cretheia 8. 112,
Cretheia (voc. f.) 2. 611.
Cretheus
Cretheus 1. 740; 5. 477,
Cretheos 1. 42.
Crethides
Crethiden 6. 609.
crimen
crimine 1. 696; 2. 80; 3. 298 (sine
crimine K; BGL potius nunc), 493; 4.
430; 5. 658; 6. 87,
crimina (acc.) 4. 478.
crinio
crinita (nom. f.) 5. 370.
crinis
crinis (nom.) 3. 526; 6. 62,
crimen 1. 205, 612; 2. 103; 8. 7, 68 (KG;
B virgam; L vimen),
crine 3. 132; 6. 129, 144, 189, 643,
crines (acc.) 1. 218, 293, 412, 449; 3.
264, 286; 6. 176, 563; 7. 250; 8. 348,
crinibus 2. 42; 4. 413; 5. 415; 6. 618.
crispo
crispans (f.) 1. 311.
crista
crista (abl.) 3. 62,
cristas 3. 176; 5. 563; 7. 467,
cristis 7. 616; 8. 61.
Crobialus
Crobiali 5. 102.
croceus
croceo (abl. n.) 8. 234,
croceos 5. 590,
croceis (f.) 4. 23.
Cromna
Cromnae (gen.) 5. 105.
crudelis
crudelis 1. 695; 6. 561,
crudelis (nom. f.) 2. 484; 3. 611; 4.
459; 7. 341; 8. 94,
crudelis (n.) 5. 143,

crudele 3. 302,
crudelia (acc.) 5. 271.
crudesco
crudescit 3. 210 (L; KBG crebrescit),
crudescere 2. 509.
crudus
crudi 4. 250 (L; KBG crudis); 6. 97,
crudi 2. 542,
cruda 7. 318 (L; KBG una),
crudo 6. 82,
crudis (abl. m.) 4. 250 (KBG; L crudi).
cruentus
cruentus 6. 654,
cruento (abl.) 8. 395,
cruenta (abl.) 2. 27,
cruentis (m.) 2. 156,
cruenta 8. 346,
cruentis (f.) 2. 303.
cruor
cruor 1. 735; 2. 233; 6. 185, 724; 7.
359,
cruorem 1. 818, 822,
cruores (acc.) 4. 330; 5. 585; 6. 614,
705; 7. 552; 8. 241.
cubile
cubile 5. 154,
cubili 4. 464,
cubile 2. 137, 345; 7. 21,
cubili 6. 689; 7. 116; 8. 9,
cubilia (acc.) 3. 37; 5. 144.
culmen
culmen (acc.) 2. 179,
culmine 5. 445,
culmina 4. 260,
culmina 5. 646.
culpa
culpa 7. 386,
culpae 4. 356,
culpae 3. 392,
culpam 3. 407; 4. 477; 6. 744.
culpo
culpanda (nom. f.) 1. 244.
cultus
cultus (nom.) 4. 611; 5. 357,
cultu (abl.) 2. 646; 5. 354, 570 (K;
BGL vultu),
cultus (acc.) 1. 15; 6. 224.
cum (praepos.) (54)
1. 138, 155, 612, 617; 2. 29, 141, 183,
223, 365, 478, 551, 609; 3. 330, 358,
577, 612, 638, 723, 732; 4. 33, 66, 265,
336, 393, 502, 576; 5. 90, 158, 161, 273,
348, 478 **bis,** 603; 6. 60, 69, 74, 89, 148,
188; 7. 57 (KGL; B quam), 71, 204,
391, 458; 8. 120, 132, 205, 236, 243, 261,
268, 356, 377.
Vid. ego, tu, sui.
cum (coni.) (131)
1. c. ind.
a) prs. 1. 48, 240, 490, 594, 637, 781 (K;
BGL tum); 2. 103 (ea cum B; K eadem; GL aut), 115, 129, 130 (cum
fingis KBG; L confingis), 436, 453,
467, 507, 643; 3. 57, 91, 163, 209, 224,
419, 552, 579, 604; 4. 43, 45, 222, 281

(KBL; G dum), 286, 357 (BG; KL
tum), 564 (BG; KL ceu), 607, 626 (G;
KBL tum), 680; 5. 124, 304, 368, 369,
456, 673; 6. 169, 277, 353, 378, 402, 412,
429, 644; 7. 24, 142, 303, 359, 400, 623,
648; 8. 56, 115, 177, 230, 446 (cum
tollit KBG; L contollit),
b) imperf. 4. 748,
c) fut. 1. 16, 171 bis, 181; 2. 338; 4. 524,
d) perf. 1. 337, 622, 624, 641, 682, 704,
726, 765; 2. 36, 51, 75, 90 (KG; BL
dum), 458; 3. 384, 466, 635; 4. 384, 490,
507, 579; 5. 253, 276; 6. 532, 573, 684,
715; 7. 90, 172, 321, 564, 569; 8. 306,
461,
e) perf. et prs. 4. 60,
f) plperf. 5. 224 (B; KGL iam),
g) fut. perf. 1. 466; 3. 501; 4. 583; 5.
237; 7. 469,
    2. c. subi.
a) imperf. 1. 82, 291, 534, 535 (KL;
BG cur), 588, 589, 662 (BG; KL qui);
2. 491; 3. 353, 530, 539, 617; 4. 164; 6.
140; 7. 259, 288,
b) perf. 5. 529 (L; KBG cur),
    3. sine verb.
2. 477 (KL; BG tum); 3. 700; 4. 641,
731; 5. 403; 6. 231; 7. 332.
Vid. ceu, dum, haud, iamque, qualiter,
quam, sic, talis, tum, tunc, ut, velut,
veluti.

cumulo
cumulat 1. 204.

cunabula
cunabula (acc.) 5. 417.

cunctor
cunctatur 1. 757 (BL; KG cunctatus);
3. 606; 7. 335, 627; 8. 403,
cunctamur 3. 656,
cunctanti (m.) 1. 156 (K; BGL conanti),
cunctantem (m.) 2. 93; 4. 277,
cunctantes (m.) 7. 64,
cunctantia 7. 176,
cunctantibus (m.) 2. 377,
cunctantes (m.) 3. 613,
cunctantia 3. 693,
cunctatus 1. 757 (KG; BL cunctatur);
7. 581,
cunctata (nom. f.) 2. 320; 4. 403; 5. 392,
cunctatis (abl. f.) 7. 4,
subst. cunctantibus (dat. f.) 2. 215.

cunctus
cunctus 3. 701,
cuncta (nom.) 2. 661; 4. 64; 6. 53, 626;
7. 471,
cuncti (nom.) 1. 608; 4. 212 (K; BGL
functi); 8. 386,
cunctae 1. 815; 7. 370,
cuncta 1. 532, 557; 5. 626; 7. 641,
cunctis 1. 559; 5. 591,
cunctis (f.) 8. 199,
cunctas 2. 128; 6. 80; 8. 104,
cuncta 4. 389; 5. 228; 6. 476; 7. 518;
8. 84,

cunctis (f.) 1. 196,
cunctis 3. 451; 4. 747,
subst. cuncti (nom.) 1. 213; 3. 674; 4.
189; 5. 15, 180,
cunctae 1. 784 (G; KBL vinctae) ; 2.
187,
cuncta 2. 359; 5. 300, 362,
cunctis (m.) 5. 643; 6. 628,
cunctos 6. 36,
cunctas 2. 164,
cuncta 1. 121; 2. 223; 3. 317, 594; 4.
424; 5. 663; 6. 331, 444; 8. 449.

cuneus
cuneos 6. 632,
cuneis 3. 164.

Cupido
Cupido 8. 232.

cupido
cupido 1. 838, 845; 4. 247; 5. 536; 6. 472,
cupidine 2. 131.

cupio
cupit 5. 493; 7. 299, 409, 628, 641; 8. 5,
403,
cuperem 1. 746; 5. 534, 665,
cuperet 5. 81,
cupiens 6. 298,
cupiens (f.) 7. 434.

cupressus
cupressi (gen.) 1. 774.

cur (22)
1. 218, 535 (BG; KL cum); 2. 469; 3.
17, 76, 273, 375, 661; 4. 160, 204, 519;
5. 529 (KBG; L cum); 7. 12, 48, 280,
344, 420 (L; K dic; B nunc; G nec),
421 (K; BGL me), 439, 483, 493; 8. 165.

cura
cura 1. 179, 477; 3. 336, 397; 4. 127,
270; 5. 19, 264, 364, 533; 6. 192, 417
(cura cavere G; KB **om.**; L in peste
revinctos), 474; 7. 26, 129, 480; 8. 238,
curae 4. 541,
curae 1. 64,
curam 4. 415; 7. 350,
cura 6. 499,
cura 1. 693; 4. 354; 7. 173; 8. 76,
curae 1. 55, 759; 5. 52, 334,
curarum 1. 536,
curis 2. 161; 8. 233,
curas 1. 837; 2. 399; 3. 447, 702; 4. 489,
703; 5. 281; 6. 660; 7. 209; 8. 220,
curis 1. 329, 733; 2. 113, 137; 3. 362,
489, 623; 4. 7, 538; 5. 303, 548; 6. 623,
759; 7. 153, 241; 8. 24.

curo
curat 6. 250,
curant 6. 92.

curro
currit 3. 152,
currimus 1. 307,
curre 4. 336,
currere 1. 265; 4. 587; 5. 119, 243.

currus
currus (nom.) 2. 35; 3. 84; 6. 415,
curru (abl.) 1. 68 (KG; BL currus); 2.
266; 5. 611; 6. 370, 517, 697,

currus 6. 195, 724,
curribus 6. 416 (KGL; B orbibus),
currus 1. 68 (BL; KG curru); 2. 411;
3. 415; 5. 245; 6. 6, 105, 395, 401.
curso
cursant 4. 108.
cursus
cursus 5. 14,
cursus 4. 439,
cursum 2. 407,
cursu 1. 532; 2. 77, 612; 3. 548, 614; 4.
83; 6. 605; 8. 184,
cursus 3. 236,
cursus 1. 3, 483; 2. 49, 400; 3. 489; 5.
70, 132,
cursibus 4. 264; 6. 253, 270.
curvus
curvae 6. 424,
curvo (dat. m.) 5. 413,
curvo (abl. n.) 1. 275; 3. 636,
curvas 2. 11,
curva 1. 615; 2. 500; 3. 568; 6. 567,
curvis (m.) 4. 727.
cuspis
cuspis 1. 404, 451; 2. 618; 3. 105, 197
(BL; KG cassis); 6. 250, 259, 705,
cuspidis 3. 284; 6. 202,
cuspide 1. 392; 3. 197 (KG; BL casside); 6. 617; 7. 422.
custodia
custodia (nom.) 6. 471.
custos
custos 4. 367; 5. 356; 6. 640; 7. 517,
custodem 4. 366,
custos 4. 387 (G; KBL cantus); 8. 75.
Cyaneae
Cyaneae 4. 658, 681,
Cyaneas 1. 60; 4. 562; 5. 85, 167; 8. 181.
Cyanaeus
Cyaneae (nom.) 1. 630; 4. 638; 7. 42,
Cyaneos 2. 382; 5. 482; 8. 193.
Cybele
Cybele (nom.) 8. 240.
Cyclops
Cyclops 1. 136; 4. 287; 7. 648,
Cyclopes (nom.) 4. 104.
cycnus
cycnus 1. 432.
Cydrus
Cydrum 3. 192.
Cyllaros
Cyllaron 1. 426.
Cyllenius
Cyllenius 4. 385,
Cyllenia (nom. f.) 1. 436.
Cymaeus
Cymaeae (gen.) 1. 5.
Cymothoe
Cymothoe (nom.) 2. 605.
Cynosura
Cynosura (nom.) 1. 17.
Cynthia
Cynthia (nom.) 2. 56; 3. 558.
cyparissus
cyparissis (dat.) 7. 405.

Cyris
Cyris (nom.) 6. 80.
Cyrnus
Cyrne 6. 297.
Cytaei
Cytaei 6. 427,
Cytaeis (dat.) 5. 466.
Cytaeus
Cytaeae (gen.) 6. 156,
Cytaeis (n.) 6. 543,
Cytaeos 6. 595,
Cytaeis (f.) 6. 693.
Cythera
Cythera (acc.) 8. 229.
Cytherea
Cytherea (nom.) 2. 328; 7. 189; 8. 235.
Cytisorus
Cytisorus 5. 462.
Cytoros
Cytoron 5. 105.
Cyzicus
Cyzicus 2. 636, 656; 3. 9, 22, 60, 220,
313; 4. 441,
Cyzice 3. 326.
Daedalus
Daedalus 1. 704.
Dahae
Dahis (dat.) 2. 157.
damno
damnavit 1. 70,
damnastis 3. 260,
damnare 2. 483,
damnata 2. 16, 153,
damnati (gen. m.) 1. 787.
Danai
Danaum 1. 555; 6. 173,
Danaos 1. 371.
Danubius
Danubi 8. 293, 378.
daps
dapes 1. 137; 3. 120; 4. 634; 8. 162,
dapes 2. 155, 194; 3. 457, 569; 4. 107,
339, 429, 454; 8. 213,
dapibus 1. 62; 2. 221, 349; 4. 492.
Daraps
Daraps 6. 66, 572.
Dardanius
Dardanium (acc. m.) 2. 581,
Dardaniis (dat. f.) 2. 445.
Datis
Datin 6. 65.
de (47)
1. 41, 136, 137, 141, 332, 412, 431, 432,
555, 779, 814; 2. 449, 544; 3. 28, 126,
317, 487, 499, 619; 4. 138, 331, 348, 591,
743, 756; 5. 187, 404, 476, 500, 512; 6.
65, 137, 321, 351, 357, 640, 714, 760; 7.
45, 136, 151, 285, 356, 645; 8. 32, 344,
375.
dea
dea 2. 99, 115, 141, 175; 4. 346; 5. 378;
436; 6. 174, 488, 602, 609,
deae 5. 112, 205; 7. 237, 294; 8. 29,
deae 6. 671,
deam 1. 85; 3. 64; 7. 211, 384,

dea (voc.) 2. 302; 5. 217,
deae 1. 91, 106; 7. 272,
dearum 4. 75; 7. 151,
deas 4. 519,
deae 1. 796; 6. 41.
debeo
debuimus 2. 408; 5. 664,
debueram 3. 517,
debeat 6. 200,
debere 1. 119,
deberi 2. 570,
debitus 5. 277, 530,
debita (nom. f.) 4. 693,
debita (nom.) 3. 461,
debita 2. 552; 3. 312; 5. 21, 180; 6. 593.
decedo
decedere 2. 297, 401; 3. 736; 4. 522.
deceo
decet 6. 314; 7. 416,
decuit 7. 418; 8. 284.
decerno
decernit 7. 318 (KBG; L desaevit),
decernimus 5. 637,
decernere 4. 193; 8. 319,
decretus 3. 374,
decreta (nom. n.) 2. 433,
subst. n. decreta (acc.) 1. 536; 8. 407, 464.
decido
decidit (perf.) 2. 58,
decidat 4. 321.
decimus
decimae (gen.) 2. 54,
decima (abl.) 7. 367.
decipio
est decepta 1. 411,
deceptus 3. 22; 5. 111,
decepta 7. 161 (KGL; B defecta); 8. 418,
deceptum (acc. n.) 3. 477.
declino
declinant 3. 69.
decor
decor 5. 347; 8. 460.
decoro
decorant 3. 333.
decresco
decrescant 6. 393,
decrescere 3. 156.
decretum vid. decerno.
decurro
decurrit 3. 125, 421, 591 (KBG; L discurrit),
decurrunt 1. 186,
decurrat 1. 802,
decurrens (m.) 1. 255; 3. 526.
decus
decus 1. 114, 452; 3. 180; 4. 162, 241; 5. 378, 514; 6. 62,
decus 3. 346, 523; 5. 539, 563; 6. 470; 7. 459; 8. 117,
decus 1. 56; 2. 243, 611; 4. 630; 8. 37.
dedignor
dedignata (nom. f.) 3. 535.

dedo
deditur 2. 482.
deduco
deduxere 1. 275 (KL; BG diduxere),
deducat 6. 261,
deducere 2. 403; 4. 275.
defendo
defendite 5. 538,
defendere 1. 213; 2. 109; 7. 164,
defenditur 5. 557; 8. 353,
defensus 1. 35,
defensa (nom. n.) 4. 67.
defero
defert 4. 80,
detulit 4. 17,
deferre 2. 523,
defertur 2. 135, 535; 4. 397, 434; 6. 749; 8. 376,
delatus 4. 159,
delatum (acc. n.) 1. 122,
delata (abl.) 3. 140 (G; K delicata; BL duplicata).
defessus
defessus 7. 624,
defessum (m.) 4. 278.
deficio
deficit 3. 236; 5. 428, 446; 6. 635, 671; 7. 380,
deficiunt 3. 180; 4. 246,
deficiam 1. 331,
defecere 7. 272,
defice 2. 596; 4. 35, 592,
deficere 4. 645 (KBG; L diffugere),
defit 6. 39 (KG; BL desit),
defecta 2. 285; 7. 116, 161 (B; KGL decepta),
defectum (m.) 7. 601 (L; KBG defixum),
defecta (acc.) 2. 463, 489.
defigo
defixit 4. 226,
defixerat 5. 455; 6. 534,
defixus 5. 377; 7. 82, 407, 511; 8. 369,
defixum (m.) 7. 601 (KBG; L defectum),
defixae 6. 504,
defixa 4. 667,
defixa 5. 312.
defio vid. deficio.
deflecto
deflectere 8. 76.
defleo
deflent 3. 284,
defleta (nom. f.) 2. 79 (BGL; K dilecta); 8. 208,
defletos 5. 575,
defleta 5. 60.
deformo
deformat 3. 716.
degener
degenerem (m.) 7. 430,
degeneres (nom. m.) 6. 86,
degeneres (m.) 1. 164.
degero
degere 8. 102 (B; KGL digere).

degredior
   degreditur 6. 754 (B; KGL digreditur).
dehinc
   1. 551; 4. 760; 5. 215; 7. 596.
dehisco
   dehiscens (f.) 2. 587,
   dehiscentem (f.) 1. 624.
deicio
   deicit 1. 191; 2. 330; 6. 194, 218, 552;
   7. 514,
   deiecta 2. 470; 8. 289,
   deiecta (abl.) 1. 132; 8. 204,
   deiecta (acc.) 3. 594.
Deilion
   Deileonta 5. 114.
dein
   7. 318 (dein negat BL; KG denegat),
   588.
deinde (9)
   3. 384; 4. 273; 5. 213; 7. 20, 472, 516,
   537; 8. 109, 270.
delabor
   delabere 2. 127,
   delapsa (nom. f.) 3. 533; 7. 399 (B;
   KGL dilapsa),
   delapsa (acc.) 2. 62.
delicatus
   delicata (abl.) 3. 140 (K; BL duplicata; G delata).
deligo
   deligerit (subi.) 3. 201.
Delius
   Delius 1. 446; 3. 432.
delphin
   delphin 1. 131.
delubrum
   delubra (acc.) 1. 15; 2. 188, 301; 7. 179.
deludo
   deludit 6. 240.
demens
   demens 3. 63; 4. 556; 5. 656,
   demens (f.) 2. 204; 6. 474; 7. 12, 128,
   433.
demeto
   demetit 3. 157.
demitto
   demittit 3, 41; 4. 77; 5. 691 (KBL; G
   dimittit); 6. 64,
   demittere 1. 94; 7. 314,
   demissa (nom. f.) 1. 581; 2. 434, 635,
   demissa (acc.) 3. 640.
demum
   hic demum 4. 548,
   sic demum 4. 616,
   tum demum 3. 633.
denego
   denegat 7. 318 (KG; BL dein negat).
denique
   3. 345; 5. 17; 8. 451.
dens
   dentis (gen.) 7. 554,
   dentibus (abl.) 3. 589; 4. 215; 6. 437;
   7. 76.

denso
   densant 7. 628,
   denset 3. 207 (B; K resonat; G donat;
   L duplicat).
densus
   densus 5. 168,
   densa 3. 163 (KBG; L magna),
   densam 2. 367; 3. 575,
   densa 3. 163 (L; KBG magna), 484;
   5. 414 (L; KBG densae); 6. 229, 507,
   577,
   densi 6. 89, 683,
   densae 5. 414 (KBG; L densa),
   densa (acc.) 3. 604,
   densis 3. 87; 4. 325,
   densis 6. 583,
   densis 1. 205,
   densior (f.) 6. 76.
depello
   depellit 1. 652,
   depulit 6. 652,
   depulerat 3. 566.
depingo
   depicta (nom. f.) 6. 226.
depono
   deponere 5. 34.
depopulo
   depopulant 4. 429,
   depopulare 6. 532.
deposco
   deposcimus 5. 634,
   deposcere 1. 199.
deprecor
   deprecor 7. 454; 8. 53.
deprendo
   deprendere 1. 458, 464,
   deprensa 4. 692,
   deprensae (gen.) 4. 356.
depromo
   depromere 5. 214; 7. 450.
dequestus
   dequesta (nom. f.) 5. 448.
derigo
   derigit 6. 541 (KB; GL dirigit),
   derigimus 2. 49 (KBG; L dirigimus),
   derexit 1. 569 (B; KGL direxit).
deripio
   deripiunt 1. 825 (BG; KL diripiunt);
   2. 240 (BG; KL diripiunt),
   derepta (nom. f.) 2. 160 (BL; KG direpta),
   derepta (acc.) 6. 668.
desaevio
   desaevit 7. 318 (L; KBG decernit).
descendo
   descendit 1. 538; 3. 652; 6. 244; 8. 219,
   332,
   descendunt 7. 25,
   descendet 7. 55,
   descendere 1. 686; 3. 518, 575; 4. 353;
   7. 592.
desero
   deseris 3. 325; 6. 497,
   deserit 1. 287; 5. 445; 7. 302,
   deserat 2. 5,

desere 1. 215; 3. 181,
deseruisse 3. 488,
desertus 6. 639; 7. 560,
deserta 2. 455; 7. 103, 305,
deserto (abl. m.) 4. 84,
deserta (abl.) 8. 308,
desertos 5. 119,
desertas 2. 376,
deserta 4. 52; 6. 105.
deses
  deside (f.) 3. 660; 5. 148.
desido
  desidit 8. 329.
designo
  designat 3. 425.
desilio
  desilit 2. 198; 6. 424,
  desiliunt 2. 447,
  desiluit 4. 355.
desino
  desinit 3. 696.
despicio
  despicit 3. 678,
  despecta (nom. f.) 8. 283.
despondeo
  despondet 7. 510.
despumo
  despumat 8. 254.
destino
  destinat 2. 180, 484; 7. 317,
  destinet 1. 417.
destringo
  destrinxit 7. 330.
desum
  desum 8. 277,
  derat 2. 314; 5. 542,
  derunt 7. 68,
  defuit 1. 187, 404; 3. 294; 6. 68,
  defuimus 7. 174,
  defuerit 7. 95,
  defuerint 5. 207,
  desit 6. 39 (BL; KG defit),
  desint 4. 716.
desuper
  4. 307; 5. 175; 7. 601.
deterior
  subst. n. deteriora (acc.) 3. 647.
detineo
  detinet 7. 262.
detono
  detonet 4. 294.
detorqueo
  detorquet 1. 120; 4. 571, 685; 5. 397.
detraho
  detrahit 3. 142, 564.
detrunco
  detruncat 3. 145.
Deucalion
  Deucalion 1. 366.
deus
  deus 1. 245 bis; 2. 278, 323, 356, 435,
  625; 3. 46, 265, 271 bis, 325; 4. 484, 585,
  623, 652, 653; 5. 126, 260, 389, 428, 639;
  6. 514, 539, 657,
  dei 1. 207, 577, 842; 2. 258, 359, 421; 3.

299; 4. 72, 358; 5. 254, 409; 6. 32, 533,
673; 7. 368,
deo 1. 691; 2. 95; 3. 56,
deum 3. 85; 4. 19; 6. 539, 756; 7. 303,
dei 2. 61 (L; KBG adeo); 3. 306; 4.
667,
di 4. 567 bis; 8. 49,
deorum 1. 142, 742; 2. 441, 486; 4. 237,
460, 674, 704,
deum 1. 1, 15, 553, 683; 2. 16, 179; 3.
224, 356; 4. 86, 179 (KGL; B die), 426,
472, 477; 5. 329, 503; 6. 49; 8. 401,
deis 1. 323, 342; 2. 5, 577; 3. 413, 616;
6. 47; 7. 29,
deos 1. 212; 2. 167, 375, 512; 6. 315;
7. 228,
di 1. 667; 3. 201, 259,
deis 4. 554; 7. 71,
dis 3. 505; 6. 676.
deveho
  devectam 4. 114.
devenio
  deveniunt 4. 452,
  deveniat 7. 180,
  deveniant 1. 843.
devexus
  devexa (nom. f.) 3. 398 (vid. acc.),
  devexa (acc.) 3. 398 (vid. nom. f.),
  devexis (m.) 3. 687.
devius
  subst. n. devia (acc.) 3. 49; 8. 54.
devolo
  devolat 1. 93; 4. 204.
devolvo
  devolvunt 2. 235,
  devolvit 2. 89.
dexter
  dexter 4. 211,
  dextrum (m.) 8. 246,
  dextro 6. 701,
  dextro 1. 245,
  subst. f. dextera 1. 110; 3. 41, 144, 704;
  6. 316; 7. 94,
  dextra 3. 89; 4. 311; 5. 64; 6. 311,
  dextrae 3. 12; 4. 40; 5. 494; 6. 649,
  dextrae 3. 139; 4. 635; 7. 123, 399,
  dextram 2. 638; 3. 269; 4. 289, 289
  (KGL; B laevam); 5. 515 (L; KBG
  dona); 6. 21, 339, 366; 6. 539 (KBL; G
  dextra); 7. 293, 373, 587, 652,
  dextra 1. 334, 817; 2. 258; 3. 279; 4. 11,
  167, 622; 5. 210, 437, 6. 12, 126, 229,
  309, 539 (G; KBL dextram); 7. 468,
  476, 578, 608; 8. 324, 359,
  dextrae 1. 681; 3. 391; 6. 363,
  dextras 3. 18, 630; 7. 344,
  dextris 8. 301.
Diana
  Diana 4. 60,
  Dianae 2. 7, 301; 5. 379; 6. 73; 7. 179,
  Dianae 5. 238, 345; 8. 208.
dico
  dicavi 3. 535.

dico
   dicam 2. 439 (K; BGL diemque); 3. 377,
   dixit 1. 120, 568, 722; 2. 408; 3. 476; 4. 15, 68, 252, 629; 5. 241, 391; 6. 307, 340, 550; 7. 546; 8. 16, 356,
   dixerat 1. 182, 309, 608, 681; 2. 300, 567, 608; 3. 456, 628; 4. 337, 422, 636; 5. 210, 325, 397, 407, 690; 6. 217, 277, 315, 503, 737; 7. 141, 210, 456, 522; 8. 285,
   dic 6. 516; 7. 275, 287, 420 (K; B nunc; G nec; L cur), 478, 529; 8. 64,
   dicere 4. 547,
   dicens (f.) 6. 745; 7. 333,
   dicitur 7. 137,
   dictus 6. 125 (K; BGL ductus),
   dicta 3. 671; 6. 268,
   dictam 2. 244,
   dicta (nom.) 2. 384; 5. 152; 7. 511,
   dicta 2. 576,
   subst. n. dicta 2. 326; 3. 714; 5. 600,
   dictis 1. 39; 3. 615, 699; 5. 468; 7. 514; 8. 112 (vid. abl.),
   dicta 2. 69, 600; 4. 222, 330, 482, 735; 5. 21, 321; 7. 544, 558; 8. 445,
   dictis 1. 336; 2. 591, 663; 3. 471, 638, 690; 4. 38, 143; 5. 358, 533, 596, 671; 6. 458, 587, 602; 7. 101, 451; 8. 112 (vid. dat.), 466.
dicto
   dictat 1. 685.
dictum vid. dico.
diduco
   diduxere 1. 275 (BG; KL deduxere).
Didymaon
   Didymaonis 3. 707.
dies
   dies 1. 344, 505, 542, 655, 844; 2. 52, 107, 214, 286; 3. 248, 258, 362, 698; 4. 276, 344, 678, 730; 5. 12, 41, 157, 276 bis, 544; 6. 320, 356 (ille dies KGL; B illuvies), 628; 7. 229, 561; 8. 52, 180, 454,
   diem 1. 275, 396; 2. 76, 89, 439 (diemque BGL; K dicam); 3. 37, 175; 4. 97; 5. 413, 601; 6. 438 (ante diem KBG; L Aeetes), 734; 7. 246, 619; 8. 100, 150, 175,
   dies 7. 336,
   die 2. 281; 4. 179 (B; KGL deum); 8. 288, 416,
   dies (acc.) 1. 329; 8. 382.
differo
   differs 4. 62,
   differt 1. 753,
   distulerant 5. 460,
   differat 4. 78.
diffido
   diffide 5. 592.
diffugio
   diffugiunt 3. 255,
   diffugere 4. 645 (L; KBG deficere).
diffundo
   diffundit 3. 560; 6. 388, 745,
   diffuderis (ind.) 6. 56,

diffusa (nom. f.) 2. 104.
digero
   digere 8. 102 (KGL; B degere).
digitus
   digitis (abl.) 4. 267.
dignor
   dignatur 7. 651,
   dignata est 2. 50,
   dignetur 7. 47,
   dignare 1. 57,
   dignatus 1. 811; 4. 168.
dignus
   dignus 5. 458; 8. 29,
   digna 2. 471; 4. 588; 5. 652, 657; 8. 430,
   dignum 6. 51,
   dignum (m.) 5. 472,
   digno 7. 290,
   digna (abl.) 1. 6,
   dignis (m.) 7. 280,
   digna 1. 769; 2. 242, 421; 4. 363; 8. 277, 345,
   subst. n. digna (acc.) 2. 117,
   dignior 1. 167,
   dignior 7. 291.
digredior
   digreditur 6. 754 (KGL; B degreditur).
digressus
   digressibus (dat.) 3. 4.
dilabor
   dilapsa (nom.) 7. 399 (KGL; B delapsa),
   dilapsae (nom.) 3. 358.
diligo
   dilexisse 7. 209,
   dilecta 2. 79 (K; BGL defleta), 316,
   dilectae (dat.) 4. 363,
   dilectum (n.) 4. 401,
   dilecta (acc.) 3. 342; 6. 598; 8. 229,
   subst. m. dilecte 4. 468.
diluo
   diluerat 3. 557.
diluvium
   diluvio (abl.) 6. 394.
dimitto
   dimittit 1. 397; 5. 691 (G; KBL demittit),
   dimiserat 5. 72,
   dimiseris (subi.) 5. 539,
   dimitte 5. 286; 7. 240, 455; 8. 105,
   dimittere 6. 19; 7. 261,
   dimissa (acc.) 5. 172.
Dindyma
   Dindyma 3. 232,
   Dindyma 3. 20.
Dione
   Diones 7. 187.
Dipsas
   Dipsanta 6. 192.
Dira
   Dirae (nom.) 4. 586; 5. 445.
dirigo
   dirigit 6. 541 (GL; KB derigit),
   dirigimus 2. 49 (L; KBG derigimus),
   direxit 1. 569 (KGL; B derexit).

dirimo
dirimit 4. 664; 8. 365,
diremit 3. 188,
diremerit (subi.) 7. 540,
dirimi 1. 284.
diripio
diripiunt 1. 825 (KL; BG deripiunt);
2. 240 (KL; BG deripiunt); 4. 454,
diripiat 1. 813,
direpta (nom. f.) 2. 160 (KG; BL derepta).
dirus
dira 2. 291,
diri 4. 68,
dirae 7. 623,
diri 7. 555,
dirae 4. 79,
diram 6. 399; 8. 263 (BGL; K diro),
dirum 2. 567; 3. 172,
diro 8. 263 (K; BGL diram),
dira 8. 352,
diro 3. 132,
diros 4. 148; 6. 151; 7. 552,
diras 2. 235; 5. 72 (BG; KL om.); 7.
299,
dira 2. 172; 3. 59; 4. 106; 5. 659; 8. 399,
diris (f.) 6. 591,
diris 7. 206,
subst. f. diras 1. 804.
Dis
Ditis 1. 780; 4. 411; 6. 112,
Ditem 3. 520; 7. 313.
dis
ditem (f.) 4. 407,
dite 2. 296,
dites (nom. m.) 6. 117,
ditibus (abl. m.) 4. 360,
ditior (f.) 6. 38,
ditissimus 5. 122.
discedo
discessit 1. 570; 7. 558,
discedere 1. 285; 4. 645; 8. 79,
discedens (m.) 7. 108.
discerno
discernere 5. 394,
discreta 7. 13,
discreti (gen. m.) 2. 633.
disco
didicere 6. 291,
discat 1. 410,
discere 1. 772.
discolor
discolor (f.) 5. 564; 6. 120, 525.
Discordia
Discordia (nom.) 2. 204; 7. 468.
discordia
discordia (nom.) 6. 401.
discrimen
discriminis 5. 311; 7. 500,
discrimine 1. 503; 3. 712; 4. 296, 689;
6. 395, 545; 7. 631,
discrimina 1. 37; 3. 75; 5. 688,
discrimina 1. 217, 714; 2. 578; 4. 619;
7. 426; 8. 388.

discumbo
discumbitur 2. 190; 8. 255.
discurro
discurrit 3. 591 (L; KBG decurrit),
discurrunt 1. 312,
discurrere 6. 203.
discursus
discursibus (abl.) 3. 220; 5. 427.
discutio
discussa (abl.) 4. 700; 5. 174.
disicio
disicit 3. 162,
disiecit 3. 141,
disiecta (nom. n.) 4. 412,
disiecta 3. 222; 4. 167.
disiungo
disiungimur 2. 562.
dispello
dispulerant 6. 530,
dispulerit (subi.) 3. 89.
dispergo
dispersit 2. 76,
dispersos 6. 54.
dissilio
dissiluisse 4. 694.
dissimulo
dissimulas 7. 485,
dissimulant 2. 373.
dissipo
dissipat 6. 380; 7. 626.
dissolvo
dissolvere 1. 123.
dissonus
dissona (nom. n.) 3. 359,
dissona 5. 608.
disto
distat 8. 291.
dito
ditant 6. 145.
diu
1. 259; 6. 381, 384, 703.
diva vid. divus.
diversus
diversus 4. 387; 6. 581,
diverso (abl. m.) 3. 113, 243,
diversos 7. 577,
diversas 1. 92; 2. 284; 3. 146; 4. 640,
diversa 4. 157; 6. 299,
diversis (m.) 4. 447; 5. 309,
subst. n. diversa (acc.) 3. 182; 6. 301.
dives
dives 1. 394; 5. 590; 6. 204,
dives (f.) 5. 203,
divitis 2. 635; 4. 463,
divitis (f.) 1. 511.
divido
dividit 7. 2,
dividat 5. 57,
dividitur 1. 355,
dividimur 1. 321,
diviso (dat. m.) 6. 221.
divus
diva (abl.) 1. 403,
subst. diva 2. 120, 123, 226; 3. 488; 4. 80,
605; 5. 199; 6. 457, 467, 644; 8. 321,

divae 2. 369; 3. 235; 4. 419; 7. 395; 8. 225,
divae 3. 26; 6. 668; 7. 216,
diva (voc.) 2. 295, 612; 4. 336,
divi 5. 624,
divum (m.) 1. 27, 46, 231, 309; 3. 40, 373, 426, 668; 4. 1, 526, 577, 741; 6. 626; 7. 226; 8. 336,
divis (m.) 4. 417,
divos 1. 138, 669; 5. 484 (G. KBL clivos),
divae 3. 216,
divis (m.) 3. 303; 4. 438; 7. 498.
do
dat 1. 39; 2. 324, 497; 3. 340, 726; 4. 254 **bis,** 304; 5. 70, 97, 487; 6. 59, 62, 347, 359, 445, 557; 7. 373, 435,
dant 1. 352 **bis,** 444, 478; 2. 264, 412; 3. 5, 43, 254; 4. 292, 405; 5. 148, 182; 7. 570; 8. 173,
dabam 7. 69; 8. 97,
dabat 1. 63; 2. 226; 3. 11, 484; 4. 222; 5. 496, 506; 7. 251; 8. 214,
dabant 3. 301; 5. 21,
dabo 1. 89; 5. 541; 7. 208,
dabis 1. 19; 4. 64; 6. 500,
dabit 1. 89, 465, 466; 2. 338, 597; 4. 13; 5. 681; 6. 597; 7. 273,
dabunt 4. 568,
dedi 6. 476; 8. 107,
dedisti 7. 89; 8. 48,
dedit 1. 483, 592, 766; 2. 29 (KBG; L vehit), 69, 208; 3. 106, 738; 4. 49, 373, 543, 625, 660, 670; 5. 390, 546; 6. 470, 670; 7. 66, 279, 412, 558, 602; 8. 6, 44,
dedere 1. 254,
dederant 4. 432,
dederit 7. 273,
dem 4. 635,
des 1. 178 (si des BGL; K sedeat),
det 1. 344; 4. 124, 736; 7. 87,
demus 2. 322,
dent 4. 706; 5. 617 **bis;** 6. 733,
darem 1. 534,
dares 3. 651; 8. 11,
daret 7. 545, 615,
darent 5. 145,
dederit 6. 515,
dedissem 1. 720,
dedisset 2. 176,
da 1. 41, 87, 196, 268, 333, 604, 675, 793; 4. 360, 362; 5. 218, 515, 516, 666; 6. 465; 7. 246, 419, 550; 8. 280,
date 1. 809; 2. 336; 3. 312; 4. 634,
dare 1. 754; 3. 268, 681; 7. 18, 418 (G; KBL dari); 8. 80, 443,
daturum 6. 675,
daturam 7. 320,
datur 1. 242; 2. 121; 3. 667; 4. 141, 511; 6. 601; 7. 270, 628; 8. 381,
dabitur 4. 587, 598, 620,
danda forent 3. 409,
dari 3. 104, 542, 645; 5. 510; 7. 418 (KBL; G dare),
datus 4. 704; 5. 275,

data 1. 102; 3. 16,
datum 1. 322; 3. 688,
datum 6. 272,
datam 8. 271,
datum 8. 397,
dato 2. 303; 6. 127,
data 1. 596,
data 4. 347; 5. 260; 7. 174,
datos 3. 242,
datas 1. 560,
datis (f.) 3. 14.
doceo
docet 1. 235, 472, 848,
docebo 3. 377; 4. 558,
doceat 7. 522,
doce 2. 469; 5. 388,
docere 8. 221,
docens (f.) 2. 335,
doctus 6. 132,
doctum (m.) 1. 477,
docta (abl.) 1. 122.
docilis
docilis (nom. f.) 6. 237 **bis.**
Dodonis
Dodonida 1. 302.
doleo
dolet 4. 175 (BG; KL videt); 5. 525; 7. 161,
doluit 4. 238,
doluisse 6. 502,
dolens 5. 95,
dolens (f.) 4. 49.
Dolonius
Dolonii (gen. m.) 5. 7.
Dolopeius
Dolopeia (acc.) 2. 10.
dolor
dolor 1. 291, 327, 548; 2. 133, 165, 393; 3. 230, 282, 384, 694, 739; 7. 370; 8. 264, 290,
doloris 6. 279,
dolorem 1. 766; 3. 371; 5. 545,
dolor 4. 30,
dolore 7. 8, 475,
dolores 2. 609,
dolorum 3. 515,
dolores 1. 792; 2. 143; 5. 432.
Dolus
Dolus 2. 206.
dolus
doli 2. 123,
dolum 8. 77,
doli 1. 64, 245,
dolos 1. 714; 2. 567; 4. 354; 5. 222, 248, 291; 6. 467; 7. 92; 8. 410,
dolis 1. 485, 695; 3. 491; 6. 263.
domina
dominae 2. 345; 7. 268,
dominae 7. 181 (L; KBG dominam),
dominam 3. 23; 4. 355; 5. 377; 7. 181 (KBG; L dominae), 234; 8. 173.
dominus
domini 4. 116,
domino 1. 490,
dominum 2. 388; 8. 444,

dominos 8. 418,
dominis 6. 409, 724.
domo
  domat 1. 600,
  domant 1. 594; 6. 360,
  domui 8. 72,
  domitum (m.) 8. 66,
  domito (m.) 1. 75,
  domitas 3. 539,
  domitis (f.) 2. 423; 5. 299.
domus
  domus 1. 512, 753, 837; 2. 96; 3. 73, 399;
  4. 26, 48, 180, 213, 612; 5. 382; 6. 82, 689,
  domus 2. 593; 6. 548; 7. 444; 8. 135, 149,
  domo 2. 236 (G; KBL domos),
  domum 1. 769; 2. 163, 275; 7. 109, 502,
  domus 1. 721,
  domo 1. 6; 4. 33; 6. 487; 8. 422,
  domos 1. 584, 706, 716, 782; 2. 74, 128,
  177, 190, 211, 236 (KBL; G domo),
  263, 291, 336, 376, 394; 3. 296, 321, 731;
  4. 102, 448; 5. 234, 516, 451 (GL; KB
  domus), 684; 6. 324; 7. 16, 50, 381; 8.
  46, 323, 395,
  domus (acc.) 5. 451 (KB; GL domos).
donarium
  donaria (nom.) 5. 644.
donec (19)
    1. c. ind.
  a) prs. 2. 535 (K; B pistris; GL belua);
  3. 414; 4. 190, 309, 403; 6. 634; 8. 292,
  b) perf. 1. 496, 591; 2. 373; 3. 78; 4. 48,
  c) fut. perf. 4. 526,
    2. c. subi.
  a) prs. 1. 842; 5. 685; 8. 87, 190, 383,
  b) imperf. 2. 473.
dono
  donat 1. 473; 3. 207 (G; K resonat; B
  denset; L duplicat); 5. 7, 123 **bis**; 8.
  236,
  donant 2. 309,
  donato (abl. n.) 6. 692.
donum
  dono 1. 528,
  donum 2. 252; 3. 170; 5. 447,
  dona 5. 206, 215,
  dona 1. 551; 2. 409, 421, 472, 488, 553,
  576; 3. 177; 4. 179, 216; 5. 503, 515
  (KBG; L dextram); 6. 549; 7. 48, 418;
  8. 101,
  donis 5. 31.
Dorceus
  Dorcea 3. 159.
Doricus
  Dorica (nom. f.) 2. 572 (BGL; K
  turica).
dorsum
  dorso 8. 111,
  dorso 2. 631; 4. 178; 6. 90.
Doryclus
  Dorycli 2. 149.
dos
  dotes (acc.) 8. 337.
dotalis
  dotalia (acc.) 8. 279.

Doto
  Doto 1. 134.
draco
  draconis 8. 60, 92, 107, 438,
  draconem 2. 382; 7. 550; 8. 71,
  dracone 1. 60,
  dracones 3. 190; 7. 120,
  dracones 1. 68; 2, 276; 6. 57.
Drangaeus (KG; BL Drancaeus)
  Drangaea (nom. f.) 6. 106, 507.
Dryope
  Dryope (nom.) 3. 529.
Dryope
  Dryopes 2. 174.
dubito
  dubitaret 8. 440.
dubius
  dubius 7. 177,
  dubii 8. 340,
  dubiae (gen.) 2. 252; 7. 243 (L; KBG
  durae),
  dubium 1. 401,
  dubium 4. 272,
  dubia 5. 301,
  dubii 5. 63,
  dubiis (n.) 4. 257 (vid. abl.),
  dubios 2. 72; 6. 150,
  dubiis (f.) 1. 248; 3. 623; 4. 527,
  dubiis 4. 257 (vid. dat.),
  subst. dubios 4. 578.
duco
  ducit 1. 734; 3. 435, 554, 645; 6. 114,
  ducunt 2. 183,
  ducam 2. 134,
  duxit 1. 429; 5. 343,
  duceret 3. 540,
  duxerit 1. 307,
  duc 5. 387,
  ducere 1. 343,
  ducentem 4. 536,
  ducentem 6. 376,
  ducente (f.) 7. 348,
  ducitur 6. 490,
  ducuntur 5. 326,
  ductus 6. 125 (BGL; K dictus).
ductor
  ductor 1. 164, 240, 296, 485, 659, 835;
  2. 468; 3. 605, 717; 4. 133, 157, 703; 5.
  36, 129, 184; 6. 48; 8. 30, 308,
  ductor 3. 711.
ductus
  ductibus (abl.) 7. 168.
dudum
  5. 3 (L; KBG tum non); 8. 378.
dulcedo
  dulcedine 6. 663.
dulcis
  dulcis 6. 473,
  dulcis 7. 124,
  dulcis 4. 531,
  dulcis (f.) 8. 402,
  dulcem 1. 397,
  dulcem 3. 658,
  dulci 3. 159, 723; 5. 49,
  dulci (f.) 1. 277, 334,

dulces (m.) 4. 89,
dulcibus (f.) 3. 371,
dulces 1. 237; 4. 389, 632; 8. 82,
dulcis (m.) 7. 513,
dulces 6. 561; 7. 340,
dulcia 4. 448,
dulces (voc. f.) 4. 30,
dulcibus (n.) 1. 251.
dum (45)
   1. c. ind.
   a) prs. 1. 306 (dumque KG; BL nunc),
327, 396, 492; 2. 32, 183, 325, 347, 369
(L; KG qui; B quos), 451, 590 (K; BGL
tum); 3. 21, 680, 686; 4. 141, 281 (G;
KBL cum), 330, 515, 556, 643; 5. 96,
170, 184, 334, 336; 6. 14, 26, 201, 254,
576, 601; 7. 256, 542,
   dum . . . cum 2. 451,
   b) perf. 1. 606; 2. 90 (BL; KG cum),
      2. c. subi.
   a) prs. 3. 98; 4. 294; 5. 300; 7. 75, 76,
   b) imperf. 1. 425; 3. 651 **bis,**
      3. sine verb.
   2. 381.
   Vid. dummodo, necdum, tum, tunc.
dumetum
   dumeta (acc.) 3. 57.
dummodo
   dum . . . modo 5. 265.
duo
   duo (m.) 7. 569.
duplex
   duplicem (f.) 8. 235,
   duplices (nom. m.) 6. 509.
duplico
   duplicat 3. 207 (L; K resonat; B denset; G donat),
   duplicata (abl.) 3. 140 (BL; K delicata; G delata).
dure
   5. 196 (BG; KL durae); 8. 459.
duro
   durat 1. 844; 3. 384; 7. 359,
   durant 2. 350,
   duravimus 6. 336,
   duret 5. 24,
   durent 2. 245,
   durasset 3. 246,
   durate 1. 237,
   durare 6. 308; 7. 74, 338,
   durata 2. 158,
   duratum (m.) 7. 364 (L; KBG duratam),
   duratam 7. 364 (KBG; L duratum),
   durata (acc.) 4. 250.
durus
   durus 1. 718; 3. 181, 648; 4. 383; 6. 462,
   dura 2. 237, 355; 4. 426, 668; 6. 683; 7.
160, 310,
   durae 3. 610; 4. 486; 5. 196 (KL; BG
dure); 7. 243 (KBG; L dubiae),
   duri 6. 545,
   durae 2. 455; 6. 298, 624; 7. 202,
   durum (n.) 1. 565,
   dura (voc.) 7. 218,

duro 3. 655,
dura 1. 832; 4. 175,
dura 3. 165; 8. 465,
duris 4. 100,
duris (f.) 5. 308,
duros 5. 278; 7. 276,
duras 3. 710,
dura 3. 671 (B; KG plura; L rupta);
5. 144,
duris (n.) 4. 611,
subst. dure 4. 130,
duris (dat. n.) 7. 95,
duris (abl. n.) 4. 35.
dux
   dux 2. 64, 108, 610; 3. 151, 705; 5. 99,
118, 277, 310, 416, 437, 555; 8. 220, 433,
   ducis 1. 184, 440, 682; 2. 351; 3. 13, 240,
285, 641, 702; 5. 218, 364, 682; 7. 524,
   duci 1. 302; 2. 409, 655; 3. 370; 6. 450;
8. 39 (duci mihi K; BGL mihi iam),
   ducem 1. 227, 343, 693, 759; 2. 509, 590;
3. 70; 4. 7, 547; 5. 377; 6. 137; 7. 264,
557,
   duce 1. 19, 177, 483, 507; 5. 138, 267,
375, 395, 399; 6. 97, 209,
   duces 6. 9; 7. 629,
   ducum 1. 101; 5. 607; 6. 683, 723,
   duces 2. 643; 5. 575; 6. 15, 41, 93,
   ducibus 1. 262; 4. 554.
Dymas
   Dymantis 4. 187.
e (25)
   1. 158, 196, 221, 417, 465, 523; 2. 205,
271 (K; BGL in), 460, 513, 538; 3. 529;
4. 68, 85, 89, 199, 242 (L; K a; BG o),
661, 695; 5. 9, 61; 6. 8, 83, 681; 7. 360.
ebur
   ebur (nom.) 2. 466.
ecce (38)
   1. 207, 212, 484, 566, 686; 2. 16, 214,
311, 336, 478, 509, 587; 3. 60, 124, 257,
396, 675; 4. 22, 282, 302, 392, 565; 5. 13,
212, 618; 6. 231, 386, 575, 741; 7. 22,
194, 210; 8. 12, 32, 107, 194, 278, 434.
Echeclus
   Echeclum 3. 138.
Echion
   Echion 1. 440; 4. 134, 734; 7. 543.
Echionius
   Echionii (m.) 7. 554; 8. 343,
   Echionia (abl.) 7. 301.
edax
   edaci (abl. m.) 6. 420.
edisco
   ediscere 1. 368.
edo
   edit 7. 359 (G; KBL alit),
   edere (perf.) 5. 364.
edo
   edidit 1. 367,
   edere 4. 24.
edoceo
   edocet 6. 16,
   edocuere 3. 386.

4. 124; 5. 491; 7. 520,
nostrum 1. 150,
nobis 1. 531; 4. 623, 705; 5. 18, 553, 578
(BG; KL nodis); 6. 329, 731; 8. 183,
268, 338, 351,
nos 1. 175; 2. 256, 574; 3. 714; 5. 316,
504, 667; 7. 229; 8. 190.

egredior
egressus 4. 134,
egressa (nom.) 2. 277,
egressi (nom.) 8. 121.

egregius
egregio (abl. n.) 5. 367.

ei (6)
1. 327; 6. 624; 7. 201a (KBL; G om.),
236, 284, 483.

eia
8. 110.

eicio
eiecere 6. 411,
eiecta 8. 20 (BG; KL erecta),
eiectum (m.) 6. 727.

eiecto
eiectat 2. 30.

elanguesco
elanguit 4. 527.

Electrius
Electria (nom. f.) 2. 431.

Eleus
Elei (gen. m.) 4. 227.

elido
elisit 6. 197 (G; KBL elusit),
elisa (nom. f.) 4. 663.

eligo
electus 4. 242.

Elis
Elis 1. 389,
Elidis 1. 665.

eluctor
eluctanda (nom. f.) 8. 184.

eludo
elusit 6. 197 (KBL; G elisit),
eludat 2. 569 (L; K ludat; BG luat),
eluditur 4. 41.

Elysium
Elysium (acc.) 1. 650.

Emeda vid. **Emoda.**

emergo
emersit 5. 1.

emetior
emensas 5. 181,
emensa 4. 350.

emico
emicat 2. 543; 3. 429 (L; KBG evocat);
4. 289, 501; 6. 636,
emicuit 1. 655; 3. 582; 4. 97; 5. 92; 6.
551; 7. 397,
emicet 6. 596.

emineo
eminet 1. 317 (super eminet KBG; L
supereminet); 3. 338; 8. 227.

emitto
emittit 4. 260,
emissa (nom. f.) 2. 550; 3. 44.

Emoda (KG; BL Emeda)
Emoda (nom.) 6. 143.

en (23)
1. 226 (L; KBG et); 2. 213, 395; 3. 103,
169 (B; K et; GL i), 178, 272 (K; BGL
heu), 292 (BG; K hic; L heu), 415, 510
bis, 514, 536, 670 (BL; K et; G ast);
4. 758; 5. 315; 6. 267, 274; 7. 42, 442
(BGL; K nunc), 546 (BGL; K et),
546; 8. 60.

enim (26)
enim 1. 17 (BGL; K iam); 2. 362; 3.
16; 4. 303 (KBG; L ubi), 578; 5. 536;
8. 393,
nec enim 3. 681; 6. 488,
neque enim 1. 166, 500, 533, 587, 783;
2. 2, 102 (KBG; L neque iam), 490,
603; 3. 210; 6. 22, 37, 657; 7. 456 (KG;
BL que etenim); 8. 265,
quis enim 5. 171,
sed enim 1. 228.

Enipeus
Enipeus 1. 357; 5. 208,
Enipea 1. 83.

enitor
eniti 4. 680,
enisus 2. 462.

eno
enavimus 5. 315.

ensifer
ensifer 3. 406.

Ensis
Ensis (nom.) 2. 68.

ensis
ensis (nom.) 3. 233,
ensem 2. 252, 481; 5. 513; 6. 230, 292;
7. 147, 287; 8. 19, 360,
ense 1. 144, 225, 366, 812; 2. 182, 303;
3. 119, 157; 5. 271; 6. 127, 281, 308, 617;
7. 530, 619; 8. 310,
enses 3. 51; 5. 479,
ensibus 3. 111,
enses 1. 820; 2. 215; 5. 145,
ensibus 6. 198, 400.

Enyo
Enyo 4. 604.

eo
it 1. 411 (B; KGL et), 494 (KBL; G
ut), 508, 725; 2. 60 (L; KBG et), 111
(GL; K et; B his), 233 (KBL; G his),
348; 3. 3, 277; 4. 46, 201; 5. 89, 101 (B;
KGL hinc); 6. 341, 372, 381, 527, 724
(BGL; K est); 7. 229; 8. 285 (itque
BG; KL atque), 331,
imus 5. 636 **bis**; 6. 328,
ibat 3. 187, 431, 718; 4. 392; 5. 332, 430;
6. 375, 694, 739; 8. 126, 360 (KGL; B
nabat),
ibant 3. 675 (KB; GL ibunt); 6. 160,
ibit 4. 217; 5. 586; 7. 17, 470,
ibimus 4. 51; 5. 669,
ibunt 3. 675 (GL; KB ibant),
iit 6. 685; 8. 286 (L; KBG supplex),
eat 6. 599,
irem 3. 308,

iret 7. 294; 8. 205,
iremus 8. 168,
irent 8. 398,
isset 4. 710,
i 1. 56, 750; 2. 422 **bis**; 3. 169 (GL; K
et; B in); 4. 13, 78; 7. 162, 240; 8. 102
(B; KGL in),
ite 1. 248; 3. 448; 6. 29, 285; 8. 355,
ire 1. 271, 438, 472; 4. 330, 371; 6. 3, 15,
238; 7. 113, 134, 138, 202, 390, 577; 8. 71,
152, 198, 346, 395,
euntem 7. 106,
euntem 8. 55, 209,
itur 5. 563,
eundum est 8. 184.

Eous
1. subst.
Eoum 7. 22 (B; KGL eoo),
2. adi.
Eoae 2. 72,
Eoi (n.) 3. 539.

eous
1. subst.
eoo (abl. m.) 7 22 (KGL; B Eoum),
2. adi.
eoi 4. 96,
eoae (gen.) 2. 642; 6. 142, 699,
eoo (abl.) 5. 76,
eoo 5. 245,
eoas 4. 509,
eois (f.) 6. 690.

epulae
epulae 6. 333,
epulas 2. 96, 653; 4. 530; 8. 96, 252.

eques
eques 1. 410, 708; 5. 515, 591; 6. 229,
equitem 6. 210.

equidem (7)
1. 236, 325; 3. 270; 4. 476, 619; 8. 420,
432.

equinus
equino (abl. n.) 5. 153.

equus
equus 2. 386; 6. 256,
equi 5. 585; 6. 234, 240; 6. 377; 7. 605,
equum 1. 491; 6. 527,
equo 1. 147; 3. 21; 6. 639,
equi 1. 611; 3. 90; 6. 398,
equorum 2. 130, 508; 5. 183; 6. 161,
equum 6. 237,
equis 6. 234,
equos 2. 10, 552; 3. 499; 5. 123, 288,
413; 6. 510, 560, 582,
equis 1. 389, 539, 678; 2. 75; 4. 608; 6.
29, 35, 147, 204, 328, 523, 553; 7. 646.

era
eram 1. 781; 7. 313.

Erebus
Erebi 4. 407,
Erebum 3. 410,
Erebo 6. 292.

erebus
erebi 2. 120.

Erginus
Erginus 1. 415; 8. 177,
Erginum 5. 65.

ergo (28)
1. 31, 659, 774; 2. 407; 3. 411, 615; 4.
400, 433, 585, 755; 5. 256, 318, 542, 648;
6. 14, 41, 449, 482; 7. 4, 196, 286, 323,
407, 625; 8. 315, 321, 337, 439.

Eribotes
Eribotes 1. 402,
Eriboten 3. 478.

Eridanus
Eridani 5. 430.

erigo
erigit 1. 157 (KBG; L egerit), 658; 3.
331, 632; 6. 186 (KG; BL egerit); 7.
24; 8. 224,
erigitur 6. 748; 7. 145; 8. 367,
erecta 8. 20 (KL; BG eiecta),
erectum (m.) 1. 257.

erilis
erili (f.) 7. 124,
erilem (f.) 6. 706,
erili (n.) 4. 383,
eriles (nom. m.) 6. 413,
erilis (m.) 6. 124,
eriles (f.) 6. 108.

Erinys
Erinys 2. 281; 3. 19; 4. 74, 617; 5. 146;
7. 112, 462; 8. 396.

eripio
eripit 4. 272; 6. 619,
eripiat 4. 79,
eripe 1. 10, 88, 225; 2. 490; 4. 539; 7.
241,
ereptus 3. 316; 6. 571,
erepta 1. 287,
erepta (abl.) 2. 569 (ereptaque BG;
KL et rapta.

erro
errat 4. 576; 6. 674; 8. 365 (KG; BL
extat),
errabat 6. 295,
errabant 5. 146,
errantis (f.) 4. 419,
errantem (m.) 7. 562 (B; KGL exstantem), 578,
errantes (f.) 8. 164,
errantes 6. 583,
errantes 4. 561,
errantibus (m.) 3. 621,
erratum (m.) 4. 447.

error
error 3. 298, 579; 5. 115, 455 (KGL; B
horror); 6. 17, 277, 473,
errore 3. 407; 4. 208, 397; 5. 574; 7. 10,
erroribus (abl.) 3. 31; 4. 376.

eructo
eructat 4. 345.

erudio
erudiit 2. 50.

erumpo
erumpit 5. 465; 8. 324.

eruo
eruis 6. 131,
eruit 6. 101,
eruit 7. 329,
eruerent 5. 145,
eruta (nom. f.) 4. 761.
Erymantheus
Erymanthei (n.) 1. 374.
Erymanthus
Erymanthi 2. 495.
Erymus
Erymo (dat.) 3. 194.
Erythia
Erythia (voc.) 5. 106.
Eryx
Eryx 2. 523,
Erycis 4. 322.
escendo
escendit (perf.) 1. 206,
escendere 1. 410 (L; KBG conscendere.
et (1086)
et 1. 10, 14, 20 (KL; BG seu), 23, 24,
36, 50, 52, 54, 56, 63, 68 (et quos BL;
KG saevos), 70, 73, 74, 84, 86, 89, 93
(Thespia et K; BGL Thespiaca), 94,
95, 115 **bis**, 119, 120, 122, 128, 138, 141,
150, 155, 157, 160, 166, 171, 183, 185,
190, 201, 203, 206, 212, 213 (fremere et
KBG; L pelagi), 223, 226 (KBG; L
en), 247, 258, 263, 268, 270, 273, 274,
279, 282, 297, 315, 320, 328, 334, 350,
362, 366, 370 **bis**, 372, 376, 378, 382, 386,
389 (et levis G; K felevis; BL felixque), 389, 397, 403, 404 (G; KBL ac),
407, 411 (KGL; B it), 417, 422, 432,
449, 450, 457, (BGL; K at), 461, 464,
466, 468, 473, 483, 486, 508 (BG; KL
est), 509, 512 **bis**, 514, 516, 518, 524 (et
iunctas KBG; L adiunctas), 524, 527,
530, 531, 538, 543, 550, 554, 557, 565,
567, 568, 571, 584, 590, 595, 600, 602,
608, 611, 613, 629, 634, 638, 643, 651,
653, 656, 665, 666, 668, 671 (stare et
BG; K claret; L stare), 674, 682, 683,
685, 688, 692 **bis**, 707, 710, 713, 722,
727, 735, 738, 748, 749, 754, 758, 767,
770, 772, 775, 777, 784, 788, 792, 796,
798, 800, 804, 806, 808, 815, 816,
820, 822, 824, 834, 835, 840, 842, 845,
850 **bis**; 2. 4, 15, 20, 22, 25, 35, 37, 42,
46, 53, 58, 60 (KBG; L it), 66, 68, 70,
74, 78, 80, 83, 97, 100, 104, 105, 109,
111 (K; GL it; B his), 112, 122, 127,
128, 130, 135, 136, 140, 141, 146, 160,
161, 167 (K; BGL tum), 173, 175, 193,
194, 195, 198, 199, 201 **bis**, 203, 204,
206 **ter**, 209, 211, 215, 219, 220, 223, 233,
238, 243, 252, 256, 259, 262, 266, 267,
272, 276, 278, 284, 287, 289, 305, 321
(L; KBG ut), 323, 330, 331, 339, 348,
350, 354, 356, 358, 360, 365, 367, 368, 377,
379, 389, 394, 395, 402, 414 (KGL; B
haec), 423, 427, 433, 444, 446, 450, 461,
464, 466, 477, 486, 493, 494, 496, 497,

514, 516, 524, 526 **bis**, 528, 537 **bis**, 538,
549 **bis**, 554, 556, 561, 569 (et rapta KL;
BG ereptaque), 578, 580, 583, 586, 591,
595, 597, 603, 608, 611, 618, 620, 628,
629, 638, 640, 646, 648, 660; 3. 11, 12,
13, 25, 31, 32, 33, 35, 44, 50, 51, 56, 57,
62, 64, 65, 73, 78, 87, 96, 99, 103 (BGL;
K at), 112 **bis**, 117, 123, 129, 135, 139,
143, 149, 152, 154, 158, 169 (K; B en;
GL i), 172, 175, 179, 181, 190, 192, 195,
197, 198, 202, 205, 216, 218, 227, 228,
232, 234, 238, 239, 247, 264, 266, 278,
284, 291, 297, 303, 307, 310, 312, 316,
324, 333, 351, 361, 378, 379, 388, 390,
392 (L; KBG sed), 393, 394, 399, 404,
405, 418, 421, 424, 425, 435, 451, 456,
459, 464, 471, 474, 476, 479, 482, 495,
503, 507, 508, 513, 514, 516 (B; K **om.**;
BL ut), 520, 521, 524 **bis**, 528, 532, 539,
540, 544, 545, 554, 556, 563, 589, 591, 596,
597, 610, 612, 614, 623, 624, 625, 628
(GL; KB at), 632, 648, 657, 658, 670
(ego et K; B ego te; GL egomet), 670
(K; BL en; G ast), 680, 682, 695, 710,
711, 718, 723, 727, 731, 740; 4. 11, 15,
18, 21, 23, 28, 29, 32, 35, 37, 39, 43, 49,
52, 54, 61, 67, 76, 78, 86, 87, 88, 89 **bis**,
93, 96, 98, 100, 101, 107, 115, 116, 123,
131, 133, 136, 143, 144, 149, 156, 160,
162, 164, 168, 171, 172, 175, 178, 180,
183, 188 **bis**, 192, 198, 207, 211, 214, 221,
223 **bis**, 226, 234, 238, 246, 248, 250,
252, 254, 256, 258, 265, 266, 267 **bis**,
272, 275, 277, 282, 287, 290, 292, 299,
306, 313, 314, 319, 329, 334, 358, 375,
383, 386, 390, 392 (KGL; B at), 393,
395, 398, 404, 408, 409, 413, 418, 422,
430, 442, 453, 468, 470, 476, 480, 482,
485, 486, 490, 504, 512, 518, 524, 528,
533, 534, 535, 539, 543, 545, 546, 571,
576, 583, 596, 597, 609, 612, 615, 624
(sileo et G; K sileam; B sileo; L sine
me), 636, 646, 647, 652, 655, 662, 666,
676, 685, 688, 695, 706, 715, 716 (KGL;
B tot), 723, 730, 740, 746, 752, 757, 762;
5. 12, 24, 27, 30, 33, 46, 50, 66, 71, 74,
81, 83, 102, 104, 108, 114, 119, 122, 127,
129, 131, 146, 151 (KBL; G **om.**), 160,
161, 169, 175, 183, 193, 197, 201, 209,
220, 241, 245, 252, 260, 262, 266, 275,
278, 280, 281, 288, 294, 301, 310, 311,
319, 321, 325, 332, 337, 340, 347, 348,
355, 363 (B; KGL at), 365, 369, 370,
384, 391, 415, 424 (K; BGL hi), 427,
430, 432, 438, 443, 447, 450, 460, 472,
477, 478, 494, 509, 513, 520, 523, 525,
528, 534, 537, 543, 557, 571, 574, 577,
579, 580, 588, 592, 595, 596, 600, 604,
613, 614, 615, 616, 637, 641, 642, 643,
644, 655, 660, 661, 667, 668, 670 (K;
BGL **om.**), 672, 677, 682, 684, 685, 689,
691, 693; 6. 1, 19, 20, 27, 31 (G; KBL
gens), 49, 56, 59, 71, 74, 82, 82 (BGL;
K est), 83, 84, 85, 93, 101, 117, 118, 121,
122, 124, 129, 130, 132, 133, 136, 137,

141, 142, 144, 150, 151, 157, 159, 160,
162, 172, 178, 186, 196, 212, 214 (KG;
BL at), 231, 235, 243, 249, 251, 253,
255, 258, 267, 281, 287, 293, 306, 311,
321, 340, 341, 343, 351, 365, 368, 372,
377 (KL; BG in), 386, 393, 401, 422,
433, 438, 442, 448, 449, 451, 468, 472,
474 **bis,** 480, 489, 491, 494, 496, 502, 508,
511, 514, 520, 529, 531, 537, 541, 543, 547,
550, 556, 574, 597, 612, 620, 637, 639,
659, 660, 663, 685, 689, 699, 704, 709,
711, 724, 732, 738, 739, 741, 744, 753;
7. 2, 5, 31, 47, 52, 63, 68, 69, 77, 79, 82,
86 (K; BGL at), 88, 99, 102, 103, 106,
107, 110 (K; BGL at), 123, 124, 132,
135, 148, 152, 158, 161, 169 (fallat et
KL; B insomnem; G solvat et), 176,
181, 188, 192, 197, 199, 203, 212, 220,
228, 231, 232, 254, 264 (KBG; L ad),
267 (KGL; B ac), 272, 281, 283, 300,
304, 308, 311, 318 (L; KBG atque),
322, 324, 328, 330, 337, 343 (KG; B
heu; L te), 349, 355, 360, 363, 365, 389,
412, 414, 427, 432, 436, 444, 455, 457, 458,
460, 461, 464, 467, 471, 481, 487, 489,
491, 494, 496, 497, 501 (K; BGL si),
503, 507, 512, 514, 517, 524, 525, 528,
539, 546 (K; BGL en), 548, 551 (vellera et G; KB velleris; L quercus et),
553, 554, 563, 566, 571, 575, 578, 586,
590, 592, 599, 506, 611, 614, 617, 626,
638, 648; 8. 1, 16, 25, 29, 41, 44, 50, 55,
57, 60, 63, 66, 73, 82, 85, 91, 111, 113,
121, 141, 146, 157, 168, 170, 174, 176,
184, 188, 197, 199, 218, 231, 236, 246,
250, 251, 252, 260, 278, 286 (et remigis
KB; G regis; L et remos), 289, 290,
299, 301, 305, 308, 309, 314, 327, 341,
348 (KGL; B sed), 354, 355, 356, 359,
368, 370, 375, 386, 394, 401, 410, 429,
434 (KG; BL te), 436, 442, 447, 452,
464, 466 **bis,**
et . . . et 1. 39, 658; 2. 573; 3. 467, 576,
679, 696; 4. 370, 438; 5. 634; 6. 314, 554,
618, 649; 7. 136; 8. 269, 360, 361,
et . . . et . . . et 3. 728,
nec minus et 4. 56,
quin et 2. 416; 4. 381; 5. 524; 6. 79,
sed non et 1. 503.
etenim (5)
4. 206; 5. 70, 680; 6. 436 (haec etenim
KGL; B Aeeten); 7. 456 (que etenim
BL; KG neque enim).
etiam (49)
etiam 1. 514, 733, 771; 2. 87, 178 (L;
KBG vel iam), 222, 606, 616, 647; 3.
273, 369; 4. 69, 233, 295, 323, 397, 500,
559, 620; 5. 105, 156, 202, 231, 645; 6.
109, 291 (L; KBG eadem), 373, 461;
7. 82, 166, 201a, 226 (KBG; L ut iam),
346; 8. 41, 137,
hic etiam 1. 723,
nunc etiam 5. 80; 6. 87,
etiam nunc 5. 665 (KGL; B etiamnum); 7. 454,

quin etiam 1. 387 (KBG; L quis con-
tra), 709; 3. 444; 5. 98, 433; 6. 382 (K;
BGL quis),
tandem etiam 7. 127,
tunc etiam 2. 316; 4. 73.
Vid. quippe.
etiamnum
5. 665 (B; KGL etiam nunc).
Euarchus
Euarchus 6. 102.
Euboicus
Euboicas 1. 373,
Euboicis (m.) 6. 321.
Eumenis
Eumenidum 2. 228; 3. 54, 217, 228.
Euphemus
Euphemus 1. 365.
Euphrataeus
Euphrataeis (abl. n.) 6. 696 (K; B
Phari raris; GL pharetratis).
Euripus
Euripus 1. 454.
Europa
Europa 2. 615,
Europam 4. 727; 8. 396.
Eurotas
Eurotan 1. 430.
Eurus
Eurus 1. 613, 639; 2. 365,
Euro (abl.) 1. 538; 2. 58 (GL; KB
auro),
Euros 1. 594.
eurus
euris (abl.) 4. 421.
Euryale
Euryales 6. 370,
Euryalen 5. 612.
Eurymenae
Eurymenas 2. 14.
Eurynome
Eurynomen 2. 136.
Eurystheus
Eurystheos 1. 114.
Eurytion
Eurytion 1. 378.
Eurytus
Eurytus 3. 99, 471; 6. 569,
Euryte 1. 439.
evado
evasit 7. 570,
evadere 7. 163, 299; 8. 155,
evasisse 6. 246; 7. 504.
eveho
evectae (nom.) 2. 35.
evello
est evulsa 3. 709,
evulsam 6. 716.
everbero
everberat 6. 737.
everto
everso (abl. m.) 7. 75.
evinco
evincite 1. 248,
evicta (acc.) 2. 186.

evoco
 evocat 3. 429 (KBG; L emicat).
evolo,
 evolat 7. 644.
evolvo
 evolvit (prs.) 4. 117.
ex (20)
 1. 62, 63 (KL; BG externo), 222, 547,
 591; 2. 40; 3. 367, 551; 4. 449, 682; 5.
 304, 522; 6. 405, 705; 7. 559, 567, 611,
 647; 8. 144, 161.
exagito
 exagitent 8. 104.
exanimo
 exanimat 2. 154,
 exanimet 5. 374.
exanimis
 exanimem (m.) 6. 346,
 exanimes (acc. m.) 1. 737.
exanimus
 exanimum (nom.) 2. 465,
 subst. m. exanimum 5. 28.
exardesco
 exarserat 2. 248.
exarmo
 exarmat 7. '597.
exaudio
 exaudita (nom. f.) 4. 518.
excedo
 excedere 5. 335; 7. 440,
 excedens (m.) 1. 826.
excelsus
 excelsi (m.) 3. 604,
 excelsum (n.) 4. 333,
 excelso (m.) 4. 381; 6. 604; 7. 376,
 excelsas 3. 485,
 excelsior (f.) 1. 405.
excidium
 excidium (acc.) 5. 537,
 excidiis (abl.) 6. 395.
excido
 excidit (perf.) 4. 457, 580 (KBG; L
 accidit),
 excidat 5. 653,
 exciderit 5. 133,
 exciderint 3. 461.
excindo
 excindere 6. 468.
excio
 excite (voc.) 1. 791,
 excita (nom. n.) 6. 8,
 excitis (abl. f.) 1. 732.
excipio
 excipit 2. 253, 438; 4. 755; 5. 543, 672;
 6. 422, 572 (B; KGL exigit), 639
 (BGL; K exigit), 646,
 excepit 8. 36,
 exceptum (m.) 1. 818.
excito
 excitat 1. 50; 3. 572.
exclamo
 exclamat 7. 530.
excubiae
 excubias 3. 71; 5. 251.

excutio
 excussit 2. 185; 8. 82,
 excusso (abl. m.) 6. 209,
 excussi 1. 618; 4. 413,
 excussa (acc.) 2. 398,
 excussis (m.) 6. 399.
exedo
 exedit (perf.) 4. 470,
 exesam 2. 137.
exeo
 exit 1. 95; 4. 54; 6. 687; 8. 187,
 exibis 4. 588,
 exeat 7. 76, 549,
 exirent 4. 698.
exerceo
 exercet 3. 162.
exero
 exerta (nom. f.) 2. 207.
exercitus
 exercitus (nom. s.) 6. 457.
exhorreo
 exhorruit 2. 202; 4. 380; 6. 52.
exhorresco
 exhorruit 7. 278, 527.
exigo
 exigit 4. 390; 6. 572 (KGL; B excipit),
 639 (K; BGL excipit),
 exegit 2. 75,
 exigere 3. 382,
 exacta (nom.) 2. 475,
 exactae (nom.) 4. 633.
exilio
 exilit 3. 58, 83; 4. 50; 6. 108.
eximo
 exime 2. 256.
exilium
 exilia (acc.) 4. 351; 5. 686.
existo
 extitit 3. 622; 4. 170.
exitialis
 exitiale (acc.) 5. 261, 447.
exitium
 exitium 2. 292,
 exitio 1. 28,
 exitium 2. 102; 3. 302,
 exitia (acc.) 1. 810; 5. 625.
exitus
 exitus (nom. s.) 4. 718; 8. 185.
Exomatae
 Exomatae 6. 144,
 Exomatas 6. 146, 569.
exopto
 exoptant 4. 194.
exorabilis
 exorabile (acc.) 1. 782.
exorior
 exoritur 2. 393; 5. 438,
 exorta 4. 602,
 exorta (abl.) 4. 723.
exordium
 exordia (acc.) 6. 20.
exoro
 exoret 1. 155.

exosus
exosus 6. 390,
exosa (nom. f.) 5. 349.
expedio
expediunt 1. 313; 2. 342; 8. 302,
expediam 4. 558,
expediit 7. 277,
expediat 4. 669,
expediant 8. 383,
expedior 1. 218.
expello
expulit 3. 107; 6. 79,
expellite 8. 349,
expellere 2. 164.
expendo
expendere 1. 51 (L; KBG vel pendere).
experior
experiar 1. 559; 3. 512 (vid. subi.); 8. 51,
experiere 5. 639,
experiar 3. 512 (vid. ind.),
experiens (m.) 2. 33,
expertus 1. 567,
experta (nom.) 7. 21,
experti (nom.) 2. 51; 5. 561,
experienda (nom. f.) 5. 319.
expers
expertes (nom. m.) 6. 122.
expeto
expetit 5. 577,
expete 4. 582.
expio
expiet 2. 276.
expleo
expleri 4. 323.
explico
explicuit 8. 248,
explicito (abl. n.) 5. 560.
exploro
explorant 3. 245,
explorare 4. 134; 7. 543.
exprimo
expresserat 2. 414.
expresso (abl. m.) 4. 660,
expressa (acc.) 1. 398; 2. 654.
exquiro
exquirit 4. 734.
exsanguis
exsangui (abl. m.) 3. 280,
exsangues (acc. m.) 3. 263, 274, 310.
exseco
exsectos 7. 636.
exsequor
exsequar 2. 217 (vid. subi.); 5. 222,
exsequar 2. 217 (vid. ind.).
exsisto vid. existo.
exsolvo
exsolvet 5. 290,
exsolvat 2. 219,
exsolvere 7. 284.
exsors
exsortia (acc.) 4. 340.
exspecto
exspectat 5. 604; 7. 300; 8. 31,
exspectant 8. 406,

exspectare 6. 327,
exspectata (voc.) 4. 437,
exspectati 8. 149,
exspectata (acc.) 7. 417.
exspiro
exspirat 4. 493.
exstinguo
exstinxi 8. 106,
exstinguere 1. 31,
exstingui 3. 294,
exstinctum (acc. n.) 3. 247.
exsto
exstat 1. 657,
extat 8. 143, 365 (BL; KG errat),
exstet 5. 252,
exstantem (m.) 7. 562 (KGL; B errantem).
exstruo
exstruxit 2. 20,
exstructa (abl.) 5. 628.
exsulto
exsultet 5. 612.
exsupero
exsuperant 2. 622.
exta
exta (acc.) 1. 232, 253,
extis 1. 205; 2. 347.
extemplo (7)
1. 722; 2. 604; 4. 315, 637; 6. 753; 7. 425, 456.
externus
externa 4. 463; 5. 249,
externae 7. 444,
externo (m.) 7. 309,
externo (abl.) 5. 360,
externa 7. 422; 8. 387,
externo 1. 63 (BG; K externo; L ex taetro),
externa (acc.) 6. 407,
externis (f.) 4. 159; 5. 56.
exterreo
exterruit 5. 232; 6. 382,
exterritus 1. 778,
exterrita (nom. f.) 8. 450.
exterus
extremus 6. 277, 674; 7. 457 (L; KG extremum; B extremo),
extrema 5. 177,
extremi 3. 730,
extremae 7. 382,
extremi 5. 3, 350,
extremo (m.) 7. 154,
extremum 7. 457 (KG; B extremo; L extremus); 8. 23, 117,
extremam 6. 431,
extremum 4. 253,
extremo 4. 732; 7. 457 (B; KG extremum; L extremus), 475,
extrema 3. 197; 5. 140; 6. 700; 8. 319,
extremo 4. 177; 5. 226; 6. 163, 574, 636; 7. 4,
extremis (m.) 4. 691,
extremos 5. 82; 6. 667,
extremas 1. 293; 6. 133, 749; 7. 11, 111,
extrema 3. 64; 5. 13,

extremis 7. 560,
extremis (f.) 7. 538,
subst. n. extrema (acc.) 6. 503,
adv. extremum 4. 115.
exto vid. exsto.
extorris
extorrem (m.) 4. 427.
extra
8. 89.
extraho
extrahit 1. 278.
extremus vid. exterus.
exubero
exuberet 3. 234.
exul
exulibus (abl.) 7. 44.
exulo
exulat 6. 462.
exulto
exultat 4. 608.
exululo
exululans (f.) 8. 172.
exundo
exundat 4. 595.
exuo
exuit (prs.) 6. 253,
exuerat 3. 2,
exue 7. 492.
exuviae
exuviae 3. 721,
exuvias 3. 143; 5. 491; 6. 19, 358; 8. 65.
facies
facies 2. 394, 493; 4. 185; 8. 312,
faciem 2. 39,
facie 6. 534,
facies (acc.) 2. 216.
facilis
facilis (nom. m.) 4. 723; 5. 406,
facilem (m.) 1. 734,
facili 8. 253,
facili (f.) 5. 524,
faciles 4. 6,
faciles 1. 151,
faciles 1. 109,
faciles 6. 323.
facinus
facinus (nom.) 2. 251.
facio
facit 2. 277,
faxo 4. 191, 220; 5. 654, 670 (K; BG
fas; L fessa); 7. 177,
face 7. 179,
fit 1. 819; 5. 163; 8. 112,
fiet 4. 572 (G; KB fieret; L fuerit),
fieret 3. 490; 4. 572 (KB; G fiet; L
fuerit),
facta 1. 545; 7. 461,
factum (nom.) 2. 337,
facto (abl. m.) 4. 624,
facta (nom.) 1. 210,
facienda (nom. n.) 1. 323,
subst. n. facti 3. 262,
facta 2. 263; 3. 394,
factis 2. 564,

facta 1. 12, 347, 772; 3. 455; 6. 94, 515;
8. 1.
factum vid. facio.
facultas
facultas 1. 534; 3. 16.
falcatus
falcatos 6. 105, 387.
fallax
fallaci (f.) 1. 809,
fallax (voc. f.) 8. 275,
fallaces (acc. f.) 7. 344,
fallacibus (f.) 3. 186; 5. 631.
fallo
fallis 4. 675,
fallit 6. 713; 8. 216.
fallunt 2. 282, 349,
fallam 1. 180,
fefellit 5. 316; 6. 366,
fallat 6. 734 (BGL; K vellera); 7. 169
(fallat et KL; B insomnem; G solvat
et),
fallere 3. 182, 490; 4. 451,
falle 7. 288,
fallens (f.) 3. 319,
fallor 8. 351,
fallatur 7. 213,
falli 5. 223; 8. 409,
falsi 8. 266,
falsae 1. 717,
falsae 6. 491,
falsa 7. 151,
falso 5. 242,
falsa 4. 461,
falsos 6. 661.
falx
falcis 6. 424,
falce 7. 370.
Fama
Famam 2. 116.
fama
fama 1. 8, 30, 47, 76, 381, 411; 2. 159,
560; 3. 622, 642; 4. 735; 5. 82, 316, 506,
553; 6. 10, 137, 156; 7. 291,
famae 3. 375, 677; 6. 471,
famae 1. 178,
famam 4. 161 (L; K nomen; BG numen); 7. 310, 459,
fama 1. 100, 790; 2. 95, 640; 4. 553.
fames
fames 2. 348; 4. 456, 499,
famem 6. 614.
famula
famulae 6. 502,
famulae 7. 366,
famulam 1. 303,
famula 5. 399,
famulae 2. 341; 8. 172,
famulas 2. 114, 138; 4. 520; 7. 145.
famularis
famularibus (abl. f.) 2. 268.
famulor
famulatur 2. 146.
famulus
famuli 3. 205,
famulo 1. 447,

famulum 6. 642,
famuli 3. 458,
famulum 1. 752; 3. 20, 282,
famulis 4. 254; 6. 359,
famulis 1. 459,
adi. famulos 1. 749 (KBG; L tremulos).
far
farra (acc.) 2. 449.
Fas
Fas (voc.) 1. 796.
fas
fas 1. 118, 508; 3. 309 **bis,** 381, 414; 5.
670 (BG; K faxo; L fessa); 7. 208,
231 **bis,** 280, 419; 8. 273, 419, 443,
fas 8. 424.
fastidium
fastidia (acc.) 4. 496.
fastigium
fastigia 3. 721 (L; KBG vestigia),
fastigia 2. 235, 553; 3. 62.
fastus
subst. m. fastis (abl.) 2. 245.
fatalis
fatale (nom.) 6. 653,
fatali (abl. m.) 3. 260,
fatales (nom. m.) 6. 608,
fatales (acc. f.) 6. 219,
fatalia 5. 241.
fateor
fateor 7. 346, 518,
fatetur 4. 415,
fatentur 8. 223,
fateri 7. 7, 481,
fatenti (dat. f.) 6. 461.
fatidicus
fatidici 4. 425,
fatidicae (gen.) 6. 70,
fatidicam 1. 2,
fatidicis (abl. f.) 1. 304.
fatigo
fatigat 2. 120, 138; 3. 21; 4. 69; 7. 311;
8. 86,
fatigant 1. 636; 5. 141; 7. 348; 8. 386,
fatiget 5. 601.
fatisco
fatiscit 4. 48,
fatiscunt 3. 395,
fatiscens (m.) 7. 598.
fatum
fati 3. 379; 4. 252, 446, 709,
fatum 3. 170 (K; BGL fatis),
fato 2. 152; 3. 374, 620; 4. 159, 741; 5.
65, 544,
fata 1. 323, 541 (vid. acc.); 2. 352, 594;
3. 184, 717; 4. 121, 127, 432; 5. 87; 6.
734; 7. 133; 8. 174,
fatorum 5. 246, 308,
fatis 1. 554; 2. 593; 3. 294, 461; 4. 449;
6. 205,
fata 1. 114, 534 541 (vid. nom.), 649,
764, 768; 2. 5, 216, 572; 3. 194, 221, 250,
734; 4. 86, 458, 479, 557, 597, 624, 752;
5. 21, 43, 156, 225, 676; 6. 201, 289, 407,
550, 621; 8. 107, 135, 389,

fatis 1. 230, 744; 2. 322 (K; B laeta;
GL hospita), 446; 3. 64, 170 (BGL;
K fatum); 4. 26, 101, 485; 5. 2, 59, 102,
686; 7. 446; 8. 397.
Faunus
Fauni (nom.) 1. 105.
faux
fauces (acc.) 2. 344, 586,
faucibus 1. 784; 2. 223; 4. 504.
faveo
fave 1. 11; 5. 197,
faventem (m.) 6. 580,
.subst. m. faventes (acc.) 3. 645.
favor
favor 3. 701; 4. 228, 669.
fax
fax 3. 664 (BG; KL pax),
facem 1. 569; 3. 137; 4. 671,
face 1. 370,
faces 1. 623; 4. 412; 5. 33,
faces 1. 14, 798; 3. 96, 350; 5. 370, 379,
facibus 1. 703; 4. 393; 6. 673.
febris
febris (nom.) 7. 244 (G; K om.; B lingua; L artus).
fecundus
fecundi (gen. m.) 5. 204,
fecunda (acc.) 6. 470.
felevis
felevis 1. 389 (K; BL felixque; G et
levis).
felix
felix 1. 25, 482; 5. 383; 7. 39,
felix 1. 389 (felixque BL; K felevis;
G et levis),
felix 2. 473,
felicis (f.) 6. 598,
felix (voc. m.) 4. 329,
felices (m.) 1. 445; 7. 18,
felicia 7. 485,
felicia 6. 138,
felicibus (m.) 6. 712.
femina
femina (nom.) 5. 670.
femineus
femineum (nom.) 2. 231,
femineis (m.) 1. 318,
femineis (n.) 5. 627,
femineas 4. 603.
fera vid. ferus.
feralis
feralis (nom. m.) 5. 31,
feralibus (abl. f.) 7. 57.
ferax
ferax (m.) 6. 102.
ferculum
fercula (acc.) 3. 539.
feretrum
feretro (abl.) 5. 11.
ferinus
ferinae (gen.) 6. 379,
ferino (abl. n.) 2. 157,
subst. ferina (abl.) 3. 569.

ferio
 ferit 1. 225, 385; 3. 176, 200; 6. 99, 249,
 374, 619; 7. 148, 378; 8. 23 (KGL; B
 terit).
fero
 fero 3. 415; 4. 216 (KB; GL feram);
 6. 549; 8. 278,
 fers 7. 413,
 fert 1. 145, 263; 3. 97, 336 (munera fert
 L; KG funereae; B inferiae), 694; 4.
 458; 5. 239, 417, 694; 6. 236; 7. 112, 306,
 ferunt 1. 615; 2. 594; 3. 148, 631; 4.
 330; 5. 31,
 ferebat 1. 730; 4. 199; 7. 473; 8. 448,
 ferebant 1. 819; 4. 748; 6. 642; 7. 133;
 8. 174,
 feram 1. 807; 2. 243 (vid. subi.), 576;
 4. 216 (GL; KB fero),
 feres 4. 242,
 feret 5. 405; 6. 268,
 ferent 4. 36,
 tuli 1. 84; 3. 328,
 tulit 1. 414, 463, 826; 2. 374, 609; 3. 206,
 392; 4. 207; 5. 6, 35, 470, 499, 649; 6.
 725; 7. 216, 576,
 tulerant 3. 355,
 tulerit 4. 623; 5. 384,
 feram 2. 243 (vid. ind.),
 ferat 1. 270, 551; 4. 55, 142, 192, 439;
 5. 547; 8. 384,
 ferant 4. 47; 5. 468,
 ferret 8. 110,
 tulerit 3. 618; 4. 441,
 fer 5. 385,
 ferte 2. 600; 4. 218 (KB; GL forte);
 5. 395,
 ferre 1. 766; 2. 282, 314; 3. 438; 4. 326,
 547, 644, 678; 5. 510; 7. 297; 8. 5, 212,
 442,
 ferens 2. 460; 3. 47; 4. 19, 237, 735; 5.
 193, 466; 7. 544; 8. 135, 360,
 ferens (f.) 2. 418; 4. 496; 8. 96,
 ferentem 6. 104,
 ferentem 3. 194,
 ferentes (acc. m.) 1. 266; 6. 327,
 feror 1. 198; 6. 330,
 fertur 1. 415; 3. 588, 591; 5. 68; 6. 543;
 7. 464,
 feruntur 4. 255, 681; 6. 195,
 ferar (ind.) 2. 299,
 ferri 3. 678; 4. 56.
ferox
 ferox (m.) 3. 549; 6. 615, 741.
ferratus
 ferrata (nom. f.) 6. 90.
ferreus
 ferreus 5. 410.
ferrugo
 ferrugine 1. 775.
ferrum
 ferri 3. 100; 5. 144,
 ferrum 1. 759; 2. 228,
 ferro 1. 94, 488, 599; 2. 238; 3. 144 **bis,**
 381, 425, 670; 6. 98, 110, 574; 8. 343.

fertilis
 fertilis (gen.) 7. 608,
 fertilis (gen. f.) 6. 711.
ferus
 ferus 1. 43, 716; 5. 553; 6. 287, 303; 7.
 563,
 fera 3. 88,
 feri (gen. m.) 6. 516,
 fera (nom.) 4. 585,
 feros 7. 504,
 feras 3. 643,
 fera 1. 596; 5. 533, 651; 6. 755,
 subst. f. ferae (nom.) 3. 530, 592 (BG;
 KL feris),
 ferarum 6. 333,
 feris (dat.) 3. 592 (KL; BG ferae).
ferveo (fervo)
 fervent 1. 640,
 fervēre 1. 121; 6. 588; 7. 150.
fervor
 fervor 7. 194 (L; KBG languor).
fessus
 fessus 7. 152; 8. 79,
 fessa 3. 511; 5. 670 (L; K faxo; BG
 fas),
 fessum (m.) 1. 474; 8. 231,
 fessam 1. 830,
 fessa 3. 552,
 fesso 2. 32; 3. 664; 7. 592,
 fessi 4. 376; 5. 32,
 fessae 4. 514; 6. 77,
 fessa 4. 66, 639,
 fessis 7. 25,
 fessis (f.) 4. 20; 5. 279,
 fessos 1. 48; 6. 444,
 fessas 2. 69; 4. 326, 699,
 fessis (f.) 1. 288,
 subst. m. fesso (dat.) 4. 274,
 fessis (dat.) 4. 736; 5. 177.
festino
 festinet 1. 270.
festinus
 festina 2. 191; 3. 341; 4. 470; 6. 472,
 festinam 7. 187,
 festina (acc.) 6. 325.
festus
 festa (abl.) 2. 188; 5. 74,
 festae 8. 240,
 festis (f.) 3. 159,
 festa 2. 582; 4. 760.
fetus
 feta (acc.) 7. 367,
 subst. feta (nom. f.) 5. 149.
fetus
 fetum 4. 45,
 fetus (acc.) 7. 375.
fibra
 fibrae (gen.) 7. 356.
fibula
 fibula (nom.) 1. 433.
fides
 fides 1. 383; 2. 167, 646; 3. 598, 704; 4.
 541, 614, 744; 5. 75, 498; 7. 91, 100; 8.
 430,

fidem 2. 338; 6. 22; 8. 49, 222, 249.
fide 4. 88.
fido
fidere 1. 118; 4. 544,
fidens 1. 308; 6. 248,
fidens (f.) 8. 112,
fidentem (f.) 6. 260.
fiducia
fiducia (nom.) 1. 603; 3. 364, 669; 4. 124, 206; 7. 520.
fidus
fidus 5. 104,
fida 1. 812; 7. 355; 8. 97,
fidi (gen. m.) 8. 411,
fida (acc.) 3. 710,
fidissima 5. 63,
fidissime 8. 75, 197, 419.
figientem (?)
figientem (f.) 7. 260 (K; BGL fugientem).
figo
figit 4. 395; 7. 254, 463; 8. 368,
fixit 3. 74,
fixerat 5. 115; 7. 559,
fixa 1. 549; 6. 487,
fixum (nom.) 5. 288,
fixam 1. 157; 3. 156,
fixa 4. 281,
fixi 4. 505,
fixae 2. 260,
fixa 1. 533; 6. 442; 8. 405,
fixos 4. 708; 5. 170,
fixas 8. 195,
fixa 1. 529; 7. 104.
filia
filia (nom.) 1. 61; 7. 78.
filius
filius 5. 457.
filum
fila (acc.) 1. 409.
findo
fissa (acc.) 1. 479.
fingo
fingis 2. 130 (cum fingis KBG; L confingis),
fingit 2. 210, 318 (K; BL om.; G rumor); 3. 223; 5. 533,
fingeret 1. 662,
finxisset 4. 365 (K; BL tenuisset; G timuisset),
finge 6. 539; 8. 429,
fingere 3. 507,
fictis (dat. n.) 1. 39.
finis
finis (nom.) 1. 350; 5. 531,
finem 3. 376, 501; 4. 64, 461, 558, 581; 5. 679; 8. 384,
fine 1. 555, 768; 4. 625,
fines (acc.) 1. 589,
finibus 3. 656; 7. 361.
fio vid. facio.
firmo
firmo 3. 711,
firmat 1. 79,
firmet 5. 215,

firmate 5. 322,
firmans 2. 47,
firmans (f.) 5. 358.
firmus
firma (nom. f.) 4. 12.
fistula
fistula (nom.) 4. 384.
flabra
flabris (abl.) 6. 665.
flagellum
flagelli 7. 149,
flagello (abl.) 8. 20.
flagito
flagitat 2. 362.
flagro
flagrantes (acc. f.) 1. 755; 7. 411,
flagrantia 5. 35; 6. 669.
flamen
flamina (nom.) 2. 429; 3. 732 (BGL; K flumina); 4. 98; 5. 683; 7. 25, 506 (G; KBL flamma).
flamma
flamma 1. 235; 4. 660; 5. 227; 7. 506 (KBL; G flamina), 586; 8. 247,
flammae (gen.) 2. 338; 6. 452, 663,
flammam 1. 204; 8. 56,
flamma 3. 134,
flammae 6. 464,
flammis 2. 156; 5. 30,
flammas 1. 232; 2. 25; 3. 273; 7. 547 (K; BGL glebas), 548 (BGL; K flatus), 571; 8. 302,
flammis 3. 351, 443; 5. 55; 6. 384; 7 .74; 8. 306, 348.
flammeus
flammea (acc.) 2. 420; 3. 400; 5. 360.
flammifer
flammifero (abl. m.) 1. 4,
flammiferos 6. 434; 7. 185,
flammiferis (m.) 7. 233.
flammiger
flammigeri (gen. m.) 5. 581.
flammo
flammabat 5. 177,
flammantem (f.) 1. 568,
flammatus 8. 300,
flammata (nom. f.) 4. 655,
flammata (acc.) 1. 108.
flatus
flatus (nom.) 8. 99,
flatu (abl.) 2. 278, 508; 3. 631,
flatus 3. 699,
flatus 2. 130; 3. 278; 7. 548 (K; BGL flammas),
flatibus 3. 624, 732; 7. 583, 601.
flaveo
flaventem (m.) 3. 35.
flavus
flavus 1. 613; 4. 719,
flava 6. 226,
flavi (m.) 3. 544,
flava (abl.) 1. 70,
flavi 6. 144,
flavis (dat. f.) 8. 237.

flebilis
flebilis (nom. m.) 3. 202,
adv. flebile 2. 453; 7. 215.
flecto
flectit 3. 42; 5. 436,
flectunt 5. 695; 8. 200 (KBG; L flexu),
flexit 2. 323; 6. 651,
flexerat 4. 59; 7. 457 (se flexerat BL;
K suffecerat; G suffixerat), 489,
flectat 2. 3,
flecte 1. 216, 525; 3. 416,
flectere 3. 250; 7. 105, 172,
flexus 3. 615.
fleo
flet 2. 175; 3. 722; 5. 23,
flebat 6. 496; 7. 251, 575 (KGL; B
flerat); 8. 205,
flebant 2. 578; 5. 429,
flevit 1. 448; 4. 374, 375; 6. 318; 8. 94,
flerunt 4. 374,
flerat 7. 575 (B;KGL flebat),
flere 4. 448; 7. 200,
flens 5. 8,
flens (f.) 1. 589; 8. 6,
flentem (m.) 6. 736,
flentes 1. 316, 633,
flentes (nom. f.) 1. 527,
flentes (f.) 1. 552,
fleturus 5. 138.
fletus
fletu (abl.) 1. 643; 2. 145, 464 (L; K
flexus; B fletus; G fluctus); 5. 340; 6.
738; 7. 458,
fletus 3. 704; 7. 383, 483,
fletus 2. 172, 464 (B; K flexus; G fluctus; L fletu); 7. 269, 8. 11,
fletibus 4. 76; 7. 410.
flexilis
flexilis (nom. f.) 5. 588.
flexus
flexu (abl.) 8. 200 (L; KBG flectunt),
377,
flexus (acc.) 2. 464 (K; B fletus; G
fluctus; L fletu); 5. 185.
floreo
floret 1. 539; 5. 564; 6. 494.
floresco
florescunt 7. 363,
florescant 7. 77.
floreus
florea (acc.) 5. 343.
flos
florem 7. 356,
flore 1. 101; 6. 709,
floribus (abl.) 6. 136, 167.
fluctuo
fluctuat 3. 637.
fluctus
fluctus (nom.) 4. 44; 8. 367,
fluctu (abl.) 1. 134, 265, 453, 479; 2.
434; 3. 102; 4. 48, 687, 726; 7. 572; 8.
331, 357,
fluctus 2. 477; 4. 404; 8. 349,
fluctibus 1. 389; 4. 83; 7. 18,
fluctus 1. 632; 2. 58, 464 (G; K flexus;

B fletus; L fletu), 535; 3. 475; 4. 347;
5. 201; 6. 163; 7. 496; 8. 327, 363, 405,
fluctibus 1. 465; 2. 368, 505, 603; 6.
482; 7. 36; 8. 382.
fluentum
fluento (abl.) 4. 601 (B; KGL memento).
flumen
fluminis 5. 212, 350; 8. 121,
flumine 8. 190,
flumina 3. 732 (K; BGL flamina); 4.
21; 5. 162, 602,
flumina 2. 496; 3. 421, 595; 4. 402, 698;
5. 186, 332, 381, 485; 8. 186.
flumineus
flumineo (abl. m.) 2. 12,
flumineo 4. 721.
fluo
fluit 6. 360,
fluat 3. 98,
fluxisse 8. 241,
fluens (f.) 5. 120,
fluentis (m.) 5. 207 (KBG; L tuenti),
fluenti (abl. m.) 3. 158,
fluentia (acc.) 1. 679.
fluvius
fluvius 5. 557,
fluvio 5. 182,
fluvium 4. 597; 7. 644,
fluvio 5. 205,
fluvium (gen.) 6. 391, 443,
fluvios 3. 435; 4. 133; 5. 341; 6. 165,
fluviis 3. 227.
focus
focus 3. 116.
foedo
foedatum (m.) 2. 275,
foedata (acc.) 4. 454.
foedus
foeda (nom. f.) 6. 283, 723 (BGL; K
sera),
foeda (acc.) 4. 498; 6. 410.
foedus
foederis 8. 271,
foedus 8. 222,
foedere 5. 633,
foedera (acc.) 2. 173; 3. 291, 503; 4. 102,
215; 5. 220, 494, 662; 6. 12, 692; 7. 177.
folium
foliis 2. 450,
foliis 6. 167.
fons
fontis 3. 553; 4. 29,
fontem 3. 531,
fontes (acc.) 3. 537 (KBG; L montes);
4. 364,
fontibus 1. 692; 5. 372 (KL; BG roribus); 7. 364.
for
fatur 1. 320, 562, 786; 2. 556; 3. 289, 316,
616; 4. 61, 249, 537, 757; 5. 131 (L;
KBG fatus), 193, 615; 7. 171, 197, 436,
553; 8. 177,
fabor 4. 578; 8. 184,
fata est 7. 8,

fatus erat 1. 240,
fare 2. 132; 5. 551, 552,
fari 3. 641; 7. 409,
fantem (f.) 6. 679,
fatus 1. 204; 4. 54, 653; 5. 54, 131
(KBG; L fatur); 6. 629, 646,
fata (nom. f.) 2. 160; 7. 349, 537; 8.
444,
fandi 3. 651; 4. 560; 5. 388,
fando (abl.) 4. 170 (KGL; B quando).
foris
  fores 7. 328,
  foribus 1. 819 (K; BGL sonitu),
  fores 2. 273; 5. 417; 7. 106,
  foribus 3. 60; 7. 114.
forma
  forma 4. 111; 6. 91, 419,
  formae 6. 465,
  formae 7. 449,
  forma 2. 148; 6. 479.
formido
  formidantem (m.) 5. 432.
formido
  formidine 1. 86; 2. 267, 360; 3. 390; 4.
  10, 174, 191, 197, 626, 646, 700; 5. 188;
  6. 535; 7. 144; 8. 307.
formo
  fuerat formata 8. 288,
  formatis (abl. f.) 2. 97.
fors
  fors 2. 559; 3. 202, 392, 665; 4. 620; 6.
  265,
  forte 5. 329,
  adv. forte 4. 44, 218 (GL; KB ferte),
  507; 5. 157; 6. 750; 7. 182, 260, 370 (L;
  KBG monte); 8. 52,
  ne forte 5. 286,
  si forte 7. 273,
  si . . . forte 7. 198, 454.
forsan (7)
  1. 170, 712; 2. 151; 3. 518, 653; 7. 129;
  8. 423.
forsitan
  2. 337; 4. 567.
fortasse
  7. 472.
fortis
  fortem (m.) 3. 478,
  forti (f.) 4. 193,
  fortia 1. 315,
  fortes (m.) 1. 434,
  fortia 1. 772,
  fortibus (n.) 6. 128,
  fortior 1. 335; 8. 341,
  fortior 7. 248,
  fortissima 8. 415,
  fortissime 7. 11,
  subst. fortissime 7. 67.
Fortuna
  Fortuna (nom.) 1. 326; 2. 176, 474, 594;
  3. 293; 5. 113, 530.
fortuna
  fortuna (nom.) 3. 337; 8. 179.

foveo
  fovet 4. 7, 358; 5. 149,
  fovent 2. 92, 121,
  fovebam 1. 541,
  fovebo 1. 555,
  fovit 1. 356,
  fovisse 3. 174,
  fovens (m.) 3. 647.
fragilis
  fragilem (f.) 6. 147.
fragmen
  fragmine 3. 477,
  fragmina (acc.) 6. 250.
fragor
  fragor 1. 753, 819; 2. 389, 477, 501, 529;
  3. 218, 404; 4. 659, 665; 5. 163; 6. 753;
  7. 529; 8. 296,
  fragorem 4. 71,
  fragore 2. 619; 3. 529,
  fragores (acc.) 4. 675; 5. 482,
  fragoribus 6. 504.
fragosus
  fragosae (gen.) 4. 261 (K; BGL fragosa),
  fragosa (abl.) 2. 198; 4. 261 (BGL; K
  fragosae),
  fragosis (abl. n.) 2. 621.
fragro
  fragrat 4. 493.
frango
  frangit 1. 363; 2. 448, 604; 3. 589; 6. 358,
  frangunt 6. 354,
  fregit 4. 721; 6. 284,
  fregisset 2. 315,
  frangite 8. 355,
  frangere 1. 390,
  frangentem (m.) 2. 459,
  frangitur 6. 635,
  fracta 2. 453,
  fracto (abl.) 3. 225; 6. 707,
  fracta 3. 36,
  fracta 1. 36; 7. 583,
  fractas 6. 412.
frater
  frater 1. 370, 376, 462, 469; 3. 191, 323,
  723; 4. 172, 746; 5. 266, 461, 536; 6. 626;
  8. 136, 277, 317,
  fratris 1. 26, 214, 358; 6. 585, 730, 742;
  7. 340; 8. 427,
  fratri 3. 491; 6. 213; 8. 74,
  fratrem 1. 13; 3. 203; 7. 279; 8. 313,
  frater 2. 602,
  fratre 5. 338; 6. 69,
  fratrum 5. 688; 8. 323,
  fratribus 6. 164,
  fratres 1. 570; 6. 203; 7. 638,
  fratribus 2. 365.
fraternus
  fraterna 4. 617,
  fraternae (dat.) 1. 178,
  fraternis (n.) 2. 565,
  fraterna 1. 163, 747.
fraudo
  fraudata (nom. f.) 2. 281,

fraudata (nom.) 5. 49,
fraudata 2. 376.
fraus
fraudis 6. 680,
fraudem 6. 16; 8. 135,
fraude 4. 293, 364; 5. 112, 502; 6. 531,
743,
fraudibus (abl.) 6. 591.
fremitus
fremitus (nom.) 2. 525,
fremitu (abl.) 1. 629; 2. 307; 3. 638; 6.
89; 8. 386,
fremitus 1. 159; 6. 232,
fremitus 2. 82; 3. 237; 6. 441 (ad fremitus L; KB adfatus; G adflatus).
fremo
fremis 5. 673,
fremit 1. 702; 4. 234; 5. 520, 524; 6. 329;
7. 67,
fremunt 2. 260; 4. 687; 6. 627 (G; K
fremant; BL frement),
frement 6. 627 (BL; K fremant; G
fremunt),
fremant 6. 627 (K; BL frement; G
fremunt),
fremere 1. 213 (fremere et KBG; L
pelagi), 608,
fremens 1. 725; 3. 229; 7. 471; 8. 372,
fremens (f.) 2. 119, 645,
frementes (nom. m.) 8. 305,
frementia (acc.) 6. 182,
subst. frementum (m.) 1. 594.
frenator
frenator 6. 162.
frendo
frendens (m.) 6. 556 (BGL; K stridens).
freno
frenabat 1. 22,
frenasse 1. 68.
frenum
freno (abl.) 1. 424,
frena 6. 414 (KBG; L temo),
ifrena 1. 455, 680; 2. 388; 3. 14, 24; 5.
513; 6. 377, 696,
frenis 4. 91; 5. 133.
frequens
frequentes (nom. m.) 1. 184,
frequentes (m.) 2. 472.
fretum
fretum (acc.) 1. 186, 331 (B; KGL
polum), 587, 626, 669; 2. 14, 29, 499;
4. 221; 5. 71,
freto 7. 541 (BGL; K fretis),
freta 1. 719; 4. 711,
fretis 2. 6; 3. 94; 5. 84,
freta 1. 1, 66, 74, 154, 380, 601, 615;
3. 7; 4. 105, 336, 421, 695, 7|25; 5. 84,
196, 471, 562; 8. 22, 72, 219, 347, 391,
fretis 1. 580; 4. 749; 5. 315; 6. 221; 7.
541 (K; BGL freto).
fretus
fretus 1. 73, 403; 6. 35; 7. 439,
freta (nom.) 3. 628; 7. 165,

freti (nom.) 4. 101,
freti (voc.) 1. 721.
frigesco
frigescere 3. 368.
frigidus
frigidus 3. 178; 4. 377; 6. 259; 7. 530,
586,
frigida (nom. f.) 2. 98, 386; 4. 214; 5. 26.
frigus
frigore 3. 236; 6. 505; 7. 230,
frigora (acc.) 1. 448.
frondeo
frondens (f.) 5. 61,
frondentibus (dat. f.) 3. 456,
frondentibus (m.) 8. 287.
frons
frondis 6. 296 (GL; KB frontis),
frondem 5. 361; 6. 714,
fronde 1. 137; 2. 189; 5. 11,
frondes 3. 402,
frondes 3. 436, 708; 4. 336; 6. 153,
frondibus 4. 23, 340.
frons
frons 1. 777,
frontis 3. 50, 189; 4. 241; 6. 296 (KB;
GL frondis),
frontem 1. 385 (GL; KB fronte), 618;
4. 167; 6. 532,
fronte 1. 7, 38, 385 (KB; GL frontem);
3. 431; 4. 232, 331,
frontibus (abl.) 1. 571.
frondosus
frondosae (gen.) 2. 414,
frondosa (acc.) 3. 545.
fruor
fruitur 6. 485; 7. 121,
fruuntur 4. 762,
fruentem 4. 38, 535,
fruentem 5. 380.
frustra (10)
1. 706; 2. 602; 3. 92, 155; 4. 40, 155; 5.
28, 599, 669; 7. 221.
frustror
frustratur 7. 162,
frustratus 5. 274.
fucus
fuco (abl.) 1. 427.
Fuga
Fuga (nom.) 6. 181.
fuga
fuga 2. 284; 4. 217 bis, 315, 524, 573,
656, 707; 6. 698, 723; 7. 219,
fugae (gen.) 3. 547; 4. 154; 6. 500; 8.
119,
fugam 2. 224, 415; 4. 644; 5. 271, 355;
6. 521; 7. 126, 297, 570; 8. 5, 135, 144,
167,
fuga 3. 584.
fugio
fugis 6. 275,
fugit 1. 147, 490, 729; 2. 300; 3. 136,
180; 4. 673, 694; 5. 101; 6. 271, 573,
642 (L; KG ruit; B fuit); 8. 7, 139,
159, 265, 449, 450,
fugitis 3. 270,

fugit 6. 8,
fugimus 8. 426,
fugere 4. 491,
fugat 2. 81,
fugeret 2. 405, 474,
fugerent 3. 530,
fugerit 1. 280; 5. 136,
fuge 2. 249, 252; 4. 140,
fugiens 1. 454; 6. 253,
fugiens (f.) 2. 181; 4. 401,
fugientis (m.) 2. 430 (vid. subst.),
fugientem (f.) 7. 260 (BGL; K figien-tem),
fugiente (f.) 3. 724,
subst. fugientis (acc. m.) 2. 430 (vid. gen. **supra).**
fugo
fugent 4. 462,
fugatum (m.) 5. 233,
fugata (abl.) 2. 51.
fulgeo
fulgit 3. 703 (L; KG vulgi; B vulgat),
fulsit 4. 660; 6. 480; 7. 566,
fulsere 1. 622; 3. 466; 5. 92,
fulgere 8. 284,
fulgens (f.) 1. 301; 6. 71,
fulgentem (f.) 7. 495,
fulgentia (acc.) 8. 101,
fulgentibus (f.) 5. 513.
fulgor
fulgor 5. 243.
fulgur
fulgura 1. 692,
fulgura 8. 61.
fulmen
fulmen 2. 337,
fulminis 2. 97; 6. 56; 7. 647,
fulmen 1. 199, 372,
fulmine 6. 169,
fulmina 3. 354,
fulmina 2. 23; 4. 287, 520; 7. 362; 8. 73.
fulmineus
fulmineus 2. 501,
fulmineum (m.) 6. 230,
fulmineam 4. 671,
fulminea (abl.) 4. 167,
fulmineis (abl. m.) 7. 583.
fulvus
fulvi (n.) 3. 567,
fulvo (abl. m.) 7. 158.
fumeus
fumeus 4. 596.
fumo
fumant 2. 233, 333; 4. 285,
fumanti (abl. f.) 3. 129,
fumantes (nom. m.) 7. 283,
fumantia (acc.) 1. 816,
fumantibus (n.) 7. 644.
fumus
fumo (abl.) 4. 676; 8. 452.
funda
fundae (gen.) 3. 96,
funda 6. 193,
fundis (abl.) 6. 230 (pro fundis B; K profundis; GL profundens).

fundamentum
fundamenta (acc.) 2. 31.
funditus
4. 195.
fundo
fundit 1. 504, 572; 3. 499; 4. 707; 5. 616; 6. 30; 8. 123,
fundunt 1. 610; 3. 243; 5. 16,
fudit 4. 167,
fuderat 1. 430, 446; 2. 107,
fundat 2. 661; 6. 391,
funderet 6. 582,
fundere 3. 697; 4. 679; 7. 180; 8. 186,
fudisse 6. 139,
fundens (f.) 8. 69,
funduntur 1. 252,
fusa est 3. 555 (BG; KL lusa est),
fusus 1. 710; 4. 746; 5. 242; 7. 610,
fusa 3. 315,
fusum (acc. n.) 8. 107,
fusi 3. 147,
fusis (abl. m.) 1. 295; 8. 93.
fundus
fundo (abl.) 1. 642; 2. 630; 3. 224; 8. 366.
funereus
funereae (gen.) 3. 336 (KG; B infer-iae; L munera fert),
funerea (abl.) 7. 468,
funereas 3. 311.
funestus
funesta (nom. n.) 3. 320,
funesta 6. 431.
fungor
functi (nom.) 4. 212 (BGL; K cuncti).
funis
funem 1. 314.
funus
funeris 6. 317; 7. 442 (BGL; K funera),
funere 2. 275; 5. 226,
funera 3. 298; 5. 39; 7. 442 (K; BGL funeris),
funera 1. 792; 2. 558; 3. 29, 215, 617, 681; 6. 242, 409, 428, 631, 741; 7. 643.
furia
furiae (nom.) 8. 2,
furias 3. 692; 5. 219; 7. 161,
furiis 1. 722; 2. 80, 163, 509; 3. 590; 4. 32, 235; 5. 520; 6. 1, 293; 8. 390 (KGL; B furtis).
Furiae
Furiarum 1. 817; 8. 20,
Furiis 2. 294 (K; BGL furti); 5. 42; 7. 170,
Furias 3. 520; 4. 13.
furialis
furiale (acc.) 2. 102; 6. 670,
furialia (acc.) 7. 254.
furibundus
furibunda (nom. f.) 2. 200.
furio
furiata (abl.) 8. 445.

furo
furit 2. 146, 614; 4. 5, 151; 6. 616; 7. 315,
528, 581, 648 (KBG; L ruit),
furens 1. 144, 662; 3. 86, 638 (BGL; K
serens); 4. 204; 5. 268, 426; 6. 211,
furens (f.) 1. 318; 2. 191; 6. 543; 8. 54,
furentis (f.) 4. 742; 5. 501,
furenti 3. 71,
furenti (f.) 2. 480,
furentem 1. 14; 4. 293; 6. 719,
furentem 7. 337,
furentes (acc. m.) 7. 640,
furentia 6. 425.

Furor
Furor 7. 510,
Furorum 1. 796.

furor
furor 1. 699; 2. 314, 624; 2. 233; 4. 562;
5. 139; 7. 36,
furoris 2. 239 (GL; KB furorum); 3.
290; 6. 516,
furori 7. 154,
furores 5. 676,
furorum 2. 239 (KB; GL furoris),
furores 6. 33, 667,
furoribus 1. 727; 5. 576; 7. 470.

furtum
furtum 4. 66,
furti 2. 294 (BGL; K Furiis),
furto (abl.) 8. 155,
furtis (abl.) 2. 283, 660; 6. 531; 8. 390
(B; KGL furiis),
adv. furto 8. 229.

fusco
fuscat 1. 396.

fuscus
fuscis (abl. f.) 6. 494.

futilis
futile (nom.) 8. 354.

Galatea
Galatea (nom.) 1. 135.

galea
galeae (gen.) 6. 365, 379; 7. 626,
galeam 3. 12, 80, 176, 342; 6. 519, 738
bis; 7. 467, 577, 632, 8. 309,
galeae 1. 222; 3. 76,
galeas 6. 186,
galeis 1. 836; 6. 183.

galerum
galeri 6. 226,
galero (abl.) 4. 138.

Gangaridae
Gangaridum 6. 67.

Gargara
Gargara (nom.) 2. 360, 583.

gaudeo
gaudes 3. 116,
gaudet 5. 118; 6. 158 bis, 528; 7. 609,
gaudent 1. 501,
gaudebant 5. 439,
gauderem 1. 340,
gaudens 1. 660; 6. 546; 7. 495,
gaudens (f.) 1. 600; 2. 135; 7. 215, 351;
8. 129,
gaudentibus (abl. m.) 1. 109.

Gaudium
Gaudia (nom.) 6. 179.

gaudium
gaudia 3. 317, 655; 4. 4, 292; 6. 513;
7. 2; 8. 164,
gaudia 3. 223, 698; 4. 164, 534; 6. 662;
7. 340; 8. 296.

gaza
gaza (abl.) 6. 562.

Gelas
Gelae (gen.) 6. 208 (BGL; K om.).

gelidus
gelidus 4. 226,
gelidi (m.) 2. 515,
gelidum (m.) 6. 100,
gelida (abl.) 4. 646; 6. 140,
gelidos 3. 415,
gelidas 3. 1; 5. 155,
gelidis (f.) 5. 350,
gelidis 6. 85.

Gelonus
Gelono (dat.) 7. 236,
Geloni 6. 512.

gelu
gelu (abl.) 1. 513; 2. 158; 6. 278, 611.

gemino
geminans (m.) 4. 343.

geminus
geminae (gen.) 5. 348,
geminam 3. 66,
gemino 1. 356; 2. 427; 3. 330; 5. 442;
8. 377,
gemina 1. 285, 428; 6. 99,
gemini 3. 190,
geminae 1. 832; 2. 598,
geminis 6. 248 (vid. abl.),
geminis (f.) 4. 716,
geminos 6. 52; 7. 568,
geminas 4. 473; 5. 417; 6. 40, 64,
geminis (m.) 5. 35; 6. 248 (vid. dat.),
geminis (n.) 6. 160.

gemitus
gemitus (nom.) 2. 187; 3. 277,
gemitu 3. 473 (vid. abl.), 737 (KBG;
L gemitum); 4. 286,
gemitum 3. 737 (L; KBG gemitu);
8. 400,
gemitu 1. 473 (vid. dat.); 2. 33, 458,
609; 4. 69; 5. 168, 310, 647; 7. 458; 8. 120,
gemitus 1. 315; 2. 240; 6. 188,
gemitus 1. 550; 2. 210; 3. 262, 696; 4.
14, 135; 6. 523, 725.

gemma
gemmae (dat.) 6. 59,
gemmas 8. 236,
gemmis 2. 651; 5. 513; 6. 672, 699.

gemmifer
gemmiferae (gen.) 5. 447.

gemo
gemit 2. 553; 3. 164; 5. 37; 6. 168; 7. 368,
gemunt 1. 728,
gemuit 1. 530; 8. 9,
gemet 1. 373,
gemens (m.) 3. 642; 8. 466,

gementem 1. 47,
gementem 8. 215, 465.
gena
genae (nom.) 8. 164,
genas 1. 758; 2. 105, 142; 3. 287, 309;
4. 51; 7. 258, 411; 8. 7,
genis 2. 205.
gener
gener 3. 497; 5. 444, 459; 6. 172, 269;
8. 166,
generi 1. 524 (L; KBG generos); 8.
350,
generum 5. 235,
gener 7. 38,
generos 1. 524 (KBG; L generi).
Genetaeus
Genetaei (gen. m.) 5. 147.
genetrix
genetrix 1. 413; 3. 322; 6. 565; 8. 171,
genetrice 4. 349; 6. 223.
genitalis
genitale (acc.) 4. 91.
genitor
genitor 1. 231, 453, 503, 531; 2. 420,
488; 3. 660; 4. 415, 502; 5. 126, 393;
6. 305, 308, 742; 7. 494; 8. 10, 443,
genitoris 1. 712; 2. 410; 5. 24, 403,
genitorem 2. 288,
genitor 1. 16; 2. 290; 5. 246,
genitore 1. 527; 2. 298; 3. 112.
gens
gens 2. 595; 4. 65, 603, 611; 5. 609; 6. 31
(KBL; G et); 8. 323,
gentis 1. 15 (K; BG genti; L centum),
779; 2. 611; 3. 514, 669; 4. 10; 5. 382,
417; 7. 485; 8. 458,
genti 1. 15 (BG; K gentis; L centum),
gentem 2. 395; 3. 248; 4. 133,
gente 3. 202, 703; 4. 33, 743; 6. 74, 678,
gentes 1. 815; 4. 713; 5. 635; 6. 519, 721,
gentibus 1. 518, 648, 744; 4. 346; 5. 308,
642,
gentes 1. 173, 555; 2. 361 (KBG; L
mentes), 644; 3. 643; 5. 181; 6. 41, 747,
gentibus 1. 196; 2. 616; 6. 37.
genu
genu (abl.) 3. 525; 6. 236; 7. 595, 603,
genibus 5. 411; 8. 203,
genibus 4. 304.
genus
genus 2. 156, 231, 468, 473, 573; 4. 172,
generis 3. 630; 4. 469; 6. 594,
genus 1. 411, 562, 770; 2. 195, 317, 560;
3. 247; 4. 205, 481; 5. 194, 278, 504;
6. 390, 468; 7. 41,
genus 6. 547.
Genysus
Genyso (dat.) 3. 114.
Geraestus
Geraesto (abl.) 1. 456.
germanus
subst. germani 3. 493; 6. 75,
germanam 6. 587,
germana (voc.) 8. 271.

gero
geris 1. 399,
gerit 1. 402; 3. 440,
gerunt 3. 675,
gerebat 2. 492,
gessit 2. 420,
gessimus 4. 30,
geras 8. 15,
gerant 2. 396,
gesseris 7. 416,
gerens (m.) 1. 836; 3. 177, 590; 4. 158,
521; 5. 272; 6. 695,
gesta (nom. n.) 3. 461.
Gerus
Gerus 6. 67.
Gesander
Gesander 6. 303, 322, 365,
Gesandrum 6. 280, 371.
Gessithous
Gessithoum 6. 637.
gestamen
gestamen (acc.) 3. 344; 6. 649,
gestamine 6. 72,
gestamina (acc.) 1. 760; 6. 671.
gestatrix
gestatrix 4. 605.
gestio
gestit 3. 634.
gesto
gestat 1. 110; 6. 53, 555,
gestant 2. 653,
gestabat 1. 453,
gestans (f.) 2. 211,
gestantem (m.) 6. 134,
gestata (acc.) 8. 118.
Getae
Getae 5. 603; 6. 507,
Getis (dat.) 5. 419.
Geticus
Geticum (m.) 6. 619,
Getico (m.) 7. 645,
Geticae 2. 232,
Geticis (abl. n.) 2. 204; 5. 618.
gigans
gigans 4. 200,
gigantum 2. 18.
gigno
genui 8. 153,
genuit 6. 641,
genitus 6. 621,
geniti (nom.) 4. 438; 5. 500,
genitos 3. 505.
glacio
glaciantibus (abl. f.) 4. 722.
gladius
gladio (abl.) 1. 438; 6. 249.
Glaucus
Glaucus 2. 605,
Glauco (dat.) 1. 190; 2. 286.
Glaucus
Glaucum 3. 153 **bis.**
glaucus
glauco (abl.) 6. 296,
glauca (abl.) 2. 499,
glaucas 3. 436.

gleba
  gleba (nom.) 7. 612,
  glebas 7. 547 (BGL; K flammas).
glisco
  gliscit 2. 278,
  gliscunt 3. 632,
  gliscere 5. 371.
globus
  globus 5. 430; 6. 381,
  globos 3. 135, 217; 5. 46; 6. 299, 555.
glomero
  glomerant 6. 86,
  glomerantur 6. 187.
Gloria
  Gloria (voc.) 1. 77.
gloria
  gloria (nom.) 2. 564; 4. 163, 469; 8. 43,
  458 (gloria magni BG; K restat imago;
  L om.).
gnarus
  gnara (nom. f.) 4. 208; 7. 224 (BL;
  KG ignava),
  gnara (nom.) 4. 404.
Gorgo
  Gorgo 3. 54.
Gorgoneus
  Gorgonei (n.) 4. 605,
  Gorgoneo (abl. m.) 6. 176.
Gortyn
  Gortyna 1. 708.
gracilis
  gracili (abl. f.) 1. 123.
gradior
  graditur 8. 238,
  gradiens (m.) 4. 628.
Gradivus
  Gradivus 3. 498; 4. 281; 5. 618; 6. 1;
  8. 228,
  Gradivi 5. 650,
  Gradivo 5. 122,
  Gradive 5. 142, 251,
  Gradivo 4. 602.
gradus
  gradum 2. 454; 3. 416; 4. 305,
  gradu 2. 546; 3. 100,
  gradus (acc.) 3. 441; 5. 395; 7. 559; 8.
  131.
Graecia
  Graecia (nom.) 1. 19; 7. 41, 132, 496,
  Graecia (voc.) 8. 275.
Graiugena
  Graiugenum 2. 557,
  Graiugenas 6. 389.
Graius
  1. subst. m.
  Graius 5. 362,
  Graio 5. 362,
  Graium 7. 550 (KGL; B graios),
  Grai 1. 543; 6. 190,
  Graium 1. 498; 5. 386; 6. 758; 8. 462,
  Grais 1. 550; 2. 326; 5. 523; 8. 262, 393,
  Graios 1. 604; 7. 39, 550 (B; KGL
  Graium),
  Grais 4. 740,
  2. adi.

Graius 5. 687,
Graia 1. 507, 599,
Graiae 1. 113,
Graio (m.) 1. 56; 2. 655,
Graium 5. 255,
Graiam 5. 116; 6. 5,
Graia 1. 523; 8. 317,
Graio 1. 519; 6. 351,
Grais 1. 18,
Grais (f.) 5. 293,
Graias 1. 33; 3. 452; 4. 402; 6. 498.
gramen
  gramine 2. 487,
  gramina (acc.) 3. 528; 7. 357, 450.
gramineus
  graminea (abl.) 4. 339,
  gramineis (abl. m.) 8. 255.
grandaevus
  grandaeva 1. 736; 2. 36; 5. 356; 8. 150,
  grandaevum (nom.) 3. 267,
  grandaeva (voc. f.) 1. 796,
  subst. grandaeva (voc. f.) 7. 348.
grates
  grates (acc.) 4. 557, 630; 7. 284, 417.
gratia
  gratia (nom.) 5. 491, 499.
gratus
  grata (nom. n.) 3. 600; 7. 25,
  gratos 3. 557,
  grata 5. 287,
  gratior 5. 104; 6. 47,
  gratior 7. 219; 8. 176.
gravidus
  gravidum (m.) 5. 22,
  gravida 8. 98,
  gravido 2. 56,
  gravidae 6. 709.
gravis
  gravis 1. 23, 145, 296; 3. 148; 4. 3; 5.
  519, 535; 6. 522,
  gravis 1. 653; 3. 239; 4. 74, 311,
  grave 3. 164,
  gravem 4. 597; 5. 597, 694; 7. 646,
  gravem 3. 124; 6. 378,
  grave 1. 170, 565; 7. 555,
  gravi 1. 300; 5. 184; 7. 292; 8. 35,
  gravi (f.) 1. 817; 5. 192; 7. 393,
  graves (nom. f.) 2. 511; 4. 515,
  graves 4. 18; 7. 141,
  graves 1. 746; 2. 40,
  gravia 1. 799,
  adv. grave 5. 169,
  gravior 5. 160; 6. 65, 382; 8. 296,
  gravior 3. 214,
  graviorem (f.) 7. 465.
gravitas
  gravitate 5. 656.
graviter
  gravius 7. 591.
gravo
  gravantia (acc.) 5. 484 (K; B armantia; G creantia; L ornantia),
  gravatum (m.) 2. 568; 4. 550.

gremium
gremium (acc.) 7. 117,
gremiis (abl.) 7. 49.
gressus
gressum 6. 348,
gressibus 5. 344,
gressus 1. 183, 710; 2. 93; 3. 8; 4. 176;
7. 110; 8. 111.
grex
gregis 5. 67, 376,
gregem 3. 634,
grege 8. 129,
greges 1. 90,
gregibus 7. 392,
greges 6. 532,
gregibus 4. 199.
gurges
gurges 8. 333,
gurgitis 4. 338,
gurgite 1. 472, 657; 2. 321; 4. 114, 409,
583, 756; 5. 521.
gyrus
gyro (abl.) 6. 132.
habena
habenae (gen.) 5. 608,
habena 3. 524,
habenae 2. 35,
habenas 1. 560; 2. 270; 4. 571; 5. 436;
6. 95, 365, 391,
habenis 1. 687; 2. 507; 3. 498, 538; 4.
679; 5. 518, 586; 6. 210, 271, 303; 7. 605;
8. 139.
habeo
habes 8. 108,
habet 1. 672; 3. 45, 291; 8. 99,
habent 2. 251; 5. 676; 8. 3,
habeat 6. 628,
habeant 5. 283; 8. 424,
habe 8. 157,
habere 5. 583,
habenti (dat. f.) 1. 10,
habentes (acc. m.) 7. 35,
habendo (abl.) 6. 174.
habilis
habilem (f.) 3. 607,
habiles (acc. m.) 7. 231.
habito
habitat 1. 583; 2. 119; 4. 147,
habitare 2. 383,
habitasse 2. 177.
habitus
habitus (acc.) 3. 223 (K; B actus; G
abitus; L aestus).
hac
hac . . . hac 4. 727.
hactenus
2. 439.
Haemonia
Haemoniae (gen.) 4. 736,
Haemoniam 1. 22.
Haemonidae
Haemonidae 4. 506; 5. 127; 6. 371.
Haemonius
Haemonius 8. 338,

Haemonii 2. 425; 7. 178 (B; KGL
Aesonii), 350, 524; 8. 283,
Haemoniae 2. 353, 636, 653 (B; KGL
Aesoniae); 7. 326,
Haemonio (m.) 7. 549; 8. 16,
Haemoniam 3. 27,
Haemonio 8. 129,
Haemonia (abl.) 3. 536,
Haemoniis (f.) 5. 262; 6. 18,
Haemonios 8. 216,
Haemonias 1. 120; 7. 17 (B; KGL
Aesonias), 56,
Haemoniis 6. 448; 8. 205,
Haemoniis (f.) 2. 592.
Haemus
Haemus 1. 727,
Haemum 1. 24.
haereo
haeret 2. 353; 3. 211, 486, 641; 4. 5; 5.
376; 6. 356, 658; 7. 122, 436, 588; 8. 55,
464,
haeremus 3. 661,
haerent 1. 316; 3. 4; 6. 416, 506,
haesit 1. 571; 4. 527; 7. 79, 384,
haeserat 8. 203,
haeserit 7. 206,
haeserit 5. 573,
haerens 2. 638,
haerens (f.) 1. 762; 5. 344,
haerentem (f.) 3. 331,
haerentes (acc. m.) 6. 421,
haesura (acc.) 1. 333; 2. 408.
Hages
Hagen 3. 191.
Hagniades
Hagniades 1. 482; 2. 48.
halcyon (halcyone)
halcyonis 4. 45 (K; BGL halcyones),
halcyones 4. 45 (BGL; K halcyonis).
halitus
halitus (nom. s.) 4. 494.
Halys
Halys 5. 112, 120.
Halys
Halyn 3. 157.
Hammon
Hammon 2. 482.
harena
harenae (gen.) 4. 230,
harena 1. 442, 613; 3. 716; 4. 264; 6. 716,
harenae 7. 561,
harenis 2. 445; 4. 410, 733; 5. 100 (vid.
abl.),
harenas 1. 181, 454; 7. 111,
harenis 1. 601; 2. 428; 3. 305; 4. 686
(KGL; B ahenis), 746; 5. 100 (vid.
dat.); 6. 620.
Harpe
Harpen 6. 375.
harpe
harpen 4. 390; 7. 364.
Harpyiae
Harpyiae 4. 428, 450, 525.

harundo
harundo 3. 135; 6. 262, 687,
harundine 1. 218; 6. 564.
hasta
hasta 3. 78, 240; 6. 217; 8. 303,
hastae 6. 653,
hastae 6. 569,
hastam 1. 270; 2. 269; 3. 107, 193, 707;
6. 202, 207, 244, 253, 347 (GL; KB
astat), 518; 7. 304, 465,
hasta 1. 143, 641; 4. 281, 609; 5. 462;
6. 194, 196, 214, 572, 639; 7. 603; 8. 133,
309, 317,
hastae 1. 222; 7. 634,
hastis 6. 381,
hastas 1. 409; 6. 136, 270; 7. 746,
hastis 1. 405; 6. 583, 685; 7. 96; 8. 449.
hastatus
hastatas 6. 120.
hastile
hastilia (acc.) 6. 229.
haud (haut) (57)
haud 4. 305, 388, 477 (L; KBG quid),
741; 5. 1, 60, 254, 354, 558; 7. 60, 650;
8. 198, 291, 318, 340, 443,
haut 1. 30; 3. 414, 627; 4. 240; 5. 534;
6. 125, 312, 498; 7. 57 (GL; KB aut),
176, 416; 8. 38, 79, 266 (B; KGL aut),
354, 404,
haut alias 7. 525,
haut alius (etc.) 2. 361; 6. 757,
haud aliter 2. 47,
haut aliter . . . cum . . . pariter 1. 489,
ceu . . . cum . . . haud aliter 7. 305,
ceu . . . cum . . . haut aliter 4. 44,
qualis . . . haud aliter 7. 380,
qualem . . . haut aliter 5. 25,
qualis ubi . . . haut aliter 7. 114,
haut minus 1. 415,
haud procul 8. 185,
haud secus 4. 665; 7. 637,
haut secus 8. 34,
haut secus . . . cum 1. 704,
haud secus . . . quam 2. 385,
qualem . . . haud secus 6. 717,
ut . . . cum . . . haut secus 7. 403,
haud ullis 3. 648,
haud umquam 5. 354,
haut umquam 4. 35; 8. 412,
haud usquam 6. 417,
haut usquam 6. 76,
Vid. velut.
haurio
haurit 1. 263; 6. 554,
hauriet 7. 97,
hausit 7. 643,
hausere 1. 818,
hausta est 4. 48.
Hebe
Hebe (nom.) 8. 231.
hebeo
hebet 1. 53; 4. 41; 5. 370; 7. 156.
Hebrus
Hebri 2. 515; 4. 463; 6. 139,

Hebrum 7. 646,
Hebro 8. 228.
Hebrus
Hebro (dat.) 3. 149.
Hebrus
Hebrum 6. 618.
Hecate
Hecate 6. 495; 7. 364,
Hecates 5. 335; 6. 113; 7. 182, 521,
Hecaten 7. 353.
hedera
hederis (abl.) 2. 268.
Helice
Helice 1. 18,
Helicen 5. 71.
Helix
Helix 6. 570.
Helle
Helle 1. 50, 282; 2. 588,
Helles 1. 167, 425, 537; 3. 7,
Hellen 2. 629; 7. 57.
Henioche
Henioche (nom.) 5. 357.
Heniochi
Heniochos 6. 43.
herba
herba (abl.) 1. 426,
herbae 7. 363.
Hercules
Herculis 3. 169, 649, 673; 5. 115, 130,
Hercule 3. 532, 641, 704; 4. 84.
Herculeus
Herculeae 5. 136,
Herculeo (m.) 1. 263,
Herculeum (n.) 1. 562,
Herculeo 1. 387; 3. 529,
Herculeo 3. 600,
Herculeis (m.) 1. 435,
Herculeis (n.) 1. 118 (vid. abl.); 2. 570,
Herculeas 1. 393; 3. 713,
Herculeis (n.) 1. 118 (vid. dat.).
heros
heros 2. 373; 4. 311; 7. 410, 614; 8. 24,
109, 379,
heroum 3. 691; 4. 325.
Hesiona
Hesionam 4. 164.
Hesperia
Hesperiae (dat.) 4. 508.
Hesperius
Hesperium (m.) 8. 91,
Hesperiis (abl. f.) 7. 259 (BL; KG a
superis).
hesternus
hesternos 3. 288.
heu (45)
1. 44, 71, 150, 172, 211, 287, 442, 744,
815; 2. 146, 217, 294; 3. 177, 261, 272
(BGL; K en), 292 (L; K hic; BG en),
303, 325, 329, 562, 592; 4. 26 (L; K ac;
BG haec), 140, 371, 378, 704; 5. 51, 523,
686; 6. 45, 374, 497, 678; 7. 43, 107, 199,
309, 338, 343 (B; KG et; L te), 449,
533 **bis**; 8. 100, 370 (K; BL nunc; G
nec), 459.

heus
   4. 387.
hiatus
   hiatu (abl.) 1. 34, 638; 4. 277, 595; 6.
   552; 7. 97, 604; 8. 329.
Hiber
   Hiber 5. 166, 559; 6. 507, 750,
   Hibero (dat.) 7. 235.
Hiberia
   Hiberia (nom.) 5. 604; 6. 120.
hibernus
   hibernus 6. 612,
   hiberni (m.) 3. 578; 6. 100,
   hiberno (abl.) 6. 632 (KGL; B hiberna),
   hiberna (abl.) 4. 105; 6. 632 (B; KGL
   hiberno),
   subst. n. hiberna (acc.) 1. 552.
Hiberus
   Hiberi (n.) 2. 34,
   Hiberas 3. 730.
hic
   1. pron.
   hic 3. 193 (KG; BL hinc); 4. 165; 5.
   490, 586, 593; 6. 573 (BGL; K hunc),
   588; 7. 649,
   haec 1. 405; 2. 320 (haec imis L; KG
   saepe imis; B saepimis); 8. 146, 153,
   hoc 1. 627; 3. 297; 4. 709 (B; KL id;
   G haec); 5. 514; 8. 160,
   huic 1. 162,
   huic (f.) 2. 141, 481,
   hunc 1. 27, 43, 94, 296, 597, 779; 2. 25,
   424; 3. 338, 541; 4. 535; 5. 68 bis, 457,
   589; 6. 190 (BGL; K hinc), 213 (KGL;
   B nunc), 303 (KBG; L hinc), 646; 7.
   351, 481, 532,
   hanc 1. 134, 642, 643; 2. 126, 434, 479;
   3. 194, 533; 4. 94, 358; 6. 445, 446, 458,
   495; 7. 469; 8. 48, 140 (ad hanc B; KGL
   adhuc),
   hoc (acc.) 1. 509; 2. 229 ter, 384, 482
   bis; 3. 354, 711; 4. 253; 5. 49 bis, 495,
   677; 6. 9 (G; KBL hos), 461; 7. 201
   (KG; BL om.), 257, 338; 8. 41, 53 bis,
   397, 443,
   hac 1. 666; 5. 395,
   hoc 2. 457; 4. 301, 545,
   hi 5. 424 (BGL; K et), 475; 8. 423,
   haec 1. 531; 2. 384; 3. 352; 4. 709 (G;
   KL id; B hoc); 5. 292, 514; 7. 511; 8.
   405,
   his 2. 233 (G; KBL it); 6. 233; 7. 65,
   his 2. 111 (B; K et; GL it); 3. 447 (vid.
   n.); 4. 562,
   his 1. 528; 3. 447 (vid. f.); 5. 515 (vid.
   abl.),
   hos 1. 104; 3. 393; 4. 299, 710; 5. 115,
   605, 683; 6. 9 (KBL; G hoc), 88, 155,
   178, 239, 545, 721,
   has 2. 174; 6. 373,
   haec 1. 149 (KGL; B nec), 245, 320,
   633, 651, 674, 681; 2. 493, 567; 3. 271,
   316, 521; 4. 54, 157, 174, 416, 653; 5. 54,
   246, 397, 534, 649; 6. 26, 292, 679, 737,

   745; 7. 141, 170, 258, 268 bis, 333, 349,
   431, 488; 8. 9, 54, 195,
   his (n.) 1. 514; 5. 515 (vid. dat.); 6. 323,
   560; 6. 675,
   hunc . . . hunc 4. 284, 683,
   hunc . . . illum 6. 551,
   hanc . . . illum 6. 602,
   illum . . . hunc 6. 573 (K; BGL illum
   . . . hic),
   hi . . . hi 6. 362,
   hos . . . hos 5. 420; 8. 332,
   hi . . . alii 1. 312,
   2. adi.
   hic 2. 658 (vid. adv.); 3. 652; 4. 757;
   5. 688; 6. 214; 7. 529,
   haec 1. 21, 338; 2. 322, 414 (B; KGL
   et), 641; 3. 376, 667; 4. 26 (BG; K ac;
   L heu), 113, 145, 213 (K; BGL atque),
   317 bis, 580, 588 (BL; KG om.); 5. 57,
   353, 492; 7. 10; 8. 396,
   hoc 2. 251, 337; 4. 26, 241,
   huius (f.) 7. 501,
   hunc 3. 201, 620; 5. 545, 596 (B; KGL
   hic); 6. 735; 7. 20 (K; BGL huc), 159
   (sis hunc L; KB tecum; G tantum),
   227, 341; 8. 150, 276,
   hanc 1. 40, 250, 545, 749 (BGL; K
   hinc); 2. 48, 662; 3. 81, 707; 4. 128; 5.
   611; 6. 305, 339, 429, 744; 7. 89, 286, 441;
   8. 264, 278,
   hoc 1. 203, 267; 4. 314; 5. 18 bis; 7. 93,
   285; 8. 349,
   hoc 3. 555; 6. 549; 8. 453,
   hac 1. 227 (hac vates B; K om.; G nimia; L longa); 2. 219, 331; 3. 270; 4. 191,
   336; 6. 138, 139, 309, 332, 534; 7. 135;
   8. 76, 426,
   haccine 1. 151,
   hoc 4. 147, 212, 443; 7. 230; 8. 155, 220,
   344,
   hoccine 1. 630,
   hi 3. 699,
   hae 7. 445,
   haec 1. 114, 220; 2. 133; 3. 297, 714; 4.
   347; 5. 218, 544, 688; 8. 50,
   his (m.) 2. 559; 5. 645,
   hos 1. 321; 2. 151; 3. 475; 4. 52, 707;
   6. 725; 7. 89; 8. 351,
   has 1. 676, 846; 2. 96, 114, 428, 606, 616,
   657, 663; 3. 143, 296, 657; 4. 335, 458;
   5. 379; 6. 324, 335, 496; 7. 16, 36, 138,
   209, 269, 270, 412, 467, 497, 500,
   hascine 7. 417,
   haec 1. 814; 2. 69, 96, 335, 606, 657; 3.
   307, 538, 650; 4. 211, 250; 5. 379, 451,
   651, 665; 6. 335, 406, 436 (haec etenim
   KGL; B Aeeten), 538; 7. 71, 275, 417,
   499, 503; 8. 14, 61,
   his 2. 647; 6. 726,
   his 1. 302; 2. 126; 4. 170; 5. 75, 195, 234,
   341; 7. 58, 153, 241, 384,
   his 6. 587; 7. 451,
   hac . . . illinc 8. 378,
   hos . . . alios 6. 577,
   illam . . . has 1. 584.

hic (65)
hic 1. 52, 130, 277, 286, 383, 436 (BGL;
K hinc), 832; 2. 142, 209, 299, 302, 334,
432, 656, 658 (vid. adi.); 3. 220, 292 (K;
BG en; L heu), 406, 422, 432, 719; 4.
146, 181 (K; BGL hinc), 187, 209, 473,
501, 514, 591, 601 (GL; KB hinc), 682;
5. 113, 287 (BL; KG hinc), 418, 465,
473, 542, 596 (KGL; B hunc), 671; 6.
129, 324, 380 (KBG; L hinc), 538; 7.
92, 99, 214 (BGL; K sic), 284, 382, 396,
398 (GL; KB hinc), 610; 8. 77 (hic
stante L; KB adstante; G instante),
145,
hic demum 4. 548,
hic etiam 1. 723,
hic . . . hic 1. 144, 362; 2. 598; 5. 78,
hic . . . huc 4. 289,
huc . . . hic 5. 405.
Hidmon
Hidmon 3. 167 (K; BL Admon; G Idmon).
hiems (hiemps)
hiems 2. 435, 505, 604; 3. 152; 4. 509;
7. 52; 8. 373,
hiemps 6. 716,
hiemem 1. 197, 614, 625; 4. 725,
hiemes (acc.) 1. 546; 2. 22; 6. 335.
hinc (96)
hinc 1. 358, 360, 394, 436 (K; BGL hic),
535, 555, 585, 586, 603, 749 (K; BGL
hanc); 2. 94, 133, 447, 534, 540, 579, 627,
632, 644; 3. 72, 95, 133, 193 (BL; KG
hic), 382, 437, 483, 572, 672; 4. 130, 181
(BGL; K hic), 337, 387, 419, 481, 561,
677, 722; 5. 5, 101 (KGL; B it), 127,
190, 287 (KG; BL hic), 382, 416, 442,
672; 6. 6, 17, 20, 33, 184, 190 (K; BGL
hunc), 279, 303 (L; KBG hunc), 350,
380 (L; KBG hic), 455, 478, 642, 656;
7. 98, 189, 219, 430, 478, 593; 8. 136, 451,
hinc atque hinc 5. 309,
hinc iam 4. 601 (KB; GL hic iam),
hinc . . . hinc 3. 157; 5. 344; 6. 30, 187,
364; 7. 143; 8. 464,
hinc illinc 4. 257,
hinc . . . illinc 5. 284; 6. 413,
illinc . . . hinc 5. 529,
hinc . . . inde 1. 353; 5. 188; 7. 398
(KB; GL hic . . . inde),
inde . . . hinc 5. 147,
hinc . . . hinc . . . inde 2. 582,
procul hinc 8. 185.
hio
hianti (dat. m.) 8. 96.
Hippasus
Hippasus 1. 148.
Hippodamia
Hippodamia (nom.) 7. 276.
Hippotades
Hippotades 1. 610.
hirtus
hirta (nom. f.) 1. 777.
hispidus
hispidus 1. 613; 6. 533.

Hister
Hister 6. 329; 8. 219, 256,
Histri 4. 718; 8. 185.
hodie
3. 658.
homo
hominem 8. 34,
hominum 1. 247, 606, 673; 2. 456; 4. 65,
320, 481; 5. 278, 296, 625; 6. 323; 7. 41.
honor (honos)
honor 1. 189; 3. 651; 5. 645; 6. 145, 152
(BGL; K sonor), 296, 464, 494; 8. 237,
honos 1. 678, 736; 2. 562; 3. 357, 515;
4. 217, 551; 5. 68; 6. 109; 8. 458,
honore 1. 514; 4. 76; 5. 464, 503; 6. 736;
8. 31,
honores 2. 573,
honores 1. 129, 177 (GBL; K honoris),
850; 2. 650; 3. 205, 273, 702; 4. 29, 532;
5. 290, 625; 6. 629,
honoris 1. 177 (K; BGL honores).
honorus
honoro (abl.) 2. 199,
honoro 4. 342.
Hora
Horae (gen.) 6. 58.
hora
hora 2. 38,
hora 7. 318 (in hora K; B obire; GL
in ira),
horas 3. 48 (BG; KL horis); 5. 311;
7. 500,
horis 2. 60; 3. 48 (KL; BG horas), 417.
Horae
Horis (abl.) 4. 92.
horreo
horret 3. 252, 403; 7. 381,
horrent 6. 504; 7. 233,
horruit 1. 752, 825; 2. 52, 100, 514; 3.
171; 5. 165 **bis**, 314; 6. 686,
horrens (f.) 3. 87,
horrentem 1. 486,
horrentem 6. 175,
horrentia (acc.) 4. 425; 6. 524,
horrendus 1. 678,
horrenda 1. 210, 580; 4. 499,
horrendum (acc. n.) 2. 86,
horrenda (abl.) 5. 220,
horrendos 4. 245,
horrendas 5. 332,
horrenda 4. 606; 5. 475.
horresco
horrescunt 2. 541,
horruit 7. 573 **bis**; 8. 82,
horrescere 6. 453.
horridus
horridus 3. 263; 7. 62,
horrida (nom. f.) 2. 306, 412, 644; 3.
108, 710; 5. 587; 6. 112,
horrida (acc.) 1. 512; 3. 567; 4. 370;
6. 341.
horrifer
horriferam 5. 306,
horrifero (m.) 5. 517.

horrificus
  horrifici (n.) 2. 97,
  horrificam 2. 518,
  horrificis (dat. n.) 3. 423.
horrisonus
  horrisoni (n.) 7. 149,
  horrisonae (dat.) 2. 583.
horror
  horror 1. 621, 652, 744; 2. 24, 433; 4.
  661; 5. 455 (B; KGL error); 6. 481;
  7. 81, 266, 295, 378, 563; 8. 67, 134,
  horrore 1. 229.
hortamen
  hortamina (acc.) 6. 94.
hortator
  hortator 4. 32; 8. 232.
hortatus
  hortatibus (abl.) 3. 550; 4. 81.
hortor
  hortatur 1. 58 (KGL; B hortatus); 2.
  335; 4. 648; 5. 358; 7. 377; 8. 336,
  hortantur 1. 214,
  hortatus 1. 58 (B; KGL hortatur); 8.
  216,
  hortatum (m.) 6. 18.
hospes
  hospes 5. 8, 596; 6. 676; 7. 42, 80, 107,
  119, 143, 488,
  hospitis 4. 187; 7. 116; 8. 170,
  hospes 2. 339; 7. 68, 454; 8. 53,
  hospite 3. 288; 6. 344; 7. 1, 13, 196, 283,
  hospitibus (dat.) 2. 438; 7. 280,
  adi. hospitis (gen. f.) 5. 202.
hospitium
  hospitii 4. 614,
  hospitio 3. 293,
  hospitio 1. 661; 6. 12,
  hospitia (acc.) 4. 212,
  hospitiis 3. 18, 174.
hospitus
  hospita (nom. f.) 2. 322 (GL; K fatis;
  B laeta); 3. 272, 304; 4. 145; 5. 385,
  hospita (acc.) 1. 44; 2. 649, 662; 4. 58.
hostia
  hostia (nom.) 1. 793.
hostilis
  hostilibus (abl. m.) 6. 235.
hostis
  hostis (nom.) 2. 250, 656; 3. 45; 4. 159,
  744; 5. 396, 535; 6. 29,
  hostem 3. 589; 4. 618; 5. 569; 8. 64, 321,
  hoste 4. 284, 503; 5. 359; 8. 428,
  hostes (acc.) 1. 438; 3. 308; 5. 634; 6.
  238, 534.
huc (26)
  huc 2. 288, 319, 324, 575; 3. 82, 446; 4.
  114, 207, 519, 717; 5. 378, 479 (BGL;
  K nunc), 499; 6. 482, 580, 648; 7. 20
  (BGL; K hunc); 8. 52, 144,
  huc atque illuc 1. 639,
  huc . . . et huc 4. 266; 6. 231,
  hic . . . huc 4. 290,
  huc . . . hic 5. 404.

humilis
  humili (abl. m.) 4. 515,
  humiles (acc.) 3. 395,
  humiles 3. 426.
humus
  humus 4. 215; 5. 57; 6. 169,
  humi (loc.) 8. 93,
  humo 7. 620,
  humum 5. 8; 7. 312,
  humo 1. 710; 4. 339; 6. 650.
Hyades
  Hyadum 2. 67.
hydra
  hydrae (gen.) 3. 228; 7. 623,
  hydris (abl.) 2. 195; 6. 397.
hydrus
  hydri 6. 437; 7. 76; 8. 343,
  hydri 4. 413.
Hylaeus
  Hylaea (abl.) 6. 74.
Hylas
  Hylas 1. 110, 219; 3. 183, 184, 486, 537,
  549, 599,
  Hylan 3. 569, 571, 596 bis, 725; 4. 18.
hymenaeus
  hymenaei (nom.) 8. 149,
  hymenaeos 8. 259.
Hymettos
  Hymetti 5. 343,
  Hymetton 1. 397.
Hypanis
  Hypanis 4. 719,
  Hypanin 6. 147.
Hypanis
  Hypanin 6. 252.
Hyperboreus
  Hyperboreas 8. 210.
Hyperia
  Hyperia (nom.) 4. 375.
Hyperionides
  Hyperionide (voc.) 5. 471.
Hyperionius
  Hyperionius 2. 34.
Hypetaon
  Hypetaona 6. 637.
Hypsipyle
  Hypsipyle 2. 352, 400; 3. 342,
  Hypsipyle (voc.) 2. 244.
Hypso
  Hypso 1. 367.
Hyrcanus
  Hyrcanos 6. 203,
  Hyrcana 3. 494,
  Hyrcanis (m.) 6. 114,
  Hyrcanis (n.) 6. 79.
Iacchus
  Iaccho (abl.) 1. 140.
iaceo
  iaces 8. 98,
  iacet 1. 830; 2. 629; 4. 211, 726; 5. 209;
  7. 62, 422,
  iacent 4. 488,
  iacebant 7. 641,
  iacuere 3. 123,

iacentis (gen. m.) 4. 322, 712,
subst. m. iacentum 2. 216.
iacio
iacit 3. 443; 5. 426; 6. 208,
iecere 3. 349,
iacias 7. 75,
iace 7. 469.
iacto
iactat 2. 341; 5. 591,
iactes 5. 651,
iactata 7. 21,
iactatam 5. 295.
iactura
iactura (nom.) 6. 331.
iaculor
iaculata (nom. f.) 4. 671.
iaculum
iaculo 5. 609,
iaculo 3. 24,
iaculis (abl.) 1. 366, 486.
iam (386)
iam 1. 16 (GL; KB tu), 23, 34, 36, 52,
55, 95, 98, 100, 123, 171, 239, 329, 350,
433, 460, 496, 516, 543, 549 (BL; KG
nam), 594, 657, 675, 738, 742, 750, 754,
767, 821, 845; 2. 38, 78, 102 (L; KBG
enim), 103 (iam tum B; K tantum; G
iam tumet; L tunc avet), 131, 154, 157,
158, 178 (vel iam KBG; L etiam), 248,
282, 306, 330, 337, 355, 403, 417, 429 bis,
442, 455, 485, 487, 524, 536, 552 bis, 564,
571, 578, 584, 621, 642 (KBL; G tam);
3. 1, 33, 35, 179 bis, 214, 221, 222, 249,
257, 265, 286, 296, 360, 364, 394, 413,
450, 481, 494, 517, 530, 565, 576, 637,
666, 677, 700, 703 bis, 713; 4. 9, 26, 28,
31, 62, 65, 82, 148, 185, 192, 225, 247,
282, 284, 308, 363, 377, 433, 475, 485,
519, 546, 586, 617, 679, 697, 733; 5. 4,
22, 48, 71 bis, 82, 119, 178, 221, 224
(KGL; B cum), 270, 288, 311, 328, 360,
361, 372, 404, 424 (K; BGL hi iam),
427, 450, 469, 525, 531, 562, 603 bis,
610, 624, 638 (L; KG vel; B quin),
647 bis, 673, 691; 6. 63, 110 (L; KBG
nam), 115, 123, 124, 158, 192, 250, 494,
547, 561, 597 bis, 638, 656, 659, 674, 677,
680, 727, 743; 7. 1, 2, 14, 25, 26, 30, 46
(K; BGL me), 84, 125, 133, 177, 226 (ut
iam L; KBG etiam), 283, 291, 392, 443
(quod iam L; KBG quoniam), 473,
474, 497, 503 (BL; KG tum), 539, 541,
544, 561, 616, 629, 650; 8. 1, 5, 24, 29, 39
(mihi iam BGL; K duci mihi), 39, 100,
195, 224, 231, 240, 241 (L; KBG tam),
242, 251 (BL; KG tum), 291, 314, 411,
444,
iamque 1. 255, 294; 2. 107, 147, 168, 190,
279; 3. 70, 165, 433, 468, 613, 653, 672;
4. 198, 344, 391, 453, 509, 512, 575, 623,
657; 5. 107, 157, 273, 436, 500 (KGL;
B namque); 6. 195, 228, 299, 386, 622;
7. 296, 310, 379, 394, 432, 449, 466, 594,
598; 8. 68, 301, 330,
iamdudum 1. 227; 3. 235, 628, 676; 5.

520; 6. 456, 588, 604; 7. 237, 243, 292,
299, 489,
hinc iam 4. 601,
iam nunc 1. 308, 334; 5. 322; 8. 47,
iam pridem 1. 537; 3. 397; 4. 214; 6. 43,
467; 7. 224,
iam tandem 4. 483; 6. 749,
iam tum 3. 515,
nec iam 1. 649 (KL; BG nec tam); 2.
372; 4. 129; 8. 47,
neque iam 1. 17 (K; BGL neque enim); 3. 708,
non iam 1. 475; 7. 155,
iam iam 1. 116, 782; 4. 90, 126; 6. 756;
7. 32, 389, 408,
iam iamque 1. 223, 805,
iam . . . iam 1. 727; 2. 63, 252, 304,
346; 4. 236; 6. 319, 567; 8. 212, 214,
iam . . . iamque 1. 712; 2. 589; 3. 643;
4. 417, 443; 5. 366; 8. 345, 365,
iamque . . . iamque 5. 84; 6. 507; 7.
630,
iamque . . . iamque . . . iam 2. 124,
iamque iam 2. 530; 3. 357; 8. 88, 108,
iamque . . . iam . . . iam 2. 6,
iamque . . . cum 2. 34, 72; 3. 417, 551;
4. 58; 5. 402; 6. 375, 644, 714.
iamdudum, iamque vid. iam.
ianua
ianua (nom.) 3. 386; 4. 231; 6. 113.
Ianus
Ianus 2. 620.
Iapetus
Iapetus 4. 74,
Iapeti 1. 564.
iapyx
iapyga 3. 611.
Iasius
Iasiae (gen.) 4. 353.
Iason
Iason 1. 298; 2. 1; 3. 80, 269, 615; 4. 222,
537, 626, 648; 5. 62, 465, 469; 6. 546,
586, 645; 7. 28, 43, 221, 307, 385, 396,
576, 600; 8. 213, 316,
Iasona 2. 402, 424, 591; 6. 759; 7. 341,
451, 515.
Iaxartes
Iaxarten 5. 596.
Iazyges
Iazyges 6. 122,
Iazygas 6. 281.
ibi (10)
ibi 4. 603, 617; 5. 115, 639; 6. 81; 7. 233,
263, 639; 8. 204,
qua . . . ibi 6. 586.
icio
ictus 6. 168,
icta (nom. f.) 2. 142; 4. 48.
ictus
ictum 6. 248,
ictu 2. 359; 3. 165,
ictus (acc.) 1. 330, 619; 2. 534; 3. 187,
284; 4. 271, 306, 690, 694; 6. 652,
ictibus 2. 269.

Ida
Idae (gen.) 2. 414,
Ida 1. 549, 704 (B; KGL ora),
Vid. Ide.

Idaeus
Idaea 2. 536,
Idaeam 1. 319,
Idaea (acc.) 2. 477.

Idalium
Idalium (acc.) 8. 229.

Idalius
Idaliae (gen.) 8. 225.

Idas
Idas 1. 166, 461; 3. 471; 4. 224; 6. 342;
7. 574,
Idae (dat.) 6. 382 (B; KGL Idam),
Idam 6. 382 (KGL; B Idae).

Idasmenus
Idasmenus 6. 196.

Ide
Ide 2. 519 (KG; BL Iden), 582,
Iden 2. 519 (BL; KG Ide),
Vid. Ida.

idem
    1. pron.
idem 3. 640; 4. 522,
eadem (nom. f.) 2. 103 (K; B ea cum;
GL aut), 104 (KBG; L odio),
eadem (acc.) 2. 166; 6. 291 (KBG; L
etiam); 8. 454,
    2. adi.
idem 2. 561; 4. 193, 216, 651, 653, **744**;
5. 455, 477; 6. 405; 7. 361, 362,
eadem (nom.) 4. 742; 5. 436 **bis**; 6. 463;
8. 424,
eadem (nom.) 6. 513; 5. 582,
eadem 1. 153; 6. 404, 662,
isdem 3. 122,
isdem 2. 162; 6. 1, 241,
isdem 4. 143.

ideo (5)
3. 381, 454; 4. 128; 5. 395 (B; KGL
adeo); 6. 24.

Idmon
Idmon 1. 228, 360; 3. 167 (G; K Hid-
mon; BL Admon), 175, 440; 4. 546; 5.
2, 27, 42,
Idmonis 5. 9,
Idmone 5. 5.

Idume
Idumen 1. 12.

ieiunus
ieiuna (acc.) 8. 456.

ignarus
ignarus 2. 1; 8. 195,
ignara 7. 192,
ignaro (m.) 5. 389,
ignarum (m.) 1. 180; 3. 290,
ignari 1. 626; 3. 109; 5. 171,
ignaris (f.) 3. 172,
ignaras 1. 69.

ignavia
ignavia (nom.) 3. 376.

ignavus
ignava (nom. f.) 6. 486; 7. 224 (KG;
BL gnara).

igneus
igneus 1. 616; 2. 342,
ignea (nom.) 1. 427; 4. 508, 612; 6. 708,
ignea (nom.) 3. 210,
ignea 2. 184.

ignesco
ignescit 5. 520.

ignifer
igniferos 8. 342.

Ignipotens
subst. m. Ignipotens 5. 452,
Ignipotens 2. 80.

ignis
ignis 1. 137, 206, 221; 2. 658; 3. 137,
380; 4. 662, 755; 6. 443 (K; BL ingens;
G igni), 454; 7. 66, 97, 207, 585,
ignis 4. 67,
igni 1. 89; 3. 313; 6. 443 (G; K ignis;
BL ingens),
ignem 1. 116; 2. 449; 4. 179; 6. 657;
7. 253, 578; 8. 245, 276,
igne 1. 125, 782, 842; 2. 182; 3. 131;
5. 451,
ignes 5. 415 (KGL; B imbres); 7. 466,
ignes 1. 516, 748; 2. 65, 72, 178, 314,
354, 369, 603; 4. 353; 5. 110, 368; 6. 54,
321; 7. 568, 624,
ignibus 1. 239; 2. 236, 582; 7. 363.

ignobilis
ignobilis (nom. m.) 1. 439.

ignoro
ignorare 8. 407.

ignotus
ignota 1. 838,
ignoti 5. 319, 376,
ignoti 5. 144,
ignotum (n.) 6. 651,
ignota 2. 43; 6. 535 (L; KBG ac nota),
678; 7. 173,
ignotae 2. 241,
ignotos 7. 134,
ignotas 4. 371,
ignota 2. 592; 3. 426,
ignotis 6. 482,
ignotis (?) 4. 195,
ignotis 2. 554; 6. 131,
subst. m. ignoto (dat.) 7. 320,
ignotis (dat.) 4. 255; 6. 25.

ile
ilia (acc.) 3. 105; 4. 685; 6. 243.

Iliacus
Iliaci (m.) 4. 59,
Iliaci (nom.) 2. 246.

ilicet
2. 186; 3. 58, 730; 4. 451.

ille
    1. pron.
ille 1. 15, 24, 110, 182, 200, 202 (ille
mihi B; K illumetu; GL illum ego),
309, 348, 465, 487, 662, 716, 741, 811;
2. 30, 89, 180, 258, 300, 512, 577; 3. 25,
64, 85, 100, 106, 126, 136, 155, 171, 286,

immemorem 6. 298,
immemorem 7. 238,
immemores (m.) 3. 375, 654; 4. 6,
immemores (m.) 6. 241.
immensus
immensus 1. 497,
immensum (nom.) 5. 165,
immenso (abl. m.) 1. 538; 3. 130,
immensa (acc.) 6. 631,
immensis (m.) 7. 523.
immeritus
immeritis (dat. m.) 3. 593,
immeritis (abl. f.) 8. 158.
immineo
imminet 6. 494, 681.
immitto
immittit 2. 613,
immisit 7. 576,
immittere 7. 353,
immissus 1. 412,
immissis (abl.) 4. 421; 6. 715,
immissis (f.) 1. 687; 5. 586; 8. 139.
immo
7. 165 (L; KBG illa).
immodicus
immodicum (m.) 5. 597.
immolo
immolet 2. 569.
immorior
immoritur 6. 570,
immortua (nom. n.) 4. 182.
immortalis
adv. immortale 7. 362.
immotus
immota (nom.) 3. 97, 402, 598; 5. 111,
immota (nom.) 5. 87,
immotis (f.) 7. 405,
immotos 4. 724,
immotis (n.) 2. 572.
immunis
immunem (f.) 1. 77.
immurmuro
immurmurat 7. 312.
immutabilis
immutabile (nom.) 2. 55.
impar
impar (m.) 8. 400, 428.
impatiens
impatiens 1. 296, 778; 3. 613; 8. 381,
impatiens (f.) 2. 125; 8. 303.
impavidus
impavidus 5. 660.
impedio
impediit 8. 259,
impediat 1. 180; 7. 183.
impello
impulit 1. 610, 674; 2. 272; 3. 325; 4. 33,
486, 502; 6. 6, 150, 178, 256, 603,
impulerat 2. 529 (L; KBG impulerit),
impulerit (subi.) 2. 529 (KBG; L impulerat); 5. 164,
impellite 5. 675,
impellere 3. 95; 5. 663,
impulsus 5. 42,

impulsae (gen.) 3. 265,
impulso (abl. m.) 7. 322.
impendeo
impendet 7. 114.
impendo
impende 4. 581,
impenditur 1. 470.
imperfectus
imperfecta (nom. f.) 6. 689.
imperium
imperium 1. 668, 788; 5. 14,
imperii 1. 522,
imperio 1. 54,
imperium 4. 385, 416; 6. 475,
imperio 4. 708,
imperia (acc.) 1. 820; 4. 81,
imperiis 1. 184; 3. 40, 620; 5. 486; 7. 94.
impero
imperat 1. 246; 2. 482; 3. 437, 460; 4.
523,
imperet 4. 149; 5. 422; 7. 47.
impervius
impervia (nom. n.) 4. 711,
subst. n. impervia (nom.) 2. 642.
impiger
impiger 6. 221.
impingo
impingit 7. 401,
impingitur 3. 149,
impacta (abl.) 6. 243.
impius
impius 5. 396; 6. 214,
impia (nom.) 4. 13; 5. 686,
impia (nom.) 5. 221,
impia 3. 30; 6. 75.
impleo
implet 2. 126, 162; 3. 220; 4. 81, 123;
5. 83; 6. 527, 630, 712, 726, 738; 7. 168;
8. 31, 143, 171,
implent 2. 167; 6. 511,
implebant 2. 241,
implevit 2. 458; 4. 665; 6. 566; 7. 462;
8. 237,
impleat 1. 21; 2. 389; 6. 40,
impleri 7. 122.
implico
implicat 2. 65; 3. 390, 425; 4. 334; 5. 451;
6. 401, 489, 707; 7. 598, 638; 8. 19, 124,
implicui 4. 166,
implicuit 2. 27; 3. 272; 5. 255,
implicet 3. 31,
impliciti (gen. m.) 1. 264,
implicitos 6. 418.
implorabilis
implorabile (acc.) 1. 573.
imploro
implorat 3. 639; 6. 264; 7. 385,
implorant 4. 516.
impono
imposuit 3. 26,
imposuere 5. 30,
imponat 5. 421,
imponite 4. 461,
imponere 5. 189, 679; 6. 742,
imposta (nom. n.) 4. 186.

incesso
incessere 4. 494.
incessus
incessus (acc.) 3. 607.
incestus
incestae (gen.) 7. 150 (L; KBG infestae).
incido
incidit 3. 592; 4. 404,
incidit 4. 744,
inciderat 7. 393,
inciderant 7. 404,
incidat 3. 94.
incipio
incipit 2. 639; 6. 167, 196; 7. 195, 528, 592; 8. 225, 361,
incipiunt 8. 245,
incipiat 7. 433,
incipe 5. 217,
incipete 4. 206,
incipiens (m.) 2. 628,
inceptum (acc. n.) 5. 399,
inceptos 3. 625; 8. 259,
subst. n. incepti 6. 680,
inceptis (dat.) 3. 490.
incito
incitat 3. 63 (incitat aere B; KGL inde ciere); 4. 609,
incitet 1. 409.
incitus
incita (nom. f.) 1. 728; 3. 690; 5. 563; 6. 302.
inclementia
inclementia (nom.) 2. 648; 7. 416.
inclinis
inclinis (nom. m.) 4. 308.
inclitus
inclitus 1. 393; 4. 467,
inclita (nom. f.) 3. 703; 4. 549, 602,
inclita (acc.) 5. 480.
includo
inclusa (n.) 3. 738,
inclusa 4. 372.
incognitus
incognitus 5. 402,
incognita (nom. f.) 1. 808 (L; KBG incondita); 3. 399,
incognita (acc.) 3. 241.
incola
incola (nom.) 4. 513.
incommodus
subst. n. incommoda (acc.) 4. 86.
inconditus
incondita (nom. f.) 1. 808 (KBG; L incognita).
inconsultus
inconsulta (acc.) 4. 302.
increpito
increpitat 3. 230,
increpitant 3. 472,
increpitare 5. 267.
increpo
increpat 3. 613; 4. 3; 6. 281, 433; 7. 127,
increpuere 4. 691,
increpet 6. 744.

incresco
increscunt 1. 315.
incubo
incubat 2. 494; 4. 724 (L; KBG invenit).
incudo
incusae (gen.) 2. 339 (B; KGL incussae).
incumbo
incumbit 7. 600,
incumbunt 2. 60,
incubuit 1. 684,
incubuere 5. 162,
incumbere 3. 447; 6. 722,
incumbens (m.) 5. 594,
incumbentem (f.) 2. 503.
incurro
incurrit (prs.) 3. 111.
incus
incudibus (abl.) 4. 288.
incuso
incuso 8. 158.
incutio
incussit 5. 550,
incussae (gen.) 2. 339 (KGL; B incusae).
inde (51)
inde 1. 271, 544; 2. 13, 91, 163, 200, 545; 3. 63 (inde ciere KGL; B incitat aere), 122, 347, 362, 472, 490, 738; 4. 96, 131, 204, 254, 401, 613, 686; 5. 73, 154, 224, 271, 327, 497; 6. 109, 198, 352, 425, 529; 7. 228, 355, 424, 461, 528; 8. 20, 175, 189, 200, 243, 255, 272, 375,
hinc . . . inde 1. 353; 5. 189; 7. 399 (KB; GL hic . . . inde),
hinc . . . hinc . . . inde 2. 584,
inde . . . hinc 5. 147,
inde . . . inde 6. 374.
indebitus
subst. n. indebita (acc.) 5. 508.
indecoris
indecores (nom. f.) 3. 515; 5. 669,
indecores (m.) 1. 810.
Indi
Indi 6. 117.
indigena
indigenis (f.) 6. 294,
indigenas (m.) 6. 93.
indignor
indignantibus (abl. f.) 1. 202,
indignatus 1. 9,
indignatos 1. 801,
indignanda (nom. n.) 1. 547.
indignus
indigna (voc.) 8. 38,
indigno (m.) 2. 146,
indignos 1. 320,
subst. n. indigna (acc.) 2. 117.
indolesco
indoluisse 7. 137.
indomitus
indomitam 4. 362.

induco
inducit 1. 847,
induxere 1. 614,
inducere 2. 132,
inducto (abl. n.) 2. 109.
indulgeo
indulget 2. 356; 3. 371,
indulgent 2. 371,
indulgeat 8. 392.
induo
induit 2. 266; 8. 235,
induit 2. 20; 4. 509,
induimus 7. 91,
indue 4. 251,
induere 2. 399,
induitur 4. 94; 7. 372.
ineo
ineunt 4. 760,
inire 3. 629.
inermis
inermem (m.) 6. 255.
iners
iners (m.) 7. 591,
inertem 8. 98,
inerti (m.) 4. 169.
inexorabilis
inexorabile (nom.) 5. 320.
inexpertus
inexpertos 1. 97.
inexpletus
inexpletis (abl. f.) 6. 759.
infamis
infame (acc.) 2. 621.
infandus
infando (dat. m.) 7. 87, 415,
infando (m.) 5. 574,
infanda (acc.) 2. 173; 3. 15; 5. 219,
infandis (f.) 7. 51.
infaustus
infaustum (acc. n.) 5. 262,
infausto (n.) 8. 315,
infaustos 5. 201.
infectus
infecta (acc.) 3. 117,
Vid. inficio.
infelix
infelix 1. 727; 4. 123, 240, 441; 5. 81;
6. 406; 7. 221; 8. 136 (BL; KG inflexit),
infelix (f.) 2. 595; 3. 95; 4. 180; 5. 187,
450; 6. 490; 7. 239, 296, 371,
infelix (acc.) 1. 587; 3. 26,
infelix (voc. f.) 4. 118,
subst. infelix (voc. m.) 1. 715,
infelix (voc. f.) 8. 160.
infensus
infensus 6. 43,
infensum (m.) 1. 72,
infensa (nom.) 5. 37.
inferiae
3. 336 (B; KG funereae; L munera
fert).
infernus
inferni (n.) 2. 192,
infernae (dat.) 5. 238,
infernos 1. 850,

infernas 1. 581,
adv. infernum 1. 832 (BL; KG aeternum).
infero
infert 5. 456; 6. 387; 7. 583,
intulit 1. 281, 488; 2. 30, 217, 631; 3. 456;
7. 365,
intulerant 4. 83,
intulerit (subi.) 5. 419,
infer 2. 565,
inferte 1. 798,
infertur 7. 372.
inferus
infera (nom. f.) 3. 253,
imae 7. 626,
imi 2. 529; 7. 253,
imo (n.) 7. 618,
imum (m.) 1. 25,
imo 1. 657; 3. 224; 5. 521; 8. 366,
ima 8. 307 (B; KGL una),
imo 3. 240; 5. 36; 6. 496,
ima 4. 565,
imis (n.) 4. 410,
imos 1. 385; 2. 535,
imas 4. 118, 382; 5. 164,
imis 7. 329, 498,
imis 1. 601; 2. 119, 320 (saepe imis
KG; B saepimis; L haec imis),
imis 5. 159; 6. 170, 565,
subst. n. ima 4. 687,
ima 4. 517; 6. 199.
infesto
infestare 4. 495.
infestus
infesti 6. 686,
infestae (gen.) 7. 150 (KBG; L incestae),
infestum 6. 245,
infestam 8. 262,
infesto 6. 697; 8. 326,
infesta 6. 617; 7. 617,
infesta 2. 593; 8. 104,
infestos 2. 314; 8. 449,
infestas 4. 659,
infesta 7. 249,
infestis (m.) 4. 576,
infestis (n.) 6. 265.
inficio
infectae (gen.) 2. 496,
infecta (nom.) 7. 552,
infecta 2. 155,
infectis (f.) 7. 302,
Vid. infectus.
infidus
infidi (m.) 5. 222,
infida (abl.) 7. 102,
infidos 2. 436,
infida 2. 577.
infindo
infindit 1. 688.
infit
infit 1. 666; 2. 610; 7. 258; 8. 414.
inflecto
inflexit 8. 136 (KG; BL infelix).

infletus
infletum (acc. n.) 6. 651.
infligo
inflicta (nom. n.) 4. 282.
informis
informibus (abl. m.) 4. 245.
infra
8. 328 (G; KB intra; L inter).
infremo
infremuit 1. 707.
infringo
infringitur 5. 411,
infracta est 6. 199,
infracti (nom.) 3. 236,
infracta (acc.) 3. 287.
infundo
infusa (nom. f.) 4. 552.
ingemino
ingeminant 2. 169; 4. 328; 7. 195.
ingemo
ingemit 1. 577; 2. 402; 3. 289, 723; 4. 117,
ingemuit 3. 509,
ingemere 4. 450.
ingens
ingens 1. 679; 2. 432; 4. 320; 5. 160, 287 (BL; K **om.**; G magnus), 370; 6. 398, 443 (BL; K ignis; G igni), 481; 8. 185,
ingens 1. 29, 682; 2. 104, 201 (KGL; B angens); 4. 177, 210; 5. 232; 6. 9; 8. 89,
ingens 2. 479, 627; 3. 498,
ingentis (m.) 6. 162,
ingentis (n.) 4. 295,
ingentem 2. 329; 3. 138; 6. 345,
ingentem 3. 99; 5. 175, 619; 6. 235, 385, 573; 8. 56,
ingens 1. 212; 3. 170,
ingens (m.) 6. 103,
ingenti 1. 258, 568; 2. 391; 3. 22, 719; 5. 124; 6. 634,
ingenti 2. 519; 3. 609, 637; 5. 595; 7. 169, 519; 8. 33,
ingenti 1. 600, 830; 5. 337; 6. 553,
ingentes 6. 172,
ingentes 1. 237; 3. 84; 4. 650,
ingentia 5. 395,
ingentes 1. 772; 3. 207; 4. 244; 5. 610,
ingentis (m.) 5. 573,
ingentes 2. 225,
ingentia 8. 462,
ingentibus (m.) 6. 630, 724,
ingentibus (n.) 2. 242; 5. 313, 537.
ingero
ingerit 2. 215 (L; KBG invenit); 6. 230,
ingerat 7. 651,
ingerar (subi.) 8. 53.
inglorius
inglorius 6. 530.
ingratus
ingrata 1. 332,
ingrato (abl. m.) 1. 446,
ingratos 7. 492,
subst. m. ingrato (dat.) 7. 507.

ingredior
ingredior 1. 304,
ingreditur 1. 744; 2. 547; 5. 70.
ingruo
ingruat 3. 454.
inguen
inguine 6. 222.
inhio
inhiat 2. 531; 4. 495,
inhiantia (acc.) 5. 468.
inhorreo
inhorruit 3. 348.
inicio
inicit 3. 343; 7. 587,
iniciunt 2. 236,
iniecta 3. 562,
iniectam 2. 32.
inimicus
inimica (nom. f.) 2. 225,
inimica 1. 700; 3. 389; 8. 295, 326.
iniquus
iniqua 2. 355; 6. 645,
iniquae (gen.) 4. 23; 7. 251,
iniqui 3. 65,
iniquo (abl.) 6. 322,
iniqua 3. 492,
iniquo 5. 554,
iniquis (n.) 6. 205,
iniquos 3. 486,
iniqua 4. 152,
iniquis (m.) 4. 242.
iniussus
iniussa (nom. f.) 6. 499 (K; BGL invisa).
iniuste
4. 474 (BL; K invisum; G iniusti).
iniustus
iniusti 4. 474 (G; K invisum; BL iniuste),
iniusti (n.) 4. 122,
iniustas 1. 279,
iniusta 6. 608.
inlacrimo
inlacrimat 3. 716.
inlicitus
inlicitas 1. 197, 627.
inlido
inlidit 4. 410; 8. 447 (KBG; L instigat),
inlisit 7. 53,
inliditur 7. 585,
inlidi 2. 520,
inlisa (acc.) 4. 658,
inlisis (f.) 4. 497 (KL; BG inlusis).
inludo
inlusis (abl. f.) 4. 497 (BG; KL inlisis).
inlustris
inlustri (abl. n.) 6. 528.
innato
innatat 3. 525.
innecto
innectere 4. 253,
innexa (acc.) 6. 111.

innoxius
　innoxia (nom. f.) 1. 572.
innubus
　innuba 4. 605,
　innuba (voc. f.) 1. 87.
innumerus
　innumeri (nom.) 4. 613,
　innumerum (m.) 2. 130,
　innumeras 1. 395; 3. 332.
Ino
　Ino 8. 21.
inòpinus
　inopina (nom. f.) 5. 638.
inops
　inops (m.) 3. 609; 4. 5, 296,
　inopis (f.) 5. 685,
　inopem (m.) 1. 697,
　inopes (nom. f.) 5. 146.
Inopus
　Inopi 5. 104.
Inous
　Inoo (dat. m.) 1. 280,
　Inois (f.) 2. 607,
　Inoas 1. 521.
inquam
　inquit 1. 81, 643; 2. 48, 143, 471, 656;
　3. 103, 649, 697; 4. 51, 466, 706; 5. 378;
　6. 274, 305, 373, 482, 536; 7. 238, 467.
inrevocabilis
　inrevocabile (acc.) 6. 6.
inrideo
　inridens (f.) 5. 650.
inritus
　inritus 7. 368; 8. 23,
　inrita (nom. f.) 6. 264,
　inrita (acc.) 5. 398; 6. 304, 692.
inroro
　inrorat 7. 360.
inrumpo
　inrumpunt 1. 819,
　inrupit 2. 211.
inruo
　inruit (prs.) 4. 299; 6. 254, 287,
　inruerant 2. 247,
　inruat 5. 689.
insania
　insania (nom.) 2. 525.
insanus
　insanus 1. 140,
　insanam 1. 605,
　insano (m.) 3. 676,
　insana (nom.) 4. 641.
inscius
　inscius 5. 3 (KBG; L conscius), 541,
　inscia (nom.) 2. 278; 3. 40; 6. 317, 660,
　inscia (nom.) 4. 367.
insector
　insectans (m.) 4. 388.
insequor
　insequeris 1. 398,
　insequitur 1. 112; 2. 365; 3. 550, 639;
　4. 239, 265, 655; 6. 106,
　insequar 1. 715 (vid. subi.),
　insequar 1. 715 (vid. ind.).

insideo (insido (?))
　insedit 4. 445,
　insedimus 1. 513,
　insedisse 2. 177.
insidiae
　insidias 1. 416; 3. 506,
　insidiis 5. 631.
insignis
　insignis 1. 143; 5. 139 (KL; BG in
　signis); 6. 701 **bis,**
　insignis (nom. f.) 3. 430,
　insignem (m.) 3. 158,
　insigne 5. 229,
　subst. n. insigne 2. 112,
　insigne 2. 418; 3. 346; 6. 53,
　insignia (acc.) 4. 139.
insilio
　insilit 6. 209 (L; KB constitit; G con-
　tigit); 8. 133,
　insiliunt 4. 683,
　insiluit 2. 513.
insisto
　insiste 3. 519,
　insistere 3. 469 (L; KBG obsistere),
　insistens (m.) 4. 312.
insomnis
　insomnem 7. 169 (B; KL fallat et; G
　solvat et),
　insomnem 7. 23,
　insomni (m.) 2. 262,
　insomnes (m.) 3. 121 (L; K in quo
　omen; BG inque omen),
　insomnes (m.) 2. 223.
insomnium
　insomnia (acc.) 1. 329; 2. 140; 7. 6.
insono
　insonuit 2. 91; 3. 79; 6. 366.
insons
　insontis (n.) 1. 103,
　insontem 5. 458,
　insontem 7. 455,
　insons (voc. m.) 6. 131,
　subst. m. insontes (acc.) 3. 407.
insperatus
　insperata (abl.) 4. 293,
　insperatos 1. 130 (BGL; K sperata).
inspiro
　inspirat 7. 255.
instar
　instar (nom. m.) 4. 202.
instauro
　instaurat 5. 690,
　instaurant 3. 470.
insterno
　insternunt 3. 463.
instigo
　instigat 8. 447 (L; KBG inlidit),
　instigant 8. 223.
instimulo
　instimulat 3. 645; 4. 285,
　instimulet 2. 134.
instituo
　instituit 3. 427,
　instituet 1. 16,
　institui 1. 566,

instituit 4. 543,
instituere 4. 487.
insto
  instat 1. 30; 2. 175; 4. 39; 6. 300 (BL;
  KG intrat),
  instant 4. 643,
  instabat 6. 644,
  instent 1. 249,
  instare 1. 302; 2. 457,
  instantis (m.) 3. 615,
  instantem (m.) 3. 552,
  instante (f.) 8. 77 (G; KB adstante;
  L hic stante),
  instanti (n.) 6. 505,
  instantes (acc. m.) 1. 382.
insuetus
  insuetis (dat. n.) 2. 330.
insula
  insula (nom.) 2. 248; 7. 262; 8. 217, 377.
insulto
  insultat 4. 604,
  insultet 6. 596,
  insultans (m.) 1. 806; 3. 235.
insum
  inest 3. 681; 6. 62, 250,
  inerat 5. 402.
insuper
  4. 428; 6. 9, 57; 7. 603.
insuperabilis
  insuperabile 3. 510,
  insuperabile 3. 12.
insurgo
  insurgit 1. 450,
  insurgere 2. 82; 4. 274; 5. 671; 7. 377,
  613,
  insurgens (m.) 4. 415,
  insurgitur 2. 13.
intactus
  intactas 3. 554.
integer
  integer 2. 58, 374; 4. 275.
intemerandus
  intemeranda (nom. n.) 5. 641.
intemeratus
  intemerata (nom. f.) 4. 271.
intendo
  intendit (prs.) 4. 648,
  intenderat 8. 68,
  intendere 6. 600; 8. 362,
  intendens (m.) 1. 401; 3. 572,
  intento (abl.) 3. 591,
  intenta 5. 339; 6. 540,
  intenta 4. 257,
  intenta 5. 312,
  intentis 4. 351,
  intentis (dat. f.) 3. 103.
inter (adv.)
  5. 336; 6. 220; 8. 303, 382.
inter (praepos.) (40)
  1. 3, 138; 2. 174, 428, 481, 629, 663; 3.
  238, 608; 4. 68, 189, 299, 482, 531, 587;
  5. 13 bis, 375, 614; 6. 95 (KBG; L pernix), 110, 155, 172, 243, 434, 509, 510,
  595, 758; 7. 103, 358; 8. 56, 148, 227,

257, 328 (L; KB intra; G intra;), 336,
339, 363, 462.
interdum
  6. 668; 7. 64.
interea (26)
  interea 1. 452, 574, 752; 2. 1, 497; 3.
  113, 332, 414, 575, 726, 740; 4. 90, 414,
  529; 5. 83, 131, 259, 532, 554, 570; 8. 78,
  134, 305, 433, 406,
  nec minus interea 3. 611.
interior
  intima (acc.) 4. 512; 5. 280; 8. 410.
intermico
  intermicat 4. 662.
interpres
  interpres 6. 690.
interritus
  interritus 4. 190.
interrogo
  interroget 1. 233.
intervolo
  intervolat 2. 613; 5. 27.
intimus vid. interior.
intono
  intonat 2. 366; 3. 169; 4. 414,
  intonuit 1. 591; 2. 208; 3. 252.
intonsus
  intonso (abl. m.) 6. 643.
intorqueo
  intorquent 8. 287,
  intorto (abl. m.) 3. 727; 4. 452,
  intortis (f.) 3. 476,
  intortos 6. 563,
  intortis (m.) 8. 356.
intra (praepos.)
  7. 110; 8. 328 (KB; G infra; L inter).
intremo
  intremit 4. 609,
  intremuit 3. 73,
  intremere 2. 519.
intrepidus
  intrepidus 1. 504.
intro
  intrat 6. 300 (KG; BL instat); 7. 646,
  intrant 1. 186,
  intrarent 1. 590,
  intraverit 5. 191,
  intrare 5. 482,
  intrasse 2. 643,
  intrantem (m.) 2. 11.
inultus
  inultos 4. 14,
  inultis (n.) 6. 531.
intus
  1.608.
inutilis
  inutile (acc.) 1. 634.
invado
  invadit 6. 255; 7. 600,
  invadunt 2. 220,
  invasit 7. 605,
  invaserat 7. 295,
  invadere 3. 146; 8. 371.
invalidus
  invalidis (dat. m.) 5. 24.

inveho
invehit 2. 624.
invenio
invenit 2. 215 (KBG; L ingerit); 3.
148; 4. 135, 724 (KBG; L incubat); 6.
3, 422,
inveniunt 2. 92,
invenit 1. 239; 7. 106,
inventus 4. 365 (KG; BL inventos),
inventos 4. 365 (BL; KG inventus).
invergo
invergens (m.) 2. 610.
inverto
invertite 7. 547,
subst. n. inversa (acc.) 3. 647.
invideo
invidet 2. 607,
invidere 3. 306,
invideris (subi.) 5. 507,
invidisse 2. 375,
invisa 6. 499 (BGL; K iniussa),
invisi (m.) 6. 468,
invisae (dat.) 1. 154,
invisum (m.) 4. 474 (K; BL iniuste; G
iniusti),
inviso (n.) 4. 758 (KBG; L invito).
invidus
invida (nom. f.) 1. 509; 2. 473; 4. 100.
invigilo
invigilat 5. 257,
invigilans (m.) 2. 374.
inviso
invisere 8. 230.
invisus vid. invideo.
invitus
inviti 1. 116,
invitae 8. 224,
invito (m.) 6. 269,
invito (abl.) 3. 391; 7. 575,
invita 6. 318, 480,
invito 1. 145; 4. 685, 758 (L; KBG inviso).
invius
subst. n. invia (acc.) 4. 400.
invoco
invocat 2. 364; 7. 342.
involvo
involvunt 6. 412,
involvens (m.) 4. 264,
involvi 7. 74.
io
1. 221; 6. 29.
Io
Io 4. 346, 392, 416; 7. 111.
Iolcos
Iolcon 1. 171.
Ionius
Ionius 7. 83,
subst. n. Ionii 4. 512,
Ionium 1. 24.
Iphiclus
Iphiclus 1. 370.
Iphiclus
Iphiclo (dat.) 1. 473.

Iphinoe
Iphinoe 2. 327,
Iphinoen 2. 162.
Iphis
Iphis 7. 423,
Iphi 1. 441.
Iphitus
Iphitus 1. 363,
Iphite 3. 480.
impono
imposuit 1. 565 (KBG; L imposita est),
imposita est 1. 565 (L; KBG imposuit).
ipse
1. pron.
ipse 1. 541, 558, 596, 665, 698, 746,
777, 787; 2. 374, 377, 597, 637; 3. 13, 38,
346, 433, 554, 701, 702; 4. 69, 109, 295,
531, 559, 568, 618, 754; 5. 41, 192, 320,
367, 412, 488; 6. 42, 47, 49, 57, 194,
258, 309, 696; 7. 60 (KGL; B ipsa), 69,
73, 201 (K; BL **om.**; G ipsa), 439, 444,
603, 628, 651; 8. 48, 224, 466,
ipsa 1. 132 (BG; KL illa); 2.50, 134,
268; 4. 405, 420; 5. 291, 437 (KBG; L
ipse), 628; 6. 370, 543, 577, 589; 7. 10,
178, 201 (G; K ipse; BL **om.**), 213
(KG; B ista; L illa), 264 (KBG; L
ipsam), 288, 310, 346 **bis,** 414, 477; 8.
78, 159 **bis,** 234, 322, 352, 410 425,
ipsius (m.) 4. 185,
ipsi (f.) 7. 170,
ipsum 1. 48; 4. 487; 5. 269; 7. 46 **bis,**
82, 149 **bis,** 314; 8. 110, 358,
ipsam 2. 280; 7. 185,
ipsi 2. 165, 540; 6. 290; 8. 257,
ipsae 5. 294,
ipsa 8. 398 (G; KBL ista),
ipsis (m.) 7. 52,
ipsa 7. 60 (B; KCL ipse),
2. adi.
ipse 1. 83, 193, 246; 2. 22, 26, 277, 356,
416, 435, 605; 3. 8, 37, 150, 369, 468, 474,
498, 604; 4. 72, 246, 287 (BL; KG
Aetna), 323, 484, 555, 571, 628, 647, 694,
703; 5. 128, 229, 437 (L; KBG ipsa),
476, 540, 576; 6. 168, 423, 611, 707; 7.
142, 385 **bis,** 471, 576, 641; 8. 137, 214,
ipsa 1. 817; 2. 41, 196, 209, 324, 338,
400, 559; 3. 393, 527; 4. 363, 416, 542;
5. 33, 65, 149; 6. 71, 173; 7. 279, 393;
8. 92, 235,
ipsius 1. 29; 8. 60, 151, 190,
ipsius 6. 354, 717,
ipsius 7. 551,
ipsi (f.) 7. 250,
ipsum 1. 47, 733; 6. 592; 7. 166 (B;
KGL illum), 535 (BL; KG ipsam),
ipsam 7. 264 (L; KBG ipsa), 535 (KG;
BL ipsum), 589; 8. 406,
ipsum 8. 18,
ipso 3. 671; 4. 496; 7. 610,
ipsa 5. 138; 7. 176, 247 (KBG; L ista),
336, 599,
ipso 4. 280, 429; 7. 27,
ipsi 4. 65, 567; 8. 211, 242,

ipsae 6. 721; 7. 271,
ipsa 5. 393; 7. 551,
ipsos 7. 109,
ipsas 7. 49,
ipsa 4. 565, 644; 7. 33, 293, 536,
ipsis 2. 168,
ipsis 6. 546; 7. 300,
ipsis 7. 505.

Ira
Ira (nom.) 5. 137,
Irae (nom.) 2. 205; 5. 146.

ira
ira 1. 37, 683; 2. 165, 659; 3. 224, 384;
4. 428, 472, 580, 742; 5. 517; 7. 149, 532,
568, 636, 639; 8. 264, 290,
irae (gen.) 3. 27; 7. 599; 8. 272,
iram 3. 446; 7. 160,
ira 4. 474,
ira 1. 722; 3. 586, 637; 4. 3, 205, 294;
5. 268, 567; 6. 422, 556; 7. 34, 82, 127,
294, 316, 318 (in ira GL; K in hora; B
obire), 330 (BG; KL ore), 484, 590; 8.
374,
irae 2. 232; 4. 88, 483, 526,
irarum 1. 748,
iras 1. 550, 673; 2. 99, 315, 362; 3. 97,
237, 696; 4. 55, 273, 521; 5. 522; 6. 284,
432; 7. 335; 8. 87, 446 (L; K **om.;** B
lenit; G quaerere).

irascor
iratus 8. 146,
irato (abl.) 6. 607,
irato 2. 63,
irata (nom.) 7. 582.

Iris
Iris 7. 189,
Irim 4. 77,
Irin 7. 186.

Iris
Iris 4. 600; 5. 120.

Iron
Iron 3. 111.

Iron
Iron 6. 201.

is
1. pron.
ea 2. 103 (ea cum B; K eadem; GL
aut),
id 4. 709 (KL; B hoc; G haec); 6. 234;
7. 428,
eum 6. 115, 217,
id 8. 393,
ea (nom.) 4. 144; 5. 626,
ea 1. 240; 4. 1, 109; 5. 93, 253, 509, 510,
667; 7. 542,
2. adi.
is 6. 165,
ea 3. 664; 8. 43,
id (nom.) 3. 294,
ea (acc.) 2. 655; 3. 223, 455; 4. 330; 6.
18; 7. 108.

Issedonius
Issedoniae (nom.) 6. 750.

iste
1. pron.
iste 5. 664; 8. 58,
ista (nom.) 7. 213 (B; KG ipsa; L illa),
ista (nom.) 8. 398 (KBL; G ipsa),
ista 4. 34, 650; 5. 530, 675; 7. 139,
istis (n.) 7. 507,
2. adi.
iste 3. 698; 4. 704; 5. 544, 653; 8. 441,
ista 1. 506, 670; 2. 469; 3. 373, 699,
isti (n.) 4. 155,
istum 7. 162,
ista 7. 247 (L; KBG ipsa),
isto 7. 71,
ista 8. 149,
istas 6. 727,
istis (m.) 7. 452,
istis (n.) 7. 345.

Isthmos
Isthmon 8. 23.

ita (13)
1. 562; 3. 448; 4. 239, 360, 485, 537, 610,
624; 6. 265; 7. 83, 238; 8. 318, 408.

iter
iter 1. 586, 789; 2, 575; 4. 561; 8. 183,
iter 1. 565, 570, 717, 793, 806; 2. 44, 455,
495; 3. 42, 241, 656, 734; 4. 58, 197, 424,
690; 5. 173, 400; 7. 408; 8. 190.

itero
iterant 1. 29, 633,
iterata (nom.n.) 1. 593.

iterum (40)
iterum 1. 632; 2. 169, 395, 399, 594; 3.
387, 666; 4. 283, 302, 400 **bis**, 625, 632,
653, 707; 5. 671; 6. 238, 300, 301, 367,
584; 7. 150, 196, 202, 447, 451, 533, 625;
8. 45, 193, 285, 300, 313, 353 **bis**, 366,
iterum . . . atque iterum 7. 382,
iterum . . . iterumque 7. 12.

Itys
Ityn 3. 189.

iuba
iuba 3. 228, 740,
iubae (gen.) 6. 606,
iubae (nom.) 3. 196; 8. 88,
iubas 3. 25; 6. 111.

iubar
iubar 3. 292; 5. 410,
iubar 3. 429, 560; 4. 93; 5. 311, 331.

iubeo
iubeo 8. 71,
iubet 1. 94; 2. 650; 4. 112, 134, 176, 371;
5. 48, 190, 214, 261, 491, 556; 7. 187, 300,
553; 8. 156,
iubent 4. 489,
iubebat 3. 691,
iussistis 6. 729 (BGL; K lusistis),
iubeas 7. 281; 8. 459,
iubeat 6. 437,
iussisset 7. 424,
subst. m. iubenti (dat.) 1. 58,
iussi sumus 8. 42,
iussus foret 7. 134,
iussus 4. 165,
iussa 1. 592,

iusso (dat. m.) 5. 481,
iussa 3. 234,
iussae 4. 523,
iussos 1. 66, 4. 438,
iussas 3. 508,
iussa 1. 74,
subst. n. iussa 1. 115; 7. 92,
iussa 1. 200, 689, 754; 3. 47; 5. 492, 659;
7. 61, 71, 95, 429,
iussis 1. 820; 7. 138.
iucundus
iucunda (voc. f.) 7. 336.
iugalis
iugalem (f.) 8. 245,
iugale 8. 222,
iugali (f.) 4. 354,
iugales (nom. f.) 5. 443,
iugales 1. 226,
iugales 2. 344.
iugerum
iugera (acc.) 6. 130.
iugis
iugi (abl. n.) 5. 485 (B; KGL vigili).
iugulum
iugulo (abl.) 3. 154.
iugum
iugi 2. 31; 3. 566; 4. 110,
iugo (abl.) 3. 403; 4. 203,
iuga 4. 66, 228, 286; 6. 392,
iugis 2. 19,
iuga 1. 3; 2. 621, 633; 3. 401, 521, 584;
4. 594, 631, 647, 658, 685; 5. 105, 183,
343, 431, 489; 6. 388, 426; 7. 367, 596,
iugis 2. 333, 635; 3. 466, 627, 709; 4.
692; 8. 448.
Iulus
Iulos 1. 9.
iungo
iungit 1. 240; 4. 29; 6. 143,
iungunt 1. 636; 4. 701,
iungam 8. 342,
iunget 4. 215,
iunxit 6. 265,
iunxere 3. 14; 6. 182,
iunxerit 5. 384,
iungat 3. 505,
iungeret 2. 491; 6. 692,
iungere 1. 165, 198, 520; 3. 309; 5. 515;
6. 436; 8. 437,
iunxisse 6. 484,
iungens (f.) 1. 163,
iungi 1. 124; 2. 324,
iuncta 4. 464; 5. 345,
iuncto (abl.) 7. 374,
iuncta (abl.) 6. 12,
iunctos 3. 8,
iunctas 1. 524 (et iunctas KBG; L
adiunctas); 3. 18,
iunctis (f.) 2. 319,
iunctis 4. 304; 5. 59,
subst. m. iunctis (dat.) 2. 561.
Iuno
Iuno 1. 96; 2. 3; 3. 184, 487, 509, 534,
611, 665; 4. 7, 55, 354, 359, 416, 682;
5. 183, 280, 286, 363, 401; 6. 429, 450,

590, 650, 680; 7. 154, 186 (BG; KL
tunc), 190, 442; 8. 318,
Iunonis 4. 27, 392,
Iunonem 2. 85; 4. 3,
Iuno 1. 215,
Iunone 1. 73; 6. 578.
Iunonius
Iunonia (nom.) 8. 231,
Iunonia (nom.) 8. 383.
Iuppiter
Iuppiter 1. 82, 247, 344, 466; 2. 52, 84,
305, 358;3. 19, 91, 131, 401, 465, 697;
4. 219, 365, 560; 5. 163, 304; 6. 49, 170,
391, 653; 8. 266,
Iovis 1. 156, 303, 663, 690, 788; 2. 416;
3. 89, 225, 385, 578, 620, 667; 4. 28, 75,
127, 256, 327 **bis**, 414, 417 (B; KGL
Phari), 479, 520, 542, 551, 580, 684,
708, 757; 5. 110, 147, 204, 280, 550, 572,
653; 6. 53, 91, 137, 463, 636; 7. 568,
Iovi 1. 730, 795; 2. 434; 4. 391,
Iovem 2. 363; 560; 4. 61, 70, 352, 360;
5. 623,
Iuppiter 4. 122; 6. 730,
Iove 1. 133, 372; 4. 313; 5. 478; 6. 608,
621.
Iuppiter
Iuppiter 5. 371.
iurgium
iurgia (acc.) 3. 638 (modo iurgia K;
BL periuria; G in iurgia).
iuro
iuro 7. 500,
iurasse 8. 423,
iuratos 6. 96.
ius
iuri 5. 509 (B; KGL vero),
ius 5. 627,
iura 8. 401,
iura 2. 309; 3. 651; 4. 103; 5. 674; 6. 126.
iuste
iustius 3. 297.
iustus
iustae (nom.) 3. 515 (KBG; L lusae),
iustis (f.) 7. 419 (L; KBG iustas),
iustas 7. 419 (KBG; L iustis),
subst. n. iusti 1. 534; 5. 498,
iusta (acc.) 1. 459; 3. 367; 5. 6.
iuvenca
iuvencae (gen.) 4. 350, 357,
iuvencam 1. 190,
iuvenca 2. 331; 4. 398.
iuvencus
iuvenci (nom.) 3. 57,
iuvencis (dat.) 1. 36.
iuvenis
subst. m. iuvenis (gen.) 1. 710; 2. 265;
5. 526; 7. 350,
iuveni 3. 517, 546; 6. 313; 7. 458; 8. 130,
iuvenem 1. 31, 38, 47, 58, 153, 281; 2.
554; 3. 352; 4. 136; 5. 429, 659; 6. 693;
7. 79, 188, 316, 345,
iuvenis 7. 11,
iuvenes 1. 252; 4. 174,
iuvenum 1. 473; 3. 163,

iuvenes 1. 78, 720,
iuvenes 4. 206, 477; 6. 285.
iuventa
iuventae 1. 101, 113; 4. 233, 318; 5. 365;
7. 339; 8. 460,
iuventae 1. 347; 7. 224,
iuventam 6. 695,
iuventa 3. 324, 682; 5. 257; 7. 512; 8. 26,
257.
iuventus
iuventus 1. 599; 3. 628; 4. 655, 668; 5.
558; 6. 231; 7. 556.
iuvo
iuvat 2. 387; 3. 368; 4. 326; 6. 339,
iuvant 1. 702; 2. 585; 5. 626; 6. 227, 751,
iuvabant 8. 162,
iuvabis 4. 618,
iuvabunt 3. 714,
iuvit 1. 376,
iuvimus 5. 661,
iuvere 3. 85,
iuves 1. 21,
iuvet 1. 249; 4. 420; 5. 687; 7. 275, 504;
8. 80,
iuvaret 3. 701; 8. 169,
iuvare 4. 568.
iuxta (adv.) (8)
1. 582, 606, 705; 4. 424; 5. 393, 571, 572;
7. 404.
iuxta (praepos.)
2. 193; 5. 187, 457; 6. 50.
labefacio
labefacta (nom. f.) 7. 175; 8. 357.
labes
labes 7. 386,
labem 2. 239; 3. 377,
labes (nom.) 5. 236.
labo
labat 3. 164,
labant 3. 75; 4. 565 (BGL; K labent),
labent 4. 565 (K; BGL labant),
labantem (f.) 1. 542,
labantia (acc.) 3. 150 (G; KL natantia;
B liquentia),
subst. m. labantibus (dat.) 6. 473.
labor
labitur 5. 3; 6. 563, 663; 8. 116,
labuntur 1. 290,
laberer 7. 259,
labere 5. 639,
labens (f.) 2. 425,
labentis (m.) 6. 377,
labentem (m.) 4. 311,
labentibus (abl. f.) 5. 55,
lapsus 1. 399; 5. 253,
lapsa 6. 366,
lapso (m.) 6. 654,
lapsum (m.) 1. 831,
lapso (m.) 8. 331,
lapsae 4. 503,
lapsis (abl. m.) 6. 541,
subst. m labentum 3. 219.
labor (labos)
labor 1. 143; 2. 618; 3. 350, 473, 510,
574; 4. 50, 89, 470, 545, 638, 705; 5. 49,

141, 169, 453, 542, 688; 6. 713; 7. 520,
labos 6. 352, 361,
laboris 1. 235; 5. 18, 514; 7. 72,
laborem 7. 159, 413 (KL; BG laborum); 8. 78, 117,
labor 4. 329,
labore 7. 534,
labores 5. 38, 364,
laborum 3. 367; 6. 548; 7. 15, 413 (BG;
KL laborem), 417; 8. 182,
labores 1. 172, 247, 320, 473, 564; 2. 79,
409; 3. 625; 4. 420, 539; 5. 132, 194, 278,
448, 486, 575, 617; 6. 24, 599, 736; 7. 131,
200, 276, 439,
laboribus 2. 285.
laboro
laborat 6. 224,
laborantis (f.) 2. 495,
laborantes (acc. m.) 4. 656,
laborati (n.) 5. 225.
lac
lacte 2. 157.
Lacaena
Lacaenae (gen.) 7. 150.
lacer
lacera (nom. f.) 1. 49,
laceras 3. 314.
lacero
lacerat 1. 719; 6. 401; 7. 636,
laceret 1. 813.
lacertus
lacertis 1. 435,
lacertos 6. 525,
lacertis 1. 135, 441; 3. 20 (KGL; B
catervis); 4. 375; 8. 93.
lacesso
lacessit 5. 571,
lacessitis 4. 207.
Lacon
Lacon 1. 421; 4. 254; 6. 255,
Laconi 4. 340.
lacrima
lacrimae (nom.) 1. 238, 724; 4. 218,
lacrimis 2. 161; 3. 371, 688,
lacrimas 1. 767; 2. 299, 428, 563; 3. 366,
395; 5. 13, 30,
lacrimis 2. 141, 169; 3. 283, 601; 4. 11,
42, 51, 169; 5. 647; 7. 258.
lacrimo
lacrimans 3. 9, 606,
lacrimans (f.) 2. 408.
lacus
lacum 6. 68,
lacus 1. 556,
lacus 4. 379; 5. 148; 6. 566.
laedo
laedere 2. 434,
laesi (nom.) 2. 250.
laetabilis
laetabile (nom.) 6. 606.
laetitia
laetitiae (gen.) 7. 28.
laetor
laetatur 1. 500,
laetabere 7. 414,

laetarer 4. 752,
laetantibus (dat. m.) 1. 274,
laetatus 4. 737,
laetata (nom. f.) 1. 134.
laetus
laetus 1. 161, 182, 264, 485; 2. 98, 415,
556; 3. 200, 474, 659; 4. 342, 532; 5. 69,
416, 444; 6. 266,
laeta 1. 30, 170; 2. 299, 322 (B; K fatis;
GL hospita); 3. 633; 4. 162, 540; 5. 1;
6. 477, 543, 659; 7. 487; 8. 240,
laetae (gen.) 3. 464,
laeto (abl.) 5. 570,
laeto 1. 309,
laeti 1. 188, 250, 610; 2. 370, 441; 8. 223,
laetae 2. 189,
laetos 4. 116,
laeta 2. 110; 5. 423; 7. 512,
laetis (m.) 4. 31, 81,
subst. m. laetis 8. 252,
laetos 2. 649.
laevus
laevi (m.) 3. 521,
laevum 6. 246,
laevom (n.) 1. 353,
laevum (acc.) 8. 189,
laevo 5. 160,
laevo 1. 623; 6. 69,
laevos 2. 387,
subst. f. laevam 4. 289 (B; KGL dextram),
laeva 2. 589,
subst. n. laevum (acc.) 4. 211,
adv. laevum 1. 156.
Lageus
Lagea (nom. n.) 6. 118.
lamna
lamna (abl.) 1. 123.
lampas
lampada 1. 840; 3. 125; 8. 262, 278,
lampade 7. 366.
Lampsacus
Lampsacus 2. 623.
lancea
lancea (nom.) 3. 588; 6. 124, 302.
langueo
languent 1. 315; 7. 466,
languentis (f.) 4. 40,
languentes (acc. f.) 7. 24,
languentia 4. 388.
languesco
languescit 7. 361,
languescunt 3. 236.
languor
languor 7. 194 (KBG; L fervor).
Laomedon
Laomedon 2. 552.
Laomedonteus
Laomedonteos 2. 474.
lapis
lapis 2. 467.
Lapithes
Lapithes 5. 515; 7. 606,
Lapithae (nom.) 5. 652,
Lapithas 4. 280.

lapsus
lapsu (abl.) 1. 91, 686.
laquear
laquearia (acc.) 5. 243.
laqueus
laqueis (abl.) 6. 133.
lar
laris 3. 375,
larem 4. 45,
lares 2. 246,
laribus (dat.) 3. 175.
largior
largitur 2. 650.
largus
largus 1. 735; 4. 551; 6. 723.
lasso
lassat 6. 174,
lassant 3. 661,
lassatur 1. 707,
lassatus 1. 419,
lassatas 2. 262.
lassus
lassa (nom. f.) 7. 561.
Latagus
Latagum 5. 584; 6. 572.
late (6)
1. 841; 3. 129, 584; 4. 282, 320; 6. 104.
lateo
latet 2. 258; 3. 108; 6. 195; 7. 59,
latent 4. 309,
latuit 6. 533, 609,
latuere 6. 703,
lateant 6. 392,
latentem (f.) 7. 252,
latentia (acc.) 1. 128.
latex
latices (acc.) 1. 666; 4. 533.
Latius
Latias 1. 21,
Latiis (m.) 2. 245.
Latmius
Latmius 8. 28.
Latona
Latona (nom.) 4. 60.
Latonius
subst. f. Latonia (nom.) 3. 415; 6. 159.
latratus
latratu (abl.) 6. 112.
Latris
Latris 6. 121.
latus
latum (acc. n.) 1. 585; 3. 240,
lato (m.) 6. 552,
lata (acc.) 2. 490; 5. 594,
latis (n.) 6. 508.
latus
latus 3. 50; 5. 165; 6. 383,
lateri 2. 504; 3. 486,
latus 1. 124, 619; 2. 619; 3. 61; 4. 304,
378; 5. 102, 135; 6. 243, 258; 7. 479; 8.
189, 375,
latere 6. 202,
latera (acc.) 3. 87; 4. 693.
laurea
laurea (nom.) 1. 6.

Laurens
Laurentibus (abl. f.) 6. 410.
laurus
laurus 1. 386,
laurum 4. 548,
lauro 3. 434; 4. 334,
laurus (acc.) 1. 209.
laus
laudis 1. 717,
laudi 7. 67,
laus 2. 243,
laude 1. 105; 2. 148; 3. 677; 4. 342; 5. 296; 6. 594; 7. 290,
laudes (acc.) 6. 94,
laudibus 1. 476; 5. 83; 6. 546 (KGL; B caedibus).
lavo
lavet 4. 153,
lavitur 4. 229,
lotos 2. 276.
laxo
laxat 8. 334,
laxent 4. 720,
laxantur 2. 35.
lea
lea (nom.) 3. 737.
leaena
leaenae (gen.) 6. 148.
Learchus
Learcho 1. 280,
Learchum 3. 68.
Leda
Ledae (gen.) 1. 562.
legio
legio 6. 48, 508; 7. 573,
legiones (acc.) 6. 402.
lego
legatos 6. 15.
lego
legit 1. 314; 5. 326 (B; KGL petit),
legunt 2. 13, 452; 3. 36,
legam 4. 364,
leges 2. 152,
legi 1. 510,
legit 4. 521; 5. 464,
legere 4. 112,
legens (m.) 1. 711; 4. 440,
legitur 2. 428,
lectum (acc. n.) 3. 5,
lecto (n.) 4. 591,
lectos 4. 735; 6. 405,
lectas 3. 431,
lecta 6. 559.
Leleges
Lelegum 3. 204.
Lemnos
Lemnos 2. 79, 95, 431; 4. 440,
Lemni 2. 90, 108,
Lemno 2. 101, 323,
Lemnon 1. 392; 2. 127, 198, 311,
Lemno 2. 164, 401.
lenio
lenit 3. 40; 8. 466 (B; K om.; G quaerere; L iras).

lenis
lenis (nom. f.) 1. 840,
leni (abl.) 3. 32,
leni (f.) 4. 386,
lenibus (abl. n.) 6. 665.
lentus
lenti (m.) 7. 213,
lentum (m.) 7. 597,
lento (m.) 1. 124,
lentis (dat. f.) 3. 211 (vid. abl.),
lentis (f.) 3. 211 (vid. dat.).
leo
leo 1. 757; 3. 588, 636; 6. 347, 613,
leonis 3. 720,
leoni 1. 263,
leonem 2. 459; 3. 24; 8. 126,
leones 8. 456,
leonum 3. 237,
leones 3. 706.
Leodocus
Leodocus 1. 358.
Lerna
Lernae (gen.) 1. 35; 2. 496; 3. 511.
Lesbos
Lesbos 3. 7.
letalis
letalis (nom. m.) 4. 508,
letales (acc. f.) 2. 155.
Lethaeus
Lethaei (gen. m.) 8. 84.
Lethe
Lethen 2. 483.
letifer
letifer 6. 342,
letifera (abl.) 1. 192,
letiferis (abl. f.) 8. 17,
subst. m. letifer 4. 525.
Letum
Leti 2. 206,
Leto (dat.) 8. 74.
letum
leti 1. 32, 714, 773, 808; 3. 253 (B; KGL belli), 386; 4. 113, 231, 514; 6. 178, 337,
leto 1. 633 (vid. abl.), 786; 6. 272; 7. 314,
leto 1. 633 (vid. dat.), 821; 4. 168; 7. 453.
lēvis
levi (abl. n.) 1. 290.
levis
levis 3. 167, 523, 554; 6. 665, 697; 7. 24 (KGL; B sero),
levis 1. 389 (et levis G; K felevis; BL felixque); 6. 197, 472; 7. 259,
leve 3. 627,
levi (n.) 5. 609,
levem 1. 71,
levem 6. 704,
levi 6. 376,
levi 5. 462; 6. 748,
levi 3. 257 (BGL; K autem); 6. 672,
levibus (m.) 6. 326,
leves 3. 33,
leves 1. 409, 783; 3. 126,
levibus (n.) 2. 447,
levior 2. 323; 6. 524,

levior 7. 156 (KBG; L propior),
levioris (m.) 6. 240,
leviore (n.) 1. 338.
levitas
levitate 5. 270.
levo
levat 2. 448 (KBG; L locat); 4. 502;
8. 352,
levant 3. 263; 6. 89; 7. 512,
levet 6. 276,
levare 7. 408,
levantis (gen. m.) 4. 166.
lex
lex 4. 209,
legem 1. 213; 4. 75,
lege 1. 833; 2. 357; 4. 709, 753; 6. 445;
7. 427,
legum 4. 102.
Lexanor
Lexanoris 6. 686.
libamen
libamine 1. 204,
libamina (acc.) 5. 192.
libeo
libet 6. 476; 7. 50,
libuit 8. 268.
Liber
Liber 1. 567.
liber
liber 3. 470; 4. 306; 6. 330; 7. 541.
libertas
libertas 1. 601.
libo
libat 1. 666; 2. 194; 5. 615,
libavit 3. 457; 4. 17,
libans (m.) 1. 193,
libato (abl. m.) 1. 740.
libum
liba (acc.) 4. 339.
Libya
Libya (abl.) 1. 588.
Libye
Libyes 7. 607.
Libycus
Libycum (acc. n.) 2. 619,
Libyco (n.) 6. 411.
Libys
Libys 1. 512.
liceo
licet 2. 644; 3. 387; 4. 459; 5. 686 (quam
tum licet B; K quantumlibet; G quantum licet; L quantum luet),
licebit 4. 584,
liceat 2. 297; 5. 293; 8. 416.
lignum
ligno (abl.) 6. 98, 251.
ligo
ligat 2. 268; 4. 94; 5. 149,
ligant 5. 11,
ligari 5. 190.
lilium
lilia (nom.) 6. 492.
limen
limen (acc.) 7. 22 (KGL; B lumine),
limine 1. 375, 709, 823, 848; 2. 237, 255,

260; 3. 679; 6. 354; 7. 4, 382,
limina 2. 136,
limina 1. 676; 4. 28 (K; BG lumina; L
numina); 5. 408, 695; 7. 110; 8. 334.
limes
limite 4. 614; 6. 361.
lingua
lingua 7. 244 (B; K om.; G febris; L
artus),
lingua 3. 632; 5. 597; 8. 63, 86, 352,
linguis 2. 433; 6. 58,
linguas 1. 61,
linguis 2. 122; 3. 458.
linquo
linquo 8. 46,
linquis 2. 290, 424,
linquit 1. 407; 3. 117; 7. 102,
linquimus 1. 543,
linquet 1. 181,
liquerunt 4. 98,
liquerat 1. 661; 5. 230,
linquam 1. 560,
linquerit 1. 697,
linque 2. 274; 4. 597,
linquite 1. 631; 3. 144,
linquere 7. 231,
liquisse 6. 140; 7. 502,
linquens 1. 280; 3. 59; 4. 131,
linquens (f.) 5. 441,
linquente (f.) 1. 706,
linquitur 6. 84 **bis**, 689; 7. 643,
linqui 2. 394.
linteum
lintea (acc.) 4. 83.
linum
lini 6. 225.
Lipare
Lipares 2. 96.
liqueo
liquentia (acc.) 3. 150 (B; KL natantia;
G labantia).
liquidus
liquidi (m.) 4. 16,
liquido (abl. n.) 6. 710,
liquidi 2. 467.
liquor
liquuntur 6. 247 (KGL; B tinguntur).
litus
litus 2. 74,
litoris 1. 330; 2. 494; 4. 613, 628,
litus 2. 632,
litore 1. 136, 189, 250, 275, 365, 494,
628, 801; 2. 90, 392, 406, 446; 3. 248, 570,
602, 700, 730; 4. 147, 177, 442, 505, 590;
5. 40, 87, 130, 245; 6. 412; 7. 260, 270,
343; 8. 220, 311, 327, 344,
litora 1. 606; 3. 416; 4. 99, 715; 5. 153;
8. 138, 207,
litoribus 2. 505,
litora 1. 123, 183, 207, 423, 614, 652;
2. 326, 366, 400, 436, 451, 546, 558, 580;
3. 8, 219, 261, 267, 308, 311, 372, 425,
484, 568, 643; 4. 133, 425, 606, 636, 698,
732, 736, 742, 750; 5. 117, 174; 6. 597;
7. 35; 8. 161 (BG; K Colchida; L om.;

359, 432,
litoribus 2. 139 (KG; BL velleribus).
lituus
litui (gen.) 6. 180,
lituum (gen.) 6. 166, 504,
lituos 1. 268; 5. 654; 6. 108.
liveo
liventia (acc.) 1. 63.
loco
locat 2. 266, 448 (L; KBG levat); 3.
445; 6. 254, 370,
locant 3. 334, 462,
locavit 2. 257, 346.
locus
locus 2. 493; 4. 451; 5. 492 (KBG; L
loco), 509; 8. 148,
loci 1. 778; 2. 112, 328, 340,
loco 3. 428,
locum 2. 412; 4. 654; 6. 386,
loco 1. 671 (L; KBG opus), 677; 2. 99;
3. 105, 121, 211; 5. 492 (L; KBG locus);
6. 23; 7. 175, 480,
loca 4. 278,
locorum 4. 208, 349; 5. 389,
locis 1. 794; 2. 559,
locos 1. 541, 558; 2. 39, 67, 301 (BGL;
K lucos); 3. 214; 4. 557; 8. 200,
loca 1. 850; 3. 538, 643, 685; 4. 318; 5.
180; 7. 491,
locis 2. 308, 647; 3. 660, 720.
longe (22)
longe 1. 288, 461, 653, 838; 3. 37, 123,
337, 432, 479; 4. 203, 412, 510; 6. 579;
7. 30, 264, 394, 495, 542; 8. 414,
longius 3. 571; 4. 714; 8. 199.
longinquus
longinqua 2. 286,
longinqui (gen. m.) 4. 698.
longus
longus 1. 23; 2. 368, 618,
longa 2. 8, 303; 6. 320,
longum 2. 596,
longae 4. 536,
longi 2. 114; 7. 361,
longo (m.) 1. 127,
longum (m.) 1. 325; 6. 754; 8. 78,
longo 3. 43 (BGL; K longa), 93, 738;
4. 323; 5. 216, 556,
longa 1. 227 (L; K **om.**; B hac vates;
G nimia), 395; 2. 386; 4. 378; 8. 14, 299,
longo 2. 140, 631; 3. 354,
longa 2. 642 (KBG; L regna),
longarum 7. 26,
longis (m.) 1. 316 (vid. abl.),
longos 3. 356; 8. 118,
longas 3. 482, 602; 8. 128,
longa 3. 43 (K; BGL longo), 405, 596;
5. 649, 685; 7. 6,
longis 1. 316 (vid. dat.); 5. 120, 384; 6.
511; 7. 62,
longis 1. 728; 2. 550, 562; 8. 291,
longis 4. 711; 5. 505,
adv. longum 3. 547; 4. 436; 6. 332,
longior (f.) 6. 62,
longius (nom.) 8. 303,

longissima (nom. f.) 3. 683; 5. 363; 7.
564,
longissima (acc.) 1. 559.
loquax
loquax (m.) 4. 479.
loquor
loquor 8. 47,
loqui 5. 403; 7. 118,
loquentis (f.) 7. 293,
loquentem (m.) 1. 268,
locutus 8. 36,
locuta 7. 472,
locuti (gen. m.) 5. 4.
lorica
lorica 6. 233,
loricam 4. 94.
lotus vid. lavo.
lubricus
lubricus 2. 555,
lubrica (acc.) 1. 232.
luceo
lucet 1. 841,
lucent 6. 492,
lucebis 1. 16,
lucentia (acc.) 6. 574; 8. 452.
Lucifer
Lucifer 6. 527.
lucifer
luciferae (gen.) 7. 179,
luciferas 5. 370 (KL; BG luctiferas).
luctamen
luctamine 2. 234; 3. 39; 6. 510.
luctifer
luctifer 3. 454,
luctiferas 5. 370 (BG; KL luciferas).
luctificus
luctificum (nom.) 3. 292,
adv. luctificum 3. 349.
luctor
luctantia (acc.) 8. 85,
luctatus 1. 205.
luctus
luctus 4. 88,
luctus 1. 526, 713; 2. 1,
luctum 1. 201; 3. 319; 8. 135,
luctu 3. 368, 585, 719, 740; 4. 169, 598;
6. 4, 211; 7. 132,
luctus 5. 236,
luctus 5. 5.
lucus
lucus 5. 641,
luco (abl.) 5. 237, 251; 7. 188,
luci 2. 360,
lucis 5. 645 (K; B suus at si; G suus
ast; L suus atque),
lucos 1. 750; 2. 301 (K; BGL locos);
6. 73; 7. 46; 8. 24,
lucis 5. 335, 629; 6. 114, 495; 8. 102.
ludo
lusistis 6. 729 (K; BGL iussistis),
luserat 5. 110,
ludat 2. 569 (K; BG luat; L eludat),
luserit 6. 13,
lusa est 3. 555 (KL; BG fusa est),
lusae (nom.) 3. 515 (L; KBG iustae).

ludus
ludus 3. 56; 5. 443,
ludo 1. 294,
ludo 1. 251, 423; 2. 581; 4. 607.
lues
lues 2. 291; 3. 246, 373; 4. 503, 592; 5. 15,
luem 4. 432; 6. 400,
lue 4. 529.
lugeo
lugebit 1. 443.
lugubris
lugubre (nom.) 8. 58.
lumen
lumen 6. 480 (BGL; K numen),
luminis 4. 702; 5. 409; 6. 246,
lumen 1. 572,
lumine 1. 105; 3. 100, 132, 257; 4. 248; 5. 348, 483 (K; BGL numine); 7. 22 (B; KGL limen), 334.
lumina 1. 276, 300; 4. 368, 640, 667 (BL; KG numina); 5. 50,
lumina 1. 129, 132, 334, 758, 822; 2. 185, 464, 500; 3. 69, 279, 718; 4. 28 (BG; K limina; L numina), 71, 168, 389, 449, 759; 5. 247, 340; 6. 277, 584; 7. 105, 292, 436, 483, 536 (KBG; L volumina); 8. 60, 65, 85, 204.
Luna
Luna (nom.) 1. 284; 3. 196; 8. 30.
luna
luna 2. 287,
lunae (gen.) 7. 330,
lunam 2. 367; 6. 447.
luo
luit 3. 407,
luet 4. 34; 5. 546, 686 (quantum luet L; K quantumlibet; B quam tum licet; G quantum licet),
luat 2. 569 (BG; K ludat; L eludat),
luant 3. 455,
lueret 8. 399,
luerim 1. 674.
lupus
luporum 1. 455,
lupis 3. 635,
lupis 8. 456.
lustralis
lustralia (acc.) 3. 414.
lustramen
lustramina 3. 409,
lustramina 3. 442.
lustrificus
lustrifico (abl. m.) 3. 448.
lustro
lustrat 6. 576; 7. 126, 334,
lustrant 3. 388; 4. 248 (lustrant tum L; KBG lustrarunt),
lustrarunt 4. 248 (KBG; L lustrant tum),
lustrate 3. 312,
lustrare 7. 181,
lustrasse 3. 682,
lustrans 4. 234; 6. 299,

lustrans (f.) 6. 658,
lustrantia (acc.) 5. 332.
lustrum
lustra (acc.) 1. 104, 490; 3. 68, 242, 593, 733; 4. 52, 370; 8. 27.
lustrum
lustris (abl.) 2. 572.
lux
lux 2. 566, 664; 3. 188; 4. 664, 731; 5. 1, 178, 318, 466, 606; 7. 23,
lucis 1. 789; 2. 642; 3. 48; 4. 427; 6. 733; 7. 339, 413, 493,
lucem 1. 325; 6.. 560; 7. 487,
luce 1. 486; 2. 51, 68, 198, 587; 3. 214, 558; 4. 458, 673; 5. 328, 365; 8. 57.
luxuries
luxuriem 7. 66.
luxurio
luxurians 6. 614,
luxurians (f.) 4. 496.
luxus
luxu (abl.) 2. 131, 371.
Lyaeus
Lyaei 1. 411; 2. 265; 5. 74.
Lycaeus
Lycaei (gen. m.) 6. 533.
Lyce
Lycen 6. 374.
Lycormas
Lycormae (gen.) 3. 544.
Lyctius
Lyctius 3. 729.
Lycurgus
Lycurgum 1. 729.
Lycus
Lycus 4. 173, 719 (GL; KB Tyres), 737; 5. 8,
Lyci 4. 589; 8. 215,
Lyco (dat.) 5. 62.
Lydus
Lyda (nom. f.) 4. 369.
lympha
lympha (abl.) 3. 422.
lympho
lymphaverat 3. 46,
lymphata (acc.) 6. 166.
Lynceus
Lynceus 1. 462, 467.
lynx
lynces (nom.) 2. 260 (K; BGL tigres).
lyra
lyrae (gen.) 1. 409,
lyram 5. 100.
Lyrceius
Lyrceia (nom. f.) 4. 355.
Macetes
Macetum 1. 96.
machina
machina (nom.) 6. 383.
Macrones
Macrones (nom.) 5. 151.
macto
mactat 2. 230,
mactantur 3. 439.

mactus
adv. macte 6. 547.
macula
maculis (abl.) 2. 105.
maculo
maculaverit (subi.) 4. 369,
maculatam 6. 704.
madeo
madent 4. 754,
maduerunt 3. 391,
maduere 6. 709,
madens 6. 415,
madens (f.) 1. 225; 5. 454,
madentem (f.) 2. 274.
madidus
madido (abl. m.) 1. 653,
madidis (abl. m.) 5. 415.
Maeotis
Maeotis 6. 565,
Maeotin 6. 154.
Maeotius
Maeotia (nom.) 6. 38,
Maeotia (nom.) 4. 720.
maereo
maeret 1. 335; 2. 466; 6. 626 (GL; KB
maerens); 7. 116, 197; 8. 209, 369,
maerent 3. 722,
maerens 3. 330, 695; 6. 626 (KB; GL
maeret),
maerens (f.) 2. 343,
maerentem 4. 136,
maerentem 7. 256.
maestus
maestus 2. 552; 4. 50,
maesta 1. 442, 753; 2. 289; 3. 318; 4. 43;
5. 188; 6. 73, 149, 433,
maesti 1. 712,
maestae (gen.) 1. 664; 2. 174 (KGL;
B maesta); 3. 608; 7. 635,
maesto (abl.) 4. 60; 5. 352; 6. 622,
maesta 2. 174 (B; KGL maestae); 4.
69; 7. 82,
maesto 1. 626; 4. 248 (GL; KB maestos),
maesti 2. 360 (K; BGL Moesi); 3. 333;
5. 63,
maestae 6. 505,
maestis 3. 364,
maestis (f.) 8. 233,
maestos 1. 739; 2. 608; 4. 248 (KB; GL
maesto); 7. 105,
maestas 5. 16; 8. 362,
maestis (m.) 8. 455,
maestis (n.) 3. 601,
maestissimus 4. 183; 5. 567,
maestissima (nom. f.) 2. 493.
magicus
magico (abl. m.) 6. 151; 7. 389,
magica 7. 212,
magico 8. 351,
magicis (abl. f.) 6. 449,
magicis 7. 327.
magis (36)
magis 1. 74, 176, 548; 2. 60, 209, 398,
522; 3. 113, 208 **bis**, 216, 271, 362; 4.

545, 752; 5. 126, 368, 563; 6. 461, 600,
718; 7. 75, 241, 337, 355, 622; 8. 227,
398,
magis atque magis 1. 742; 6. 206; 7.
65, 473.
Vid. quam.
magister
magister 2. 391; 3. 468; 7. 83,
magistri 1. 410; 4. 269, 329; 5. 210; 8.
202, 286 (L; KBG magistris),
magistro 1. 465,
magistro 1. 269,
magistri 3. 109; 5. 66,
magistris 1. 18; 7. 400; 8. 286 (KBG;
L magistri),
magistros 1. 382; 6. 536.
magistra
magistram 6. 501,
magistra 6. 578.
magnanimus
magnanimus 1. 634; 3. 646,
magnanimi (m.) 3. 707,
magnanimum (m.) 7. 556,
magnanimi 3. 243,
magnanimis (m.) 6. 125,
magnanimos 6. 116, 637,
magnanimis (f.) 4. 328.
Magnes
Magnes 2. 9.
magnus
magnus 2. 523; 3. 202; 5. 92, 179, 208,
287 (G; **om.**; BL ingens),
magna 3. 163 (L; KBG densa); 5. 40,
magni 1. 44; 2. 149; 3. 563, 667; 4. 90,
186, 319, 513; 5. 300, 378; 6. 294, 500;
7. 214; 8. 282, 458 (gloria magni BG;
K restat imago; L **om.**),
magnae 1. 737; 5. 108, 504; 7. 238,
magni 1. 50; 6. 576,
magno 4. 119,
magno 1. 668,
magnum 3. 160; 5. 487; 6. 40,
magnum 2. 184; 8. 459,
magne 4. 63; 5. 624, 644; 8. 350,
magnum 8. 37,
magno 3. 95, 566, 606, 639; 4. 76, 444,
602; 5. 571; 6. 4, 279, 353, 611, 744; 8.
367, 428,
magna 1. 104, 272, 349; 3. 163 (KBG;
L densa); 5. 282,
magno 4. 666; 5. 227; 7. 13,
magni 5. 364,
magna 5. 599,
magnorum (m.) 1. 476, 790,
magnis (m.) 1. 1, 341; 3. 412,
magnis (n.) 1. 554; 5. 661,
magnos 1. 462, 769; 8. 339,
magnas 4. 521,
magna 5. 307; 6. 500, 548,
magnis 2. 365, 539; 6. 521,
magnis 1. 658; 2. 222; 5. 83,
magnis 4. 669; 5. 273, 686,
adv. magnum 1. 262,
maior 3. 137; 8. 74,
maior 1. 7; 2. 206, 226, 264,

maria 8. 372,
maria 4. 644 **bis,** 704; 5. 660; 8. 352.
Mariandyni
Mariandynum 4. 171.
Mariandynus
Mariandynis (dat. f.) 4. 733.
maritus
mariti 2. 425; 3. 314; 8. 283,
marito(dat.) 8. 16,
maritos 2. 343.
marmor
marmore 1. 313; 5. 187; 6. 568.
Mars
Mars 6. 28,
Martis 3. 90, 151; 5. 130, 228; 6. 156,
336,
Martem 1. 223; 2. 100; 8. 403 (L; KG
mortem; B que moram),
Marte 1. 810; 5. 276, 601; 6. 39, 436,
602, 751; 8. 395.
Martius
Martius 2. 388; 3. 83; 7. 62, 610,
Martia (nom.) 1. 319; 3. 53, 635; 6. 66,
Martia (nom.) 5. 640.
massa
massae (gen.) 2. 339,
massa 4. 612.
Massagetes
Massageten 5. 125.
Massylus
Massylus 3. 728.
Mater
Matris 7. 635.
mater
mater 1. 428, 493; 2. 203, 536; 3. 660;
6. 149; 7. 171, 199, 376; 8. 140,
matris 2. 87, 153; 3. 47, 265; 6. 58; 7.
148, 303,
matri 4. 34, 241,
matrem 1. 348; 5. 656,
mater 5. 353; 7. 242, 248,
matre 1. 355; 3. 709; 7. 621,
matres 1. 494; 7. 113; 8. 141,
matrum 1. 315; 2. 80, 186, 306; 3. 282,
315,
matribus 1. 324,
matres 2. 133; 3. 247,
matribus 1. 155.
materies
materiem 1. 831.
maternus
materna 2. 325; 6. 224,
materni (m.) 5. 514,
materno (abl.) 5. 266,
materna (abl.) 5. 104; 6. 564.
maturus
matura (nom.) 1. 54,
matura (nom.) 7. 456.
Maurus
Mauri 3, 587.
Mavors
Mavors 5. 667, 671; 6. 178, 280; 7. 645,
Mavortis 6. 694; 7. 519, 544.

Mavortius
Mavortia (nom. f.) 2. 208; 5. 89,
subst. f. Mavortia (nom.) 5. 612.
maximus vid. magnus.
meatus
meatus (nom. s.) 3. 403.
Medea
Medea 5. 239, 257, 330; 6. 44, 157, 276,
439, 575, 667, 757; 7. 252, 381, 409, 632,
637; 8. 92, 203,
Medea (voc.) 7. 589; 8. 142, 312.
medicabilis
medicabile (acc.) 4. 87.
medicamen
medicamina (acc.) 7. 458; 8. 17.
meditor
meditetur 1. 408,
meditantem (f.) 4. 381.
medius
medius 1. 456; 2. 444; 3. 482,
medii 2. 584; 3. 559; 5. 412, 499,
mediae 1. 510; 2. 419; 3. 689; 6. 228,
medii 6. 312, 739,
mediae 1. 487; 5. 402,
medium 2. 266; 6. 251, 364,
mediam 2. 135, 298; 6. 244, 285; 8. 35,
medium 3. 136, 656; 4. 154; 6. 341,
medio 2. 629; 3. 35, 108, 337, 725; 4.
562, 573, 756; 5. 34, 121, 186, 549; 6.
679; 7. 8, 508, 604,
media 1. 821; 3. 49 (L; KBG ad medias), 326; 5. 317; 6. 180,
medio 1. 574, 696; 3. 360; 5. 667; 6. 26,
328, 352, 452, 545, 568; 8. 144,
media 4. 185,
mediis 1. 590; 4. 82; 7. 18,
mediis (f.) 2. 413,
medios 1. 3, 438; 2. 277; 3. 83; 4. 676,
690; 5. 569; 6. 238; 7. 103,
medias 2. 76, 174, 613; 3. 49 (ad medias
KBG; L media); 4. 587; 7. 469,
media 4. 68, 110, 482; 8. 56, 336,
mediis 1. 465; 3. 280, 633; 4. 390, 740;
5. 552; 7. 36, 363,
mediis 1. 571; 2. 3, 532; 3. 44, 417; 4.
198, 492, 518, 695; 7. 403,
mediis 1. 148; 2. 341; 4. 487, 748, 760,
subst. m. medium 2. 346,
medios 3. 440; 4. 531; 7. 634; 8. 257,
subst. n. medium (acc.) 4. 256.
Medon
Medon 3. 118.
Medores
Medores 6. 211.
Medus
Medus 5. 604,
Medum 5. 125.
Medusa
Medusae (gen.) 6. 396.
mel
mellis 6. 145,
mella (acc.) 1. 63; 8. 97.
Melanthus
Melanthum 3. 203.

Melas
Melas 5. 461; 6. 196, 197, 199.
Meleager
Meleagre 1. 435; 6. 719.
Melie
Melie (voc.) 4. 119.
melior vid. bonus.
membrum
membra 6. 362,
membris 3. 680,
membra 1. 813; 3. 378, 423; 5. 29, 244,
membris 6. 610.
memini
memini 8. 181, 182,
meminit 8. 22,
meministis 5. 80,
meminere 8. 242,
memento 4. 601 (KGL; B fluento),
meminisse 1. 249, 773; 2. 81; 3. 580; 5.
583; 7. 204, 481.
memor
memor 1. 46; 2. 422; 3. 649; 4. 37, 593;
5. 4; 7. 477,
memor (f.) 4. 396; 7. 159, 477,
memori (m.) 3. 397,
memorem 5. 528,
memorem 1. 826,
memori (n.) 4. 314,
memores (nom. m.) 4. 84,
memores (acc. f.) 3. 449.
memoratrix
memoratrix 6. 142.
memoro
memorat 2. 66, 649,
memorant 2. 26,
memorabere 3. 170 (L; KBG mirabile),
memorem 4. 445, 600, 718; 5. 606; 6. 36,
memorate 5. 131,
memorare 5. 474,
memoranda (nom. f.) 7. 549,
memoranda (voc. n.) 4. 328.
Memphis
Memphis 3. 361,
Memphin 4. 407.
mendax
mendaci (m.) 6. 501,
mendacem (m.) 7. 650.
Menippe
Menippen 6. 377.
Menoetius
Menoetius 6. 343.
mens
mens 1. 199, 694; 3. 256, 301, 365, 393;
4. 208, 544; 5. 50, 218, 303, 319; 6. 439,
463; 7. 5, 14, 157,
mentis 2. 252; 7. 243,
menti 1. 548; 2. 310; 3. 397 (L; KBG
vati); 8. 160,
mentem 3. 631; 4. 479, 568; 5. 550; 7.
194, 245, 473,
mente 1. 272, 329, 802; 3. 174, 735; 4.
175, 255; 5. 254, 524; 6. 453; 8. 445,
mentes 2. 186,
mentibus 6. 181,

mentes 1. 76; 2. 361 (L; KBG gentes);
4. 103; 6. 476,
mentibus 3. 283.
mensa
mensae 3. 608; 4. 67, 341, 534,
mensae 7. 124,
mensae 1. 142; 2. 651,
mensis 2. 416; 3. 159,
mensas 2. 190; 3. 117, 570; 5. 580, 690;
8. 230,
mensis 4. 497.
mensis
mensis (nom.) 7. 230 (KG; B metis;
L Pontus).
mentior
mentita 6. 698; 7. 211,
mentitae (gen.) 7. 155,
mentitas 3. 618.
mentum
mento (abl.) 2. 150.
meo
meat 7. 543 (BG; K quaeat; L parat),
meant 6. 362.
mereo
merui 8. 431 (KBG; L vetui),
meruere 1. 519; 5. 38,
meruisse 8. 467(KL; BG metuisse),
merenti (dat. f.) 2. 101,
erunt meritae 4. 526,
mereri 1. 197,
meriti 5. 223 **bis,**
meritae 4. 259,
merito 1. 649,
meritae 2. 145,
meritum 7. 421,
meritam 2. 310; 8. 223,
merito 4. 754,
merita (abl.) 7. 484,
meritis 5. 541,
meritis 7. 509,
meritis 1. 797; 7. 267,
meritos 1. 508, 726; 2. 213; 3. 702; 6.
735,
meritas 1. 677; 2. 99; 6. 730,
subst. n. meriti 2. 81; 5. 492; 7. 28, 501,
meritis (dat.) 8. 42,
subst. m. meritos 3. 390.
mergo
mergimus 8. 66,
mergunt 2. 7,
mergere 1. 604,
mersa 8. 274,
mersum (m.) 7. 38,
mersis (abl. f.) 6. 393.
meritus vid. mereo.
merus
subst. n. meri 3. 66,
mero 1. 294; 5. 594,
mero 1. 271 (KG; B viae; L animis).
Messeis
Messeides (nom. f.) 4. 374.
messis
messis (nom.) 7. 549,
messes 7. 69,

messibus 1. 682,
messes 7. 469.
met vid. ego, tu, sui.
meta
  metas 2. 34; 4. 512; 6. 310 (KBG; L
  telas),
  metis 7. 230 (B; KG mensis; L Pontus).
metallum
  metallo (abl.) 1. 261; 5. 230, 632; 6. 672,
  metallis (abl.) 6. 131.
Methone
  Methone (nom.) 1. 388.
metior
  metire 2. 480,
  mensi (nom.) 5. 475.
meto
  metit 7. 367, 621 (L; KBG premit),
  metam (ind.) 3. 671.
metuo
  metuis 8. 77,
  metuam (ind.) 4. 634,
  metuat 1. 418; 7. 178,
  metuant 5. 648,
  metuisset 6. 219,
  metuisse 8. 467 (BG; KL meruisse),
  metuens 1. 509,
  metuens (f.) 1. 331; 6. 459,
  metuentes (acc. f.) 6. 87,
  sit metuenda 4. 610,
  metuendus 8. 218.
metus
  metus 1. 23, 327, 557, 693, 838; 2. 16,
  225, 369; 5. 360; 6. 474; 7. 182,
  metus 3. 329; 4. 201,
  metum 2. 440 (KBL; G metus); 3. 428;
  7. 350,
  metu 1. 179, 802; 3. 94, 254, 269, 405,
  576, 602, 712, 739; 4. 186, 265, 514, 639;
  5. 298, 392, 427; 6. 719; 7. 80, 192, 526,
  metus 4. 181; 6. 408; 7. 242; 8. 198,
  metus 1. 31, 308, 402, 734, 741; 2. 21, 38,
  45, 118, 277, 440 (G; KBL metum); 3.
  53, 395; 4. 703; 5. 286; 6. 660.
meus
  meus 1. 566, 647, 750; 2. 384, 658; 5.
  393; 7. 17, 55, 423; 8. 439,
  mea 1. 53, 518, 563 (KL; BG me),
  mei 1. 799, 811; 5. 130, 517; 8. 273, 427,
  meae 3. 659,
  meo 4. 577; 6. 307,
  meae 1. 549; 7. 67; 8. 40,
  meo 4. 464; 7. 140, 164,
  meam 4. 120,
  meum 5. 486; 7. 130 (KBL; G mecum),
  mea (voc.) 5. 677; 6. 499,
  mea 3. 294; 5. 207; 7. 414,
  meo 2. 244; 5. 545,
  meae 1. 544,
  mea 1. 605; 3. 297,
  meorum 6. 475,
  mearum 1. 536,
  meorum 5. 246,
  meis (n.) 5. 535; 6. 625 (vid. abl.),
  meos 7. 46, 269; 8. 12,

meas 8. 337,
mea 1. 347, 643; 2. 600; 3. 260; 4. 211,
445, 450, 586, 741; 5. 674; 7. 182, 274,
447; 8. 435,
meis (m.) 5. 629,
meis (n.) 4. 753; 6. 625 (vid. dat.); 7.
291,
subst. m. meorum 1. 201; 8. 46,
meos 3. 270; 5. 503.
mico
  micat 2. 55; 5. 410; 8. 73, 122, 310, 333,
  micant 3. 558; 6. 404, 605; 7. 631 (K;
  BGL volant),
  micet 5. 203,
  micent 3. 76.
migro
  migrantibus (dat. n.) 8. 201.
miles
  miles 7. 77,
  miles 6. 55,
  milite 8. 356.
militia
  militam 1. 40.
mille
  mille (nom. f.) 5. 316,
  mille (acc.) 1. 382,
  mille 1. 754; 2. 129,
  mille 1. 715; 2. 503; 6. 37; 7. 271,
  mille (m.) 1. 727,
  subst. n. milibus 7. 622,
  milia 6. 167, 172,
  milibus 5. 273 (KBG; L molibus); 6.
  60.
mina
  minae (nom.) 3. 354; 4. 650; 5. 359; 8.
  2,
  minas 1. 27, 216, 606, 768; 2. 21; 3. 446,
  449 (KL; B animos; G animas); 5.
  256, 650; 6. 306,
  minis 3. 511; 5. 341; 8. 413.
minax
  minax (f.) 3. 579,
  minaci (abl.) 5. 519,
  minaci (f.) 1. 722,
  minacibus (abl. n.) 5. 259.
Minerva
  Minervae (gen.) 5. 504; 8. 203.
minister
  minister 5. 694,
  ministro (abl.) 2. 417,
  ministri 1. 253, 689; 2. 652; 3. 121
  (KGL; B sinistrum); 8. 242.
ministerium
  ministeria (acc.) 3. 710.
ministra
  ministram 2. 123.
ministro
  ministrat 3. 38; 4. 8; 6. 216.
Minoius
  Minoia (nom. f.) 1. 706; 7. 279.
minor
  minatur 4. 289; 8. 459,
  minantem 1. 337; 3. 552; 7. 597; 8. 358,
  minantem 6. 519; 7. 577,

minanti (n.) 4. 178,
minantes (nom. m.) 7. 653.
minor vid. **parvus.**
minus (13)
  minus 5. 641; 6. 659,
  haut minus 1. 415,
  nec minus 2. 426, 542; 3. 267; 5. 375,
  416; 6. 350, 542; 7. 23,
  nec minus et 4. 56,
  nec minus interea 3. 611.
  Vid. quam.
Minyae
  Minyae 1. 184, 519; 2. 370; 3. 272, 284;
  4. 6, 82, 246, 529, 693; 5. 28, 167; 6.
  427; 8. 212, 307, 378, 385, 415,
  Minyis 1. 274, 439, 621; 2. 15; 3. 219,
  256; 4. 423; 5. 290, 298, 507; 7. 90; 8.
  176,
  Minyas 1. 227, 310; 2. 324, 437; 3. 74,
  363; 4. 98, 298, 433; 5. 47, 455, 620, 634,
  679; 6. 4, 16, 116, 436, 482, 595; 7. 26,
  115, 189, 474; 8. 227, 319, 328 (KBG; L
  Colchos), 371,
  Minyis 3. 347.
mirabilis
  mirabile (acc.) 3. 170 (KBG; L memorabere).
miraculum
  miracula (acc.) 5. 451.
miror
  miraris 7. 444,
  miratur 2. 638; 3. 692; 4. 246, 534; 5.
  568; 6. 720,
  mirantur 1. 849; 2. 554; 5. 173,
  mirabar 7. 264,
  mirabere 1. 382; 2. 339; 4. 53,
  mirabitur 7. 471,
  mirata est 7. 337 (KGL; B miserata
  est),
  mirere 5. 584,
  miretur 1. 269,
  mirans (m.) 4. 324,
  miranti (m.) 5. 470, 597,
  mirantem (f.) 6. 489,
  mirantibus (f.) 4. 313,
  mirantia 4. 759,
  miranda (acc.) 1. 149 (KBG; L mirata),
  mirata (nom.) 2. 351; 5. 374; 6. 446;
  7. 78,
  mirati (nom.) 5. 150,
  mirata (acc.) 1. 149 (L; KBG miranda),
  subst. n. miranda (acc.) 2. 467.
mirus
  mira (nom. f.) 4. 551; 5. 226.
misceo
  miscet 6. 166, 631; 7. 373 (pavens . . .
  oscula miscet K; BGL vocemque . . .
  paventem),
  miscent 1. 635; 5. 60,
  miscebant 6. 428,
  miscuit 4. 518; 7. 406,
  miscere 1. 247, 586; 3. 310, 381,
  miscentur 4. 657,

mixta 6. 200,
mixtum (m.) 5. 305,
mixta (voc.) 4. 119,
mixto (n.) 5. 99,
mixti 2. 240,
mixtae 6. 188,
mixtas 4. 686 (B; KGL mixtis),
mixtis (f.) 4. 686 (KGL; B mixtas).
miser
  miser 5. 654; 6. 324; 7. 81, 138, 304; 8.
  408,
  miserae 1. 292; 2. 578; 4. 45, 86, 395;
  7. 152,
  miseri 4. 113 (K; BGL miseris),
  misero 4. 451, 490; 6. 215, 316, 629; 7.
  317, 455,
  miserae 2. 531; 6. 586; 7. 107; 8. 4,
  misero 6. 669,
  miserum 7. 411,
  miseram 7. 241,
  miserum 2. 294 (L; KBG serum),
  miser 1. 225; 7. 533,
  misero 1. 637; 3. 740,
  misera 6. 418,
  misero 2. 234; 4. 153; 6. 510,
  miseri 6. 128 (miseri tam KBG; L
  miserandi), 648; 8. 154,
  miserae 3. 69, 592; 6. 666,
  miseris 1. 573, 631; 4. 597; 6. 656,
  miseris (f.) 1. 648,
  miseros 1. 150, 449, 665; 3. 273, 392; 5.
  349; 7. 638,
  miseras 3. 250; 4. 107, 500,
  misera 3. 316,
  subst. misero (m.) 2. 284,
  misera (voc.) 6. 498,
  miseris (m.) 1. 685; 4. 113 (BGL; K
  miseri), 470; 6. 733,
  miseros 2. 154,
  miseri 2. 378,
  miserrima (nom. f.) 4. 455.
misereo (misereor)
  miserent 2. 92,
  miserebitur 7. 286,
  miserere 1. 326; 2. 253, 256; 8. 420.
miseresco
  miserescite 4. 446.
miseror
  miseratur 8. 55, 250,
  miserantur 8. 207,
  miserata est 7. 337 (B; KGL mirata
  est),
  miserans (m.) 4. 481,
  miserantem (m.) 2. 558,
  miserantibus (f.) 1. 281,
  miserantes (m.) 1. 72,
  miseratus 2. 496; 4. 2,
  miserata (nom. f.) 2. 19; 3. 195; 5.
  278; 7. 142, 413,
  miseranda 6. 688; 7. 121; 8. 9,
  miserande 6. 319,
  miserandi 6. 128 (L; KBG miseri tam),
  miseranda (nom.) 6. 362,
  subst. miserande 3. 116, 290; 8. 99,
  miseranda (voc. f.) 7. 235.

missilis
 subst. n. missile (acc.) 6. 340, 540,
 missilibus (abl.) 6. 191.
mitesco
 mitescat 5. 518,
 mitescere 7. 281.
mitis
 mitis 4. 740,
 mitis (nom.) 2. 305; 7. 3,
 mites (m.) 4. 706,
 mitia (nom.) 2. 646,
 adv. mite 8. 10 (L; KBG ille),
 mitior (m.) 4. 591.
mitra
 mitra (abl.) 2. 271; 5. 148.
mitto
 mittit 2. 75; 3. 401; 5. 546; 6. 620; 7.
 587 (KG; B mulcet; L prendit),
 mittunt 5. 88,
 misit 1. 815; 6. 66; 8. 35, 131,
 misere 1. 545,
 mittet 1. 19; 7. 448,
 miserat 1. 474; 6. 42, 406,
 misisset 3. 313,
 mitte 1. 308, 741; 4. 471; 6. 334 **bis**,
 538,
 mittere 4. 489; 5. 262,
 mittitur 3. 474,
 mittimur 1. 152,
 mittatur 7. 98,
 missus 1. 360; 4. 312,
 missa (nom. f.) 2. 440,
 missos 1. 625.
modo (29)
 modo 1. 211; 2. 245, 290, 404; 3. 328,
 638 (modo iurgia K; BL periuria; G
 in iurgia); 4. 360, 739; 5. 265, 507; 6.
 407; 7. 146, 259, 468, 574, 632; 8. 211,
 241, 349, 417,
 modo (= dum modo) 3. 233; 4. 192; 5.
 205; 8. 51,
 modo (c. impv.) 7. 61,
 modo . . . modo 6. 543, 616.
 Vid. dummodo.
modulor
 modulatur 4. 386.
modus
 modus 1. 294; 4. 476; 8. 272,
 modum 4. 584; 5. 388,
 modo 3. 555; 5. 675; 7. 139,
 modis (abl.) 3. 122, 393; 6. 446.
moenia
 moenia 1. 477; 5. 394; 6. 329,
 moenibus 2. 565; 8. 276,
 moenia 1. 92, 753, 846; 2. 250, 340, 394;
 3. 63, 247; 4. 58; 6. 490; 7. 191, 374, 380,
 538,
 moenibus 2. 308; 3. 229; 7. 90, 423.
Moesus
 Moesus 6. 162,
 adi. Moesi (nom.) 2. 360 (BGL; K
 maesti).
moles
 moles 1. 127,
 molis 3. 479; 7. 599,

molem 1. 499, 599, 829; 2. 32, 353, 518;
 6. 104, 349,
 mole 1. 758; 2. 28; 4. 232, 322; 5. 282,
 365; 6. 673; 8. 98,
 molibus (abl.) 1. 581; 5. 273 (L; KBG
 milibus).
molimen
 molimine 6. 34.
molior
 molitur 3. 154, 491; 5. 248; 6. 431, 650,
 molimur 5. 625,
 moliar (subi.) 6. 625,
 moliri 1. 94.
mollio
 molliri 1. 125.
mollis
 mollem (f.) 7. 304,
 molli 1. 686; 6. 239,
 molli 1. 252, 480; 6. 233; 7. 127,
 molli 1. 365, 430,
 molles (acc.) 7. 295,
 molles 6. 365.
moneo
 monet 3. 580, 614,
 monebat 7. 324,
 monebo 5. 677,
 monuit 3. 79,
 moneas 5. 54,
 moneant 6. 17,
 mone 1. 5; 6. 34,
 monens (m.) 5. 260,
 monentis (m.) 3. 327,
 monentem (m.) 4. 142,
 monenti (n.) 5. 65,
 subst. n. monitis 7. 187, 349,
 monitis 2. 385; 4. 569; 6. 117.
Moneses
 Monesen 6. 189.
Monesus
 Monesi 6. 651.
monile
 monile (acc.) 8. 18,
 monilia (acc.) 6. 668.
monitum vid. moneo.
monitus
 monitu (abl.) 1. 184, 231; 4. 27,
 monitus 1. 29; 4. 187,
 monitus 1. 475; 4. 523; 5. 127.
mons
 mons 6. 84,
 montis 1. 484; 2. 633; 3. 521, 604, 695;
 4. 96, 260; 5. 169; 6. 383, 634,
 montem 4. 316, 508,
 monte 1. 593; 3. 28; 5. 161; 7. 370
 (KBG; L forte),
 montes 1. 556; 3. 585; 4. 65, 583,
 montibus 1. 590,
 montes 1. 198, 656; 2. 20, 39, 381; 3.
 257 (L; KBG portus), 484, 537 (L;
 KBG fontes); 4. 52, 248, 645, 707; 8.
 193, 216,
 montibus 2. 479, 620; 3. 332, 353, 591,
 652, 687; 4. 21, 202, 576, 677, 755; 5.
 172, 253, 425; 6. 220, 321; 8. 289.

monstrifer
monstriferae (dat.) 5. 43,
monstriferae 2. 498,
monstriferis (abl. m.) 5. 221.
monstrificus
monstrificae (nom.) 6. 153.
monstro
monstrat 1. 848 (KG; BL monstra);
2. 61 (KBG; L monstrant); 3. 435; 8.
324,
monstrant 2. 61 (L; KBG monstrat),
monstrabat 7. 253,
monstrarat 6. 205,
monstrantem (m.) 5. 572,
monstrantia (nom.) 1. 276,
monstrata (nom.) 7. 366,
monstrata (nom.) 7. 390 (G; KBL
montana),
monstrata 5. 407.
monstrum
monstrum 2. 479,
monstri 1. 374; 2. 514; 3. 567; 4. 188,
605; 6. 45; 7. 536,
monstro 4. 155, 750,
monstrum 5. 657; 6. 6,
monstra 1. 848 (BL; KG monstrat);
7. 522,
monstris 2. 217; 3. 512; 4. 456; 7. 267,
420,
monstra 1. 33; 2. 17; 3. 29, 356, 610,
665; 4. 462, 506; 5. 482; 6. 437,
monstris 2. 248, 489; 3. 261; 4. 370; 5.
259, 329; 6. 470; 7. 345.
montanus
montana (nom. n.) 7. 390 (KBL; G
monstrata).
monumentum
monumentum (acc.) 5. 229; 6. 500; 8.
119.
Monychus
Monychus 1. 146.
Mopsus
Mopsus 1. 207, 384; 3. 98, 378; 4. 546;
5. 9, 95; 8. 248, 398,
Mopso 1. 234,
Mopsum 3. 372.
mora
mora 2. 303; 3. 490, 599 (BGL; K morae); 4. 129, 572; 5. 60, 548, 558; 6. 97,
733; 7. 219, 514; 8. 112,
morae (gen.) 3. 599 (K; BGL mora),
613; 8. 303,
moram 8. 403 (que moram B; KG
mortem; L Martem),
morae 8. 192,
moras 1. 306; 2. 356, 407; 3. 174, 375,
503 (L; KBG nefas), 574, 626, 657; 4.
458, 627; 5. 546; 6. 127, 290; 7. 33, 576;
8. 105.
morbus
morbi (nom.) 2. 475,
morbis (abl.) 5. 2.
moribundus
moribundus 6. 273,
moribundae (gen.) 5. 175.

morior
moriere 3. 105; 4. 243,
moreretur 7. 135,
mori 4. 382; 6. 241; 7. 352, 537; 8. 316,
453,
moriens (m.) 6. 244, 315,
moritura 7. 335,
moriturum (m.) 6. 630,
morituram 7. 484,
subst. m. morituri (gen.) 7. 266.
moror
moratur 3. 70, 486; 6. 615,
moramur 3. 273,
morantur 2. 169; 3. 335; 5. 28,
morabor 7. 60,
morari 3. 328; 7. 178,
morantis (m) 7. 33 (KGL; B moventis),
morantem 5. 156 (KG; B novantem;
L moventem),
morantem 4. 371,
morantes (acc. m.) 6. 280,
morantis (m.) 1. 350,
morantes 3. 381,
moratus 1. 522; 4. 243,
moratis (abl. m.) 1. 459.
Mors
Mors (voc.) 1. 327.
mors
mors 1. 803; 2. 469 (BG; KL sors); 4.
147; 5. 26,
mortis 1. 648; 6. 109, 125,
morti 4. 129,
mortem 6. 655; 8. 403 (KG; B que moram; L Martem), 431,
morte 1. 821, 824; 3. 327; 4. 459; 7. 282,
285, 314, 337, 342, 414,
mortes (nom.) 7. 332.
morsus
morsu (abl.) 2. 459.
mortalis
mortalia 3. 93; 4. 201,
mortales (f.) 1. 837; 2. 361,
mortalia 3. 378, 674,
subst. m. mortalibus (dat.) 4. 95, 526;
7. 568.
mos
mos 5. 582; 6. 125; 7. 95,
morem 2. 90,
more 1. 779; 3. 126; 4. 138; 5. 404; 6.
640; 8. 32,
moribus (abl.) 3. 646 (pro moribus L;
KBG potioribus).
**Mossynoeci (KG; B Mossonychi; L
Mossyni)**
Mossynoeci 5. 151.
motus
motu (abl.) 1. 578 (BGL; K motus); 3.
113, 244, 686; 6. 382 (L; KBG nutu),
motus (acc.) 1. 525; 3. 73,
motibus 5. 309.
moveo
movet 2. 102; 3. 415, 612; 4. 40; 5. 19,
99, 398; 6. 10, 70, 403; 7. 59, 131; 8.
352, 455,

movent 1. 616; 2. 328; 4. 219; 8. 402, 416,
movebant 2. 110; 5. 21, 296,
movebo 3. 520; 5. 291,
movebimus 5. 44,
movit 3. 19, 466, 494; 6. 74; 7. 222; 8.
210,
movimus 5. 661,
moverat 2. 357,
moveat 1. 757,
moverem 6. 728,
moveret 3. 540 (B; KGL moventem),
moverit 5. 529,
move 4. 13,
movens 5. 228, 305; 6. 37, 623,
movens (f.) 3. 61,
moventis (m.) 7. 33 (B; KGL morantis),
moventem (m.) 3. 540 (KGL; B moveret); 5. 78, 156 (L; KG morantem;
B novantem), 303 (K; BGL novantem); 6. 535,
moventes (nom. m.) 2. 477,
moture 1. 393,
movetur 2. 522 (KG; BL moveri); 6.
718,
moverer 7. 288,
moveri 2. 522 (BL; KG movetur); 7.
203,
motus 1. 578 (K; BGL motu),
mota 7. 175,
motum (nom.) 2. 513 (vid. acc.),
motum (n.) 2. 513 (vid. nom.),
mota 4. 609,
moto 4. 657 (L; KBG toto),
moti 4. 174; 5. 464,
motas 3. 238,
motis 3. 624,
motis 2. 122,
motis 2. 73; 3. 232,
movendis (dat. n.) 6. 14,
movendo (abl.) 1. 558.
mox (38)
1. 64, 300, 371, 556, 645, 745; 2. 71, 87,
122, 134, 349, 415, 575; 3. 520; 4. 36,
197, 216, 341, 360, 505, 524, 528; 5.
105, 136, 235, 338, 683; 6. 42, 139, 513,
7. 366, 484; 8. 14, 132, 137, 252, 414.
mugio
mugire 2. 498; 7. 591.
mugitor
mugitor 3. 208.
mulceo
mulcet 1. 299; 4. 358; 7. 587 (B; KG
mittit; L prendit),
mulcent 2. 140,
mulcebat 3. 718,
mulcere 8. 465,
mulcens 4. 443,
mulcens (f.) 1. 643.
Mulciber
Mulciber 2. 315; 5. 433.
mulctrum
mulctra (nom.) 6. 145.

multifidus
multifidus 4. 661,
multifidum (acc. n.) 4. 93,
multifidas 1. 61.
multus
multus 3. 693,
multo (abl.) 1. 140; 6. 704; 7. 458,
multa 1. 613, 775; 2. 465; 3. 716; 5. 6,
588,
multo 6. 358,
subst. n. multa (acc.) 1. 174; 4. 84; 5.
303, 597 (K; BGL nulla),
adv. multum 1. 459,
adv. multo 2. 209,
adv. multa 1. 757; 4. 371,
plures (acc. f.) 8. 389,
plura 3. 671 (KG; B dura; L rupta);
4. 619,
subst. n. pluris 3. 626,
plura (acc.) 1. 174; 2. 576; 4. 243,
adv. plus 7. 60,
plurimus 1. 677,
plurima (nom. f.) 2. 663; 6. 223, 262.
mundus
mundi 2. 41; 4. 564,
mundo 1. 501, 563,
mundum 1. 831,
mundo 1. 246; 3. 418.
munus
muneris 4. 366,
munere 1. 478, 660; 2. 69; 4. 23; 5. 449,
munera 7. 226,
muneribus 8. 42,
munera 2. 330; 3. 276, 313, 336 (munera
fert L; KG funereae; B inferiae); 4.
362; 5. 14, 30, 511; 7. 446, 482,
muneribus 3. 10.
murex
murice 3. 340, 727; 5. 360; 6. 704.
murmur
murmur 8. 354,
murmur 5. 469; 7. 606,
murmure 1. 626; 3. 588; 4. 239; 7. 464,
murmura (acc.) 1. 596; 2. 338; 5. 121,
651; 8. 211.
murra
murra (abl.) 8. 347.
murus
muri (gen.) 2. 553; 6. 383,
murorum 6. 503,
muros 2. 491; 5. 274; 6. 484; 8. 269,
muris 1. 593; 3. 52; 4. 102; 6. 575, 681,
753.
Musa
Musa (voc.) 3. 213; 6. 34, 516,
Musarum 5. 693.
mutabilis
mutabile (acc.) 1. 761.
mutator
mutator 6. 161.
muto
mutat 6. 443, 614,
mutabere 6. 269,
mutandum (nom.) 8. 183,
mutata (nom. f.) 4. 398; 7. 211.

mutuus
mutua (acc.) 1. 550; 5. 624.
Mycael (K; BGL **Mycaei**)
Mycael 6. 129.
Mycenae
Mycenae 3. 655,
Mycenas 1. 552.
Mycenaeus
Mycenaeis (abl. n.) 1. 381.
Mycene
Mycenes 5. 645.
Mygdon
Mygdonis 3. 320.
Mygdonius
Mygdoniae (gen.) 3. 47,
Mygdonios 8. 239.
Myrace
Myracen 6. 50.
Myraces
Myraces 6. 690, 717.
myrtus
myrtus 3. 524.
Mysia
Mysia (nom.) 3. 484.
nam (31)
1. 27, 395, 399, 445, 549 (KG; BL iam);
2. 179, 278, 644; 3. 345, 564, 568; 4. 158,
227, 463, 476, 692, 709, 717; 5. 144, 389,
556; 6. 110 (KBG; L iam), 265, 330
(L; KBG nunc), 589; 7. 16, 170, 488;
8. 139, 160, 377.
namque (18)
1. 13, 49 (K; BGL meque); 2. 490, 570,
630; 4. 155, 471; 5. 292, 333, 395, 477,
500 (B; KGL iamque), 540; 6. 123; 7.
136; 8. 42, 180, 397.
naris
naribus (abl.) 1. 221.
nascor
nasci 1. 133,
nascentibus (dat. n.) 6. 451,
subst. natus 1. 149; 4. 313; 6. 127, 306
(KBL; G nato),
nata 2. 229, 306; 3. 544; 4. 683; 5. 648,
687,
nati 1. 264, 503, 799, 811; 3. 81; 4. 2,
17, 115; 6. 311; 8. 22,
natae 1. 522; 5. 219,
nato 1. 509; 6. 288, 306 (G; KBL natus), 316, 652,
natum 1. 407, 739, 764, 769, 846; 2. 551;
4. 131; 6. 300, 566, 624,
natam 7. 101,
nate 1. 320, 713; 4. 125,
nata 5. 677; 7. 229, 550; 8. 145, 162,
nato 1. 373, 731,
nati 1. 729; 2. 203; 4. 89; 6. 627; 7. 486
(KBL; G natae),
natae 2. 247; 7. 486 (G; KBL nati),
natorum 2. 308, 395; 5. 23, 83; 6. 475,
natis (m.) 1. 1; 6. 286,
natos 1. 150, 553; 2. 181, 185; 5. 572;
6. 337; 8. 251,
natas 5. 614; 7. 49; 8. 148 (KGL; B
nuptas), 156.

natalis
natale (nom.) 6. 62,
natales (acc. f.) 3. 321.
nato
natantia (acc.) 3. 150 (KL; B liquentia; G labantia).
natus vid. nascor.
Naubolides
Naubolides 1. 362.
naufragus
naufragus 8. 360,
naufraga (nom. f.) 1. 584.
Nauplius
Nauplius 1. 372; 5. 65.
nauta
nautis 1. 276, 573; 3. 577,
nautas 2. 436; 7. 262.
nauticus
nauticus 1. 187.
navalis
navalem (m.) 8. 298.
navita
navita (nom.) 2. 443.
navo
navet 3. 145.
ne (42)
1. c. subi.
1. 200 (KGL; B nec), 472; 2. 3, 5; 4.
37, 606; 5. 240 (BGL; K neu), 286,
401, 507; 6. 316, 335, 436, 743; 7. 80, 81,
183, 201a (KB; G **om.**; L vel), 273,
274, 415, 551 (L; KB in; G quin); 8.
282,
nequis (etc.) 1. 179, 478, 509; 3. 490;
8. 51,
ne . . . neve 3. 306,
2. c. impv.
1. 215; 2. 251, 596; 4. 125, 154, 218
(KB; GL nec), 581, 592; 5. 592; 7. 288,
449; 8. 12, 436,
Vid. forte.
ne (36)
ne 1. 151, 506; 2. 180, 403; 3. 230, 294,
300 **bis**, 703; 4. 63, 120, 242, 243, 467,
633; 6. 675; 7. 50 **bis**, 200 (GL; KB ve),
331, 386, 417, 490, 541; 8. 149, 441, 467,
-n 2. 292; 3. 499,
ne . . . an 1. 71, 630, 759; 3. 374; 4.
157; 7. 131, 413.
Neaera
Neaerae (gen.) 2. 141.
Nealces
Nealcen 3. 191.
nebula
nebulam 5. 465; 6. 745.
neco
necat 6. 638 (BGL; K notat).
nec (neque) (390)
nec 1. 38, 64, 84, 133, 149 (B; KGL
haec), 174, 175, 198, 200 (B; KGL ne),
304, 321, 327, 332, 368, 403, 413, 439,
521, 525, 546, 582, 601, 615, 699, 701,
716, 764, 799, 810, 813; 2. 49, 56, 80,

84, 95, 149, 170, 232, 303, 314, 327, 345, 355, 558, 607, 634, 662; 3. 5, 75, 120, 161, 173, 255, 299, 335, 362, 460, 518, 555, 599, 669, 714; 4. 14, 53, 119, 124, 163, 173, 185, 200, 218, 218 (GL; KB ne), 243, 251, 300, 331, 399, 414, 447, 458, 477, 483, 491, 499, 540, 546, 578, 603, 619, 621, 634, 639, 675 (L; KBG vel), 696, 715 (KBG; L sed), 730; 5. 21, 45, 75, 264, 400, 479 (que nec BGL; K neque), 489, 539, 541, 542, 568, 601, 633, 639, 648, 666, 678; 6. 2, 25, 52, 55, 73, 92, 99, 156, 176, 192, 250, 273, 320, 329, 332, 357, 411, 430, 452, 469, 519, 524, 537, 548, 568, 570, 609, 661, 682, 703; 7. 7, 19, 68, 94, 95, 130, 172, 182, 229, 233, 274, 340 (GL; KB non), 354, 361, 387, 420 (G; K dic; B nunc; L cur), 430, 435, 445, 482, 487, 622, 642, 651; 8. 22, 80, 96, 99, 103, 112, 167, 198, 206, 225, 277, 303, 310, 339, 347, 370 (G; K heu; BL nunc), 390, 395, 409, 413, 418,
necdum 1. 53, 102; 2. 517 (KBG; L nox tum); 3. 366, 622 (BGL; K nec tum); 4. 208, 563; 5. 257; 6. 181; 7. 154, 619,
dum . . . necdum 1. 607,
necdum . . . nec 3. 317,
nec enim 3. 681; 6. 488,
nec iam 1. 649; 2. 372; 4. 129; 8. 47,
nec minus 2. 426, 542; 3. 267, 630; 5. 375, 416; 6. 350, 542; 7. 23,
nec minus et 4. 56,
nec minus interea 3. 611,
nec. . . nec 1. 118, 261; 2. 479; 3. 70, 88, 122, 345, 383, 452, 454, 622; 4. 204, 232, 278, 396, 547; 5. 58, 112, 206, 316, 359, 497, 553, 558, 562; 6. 36, 98, 163, 174, 482, 594, 605, 713; 7. 104, 297, 339, 433; 8. 3, 179, 320,
nec . . . nec . . . nec 3. 733; 4. 227; 8. 270,
nec . . . neque 2. 623,
nec non 2. 664,
numquam . . . nec 3. 401,
nec tamen 5. 501, 586,
nec tum 3. 622 (K; BGL necdum),
nec ullus (etc.) 1. 539; 2. 479; 3. 317; 4. 130; 5. 359, 662; 6. 76, 146; 7. 339; 8. 4, 271, 435,
nec . . . umquam 1. 118; 3. 452,
nec usquam 6. 500,
nec vero 1. 470; 4. 703, 751,
neque 2. 641; 3. 288; 4. 642; 5. 320, 627; 6. 417, 499; 8. 196,
neque enim 1. 166, 500, 533, 587, 783; 2. 2, 102, 490, 603; 3. 210; 6. 22, 37, 657; 7. 456 (KG; BL que etenim); 8. 265,
neque iam 1. 17; 3. 708,
neque . . . nec 2. 490; 3. 570, 708; 4. 128, 427, 679; 5. 479 (K; BGL que nec . . . nec), 652; 6. 615,
neque . . . nec . . . nec 8. 248,
neque . . . neque 1. 33; 3. 262; 7. 319,
sed neque 8. 247,

neque ullus (etc.) 1. 33, 533; 2. 166; 6. 37,
Vid. sed.
necdum vid. nec.
nectar
nectare 1. 396; 4. 15.
necto
nectunt 3. 374,
necte 3. 503,
nectentem (m.) 5. 79,
nectuntur 6. 297,
nexas 6. 136 (KGL; B nexis),
nexis (m.) 6. 136 (B; KGL nexas).
nefandus
nefandae (gen.) 1. 779; 2. 396,
nefandam 3. 385,
nefando 4. 516; 8. 390,
nefanda (abl.) 4. 32.
nefas
nefas 1. 808, 834; 3. 186, 258, 503 (KBG; L moras); 4. 624, 692; 5. 39; 8. 159, 168, 267, 434,
nefas 1. 598, 747; 2. 101, 210, 568; 3. 284, 301; 6. 453; 8. 108.
nego
negat 3. 736; 5. 264, 554; 7. 306, 318 (dein negat BL; KG denegat),
negant 5. 29,
negabo 6. 628,
negem 5. 287,
negaret 4. 364,
negatum (m.) 5. 102.
Nelides
Nelides 1. 388; 4. 224.
Nemea
Nemeae (gen.) 8. 125.
Nemee
Nemees 2. 495,
Nemeen 3. 511.
nempe (10)
3. 513, 674, 675; 4. 462; 6. 282 **bis**; 7. 414, 440, 441; 8. 49.
nemus
nemus 1. 577; 2. 304, 598; 4. 26,
nemoris 7. 403; 8. 25,
nemus 1. 122, 685, 755; 2. 549; 3. 181, 531; 5. 254, 637; 6. 497; 7. 167; 8. 31, 78,
nemora 1. 728; 3. 467,
nemorum 3. 48, 444, 523, 595; 6. 633,
nemora 1. 664; 2. 478.
Nephelaeus
Nephelaei (n.) 1. 56.
nepos
nepos 5. 687,
nepotem 1. 737,
nepotes 5. 500; 6. 291,
nepotum 1. 790,
nepotibus 1. 249,
nepotes 1. 523; 2. 594; 3. 14 (K; BGL penates); 8. 398.
Neptunius
Neptunius 1. 363,
Neptunia (nom. f.) 1. 415; 2. 617; 4. 213, 256; 5. 164.

Neptunus
Neptunus 1. 212, 641; 2. 26, 491, 497; 4. 114,
Neptuni 4. 150, 213,
Neptuno 4. 109,
Neptune 1. 456,
Neptuno 5. 478.
neque vid. nec.
nequeo
nequit 1. 595; 4. 323, 544; 7. 122,
nequeat 1. 804; 4. 220; 5. 670 (nequeat sic KBG; L cedam tibi).
nequiquam (14)
1. 287, 721; 4. 139; 5. 198; 6. 250, 257, 623, 643; 7. 27, 153, 197, 334, 382; 8. 139.
Nereus
Nereus 1. 658,
Nerea 1. 450.
nervus
nervo (abl.) 1. 437; 3. 182; 6. 376.
nescio
nescio 7. 60, 323; 8. 441,
nescis 7. 341,
nescit 6. 200,
nesciat 7. 140.
nescius
nescius 3. 188; 4. 253, 709; 6. 45; 7. 80,
nescia (nom. f.) 1. 515; 6. 491, 587.
Nessus
Nessus 1. 147.
Nestor
Nestor 3. 143 (KGL; B nostro),
Nestoris 6. 569,
Nestora 1. 145,
Nestor 1. 380.
Neurus
Neurus 6. 122.
neve (neu)
1. c. subi.
neu 5. 240 (K; BGL ne),
ne . . . neve 3. 308,
2. c. impv.
neve 6. 539,
neu 7. 225.
nex
necis 6. 419,
neci 1. 696; 2. 456; 6. 557; 7. 279,
necem 3. 386; 6. 191,
nece 5. 339; 6. 626,
neces (acc.) 3. 381.
nexus
nexu (abl.) 6. 341,
nexibus 6. 260 (vid. abl.),
nexus 7. 626,
nexibus 6. 260 (vid. dat.); 7. 535.
ni
c. subi.
2. 315; 5. 654; 6. 740.
nidus
nido (abl.) 7. 376.
niger
niger 1. 578, 783; 2. 45, 365; 4. 452; 7. 647,
nigram 2. 106,
nigro 1. 147; 3. 404,

nigra 6. 716,
nigro 1. 816; 6. 111,
nigris (abl. f.) 2. 195,
nigris 2. 332.
nigresco
nigrescunt 4. 260.
nigro
nigrantem (m.) 1. 13,
nigrantia (acc.) 4. 697.
nihil (nil)
nil 5. 298, 299,
nil 1. 46, 702 **bis**; 3. 231, 394, 641; 8. 154, 420,
nihil (acc.) 5. 543; 6. 488; 7. 388,
adv. nil 1. 605; 3. 560; 7. 248.
Nilus
Nilus 1. 20; 4. 409; 8. 91,
Nili 3. 361; 7. 607,
Nile 4. 346.
nimbosus
nimbosum (acc. n.) 2. 357 (L; KBG nimboso),
nimboso (n.) 2. 357 (KBG; L nimbosum).
nimbus
nimbus 4. 452,
nimbo 4. 263,
nimbo 1. 83; 2. 115,
nimbi 1. 584,
nimborum 1. 612; 6. 505,
nimbos 2. 371; 4. 662,
nimbis 2. 198; 3. 102; 6. 715.
nimis
7. 160.
nimius
nimio (m.) 8. 436,
nimio (abl.) 1. 179,
nimia (abl.) 1. 227 (G; K om.; B hac vates; L longa),
adv. nimium 5. 4, 50; 7. 336; 8. 411.
Nisaeus
Nisaeum 3. 198.
nisi
1. c. subi.
nisi 7. 200,
2. c. abl. absol.
nisi 1. 305.
nisus
nisu (abl.) 5. 157.
niteo
nitet 2. 65,
niteat 2. 68,
nitentes (acc. m.) 5. 412,
nitentia 3. 422.
nitidus
nitidus 3. 467,
nitidi (m.) 3. 553,
nitidum 5. 565,
nitidum 3. 429,
nitidis (abl. m.) 1. 135 (K; BGL nudis).
nitor
nititur 1. 358,
nitentem (m.) 7. 590.

nivalis
nivali (abl. m.) 5. 204.

niveus
nivea (abl.) 2. 271,
niveo 1. 431,
nivei 1. 90,
niveum (m.) 6. 102,
niveos 1. 219.

nix
nix 7. 563,
nivem 5. 306; 6. 325,
nive 5. 174,
nives 1. 691,
nives 7. 358.

no
nabat 8. 360 (B; KGL ibat).

Noas
Noae (gen.) 6. 100 (BG; KL Novae).

nobilis
nobilis (m.) 1. 367,
nobile (nom.) 1. 359.

noceo
nocens (f.) 2. 327; 7. 461; 8. 426,
nocendi 3. 488.

noctivagus
noctivagum (acc. n.) 2. 44.

nocturnus
nocturnus 6. 538 (L; KBG nocturnis),
nocturna 3. 19 (vid. acc.),
nocturnae (gen.) 7. 521,
nocturna (nom.) 3. 52,
nocturnis (f.) 6. 538 (KBG; L nocturnus),
nocturnis (f.) 6. 440,
subst. n. nocturna (acc.) 3. 19 (vid. nom. f.).

nodosus
nodosi (n.) 2. 534; 8. 298.

nodus
nodo (abl.) 6. 63,
nodis (abl.) 3. 124; 5. 578 (KL; BG nobis); 6. 378.

nomen
nomen 2. 468; 4. 185,
nominis 4. 735,
nomen 1. 540; 3. 171, 563; 4. 136, 161, 161 (K; BG numen; L famam), 313, 465; 5. 100; 7. 130,
nomine 2. 329, 586; 3. 600; 4. 419, 649; 5. 152, 589; 6. 36; 7. 39; 8. 174, 217,
nomina 1. 790; 4. 225, 347,
nomina 1. 352; 2. 466; 3. 426, 725; 5. 61, 119, 480, 655; 7. 275; 8. 463.

non (268)
non 1. 113, 127, 153, 164, 186, 198, 202, 229, 244, 284, 338, 372, 383, 411, 418, 441, 503, 510 **bis**, 625, 647, 716, 720, 788, 810, 828; 2. 44, 45, 48, 51, 61, 120 **bis**, 142, 148 **ter**, 182, 250 **bis**, 278, 283, 296 **ter**, 305, 313, 317 **bis**, 355, 374, 456, 471 (KBL; G nos), 473 (G; KBL nos), 505, 506, 522, 524, 557, 601, 641; 3. 17, 39, 53, 54, 85, 206, 215 **bis**, 305, 326, 355, 356, 378, 471, 644, 649, 664, 667, 696, 699 **bis**; 4. 1, 100, 102, 145, 179 **bis**,
423, 444, 461, 463, 472, 474 (BL; KG nunc), 534, 556, 610, 621, 714, 718 (KG; BL num), 730; 5. 3 (tum non KBG; L dudum), 35, 57, 127, 150, 218 **bis**, 284, 359, 368, 371, 481, 508, 545, 598 **bis**, 599, 614, 627, 628 (K; BGL num), 633, 649, 651, 652; 6. 24, 68, 69, 101, 107, 134, 215, 225, 226 **bis**, 238, 241, 269, 272, 290, 317, 326, 363, 400, 406, 410, 420, 421, 429, 463, 471, 472, 499, 537, 567 **bis**, 652, 672 **bis**, 692, 725; 7. 3, 10, 38, 48, 58, 83, 89 **bis**, 105, 135, 140, 161 (L; KBG nunc), 231, 236, 238, 267, 280, 340 (KB; GL nec), 345, 428, 439, 447 (KG; BL nunc), 459, 494, 503, 504, 576, 581, 584, 604; 8. 12, 95, 154, 155, 165, 194, 209, 290, 335, 350, 390, 411, 417, 423, 424, 425, 431, 439, 458 **bis**, 460,
non aliter 3. 737; 4. 236, 368; 5. 408,
non alius (etc.) 3. 644; 6. 451,
non aliud quam 8. 316,
non amplius 6. 426,
at non 3. 362; 6. 529,
nondum 1. 110, 602, 662; 4. 160, 346; 5. 349, 452, 660; 6. 130; 7. 396, 406, 518; 8. 146,
nondum ullis 1. 276,
non alter (etc.) 1. 191; 6. 419,
non iam 1. 475; 7. 155,
non . . . iam 2. 282,
non magis 6. 718,
nec non 2. 664,
non quemquam 7. 203,
non tantum 1. 46; 8. 186,
non ullus (etc.) 1. 26, 229; 2. 244, 296; 3. 685; 4. 102, 146, 174, 590; 7. 204, 333 (qua non KGL; B cistam), 386; 8. 39, 162, 163, 381,
non umquam 2. 434; 7. 461,
non unus (etc.) 4. 598; 8. 186, 307,
non usquam 6. 300,
Vid. aliter, secus, sed.

Nonacrius
Nonacria (nom. f.) 4. 141.

nondum vid. non.

nonne
3. 297.

nosco
noscunt 4. 278; 5. 180,
novimus 4. 438; 6. 327,
norat 7. 325,
nossem 7. 40,
norit 1. 417,
nosse 3. 17,
noscentibus (dat. m.) 5. 452,
noscere (fut.) 4. 314,
notus 6. 123, 656,
nota 4. 453,
notae (gen.) 5. 150,
notum (n.) 2. 418,
noto 3. 6; 4. 284,
nota 2. 141, 226; 6. 535 (ac nota KBG; L ignota),

notae 3. 258; 8. 176,
nota 4. 228,
notis (n.) 3. 43,
notas 1. 257; 3. 595,
nota 1. 836; 4. 242, 549; 5. 660,
notis (f.) 1. 447,
notis 7. 354,
notior (f.) 2. 95.

noster
noster 1. 534, 814; 2. 561, 607,
nostra 1. 505; 3. 396, 674; 4. 471, 544;
5. 248; 6. 460; 7. 65, 261,
nostrum 2. 251,
nostri 1. 41, 114, 713; 5. 19; 7. 136, 521
(KBL; G vestri), 532; 8. 432,
nostrae 1. 117, 718; 2. 488, 558,
nostri 7. 500,
nostro 3. 313; 4. 468; 6. 483,
nostrae 4. 475,
nostram 1. 270,
nostrum 6. 497,
nostrum (voc.) 6. 547,
nostro 1. 827; 2. 424; 4. 126; 5. 473,
nostra 5. 500; 6. 214, 743; 8. 166,
nostro 1. 342, 525; 2. 480; 3. 143 (B;
KGL Nestor), 450; 5. 295; 7. 343,
nostri 1. 628; 3. 455; 5. 38,
nostra 5. 632; 7. 175,
nostris 1. 249; 5. 668,
nostris 2. 639; 4. 484; 5. 508; 8. 49,
nostris 1. 332; 2. 593; 3. 678 (KGL; B
nostri); 5. 542 (vid. abl.); 7. 245,
nostros 1. 172, 516; 2. 143, 159; 4. 420,
539; 5. 288; 6. 268; 7. 68; 8. 37,
nostras 1. 680, 804; 2. 219; 4. 53; 7. 437,
nostra 1. 20, 791; 3. 650; 4. 219; 6. 597;
7. 61, 481,
nostris (f.) 1. 155,
nostris 1. 211; 3. 510; 4. 437; 5. 542
(vid. dat.); 8. 97, 157,
subst. n. nostra (acc.) 5. 390.

nota
notas 2. 466.

noto
notat 3. 99; 4. 287, 389; 6. 638 (K;
BGL necat),
notant 2. 312,
notato (abl. m.) 6. 206.

Notus
Notus 1. 612, 640; 6. 494,
Noti (gen.) 2. 506,
Notos 1. 652,
Notis 1. 646.

notus
notus 3. 93; 5. 438,
noto (abl.) 5. 73,
noti 6. 411,
notos 8. 173,
notis 4. 106.

notus vid. nosco.

novalis
subst. novales (nom. f.) 7. 77,
novalia 6. 118,
novalia 7. 609.

Novas
Novas 4. 719 (KBG; L Rhoas),
Novae (gen.) 6. 100 (KL; BG Noae).

novem
5. 326.

noverca
novercae 3. 506, 580, 610; 5. 188,
novercae (dat.) 1. 287; 5. 43.

novitas
novitate 2. 83.

novo
novat 1. 112, 774; 3. 423,
novant 2. 309; 4. 530,
novantem (m.) 5. 156 (B; KG morantem; L moventem), 303 (BGL; K
moventem).

novus
novus 2. 393; 4. 552; 6. 228; 7. 194; 8.
237, 259,
nova 1. 672; 3. 188; 4. 283; 5. 466,
novae (gen.) 1. 648,
novum 6. 635,
novam 1. 599; 2. 200,
novo 1. 311; 2. 441; 4. 503,
nova 1. 706; 2. 183; 5. 365; 6. 531; 7.
125, 144, 290,
novo 6. 153,
nova 4. 4, 283,
novorum (m.) 5. 128,
novis (n.) 2. 180,
novos 2. 369,
novas 6. 372, 603,
nova 1. 114; 2. 636; 3. 29 **bis**, 665, 733;
4. 424, 525, 534; 5. 118,
novis (m.) 8. 45,
novissimus 1. 461; 4. 694,
novissima (acc.) 5. 77.

Nox
Nox 6. 752,
Nocti 5. 398,
Nocte 3. 252.

nox
nox 1. 617, 670; 2. 338, 517 (nox tum L;
KBG necdum), 572, 663; 3. 32, 206,
211, 291, 363, 730; 5. 71, 94, 278, 298,
369, 566; 6. 14; 7. 3, 11, 70, 393, 408,
540; 8. 455,
noctis 1. 416; 2. 45, 288, 291, 350, 397;
3. 212, 217, 398; 4. 82, 424; 5. 231; 7.
313, 403, 501,
nocti 1. 611; 7. 372,
noctem 1. 251, 277; 2. 59, 89, 579, 662;
3. 127, 575; 4. 517, 663; 5. 107, 329, 601,
691; 6. 435; 7. 246, 598; 8. 175,
nocte 1. 774; 2. 192, 281, 657; 3. 30, 49
(L; KBG noctes), 227; 4. 105; 5. 74,
140, 443; 6. 158, 464; 7. 400; 8. 25, 95,
416,
noctes (acc.) 2. 219; 3. 49 (KBG; L
nocte); 5. 48, 332; 8. 382,
noctibus 3. 603; 5. 46, 252; 7. 166.

noxius
noxia (nom. f.) 8. 106.

nubes
nubes 3. 500; 4. 495,
nubem 2. 15; 3. 91, 465; 5. 93, 619; 6. 88,
nube 1. 396, 515, 706; 2. 500, 522; 3. 66, 129, 573; 4. 259; 6. 210; 7. 567; 8. 81,
nubes 4. 729,
nubibus 8. 115,
nubes 2. 516; 8. 451,
nubibus 1. 279, 826; 2. 119; 4. 77, 273, 661.

nubifer
nubiferi (m.) 2. 506,
nubiferam 8. 214,
nubifera (abl.) 4. 599.

nubilus
subst. n. nubila 1. 656; 6. 355,
nubila 1. 10, 151, 307, 467, 568; 3. 238; 4. 94, 149; 6. 179; 8. 30, 56, 72.

nubo
subst. f. nuptae .4. 164,
nuptae (dat.) 4. 362,
nuptas 8. 148 (B; KGL natas).

nudo
nudata (nom. f.) 5. 135,
nudatis (abl. m.) 3. 332.

nudus
nudus 1. 583,
nuda 3. 61; 5. 498,
nuda 5. 437,
nudo 4. 225,
nuda (acc.) 1. 696,
nudis (m.) 1. 135 (BGL; K nitidis),
nudis (n.) 2. 171.

nullus
nullus 2. 57; 4. 315; 6. 464; 7. 244, 387; 8. 209,
nulla 1. 548, 845; 3. 365, 704; 4. 19, 184, 217, 614; 5. 597 (BGL; K multa); 6. 440; 7. 244, 356, 386, 628; 8. 209, 364, 430,
nullum (m.) 4. 63,
nullum 6. 453,
nullo 3. 291, 593; 7. 534,
nulla 4. 511, 550; 6. 562,
nullo 4. 296; 6. 275, 395; 7. 47,
nulli 3. 704; 7. 483 (KB; GL nullos),
nullae 3. 454, 720; 5. 334; 8. 162,
nulla 3. 654,
nullos 3. 242, 517; 5. 290; 6. 453; 7. 39, 483 (GL; KB nulli); 8. 251,
nullas 5. 662; 7. 284,
nulla 8. 100, 101,
nullis (n.) 1. 697; 6. 276; 8. 430,
subst. nullus 7. 506,
nulla (abl.) 5. 346.

num (6)
1. 152 (B; KGL nunc), 519; 3. 76; 4. 718 (BL; KG non); 5. 530, 628 (BGL; K non).

numen
numen 1. 50; 6. 480 (K; BGL lumen),
numinis 2. 432,
numen 3. 428; 4. 161 (BG; K nomen; L famam); 5. 245; 8. 225,

numine 2. 48, 606; 3. 235, 664, 711; 4. 101, 540; 5. 483 (BGL; K lumine); 7. 323; 8. 195,
numina 1. 674; 2. 485; 4. 34, 667 (KG; BL lumina); 5. 38; 7. 391,
numina 3. 639; 4. 28 (L; K limina; BG lumina), 411, 549.

numerosus
numerosa (nom. f.) 1. 436; 5. 40.

numerus
numero 5. 199,
numero 5. 326; 6. 36; 8. 320,
numeris (abl.) 4. 87.

numquam (15)
2. 64; 3. 109, 230, 400; 4. 168, 525, 550; 5. 297; 6. 39, 335; 7. 94 (KBL; G quamquam), 261, 429; 8. 16, 227.

nunc (52)
nunc 1. 20, 67, 114, 117, 152 (KGL; B num), 170, 198, 216 **bis**, 243, 306 (BL; KG dumque), 344, 392, 507, 523, 698, 719; 2. 113, 242, 295, 421, 565, 659; 3. 15, 25 (KG; BL tunc), 169, 181, 241, 298 (potius nunc BGL; K sine crimine), 299, 318, 514, 686, 705 **bis**, 706; 4. 4, 28, 79, 123, 124, 420, 444, 469, 474 (KG; BL non), 478, 513, 522, 538, 573 (BL; KG tunc), 603, 633, 649; 5. 17, 20, 52, 129, 171, 198, 217, 238, 247, 284, 479 (K; BGL huc), 526, 631, 681; 6. 213 (B; KGL hunc), 289, 312, 330 (KBG; L nam) , 461, 476, 563, 594; 7. 9, 39, 65, 161 (KBG; L non), 182, 198, 203, 223, 232, 316, 341 (qui nunc est G; KL quicumque est; B primaevum), 342, 354, 417, 420 (B; K dic; G nec; L cur), 422, 442 (K; BGL en), 442, 445, 447 (BL; KG non), 463, 467; 8. 10, 64, 71, 73, 74, 98, 102, 168, 188, 351, 370 (BL; K heu; G nec), 434, 443,
nunc etiam 5. 80; 6. 87,
etiam nunc 5. 665 (KGL; B etiamnum); 7. 454,
iam nunc 1. 308, 334; 5. 322; 8. 47,
nunc . . . nunc 1. 639; 2. 396; 3. 594, 602; 4. 342; 5. 523, 572; 6. 153, 416, 581, 637, 697; 7. 512, 547,
nunc . . . nunc . . . nunc 8. 123,
nunc primum 2. 639,
nunc quoque 8. 440.

nuntius
nuntia 1. 46,
nuntia (voc.) 1. 794,
nuntia (acc.) 1. 440,
subst. nuntius 1. 597; 2. 142, 540; 3. 666; 4. 170; 5. 249, 401; 7. 98.

nuper
3. 320; 4. 652 (nuper erat B; KG perculerat; L caecus erat).

nurus
nurus (nom.) 2. 160; 4. 369,
nurum 1. 739, 847,
nurus (nom.) 2. 247; 3. 358; 8. 141,
nuribus (abl.) 1. 745; 2. 111.

nusquam
    4. 201, 451; 7. 85 **bis.**
nuto
    nutat 3. 469, 686; 6. 169; 8. 88,
    nutantem (f.) 7. 153.
nutrimentum
    nutrimenta (nom.) 6. 571.
nutrio
    nutribam 8. 97,
    nutrierat 6. 205, 710,
    nutritum (acc. n.) 6. 340,
    nutrita (acc.) 7. 357.
nutrix
    nutricem 5. 352.
nutus
    nutu (abl.) 1. 85, 194, 507; 3. 251; 4.
    761; 6. 382 (KBG; L motu); 7. 499.
Nyctelius
    Nyctelii 6. 755.
Nympha
    Nympha 4. 27,
    Nymphae (gen.) 3. 561; 4. 23,
    Nympha (voc.) 3. 536,
    Nymphae 5. 381,
    Nympharum 3. 181,
    Nymphis 3. 542,
    Nymphas 3. 522.
nympha
    nympha 5. 110,
    nymphae (gen.) 6. 52; 8. 217,
    nympha 5. 478,
    nymphae 4. 399.
o (52)
    1. 7, 113, 168, 194, 215, 242, 250 (G;
    KL **om.**; B in), 336, 721 **bis;** 2. 55, 113
    bis, 143, 218, 274, 322 (B; KGL **om.**),
    378, 404, 485, 639; 3. 617; 4. 30 **bis,**
    206, 242 (BG; K a; L e), 327, 328, 436,
    460, 469, 553, 630, 674; 5. 233, 550; 6.
    547, 676; 7. 135, 198 (L; KBG si), 217,
    229, 336, 534; 8. 10, 37, 75 (que o L;
    KBG quoque), 181, 183, 264, 269, 439.
obeo
    obit 3. 179, 710; 4. 234,
    obibam 7. 69,
    obibo 7. 486 (BGL; K abibo),
    obire 7. 318 (B; K in hora; GL in
    ira).
obex
    obice 1. 702.
obicio
    obicis 5. 627,
    obicit 6. 679; 7. 460, 524,
    obiciat 8. 388.
obitus
    , obitus (nom. pl.) 6. 184,
    obitus 1. 769, 810; 6. 515.
obliquus (oblicus).
    obliqui (m.) 1. 484,
    oblicum (n.) 1. 619,
    obliqua (nom.) 2. 7 (vid. acc.),
    obliqua 2. 7 (vid. nom.).
obliviscor
    oblita 3. 664; 8. 238,
    oblitae 4. 532,

obliti (n.) 2. 389,
    oblitos 1. 792.
oblivium
    oblivia (acc.) 4. 536.
obnitor
    obnixus 7. 595,
    obnixa (nom. f.) 6. 236, 356; 7. 157.
obnubo
    obnubit 2. 254; 7. 584,
    obnubens (m.) 5. 97.
oborior
    obortis (abl. f.) 7. 258.
obruo
    obruit 1. 319 (L; KBG obruat); 2. 534;
    7. 96 (B; KGL obruet),
    obruet 7. 96 (KGL; B obruit),
    obruit 3. 480; 4. 160,
    obruat 1. 319 (KBG; L obruit); 2. 144,
    obruar (subi.) 8. 13.
obscurus
    obscurae (gen.) 3. 526,
    obscura (abl.) 4. 135; 6. 193.
obsecro
    obsecrat 1. 782.
obsequor
    obsequitur 3. 508.
obsideo
    obsidet 2. 238; 5. 396; 8. 380,
    obsessum (acc. n.) 4. 696.
obsisto
    obsistere 3. 469 (KBG; L insistere);
    8. 404.
obstipesco
    obstipuit 4. 141.
obsto (opsto)
    obstat 1. 518; 5. 668,
    opstat 1. 318,
    obstantia (acc.) 2. 4.
obstringo
    obstrinxit 7. 602.
obtendo
    obtendit (prs.) 2. 450 (B; KGL osten-
    dit).
obtineo (optineo)
    optenta (abl.) 3. 718.
obtutus (optutus)
    optutu (abl.) 4. 324,
    obtutu 7. 88.
obvius
    obvius 1. 389; 2. 437; 3. 440; 6. 207; 7.
    400, 578, 621,
    obvia (nom.) 1. 447; 2. 166, 550; 4.
    657; 6. 316; 8. 116, 130,
    obvia (nom.) 8. 372,
    obvia 2. 313; 3. 79, 583.
occido
    occidis 7. 338,
    occidit (perf.) 3. 322; 4. 753,
    occideras 7. 441,
    occidat 7. 282.
occiduus
    occiduo (dat. m.) 5. 615,
    occiduis (abl. m.) 2. 620.
occubo
    occubat 3. 111.

occulo
occulit 8. 315,
occulerat 2. 280,
occulta (nom. f.) 7. 193.
occultus vid. occulo.
occumbo
occumbes 3. 169 (K; BGL occumbens),
occumbite 6. 286,
occumbere 1. 633; 6. 126, 309; 7. 427,
occumbens (m.) 3. 169 (BGL; K occumbes).
occupo
occupat 1. 39. 159, 354, 461; 2. 137, 521;
3. 86, 154, 168; 4. 321, 664; 6. 198, 398;
7. 254; 8. 413,
occupet 8. 87.
occurro
occurrit 3. 433; 6. 586; 7. 223,
occurrunt 7. 402,
occurrere 4. 112, 194, 678; 7. 267, 627,
occurrens (f.) 2. 46.
Oceanus
Oceanus 1. 9, 589,
Oceani 3. 404; 4. 91,
Oceano (abl.) 5. 411, 565.
Ocheus
Ocheus 6. 200.
Ochus
Ochum 3. 148.
ocior
ocior (f.) 2. 60,
adv. ocius 3. 508; 4. 143, 643.
Ocreus
Ocrea 6. 251.
oculus
oculis 5. 27; 8. 52,
oculos 1. 120, 298, 561, 771; 2. 227, 470;
3. 41; 4. 18, 131, 189, 435; 6. 580, 723;
7. 30, 214, 247, 306, 396; 8. 60, 76,
oculis 1. 495, 795; 2. 40, 45; 3. 367, 551;
4. 1, 290, 506; 6. 658.
odi
odit 7. 204; 8. 250,
odere 5. 454,
oderis (subi.) 5. 655; 6. 26; 7. 140.
Odium
Odia (nom.) 5. 145.
odium
odium 4. 742,
odium 6. 20,
odio 2. 104 (L; KBG eadem),
odia 4. 254,
odiis 3. 664,
odiis 1. 65; 3. 510; 7. 93, 255.
odor
odor 4. 455, 493,
odores (acc.) 5. 590.
odoro
odorato (abl. m.) 6. 129.
Odrussa
Odrussa (nom.) 5. 594.
Odrysius
Odrysius 1. 470; 5. 99,
Odrysiae (gen.) 4. 467,
Odrysio (abl. n.) 5. 439.

Oeagrus
Oeagri 4. 348.
Oebalides
Oebalides 4. 294.
Oebalius
Oebalius 4. 228,
Oebalium (m.) 1. 422,
Oebaliam 6. 220,
Oebalia (abl.) 4. 272.
Oebasus
Oebasus 6. 245.
Oenides
Oenides 3. 690 (KGL; B Oenidae); 4.
33; 6. 343,
Oenidae (gen.) 3. 690 (B; KGL Oeni-
des).
Oenotria
Oenotria (nom.) 1. 589.
offero
offert 3. 546, 612; 7. 597,
optulit 1. 310,
offerre 7. 46,
oblati (n.) 5. 539,
oblato (n.) 4. 403,
oblatum (m.) 3. 176,
oblato 3. 614,
oblata 5. 235; 8. 394,
oblata (nom.) 7. 328,
oblatis (abl. m.) 3. 605; 7. 31.
offundo
offusa (nom.) 5. 466,
offusae (nom.) 4. 482.
Ogygius
Ogygii (gen. m.) 2. 623,
Ogygias 8. 446.
Oileus
Oileus 1. 372.
Olbus
Olbum 6. 638.
olea
oleam 6. 712.
Olenides
Oleniden 3. 204.
Olenius
Olenii 2. 163.
Olenius
Olenii 3. 106.
oleo
olentis (acc. m.) 8. 348.
olim (14)
1. 35, 53, 72, 381, 393, 573, 586, 773; 4.
121, 321; 5. 383, 434; 6. 61; 8. 255.
oliva
olivae (gen.) 5. 361,
oliva 3. 424.
olivum
olivo (abl.) 6. 358.
olor
olorum 6. 102.
Olympus
Olympi 2. 38, 66; 3. 380; 5. 378; 7. 378,
Olympo 5. 413,
Olympum 1. 25,
Olympo 1. 4, 199; 2. 85; 5. 1, 691; 7. 158.

opus 1. 170, 429; 2. 358; 3. 145, 199,
operum 1. 475; 3. 672; 4. 545; 5. 455; 6.
633.

ora
orae (gen.) 4. 467,
oram 4. 613; 8. 376,
ora 1. 704 (KGL; B Ida),
orae 5. 202,
oris 4. 335, 484; 5. 277,
oras 1. 2; 2. 11, 575; 3. 508; 4. 115, 207,
702 (BL; KG oris); 5. 73; 6. 749; 7.
36, 42,
oris 1. 394, 715; 2. 423, 562, 615, 632;
3. 204, 573, 653; 4. 5, 159, 170, 219, 589,
702 (KG; BL oras); 5. 56, 195, 459; 6.
49, 462, 690; 7. 119, 219, 259 (L; KBG
auris).

oraculum
oracula (nom.) 1. 743.

orbis
orbis (gen.) 1. 452,
orbem 2. 628; 3. 437; 4. 447; 5. 92, 255;
5. 315; 6. 246, 345, 367; 7. 227; 8. 91,
246,
orbe 1. 566; 4. 745; 5. 473; 6. 33, 7. 35;
8. 71,
orbibus 6. 416 (B; KGL curribus),
orbes 2. 387; 3. 178, 347, 739; 4. 235,
orbibus 6. 239; 7. 560 (KBG; L oribus).

orbita
orbita (nom.) 6. 442.

orbo
orbatae (nom.) 8. 457.

orbus
orba (abl.) 6. 47,
orbi 6. 724.

Orcus
Orci 1. 784.

ordior
orsa est 8. 45,
orsus 5. 552,
orsa (nom. f.) 2. 210; 5. 392, 403,
subst. n. orsis 4. 572,
orsa 1. 21; 2. 243 (GL; KB ora); 5.
195, 291, 470.

ordo
ordo 2. 217; 4. 183; 5. 680,
ordine 1. 295, 387, 443, 532; 2. 500; 3.
593, 675; 4. 449; 5. 181, 216, 265, 577;
7. 433.

Orestes
Orestes 7. 148.

orgia
orgia (nom.) 2. 282.

orichalcum
orichalca (acc.) 3. 61.

origo
origo 5. 382,
origine 4. 120.

Orion
Orion 1. 647; 2. 62, 508; 4. 123.

orior
oritur 1. 681; 3. 463,
ortus 4. 669,
orta 3. 258; 7. 23,

orte 5. 204,
subst. m. oriens 3. 411.

Orithyia
Orithyiae (gen.) 1. 468.

ornatus
ornatus (acc.) 6. 466.

orno
ornatur 5. 449,
ornantia (acc.) 5. 484 (L; K gravantia; B armantia; G creantia).

ornus
ornum 3. 565 (K; BGL ornos); 7. 535;
8. 113,
orno 7. 169,
ornos 1. 406; 2. 6; 3. 485, 565 (BGL;
K ornum).

Ornytus
Ornyte 3. 173.

oro
oro 1. 344; 4. 173; 6. 305, 733; 7. 96,
477; 8. 103,
orat 3. 447, 629,
orant 4. 66,
orans (m.) 3. 640; 8. 285,
oranti (m.) 5. 519 (BL; KG orantem),
orantem (m.) 4. 38, 74; 5. 519 (KG;
BL oranti),
orantis (f.) 4. 258.

Orpheus
1. subst.
Orpheus 1. 187, 470,
2. adi.
Orphea (abl.) 2. 426.

ortus
ortu (abl.) 2. 367; 7. 539,
ortus (acc.) 3. 246; 5. 308, 418.

os
os (acc.) 3. 168; 5. 212,
ore 1. 711, 830; 2. 57, 645; 3. 137; 4.
190, 234, 379, 429; 5. 100, 180, 367,
373; 6. 674, 705; 7. 67, 152 (L; KBG
ora), 330 (KL; BG ira), 462, 528; 8.
36,
ora 3. 216; 4. 639; 5. 219; 6. 604,
ora 1. 263, 292, 424, 595, 636, 807; 2. 30,
125, 212, 243 (KB; GL orsa), 463, 501;
3. 25, 140, 190, 263, 264, 314, 338, 590,
641, 674; 4. 19, 160, 166, 227, 241, 262,
291, 300, 323, 357, 395, 491, 664; 5. 128,
313, 336, 379, 387, 409, 417, 466, 572;
6. 37, 718; 7. 34, 79, 115, 152 (KBG;
L ore), 277, 294, 369, 408, 431, 512,
513, 594; 8. 26, 80, 121, 151, 188, 212,
273, 442, 457,
oribus 7. 560 (L; KBG orbibus).

os
ossa 3. 166; 4. 183 (ossaque KBG; L
corpora),
ossa 3. 383; 4. 244; 5. 55, 58; 7. 207,
ossibus 7. 253.

osculum
oscula (acc.) 1. 264; 2. 168 **bis**; 3. 561;
4. 373, 702; 7. 123, 216, 255, 373 (pavens . . . oscula miscet K; BGL vocemque . . . paventem); 8. 6, **44.**

Ossa
Ossa 2. 16; 5. 496,
Ossa 7. 606.
Ossaeus
Ossaeae (gen.) 1. 448.
ostendo
ostendit 1. 434; 2. 450 (KGL; B obtendit),
ostendebat 1. 256 (KGL; B ostentarat),
ostendet 2. 566 (B; KGL ostendat),
ostendat 2. 566 (KGL; B ostendet),
ostende 7. 269,
ostendere 3. 603; 5. 178; 6. 176; 8. 199,
ostendens (m.) 2. 86.
ostento
ostentat 6. 61, 544,
ostentarat 1. 256 (B; KGL ostendebat),
ostentans (m.) 4. 757.
ostium
ostia (acc.) 1. 716; 2. 574, 597; 5. 184, 307, 440; 6. 51; 7. 85; 8. 128, 187, 292, 293, 371.
ostrifer
ostrifero (abl. m.) 1. 456.
ostrum
ostro (abl.) 2. 342, 472; 3. 118, 339; 4. 369.
Otaces
Otaces 6. 121.
Otaxes
Otaxes 6. 529.
Othrys
Othrys 6. 392,
Othryn 1. 24.
otium
otia 3. 449,
otia 1. 500; 3. 614; 5. 423.
Otreus
Otreos 4. 162.
ovatus
ovatus (nom. pl.) 6. 187.
ovile
ovilibus (abl.) 2. 73.
ovis
oves (nom.) 3. 439.
ovo
ovat 2. 507; 4. 342,
ovans 1. 485 (L; KBG avens); 3. 223; 5. 68,
ovans (f.) 8. 462,
ovante (m.) 2. 545,
ovanti (n.) 4. 418,
ovantum (m.) 3. 692,
ovantes (m.) 4. 297; 7. 649,
ovantia 1. 806.
pabulum
pabula (acc.) 2. 9; 4. 68, 106, 379, 450, 525, 586; 8. 63.
pacifer
paciferae (gen.) 4. 139.
pacisco (paciscor)
pactus 6. 560,
pacta 5. 240; 6. 44,
pacti 6. 585,

pactae (gen.) 6. 274,
pacta (abl.) 3. 495,
subst. n. pacti 8. 401,
pacta (acc.) 6. 5; 8. 221.
pacta vid. pacisco.
Padus
Padus 8. 90,
Padi 1. 527.
paean
paeana 6. 512.
paelex
paelex 4. 357; 5. 449,
paelice 2. 153; 5. 446.
paeniteo
paenitet 5. 673.
Paeones
Paeonas 4. 280.
Pagasae
Pagasas 5. 191; 8. 451.
Pagasaeus
Pagasaea (nom. f.) 5. 435; 7. 556; 8. 378.
Pagaseius
Pagaseia (nom. f.) 1. 422.
palaestra
palaestris (abl.) 4. 328.
palam
5. 630.
palatium
palatia (nom.) 2. 246.
palear
palearia (acc.) 4. 406.
palla
palla 1. 385; 3. 525,
pallam 2. 106; 5. 447,
palla 1. 132; 3. 718; 8. 204.
Palladius
Palladiam 5. 206; 8. 292,
Palladia 1. 457; 8. 463,
Palladio 1. 478,
Palladii 6. 408,
Palladios 7. 624.
Pallantis
Pallantidos 2. 72 (B; KGL Atlantidis).
Pallas
Pallas 1. 530, 642; 4. 682; 5. 183, 293, 649, 652; 6. 173, 740,
Palladis 2. 53,
Pallados 4. 555; 5. 345; 8. 224,
Pallada 1. 126; 3. 489; 4. 238; 5. 626,
Pallas 1. 87, 215,
Pallade 1. 73.
Pallene
Pallene (nom.) 2. 17.
palleo
palluit 5. 347,
pallens (m.) 1. 775,
pallentem (m.) 1. 824; 3. 192; 5. 105,
pallentes (acc. f.) 3. 287,
pallentia 4. 490, 701; 7. 79,
pallentibus (f.) 2. 205.
pallesco
pallescit 7. 586,
pallescere 2. 526.

pallidus
pallida (nom. f.) 7. 375 (KG; BL callida),
pallida (acc.) 3. 59.
pallor
pallor 3. 576,
pallore 1. 229.
palma
palmis 8. 44 (vid. abl.),
palmas 1. 80; 2. 36, 469; 4. 165, 253,
326, 473; 5. 189; 8. 140,
palmis 1. 288; 8. 44 (vid. dat.).
palmes
palmite 3. 5.
palor
palantia (acc.) 4. 506.
palus
palus 2. 202 (KBG; L pavet); 6. 158;
8. 209.
pampineus
pampineam 2. 269,
pampinea (abl.) 5. 79.
Pan
Pan 3. 47, 48,
Panis 6. 538 (que Panis L; KBG rapinis).
Panchaia
Panchaia (nom.) 6. 119.
pando
pandit 1. 397; 4. 197; 8. 187,
pandebat 1. 740,
pandet 1. 12,
panderet 1. 449 (B; KGL perderet),
pande 1. 526; 2. 617; 3. 16,
pandite 5. 203,
pandere 4. 559; 7. 46,
pandentes (acc. m.) 7. 474,
panditur 2. 579,
panduntur 4. 99,
pandi 2. 649; 7. 553,
passos 2. 502.
Pangaea
Pangaea (nom.) 2. 359.
Pangaeus
Pangaea (abl.) 1. 575, 598,
Pangaea (acc.) 4. 631.
pango
pepigit 7. 652,
pepigere 8. 154.
Panope
Panope 1. 134,
Panopes 2. 589.
papilla
papillae (gen.) 6. 374.
par
par 3. 473; 5. 43; 6. 109,
par (f.) 1. 111, 668; 2. 149; 4. 456,
parem 1. 733,
parem 6. 289, 452,
pari 3. 548,
pari (f.) 6. 722,
pares (m.) 2. 646, 652; 3. 668, 703; 4. 743,
paria 5. 600,
pares 1. 540; 5. 194,

pares 1. 550,
paribus (m.) 6. 203,
paribus (n.) 6. 157, 394.
paratus
paratu (abl.) 2. 510, 651.
Parcae
Parcae 1. 502; 5. 531; 6. 693.
parco
pepercerit (ind.) 7. 207,
parce 4. 475 (L; KBG ante), 475; 6. 307; 7. 225.
parcus
parco (abl. m.) 2. 70.
parens
parens 1. 724; 3. 178, 323; 5. 383; 6. 127,
parens (f.) 1. 650; 2. 19, 229; 3. 276;
4. 46; 6. 710; 8. 143,
parentis (m.) 1. 179, 383; 4. 80, 186,
227; 6. 297, 404 (BGL; K parentes);
7. 532; 8. 52, 261,
parenti 2. 296; 3. 346; 4. 109, 343, 468;
5. 615; 6. 215, 483; 7. 415, 455,
parenti (f.) 3. 734,
parentem (m.) 2. 559; 5. 22, 441; 7. 140,
parens 1. 791; 2. 293,
parens (f.) 1. 797,
parentes 6. 404 (K; BGL parentis),
643; 8. 154,
parentum 1. 237, 326, 544, 824; 2. 307,
340, 471, 481,
parentibus 1. 97; 7. 122,
parentes 5. 349; 6. 444; 7. 50, 103, 502.
pareo
paret 3. 49 (L; KBG patet),
paruimus 6. 291,
parere 5. 489; 7. 154, 187,
paretur 1. 252.
pario
pariet 3. 376,
parta 7. 291,
parta (abl.) 3. 677.
pariter (45)
1. 96, 135, 297, 367, 408, 409, 427, 494,
616; 2. 31, 202, 247, 392; 3. 323, 388,
421, 521; 4. 683, 762; 5. 39, 161, 180, 241,
282, 462, 587; 6. 32, 190, 211, 343, 380,
530, 565, 616; 7. 459, 569, 612; 8. 2, 169,
172, 244, 246, 281, 325, 426,
Vid. haud, velut.
Parium
Parium (acc.) 2. 621.
Parius
Parius 2. 466,
Pario (abl. n.) 5. 187 (KGL; B parvo).
parma
parmae (gen.) 1. 486,
parmas 6. 99.
Parnasius
Parnasia (nom. f.) 3. 618.
Parnasus
Parnasi 6. 392.
paro
paras 1. 649,
parat 1. 326, 748; 2. 125; 4. 289; 5. 537;
7. 532, 543 (L; K quaeat; BG meat),

parant 8. 252,
parabas 6. 731,
parabat 4. 480,
paret 5. 580,
parantem (m.) 7. 32 (KBL; G paratas); 8. 444,
parari 2. 390,
parandos 6. 430,
parato (dat. m.) 1. 174,
paratae (nom.) 2. 222; 6. 756,
parata 1. 691,
paratis (m.) 1. 180,
paratas 2. 134; 7. 32 (G; KBL parantem),
paratis (m.) 1. 125.

Parthaonides vid. Porthaonides.

Parrhasius
Parrhasio (abl. n.) 4. 138.

pars
pars 2. 236, 414, 553; 3. 631; 4. 322, 643, 692; 7. 441 (BGL; K cras),
pars . . . pars 2. 221, 447, 633, 653; 3. 278, 462; 5. 10; 7. 554; 8. 254,
partem 1. 475; 3. 440 (KBL; G partim); 6. 379,
parte 1. 17, 140, 479, 522, 579; 3. 314; 4. 639; 6. 265, 615.

Parthenius
Parthenium 5. 103.

Parthi
Parthis (dat.) 6. 691.

partim
3. 439, 440 (G; KBL partem).

partior
partitur 6. 425,
partita (nom. f.) 7. 159.

partus
partu (abl.) 5. 149.

parumper (5)
5. 391; 6. 493; 7. 74, 104; 8. 77.

parvus
parvus 1. 268; 3. 599,
parva 1. 388; 2. 564; 3. 669; 5. 23,
parvi 8. 22,
parvi 3. 379,
parvum (m.) 1. 399; 2. 551,
parva 5. 545,
parvo 5. 187 (B; KGL Pario); 8. 273,
parvi 6. 291,
parvos 1. 225,
minor (f.) 1. 582; 7. 349,
subst. minus (acc.) 3. 630,
minores (nom. m.) 3. 455,
Vid. nec.

pasco
pascit 1. 678 (KBG; L pascet); 2. 450, 487; 7. 52,
pascet 1. 678 (L; KBG poscit),
pascitur 2. 658.

pascuus
subst. n. pascua 6. 537; 7. 233,
pascua 2. 546; 4. 363; 6. 435.

passim
1. 472; 3. 222.

passus
passu (abl.) 1. 258; 3. 61; 4. 140; 5. 351; 7. 374; 8. 54,
passus (acc.) 3. 486,
passibus 3. 357; 5. 375; 6. 489.

pastor
pastor 1. 549; 3. 101,
pastore 1. 444,
pastores (nom.) 1. 159; 2. 539.

pateo
patet 1. 835; 3. 49 (KBG; L paret), 386,
patent 4. 713,
patuerunt 6. 541,
patuere 1. 64; 7. 328,
pateant 1. 556,
patens (f.) 1. 833,
patentem (m.) 1. 364,
patentes (acc. f.) 5. 84.

pater
pater 1. 90, 356, 379, 401, 498, 651, 751, 846; 2. 23, 94, 117, 199, 271, 413, 605; 3. 68, 249, 565, 726; 4. 1. 132, 258, 399, 517, 571, 609; 5. 138, 209, 406, 672; 6. 175 (KGL; B putat), 178, 204, 210, 283, 622; 7. 17, 115, 144, 420, 472; 8. 146,
patris 1. 392, 458, 828; 4. 138 (KBG; L patriae), 319, 385; 5. 336, 622; 7. 163 (B; KG precor; L procax), 215, 429, 484; 8. 3, 273, 340, 432,
patri 1. 193, 256; 2. 265; 6. 269, 571; 7. 550,
patrem 1. 696; 2. 512, 581; 3. 320; 4. 516; 6. 675; 7. 101, 309,
pater 1. 11, 525, 669, 679; 2. 250, 256; 3. 81; 4. 25, 65; 5. 18, 644; 6. 288; 7. 345; 8. 12, 70, 182, 350,
patre 2. 404,
patres 1. 628; 8. 281,
patrum 1. 316; 2. 377, 563,
patres 1. 72, 150, 761; 5. 269, 464.

patera
pateram 1. 660,
patera 5. 192,
pateras 3. 13,
pateris 1. 818; 2. 348.

paternus
paterni (n.) 1. 773; 6. 640,
paterna 4. 631; 6. 486,
paterno 6. 86,
paternae 5. 479,
paternis (f.) 4. 125,
paternis 5. 404,
paternos 1. 243,
paternis 6. 575,
paternis 6. 293,
paternis 2. 309; 5. 240.

patesco
patescunt 4. 585,
patescat 3. 217.

patior
patitur 4. 305; 5. 400, 570,
patiere 7. 331,
patiemur 4. 14,

passa sum 7. 289,
patiare 5. 206,
paterere 1. 792; 8. 167,
pati 1. 325; 6. 126; 7. 95, 186 (BGL; K petit), 491; 8. 388, 444.
patiens 3. 206, 680; 4. 611; 8. 62 (K; BGL que pavens),
patiens (f.) 1. 236, 765,
passure 8. 100,
passus 1. 174, 426; 3. 17; 4. 262, 547; 5. 234; 7. 28,
passa 6. 469, 488,
passum (m.) 5. 197,
subst. m. passis (dat.) 5. 543.
patria
patria 3. 367,
patriae 2. 178, 243; 3. 654; 4. 138 (L; KBG patris); 7. 222,
patriae 7. 100,
patriam 2. 290, 317; 5. 551; 7. 228, 459, 493,
patria (voc.) 2. 113.
patrius
patrius 1. 432; 5. 134,
patrium 2. 157; 5. 514,
patrii 4. 493,
patriae 1. 676; 3. 12, 302,
patrii 1. 500,
patriae 4. 373; 7. 123; 8. 280,
patrium 5. 191, 397, 420; 6. 512, 700,
patrium 1. 363; 2. 549; 5. 244,
patrio 1. 439; 2. 556,
patria 2. 297; 5. 233,
patrio 3. 700,
patrii 2. 609,
patriae 1. 341; 8. 427,
patriis (f.) 4. 335; 5. 323,
patriis 1. 176; 5. 456,
patrios 1. 412; 2. 2, 283; 4. 229; 5. 432, 510; 6. 321; 7. 278; 8. 106,
patrias 1. 42; 3. 360; 4. 171; 5. 197, 449, 562; 6. 287, 758; 7. 130; 8. 46, 134,
patriis 5. 425,
patriis 2. 507; 6. 338, 727; 7. 219,
patriis 6. 171; 7. 163, 440.
patruus
patrui (gen.) 1. 216.
patulus
patulo (abl.) 6. 132,
patula (abl.) 1. 399 (KGL; B vacua).
paulatim (5)
2. 354; 4. 274, 391; 6. 635; 7. 215.
paulum (13)
2. 320; 3. 503; 4. 134, 279, 403; 5. 374; 6. 748, 755; 7. 8 (KGL; B causam), 109, 384, 581, 614.
paveo
pavet 1. 699; 2. 202 (L; KBG palus); 3. 264, 584; 4. 47, 416; 5. 5; 7. 305,
pavent 3. 237 585; 6. 442,
pavens 1. 309, 756; 8. 62 (que pavens BGL; K patiens),
pavens (f.) 5. 335; 7. 373 (pavens . . . oscula miscet K; BGL vocemque . . . paventem); 8. 449,

paventi (m.) 1. 26,
paventem (f.) 4. 9; 7. 373 (vocemque . . . paventem BGL; K pavens . . . oscula miscet); 8. 1,
paventes (m.) 1. 635,
paventum (f.) 2. 411,
paventibus (m.) 5. 297,
paventes (m.) 5. 338.
pavidus
pavidae 1. 425; 2. 87; 4. 534; 8. 32,
pavidae 4. 405 (GL; KB pavida),
pavidum **2. 257,**
pavidam 1. 622; 2. 161,
pavidum 3. 56,
pavido (m.) 1. 492,
pavidi 5. 603,
pavidae 4. 504,
pavida 4. 405 (KB; GL pavidae),
pavidis (m.) 1. 591,
pavidos 3. 706; 6. 536,
pavidas 2. 200; 4. 571; 5. 426.
pavito
pavitantem (f.) 7. 410.
Pavor
Pavor 2. 204, 281; 3. 89.
pavor
pavor 1. 799; 3. 74, 374; 4. 188, 226, 320, 664 **bis**; 5. 373, 550; 6. 398, 480; 7. 392, 401,
pavore 5. 15; 6. 506,
pavoribus (abl.) 7. 147.
pax
pax 3. 664 (KL; BG fax); 4. 20,
pacis 2. 84; 3. 659,
pacem 5. 690; 7. 652,
pace 2. 386; 4. 477, 535; 5. 380.
pecco
peccatum (nom.) 5. 674.
pecten
pectine 3. 160, 541.
pectus
pectoris 1. 435; 4. 244; 7. 253,
pectus 3. 135, 477; 4. 301; 6. 208, 341, 552, 654, 737,
pectore 1. 348, 369, 432, 491, 504, 762, 835; 2. 25, 32, 233; 3. 88, 134, 241, 287, 472; 4. 4, 89, 117, 225, 265, 372, 758; 5. 36, 281, 288; 6. 351 (B; KGL corpore), 435, 496, 673; 7. 308,
pectora 1. 605 (G; KBL pignora); 3. 440 (KBG; L tergora), 623, 719; 4. 147; 7. 177,
pectora 1. 79, 163, 214, 299, 643; 2. 47, 70 (K; BGL corpora), 491; 3. 185, 260, 310, 389, 556, 577, 581, 644; 4. 219, 358, 446, 700; 5. 310, 533, 595; 6. 110, 288, 574, 603, 623; 8. 466 (B; K tempera; G tempora; L temperat).
pecus
pecus 6. 333,
pecoris 1. 56; 2. 548; 6. 640,
pecori 3. 543; 7. 401,
pecus 3. 5, 57; 6. 537.

pecus
pecus 4. 197,
pecudis 5. 490; 6. 19; 7. 54; 8. 75,
pecudi 4. 363; 5. 189,
pecudes 3. 335 (G; KBL pecudum),
pecudum 1. 28; 3. 335 (KBL; G pecudes); 4. 341.
pedes
pedes 6. 95, 554, 639,
peditem 6. 206, 554.
pelagus
pelagi 1. 7, 213 (L; KBG fremere et),
632; 2. 512; 5. 316; 6. 355,
pelago 1. 545; 2. 390, 610; 7. 53,
pelagus 1. 169, 311, 353, 473; 3. 682; 4.
350,
pelago 1. 666; 2. 501, 617; 4. 678; 5. 108;
6. 84.
Pelasgi
Pelasgi 3. 45,
Pelasgum 2. 657; 3. 126, 221,
Pelasgos 2. 659,
Pelasgi
Pelasgum 4. 352; 5. 116 (KG; BL Pelasgam),
Pelasgos 5. 474.
Pelasgus
Pelasgi (m.) 5. 682,
Pelasgam 5. 116 (BL; KG Pelasgum).
Peleus
Peleus 1. 144, 264, 403; 3. 138,
Peleos 1. 131,
Pelea 1. 257, 266.
Peliacus
Peliacae (gen.) 8. 417,
Peliacas 1. 95, 406; 8. 451,
Peliacis (m.) 3. 353.
Pelias
Pelias 1. 22, 154, 700; 4. 555; 5. 483,
493; 7. 40, 447; 8. 155,
Peliae (gen.) 1. 162, 200; 7. 98,
Pelian 1. 848; 2. 4; 7. 92, 316.
Pelion
Pelion 2. 6 (vid. acc.),
Pelion 2. 6 (vid. nom.).
Pella
Pellae (gen.) 1. 365.
pellis
pellis (nom.) 5. 203; 7. 31,
pellem 4. 620; 8. 114, 123,
pellibus (abl.) 6. 136.
pello
pepulit 3. 466; 5. 153,
pellere 1. 837; 4. 408, 431,
pepulisse 4. 519; 5. 678,
pelli 6. 357 (KB; GL velli),
pulsus 3. 204, 368, 492; 4. 88 (L; KBG
pulsum); 5. 347,
pulsum 4. 88 (KBG; L pulsus),
pulsum 3. 127,
pulsam 2. 158,
pulso 3. 513 (B; KGL pulchro),
pulsa (abl.) 4. 197, 529,
pulsas 5. 330,

pulsa 3. 221,
pulsis (f.) 4. 288.
Pelops
Pelopis 1. 512; 7. 276.
Pelorus
Pelori 1. 579.
pelta
pelta 6. 375,
pelta 5. 135.
peltatus
peltata (nom. f.) 5. 613.
penates
penates (acc.) 2. 152, 474; 3. 14 (BGL;
K nepotes); 5. 510, 569; 7. 126, 145; 8.
37,
penates 1. 721.
pendeo
pendet 2. 427; 4. 669; 5. 20,
pendent 3. 93, 600,
pendebat 1. 481,
pependit 1. 259,
pendeat 3. 500,
pendentia (nom.) 2. 332; 5. 301.
pendo
pendit 1. 445,
pendere 1. 51 (KBG; L expendere); 7.
421,
pendi 4. 478.
Peneius
Peneia (nom. f.) 1. 386.
penes
4. 16; 5. 14.
penetralis
subst. n. penetrale (acc.) 7. 325,
penetralibus 5. 456,
penetralia 6. 478.
penetro
penetravit 4. 171,
penetraverit (ind.) 4. 582,
penetrarit (ind.) 7. 43.
penitus (5)
1. 668; 3. 377; 5. 106, 166; 7. 323.
penna
penna (abl.) 6. 421,
pennis (abl.) 1. 233; 7. 377.
pensum
penso (abl.) 2. 140.
Pentheus
Pentheos 3. 264,
Penthea 7. 301.
per (168)
1. 28, 33, 83, 91, 96, 104, 173, 207, 208,
217, 219, 271, 286, 293, 373, 438, 484,
487, 535, 545, 546, 569, 680, 753, 765,
767, 776, 843; 2. 11, 79, 115, 163, 178,
200, 273, 284, 288, 298, 393, 400, 424,
503, 516, 546, 592, 601, 631; 3. 7, 23, 49,
63, 127, 135, 136, 185, 196, 199, 219, 222,
239, 247, 254, 277, 440, 519 (BGL; K
om.), 538, 545, 582, 593, 596, 643; 4. 82,
210, 217, 252 (KB; G post; L pro), 302,
401, 421, 553, 561, 569, 613, 647 **bis**, 672,
676, 690, 707, 710, 725, 750; 5. 82, 124,
194, 200, 231, 243, 302, 329, 343, 410, 412,
440, 471, 511, 619; 6. 25, 32, 35, 105, 147,

179, 228, 234, 238, 239, 246, 285, 305,
341, 441, 492, 552, 563, 567 **bis**, 632,
654 **bis**, 670, 704, 755; 7. 6, 138, 146,
221, 266, 271, 302, 305, 367, 374, 380,
389, 402, 426, 463, 465, 469, 480, 498,
499, 500, 528; 8. 4, 8 (per antiqui BGL;
K peranti), 27, 30, 54, 110, 118, 128,
182, 219, 240, 247, 286, 391.
perago
  peragit 1. 146, 506,
  peragebat 7. 408,
  peraget 2. 384,
  peregi 7. 518; 8. 108,
  peregerat 1. 283,
  peractum (nom.) 1. 788,
  peracto (abl.) 1. 566; 6. 436,
  peracta (abl.) 2. 96.
peragro
  peragrat 6. 301.
peranti
  8. 8 (K; BGL per antiqui).
percello
  perculit 2. 91; 6. 481,
  perculerat 4. 652 (KG; B nuper erat;
  L caecus erat),
  perculerit (ind.) 4. 592.
Percosius
  Percosia (nom. f.) 3. 10.
Percote
  Percotes 2. 621.
percurro
  percurrere 6. 601,
  percurrens (m.) 6. 63.
percutio
  percutit 5. 100,
  percussit 3. 477,
  percussus 3. 573; 8. 81,
  percussa (nom.) 3. 529; 6. 278; 7. 475,
  percusso (abl. n.) 1. 369,
  percussa (acc.) 1. 495.
perdo
  perdiderit 1. 467,
  perderet 1. 449 (KGL; B panderet),
  590; 7. 316,
  perdere 7. 345, 447,
  subst. perdite 4. 140.
perdomo
  perdomitis (abl. m.) 7. 516.
pereo
  perit 6. 200,
  pereat 7. 7, 551 (GL; KB pereant),
  pereant 7. 551 (KB; GL pereat),
  perire 7. 342,
  periisse 5. 525; 7. 99,
  pereuntia (acc.) 3. 725,
  periturus 7. 307.
pererro
  pererrat 3. 537.
perfero
  perferat 8. 191 (BL; KG proferat),
  perferre 5. 491,
  perfertur 8. 113.
perficio
  perfice 7. 61,
  perfecta (nom. n.) 4. 538.

perfidus
  perfidus 6. 432; 7. 425,
  perfida (acc.) 5. 289.
perfringo
  perfringere 1. 192,
  perfracta (nom. n.) 6. 184.
perfundo
  perfudit 5. 365,
  perfusa (nom. f.) 2. 212,
  perfusi (nom.) 4. 338.
perfuro
  perfurit 8. 383.
Pergama
  Pergama (acc.) 2. 489, 570; 3. 513.
pergo
  pergis 7. 128,
  pergit 1. 31, 600, 745; 8. 404,
  pergunt 1. 531; 3. 147,
  pergat 5. 630,
  perge 3. 212,
  pergite 3. 625,
  pergere 4. 121, 175, 690; 5. 173.
Periclymenus
  Periclymenus 1. 388.
periculum (periclum)
  pericli 5. 229; 6. 474; 8. 403,
  pericula 7. 516,
  periclis 6. 678,
  pericula 1. 153; 2. 379; 7. 271,
  periclis 1. 57; 2. 293; 5. 490; 7. 533; 8.
  430.
perimo
  perimi 8. 99,
  peremptum (m.) 6. 743,
  perempto 3. 249,
  perempta 3. 709,
  perempti 3. 123,
  subst. m. perempti (voc.) 3. 448.
periurium
  periuria (acc.) 3. 638 (BL; K modo
  iurgia; G in iurgia); 7. 509.
permisceo
  permixtum (m.) 7. 255.
permitto
  permissum est 1. 169,
  permissa 8. 424,
  permissae (dat.) 8. 80,
  permissum (n.) 1. 645,
  permissa (acc.) 1. 574,
  permissis (f.) 4. 679.
permuto
  permutant 5. 424.
pernix
  pernix 1. 489; 6. 95 (L; KBG inter),
  pernix (f.) 1. 92.
pernox
  pernox (m.) 3. 117, 414.
perodi
  peroso (dat. m.) 6. 289.
perpetior
  perpetior 7. 243,
  perpetitur 4. 431,
  perpetimur 2. 180; 3. 380; 5. 489,
  perpeterer 3. 319,
  perpessa (nom. f.) 6. 754.

perquiro
  perquirere 3. 684.
perrumpo
  perrumpere 8. 193.
Perseis
  Perseidos 7. 238.
Perseius
  Perseia (nom. f.) 5. 581; 6. 495.
persequor
  persequor 8. 276,
  persequitur 6. 658,
  persequar (ind.) 8. 343.
Perses
  Perses 3. 493, 502; 5. 266, 271, 284; 6.
  15, 26, 34, 75, 725, 741,
  Persen 5. 529, 634, 678; 6. 30,
  Perse 6. 605.
Perseus
  Perseos 1. 68,
  Persea 5. 497.
Perseus
  Perseus 2. 63.
Perseus
  Perseas 7. 450.
persolvo
  persolvere 4. 630.
persono
  personat 2. 164; 3. 528.
personus
  persona (nom. f.) 4. 418.
persto
  perstas 7. 58,
  perstat 8. 85,
  perstant 7. 511,
  perstantem (m.) 4. 143.
perstringo
  perstrinxerat 7. 81,
  perstringere 7. 194.
peruro
  peruris 1. 76.
pervenio
  pervenere 7. 395.
pervigil
  pervigil 1. 481; 3. 76; 5. 141, 603,
  pervigil (f.) 4. 286; 7. 9,
  pervigilis (n.) 7. 536,
  pervigili (abl. m.) 3. 359.
pervigilo
  pervigilat 6. 224,
  pervigilant 3. 739.
pervius
  pervia (nom.) 1. 127,
  pervia (nom.) 1. 720,
  pervia 1. 1.
pervolito
  pervolitant 4. 505.
pes
  pedem 7. 112,
  pede 3. 527; 5. 160; 8. 21, 69,
  pedum 3. 244, 436,
  pedes 1. 385; 3. 167,
  pedibus 2. 258; 8. 305.
pestifer
  pestiferam 7. 334 (B; KGL pestis erat),
  pestiferas 4. 594.

pestis
  pestis (nom.) 2. 498; 4. 482, 491; 7.
  334 (pestis erat KGL; B pestiferam);
  8. 165,
  pestem 7. 252,
  peste 1. 822 (L; KBG veste); 4. 551;
  6. 417 (in peste revinctos L; KB **om.**;
  G cura cavere), 418; 7. 125,
  pestes (nom.) 3. 454.
peto
  peto 2. 297; 4. 251 (KBG; L pete); 5.
  508,
  petis 1. 392; 5. 393,
  petit 1. 162, 288, 460; 2. 306, 391; 3. 420,
  485, 508; 4. 39, 400, 528; 5. 271, 326
  (KGL; B legit), 336, 555, 665; 6. 212,
  421, 456, 688; 7. 15, 33 (ante petit K;
  B ante rapit; G ante aperit; L antevenit), 186 (K; BGL pati), 325,
  petimus 5. 321,
  petitis 7. 61,
  petunt 1. 24; 2. 74, 190, 539; 4. 505; 5.
  328; 7. 28; 8. 122, 201, 297,
  petebat 3. 128, 531; 5. 64, 341,
  petii 8. 150,
  petisti 5. 235; 7. 438,
  petivit 1. 570; 5. 502; 7. 189,
  petiere 1. 92; 7. 220,
  petas 5. 240 (B; KGL petat),
  petat 3. 695; 5. 240 (KGL; B petas),
  353; 7. 178,
  petamus 5. 282; 8. 188,
  petant 5. 531,
  peteret 4. 164,
  pete 4. 251 (L; KBG peto),
  petere 3. 459; 5. 127, 495,
  petiisse 6. 537; 8. 169,
  petens 2. 545; 3. 568, 594, 728; 6. 599,
  petens (f.) 1. 136,
  petentem (m.) 2. 557,
  petentes (m.) 5. 386,
  petentes (m.) 6. 407,
  petentibus (m.) 3. 700,
  petendum (m.) 5. 471,
  petenda (nom.) 5. 318.
Peuce
  Peuce 8. 217,
  Peuces 8. 376,
  Peucen 8. 293.
Peuce
  Peucen 8. 256.
Peucon
  Peucon 6. 564.
Phaethon
  Phaethon 3. 213,
  Phaethonta 5. 429.
phalanx
  phalanx 1. 436; 3. 97; 6. 53, 106; 7. 471,
  613,
  phalanges 6. 750,
  phalangas 6. 758.
Phalces
  Phalces 6. 88,
  Phalcen 6. 245, 554.

Phalerus
 Phaleri 4. 654; 6. 217,
 Phalere 1. 398.
pharetra
 pharetrae (gen.) 2. 521; 5. 583,
 pharetram 2. 492; 3. 161, 607,
 pharetra 2. 569,
 pharetrae 2. 511,
 pharetras 1. 634, 661; 3. 663; 5. 426,
 pharetrae 4. 30,
 pharetris 1. 708; 5. 135, 380, 559, 609.
pharetratus
 pharetratis (abl. n.) 6. 696 (GL; K
 Euphrataeis; L phari raris).
Pharius
 Pharii (m.) 2. 318 (L; KBG Phariis),
 Pharia 4. 408,
 Phariae 1. 644; 7. 113,
 Phariis (abl. n.) 2. 318 (KBG; L Pha-
 rii).
Pharus
 Phari 4. 417 (KGL; B Iovis); 5. 423;
 6. 696 (Phari raris B; K Euphrataeis;
 GL pharetratis).
pharus
 pharon 7. 85.
Phasiades
 Phasiaden 6. 640.
Phasis
 Phasis 1. 518; 2. 597; 4. 545; 5. 51, 179,
 426,
 Phasidis 1. 2, 78; 3. 306, 501, 662; 4.
 616, 706; 5. 342, 421, 440; 6. 295, 319,
 641, 643; 7. 564,
 Phasim 1. 43, 87,
 Phasin 2. 379; 7. 220,
 Phasi 5. 205, 208,
 Phaside 5. 299.
Pheraeus
 Pheraei (nom.) 1. 444.
Philyra
 Philyrae (gen.) 5. 152.
Phineius
 Phineia (acc.) 4. 504.
Phineus
 Phineus 4. 433, 444, 467, 473, 629,
 Phinei 4. 425; 5. 127,
 Phineos 5. 5,
 Phinea 4. 500, 550.
Phlegethon
 Phlegethontis 1. 735.
Phlegra
 Phlegrae (gen.) 1. 564 (BGL; K Phle-
 gram); 5. 692 (Phlegrae qui G; KBL
 Phlegraeas),
 Phlegram 1. 564 (K; BGL Phlegrae);
 6. 169.
Phlegraeus
 Phlegraeas 5. 692 (KBL; G Phlegrae
 qui).
Phlegyas
 Phlegyan 2. 193.
Phlegyas
 Phlegyas 3. 125.

Phlias
 Phlias 1. 412; 3. 149.
Phlogius
 Phlogium 5. 114.
phoca
 phocae (nom.) 5. 439,
 phocas 3. 727,
 phocis 2. 319.
Phoceus
 Phocea 3. 204.
Phoebe
 Phoebes 4. 361; 7. 366.
Phoebeius
 Phoebeius 1. 228.
Phoebeus
 Phoebeum (m.) 3. 372.
Phoebus
 Phoebus 2. 76; 3. 481,
 Phoebi 1. 383; 3. 437, 559; 4. 76, 468;
 5. 331, 403, 483, 598 (B; KGL belli);
 6. 468,
 Phoebo 2. 316; 8. 116,
 Phoebum 3. 541,
 Phoebe 1. 5,
 Phoebo 1. 230, 311; 4. 98.
Pholoe
 Pholoe 1. 140,
 Pholoen 3. 66.
Pholus
 Pholum 1. 338.
Phorcys
 Phorcys 3. 727.
Phrixeus
 Phrixeae 8. 75, 119,
 Phrixei 6. 150,
 Phrixeo (abl. n.) 5. 632,
 Phrixeos 1. 391,
 Phrixea 2. 585; 8. 267.
Phrixus
 Phrixus 1. 41, 279; 5. 225, 229, 461,
 474; 6. 446; 7. 120,
 Phrixi 1. 272, 328, 377; 4. 556; 5. 186,
 256, 263, 476, 499; 6. 11, 542, 593; 7. 14,
 136,
 Phrixo 1. 520; 2. 599; 5. 362, 509; 6. 598,
 Phrixum 5. 510, 525,
 Phrixe 1. 291; 5. 194, 197; 7. 38.
Phrixus
 Phrixus 6. 70.
Phrontis
 Phrontis 5. 460.
Phryges
 Phryges 2. 578,
 Phrygum 2. 551,
 Phrygibus 2. 485,
 Phrygas 4. 78; 7. 635.
Phrygia
 Phrygiam 2. 633.
Phrygius
 Phrygius 2. 624; 5. 694,
 Phrygiae (gen.) 4. 164,
 Phrygio (abl.) 2. 417; 3. 6,
 Phrygia (abl.) 1. 549,
 Phrygiis (n.) 3. 512,

Phrygios 1. 9; 5. 501,
Phrygias 3. 23.
Phylace
(nom.) 1. 474.
piaculum
piacula 2. 433,
piacula 1. 814; 2. 563; 4. 252.
picea
piceae (dat.) 3. 533,
piceae 3. 165.
piceus
piceo (abl.) 2. 115; 3. 195, 577,
piceo 1. 617; 2. 517,
picei 1. 622,
piceae 3. 439,
piceos 3. 135.
pictura
picturae (gen.) 1. 129.
Picus
Pici 7. 232.
pietas
pietas 1. 244; 5. 86; 6. 311, 471.
pigeo
piget 2. 81.
piger
piger 2. 387, 428.
pignus
pignora (nom.) 1. 605 (KBL; G pectora).
pilum
pilis (abl.) 6. 403.
Pindus
Pindus 5. 496.
pineus
pinea (acc.) 2. 633; 3. 521.
pingo
picta (nom.) 2. 150; 5. 609,
picto (abl. n.) 3. 11; 6. 227,
pictas 3. 340,
pictis (f.) 7. 211.
pinguesco
pinguescere 1. 426.
pinguis
pingue 4. 100,
pinguem (m.) 5. 423,
pingui 3. 286,
pingui 1. 449,
pingui 1. 204; 3. 124; 6. 39, 360,
pingues (acc. f.) 8. 247,
pinguia 1. 192; 7. 607.
piniger
piniger 6. 393.
pinna vid. penna.
pinus
pinus (nom.) 1. 687; 5. 435,
pinum 2. 48, 105, 196,
pinu 1. 457,
pinus (acc.) 1. 123.
Piresius
Piresius 1. 356.
Pisa
Pisae (gen.) 1. 664.
piscis
piscis (gen.) 1. 130.

pistris
pistris (nom.) 2. 531, 535 (B; K donec; GL belua).
Pitya
Pityam 2. 622.
pius
(pius 3. 637, 722; 4. 348,
pia 1. 750,
pii (m.) 5. 336,
piae (dat.) 2. 310,
pia (abl.) 2. 599,
piis (m.) 2. 264,
pios 2. 411; 4. 2,
pias 1. 80; 2. 249,
pia 1. 459, 685; 2. 330; 5. 6,
subst. m. piorum 1. 650, 842; 2. 256.
pix
picis 8. 302,
pice 1. 480; 8. 348.
placabilis
placabilis (f.) 4. 472,
placabile 1. 324,
placabile 5. 331.
placeo
placet 2. 150, 403; 4. 367; 6. 3, 15,
placent 1. 37; 2. 326; 6. 330,
placuit 7. 344,
placeat 3. 233,
placitum 3. 297,
placitae (gen.) 2. 509,
placitis (n.) 3. 416 (K; BGL placidis),
placitos 2. 5.
placidus
placidus 5. 197 (BG; KL brumae); 8. 14,
placida 1. 571,
placidi 1. 298, 410,
placidae (gen.) 1. 793,
placidum (m.) 1. 265 (L; KBG placido),
placido 1. 265 (KBG; L placidum); 4. 83,
placida 3. 434,
placidi 3. 457; 4. 422,
placida 3. 2,
placidis (n.) 3. 416 (BGL; K placitis),
placidas 4. 103,
placidis (f.) 1. 657; 2. 118,
placidis 2. 591, 635; 5. 533; 6. 458.
placitus vid. placeo.
placo
placat 1. 596, 781,
placare 8. 275,
placantia (acc.) 3. 408; 5. 98,
placati (gen. m.) 4. 338.
plaga
plaga 4. 210; 5. 327; 6. 37,
plagae (gen.) 1. 511.
planctus
planctus (nom.) 2. 393,
planctu (abl.) 3. 281, 359,
planctus (acc.) 1. 317; 2. 299, 481; 3. 315; 8. 239,
planctibus 2. 175; 4. 494.

plango
  plangeret 3. 298.
plangor
  plangore 3. 275; 6. 566.
planta
  plantae (gen.) 6. 702,
  planta 6. 540,
  plantis 3. 528,
  plantis 1. 840; 7. 4.
plantaris
  subst. plantaria (acc.) 1. 67.
plaudo
  plausa (nom. f.) 3. 527.
plaustrum
  plaustri 6. 331,
  plaustro (abl.) 2. 160,
  plaustris 6. 154; 8. 201,
  plaustra 2. 178,
  plaustris 6. 80.
plausus
  plausu (abl.) 4. 358.
Pleias
  Pleiadum 5. 46,
  Pleiades 2. 67 (L; KBG Pleiones).
Pleione
  Pleiones 1. 738; 2. 67 (KBG; L Pleiades).
plenus
  plenus 1. 230; 2. 507,
  plena 1. 414; 5. 182; 8. 456,
  plenum (m.) 1. 233,
  plena 5. 257; 7. 608,
  pleni 1. 298; 2. 441,
  plenas 1. 396, 646; 2. 110, 267,
  plena 1. 235,
  plenis (f.) 1. 708,
  plenior (m.) 1. 376.
Plias
  Plias 2. 406,
  Pliada 2. 357,
  Pliade 1. 647; 4. 269,
  Pliades 5. 415,
  Pliadas 5. 305.
plumbum
  plumbo (abl.) 1. 420.
plurimus, plus vid. multus.
poculum
  pocula 1. 143, 260,
  pocula 1. 139, 816; 2. 155, 194, 417, 654;
  4. 455; 5. 595, 616.
Poeantius
  Poeantia 1. 391,
  Poeantia (nom.) 3. 722.
Poena
  Poena (voc.) 1. 797.
poena
  poena 1. 848,
  poenae (gen.) 4. 64, 259 (B; KGL
  pugnae), 486, 536, 584,
  poenam 2. 86 (K; BGL poenas); 6.
  351,
  poenis 3. 389 (vid. abl.); 4. 461; 7. 509,
  poenas 1. 51; 2. 86 (BGL; K poenam);
  4. 13, 430, 758; 5. 38; 6. 730; 7. 421;
  8. 443,

poenis 3. 389 (vid. dat.); 4. 425, 550;
  7. 147, 357 (K; B ponti; G Ponti; L
  ventis).
polleo
  pollens (f.) 6. 85.
polluo
  polluerunt 4. 457.
Pollux
  Pollux 3. 149, 330, 667, 723; 4. 190, 225,
  271, 299, 303, 312, 331, 757; 8. 245,
  Pollux 1. 220.
polus
  polus 2. 199; 5. 107, 193,
  poli 1. 17; 2. 120, 357, 487; 4. 236, 643;
  5. 227; 8. 58, 334,
  polo 1. 829,
  polum 1. 265, 331 (KGL; B fretum),
  586; 3. 2,
  polo 1. 284; 2. 62, 89; 3. 196, 533; 4.
  527; 5. 638,
  poli 1. 622.
Polyphemus
  Polypheme 1. 457.
Polyphemus
  Polypheme 4. 107.
Polyxo
  Polyxo 2. 316.
pondus
  pondere 1. 289, 374, 830; 3. 564; 4. 290,
  pondera (acc.) 1. 39; 3. 96.
pone (5)
  3. 70, 443; 4. 198; 5. 414; 6. 253.
pono
  ponis 7. 452,
  ponunt 8. 211,
  posuit 3. 480; 4. 378,
  posuere 4. 699,
  posuissem 1. 339,
  pone 8. 78,
  positum (m.) 5. 11,
  posito (m.) 3. 541,
  positi 1. 294,
  positas 5. 580.
Ponticus
  Pontica (acc.) 1. 800.
Pontus
  Pontus 4. 723; 7. 230 (L; KG mensis;
  B metis),
  Ponti 1. 716; 4. 318, 561, 590, 712; 5.
  165; 7. 357 (G; K poenis; B ponti; L
  ventis),
  Pontum 2. 629.
pontus
  pontus 1. 152, 496, 578, 672; 2. 201, 275,
  366, 503; 4. 211, 576; 5. 337; 6. 328;
  8. 373,
  ponti 1. 37, 702; 2. 379, 529, 574, 584,
  634; 4. 513, 656; 7. 357 (B; K poenis;
  G Ponti; L ventis); 8. 180, 183, 189,
  207,
  ponto 1. 127, 413; 3. 442; 4. 347; 5. 162
  (vid. abl.),
  pontum 1. 331 (KGL; B ventum), 471,
  651; 4. 582, 665; 5. 212,

ponto 1. 59, 75; 2. 478; 3. 35, 108, 513
(KBG; L coepto), 725; 4. 221, 562,
667; 5. 34, 162 (vid. dat.), 442; 7. 329.
poples
poplite 1. 185; 2. 93; 6. 245, 551.
populator
populator 1. 683.
populeus
populeus 6. 296,
populeae (gen.) 6. 260,
populeae (nom.) 5. 429,
populeos 5. 185.
populor
populatus 3. 307.
populus
populus 8. 281 (BL; KG populi),
populo 5. 402,
populum 1. 71,
populi 3. 455; 8. 281 (KG; BL populus),
populis 1. 10, 23, 440, 559, 845; 2. 642,
populos 1. 833; 2. 296, 363, 439; 3. 352;
4. 510; 5. 405.
porrigo (porgo)
porrigit 6. 553,
porrexerat 3. 567,
porrigat 3. 234,
porgens (m.) 2. 655,
porrecta (nom. f.) 6. 234.
porro
7. 167.
porta
porta 3. 70, 253,
portae (gen.) 1. 654 (BG; KL portam),
676; 7. 382,
portam 1. 609, 654 (KL; BG portae),
porta 1. 596, 847; 3. 497,
portae 1. 832,
portis (abl.) 7. 300.
Porthaonides (KL; BG Parthaonides)
Porthaonides 3. 705.
porticus
porticibus (abl.) 1. 729; 2. 191.
portitor
portitor 1. 784; 6. 159.
porto
portat 1. 420, 431; 2. 326; 7. 591,
portant 2. 429; 5. 10; 7. 555.
portus
portu 3. 42,
portum 2. 322,
portu 7. 261,
portus (acc.) 2. 405, 656; 3. 45, 257
(KBG; L montes); 8. 370, 421.
pos
6. 135 (K; BGL post).
posco
posco 3. 672,
poscit 7. 315; 8. 63,
poscunt 1. 543; 4. 194; 7. 176; 8. 434
(BL; KG possunt),
poscat 5. 527,
poscant 5. 648 (BL; KG possint),
poscere 1. 99, 609, 770,

poscens (m.) 6. 351; 7. 593,
posci 2. 552; 6. 386.
possideo
possessa (acc.) 1. 60.
positus
positu (abl.) 6. 110 (B; KGL positus),
positus (acc.) 6. 110 (KGL; B positu).
possum
possum 1. 325; 2. 292, 293; 4. 557; 7.
270, 284,
potes 2. 490; 4. 251; 7. 241, 338; 8. 41,
145,
potest 1. 13; 7. 454; 8. 364,
possumus 7. 428,
possunt 6. 357; 8. 434 (KG; BL poscunt),
potui 1. 766; 8. 280,
potuit 1. 305, 368; 3. 683; 7. 105; 8. 290,
potuere 2. 232; 6. 519,
possim 4. 569, 630 (BGL; K possem);
7. 200,
possis 5. 394,
possit 1. 463, 701; 8. 371,
possint 5. 648 (KG; BL poscant),
possem 3. 657; 4. 630 (K; BGL possim); 8. 151,
posset 7. 199, 297; 8. 439,
posse 3. 295, 645; 7. 81; 8. 394, 438,
potuisse 4. 57; 7. 100,
potens 3. 48, 151,
potens (f.) 4. 366; 6. 680,
potentis (f.) 3. 321,
potentes (acc.) 6. 466,
potentes 3. 630,
potentior (f.) 6. 440; 7. 498.
post (adv.)
2. 347; 5. 463.
post (praepos.) (14)
1. 139, 564; 2. 563 **bis**, 662; 3. 160, 405;
4. 252 (G; KB per; L pro); 5. 77, 148,
685; 6. 135 (BGL; K pos), 347; 8. 202.
posterus
postera (nom. f.) 2. 664; 4. 423,
postremum (m.) 7. 532.
postis
postes 7. 322,
postibus 3. 25,
postes 7. 109,
postibus 2. 168.
postquam (10)
c. ind.
a) prs. 3. 27; 4. 142; 5. 468; 7. 577,
b) perf. 1. 8; 2. 94, 99; 4. 32; 7. 526;
8. 92.
potens vid. possum.
potentia
potentia (nom.) 4. 16; 5. 498.
potestas
potestas 4. 12, 19; 5. 292; 6. 460; 7. 205;
8. 381, 424.
potior
potitur 1. 520; 6. 469,
potiere 6. 332,
poteretur 7. 54.

potior
potior (f.) 4. 127, 622,
potius (nom.) 2. 253; 3. 144,
subst. potioribus (abl. n.) 3. 646 (KBG;
L pro moribus),
adv. potius 3. 298 (potius nunc BGL;
K sine crimine); 4. 119, 169, 446; 5.
324; 6. 21; 7. 14, 134, 227, 287, 290, 318,
492; 8. 66.
potis
pote (nom.) 4. 680.
potius vid. potior.
poto
potantem (m.) 5. 585,
pota (abl.) 6. 67.
praecedo
praecedit 4. 198 (KBG; L procedit).
praeceps
praeceps 3. 101, 404; 4. 263, 675; 6. 256,
652, 739; 7. 85 (KBG; L prensus), 102;
8. 261,
praeceps (f.) 4. 656, 682; 6. 715,
praecipitem (m.) 2. 289,
praecipiti 1. 83; 3. 275,
praecipiti (f.) 5. 22,
praecipites (nom. f.) 4. 658,
praecipites 2. 185; 4. 57; 8. 131,
praecipites 3. 110.
praeceptum vid. praecipio.
praecipio
praecipiunt 4. 341,
praecipere 4. 408,
praecepta (acc.) 4. 751 (K; BGL praerepta),
subst. n. praecepta (acc.) 5. 263.
praecipito
praecipitat 1. 756; 2. 116, 391, 517; 4.
627; 5. 269,
praecipitans (m.) 4. 297,
praecipitata (nom. f.) 4. 642.
praecipue
2. 351; 5. 302; 6. 493; 8. 226.
praecipuus
praecipuum (m.) 1. 779,
praecipuo (m.) 5. 463,
praecipuos 4. 364.
praeclarus
praeclara (nom. f.) 2. 149.
praecludo
praeclusa (nom. f) 4. 668.
praecordia
praecordia (nom.)) 3. 632; 4. 285.
praecurro
praecurrere 1. 804; 2. 128.
praeda
praeda 6. 313,
praedae 3. 22, 549,
praedae 2. 531,
praedam 6. 191,
praeda 4. 498, 762,
praedas 7. 29, 56.
praedico
praedicti (m.) 4. 593; 7. 72,
praedicto (abl. m.) 7. 188,
praedicta (acc.) 8. 127,

subst. n. praedicta 4. 460,
praedicta 5. 256.
praedictum vid. praedico.
praedo
praedo 8. 267,
praedonis 8. 151,
praedo 1. 723; 7. 50.
praedor
praedantur 4. 429,
praeder 5. 646,
praedari 6. 339.
praedulcis
praedulce (acc.) 4. 161.
praedurus
praeduri (gen. m.) 1. 235.
praefero
praetulit 8. 246,
praelata est 8. 341,
praeferre 5. 662.
praeficio
praeficis 2. 302.
praefigo
praefixa (nom. f.) 1. 836,
praefixa (acc.) 3. 28; 4. 379.
praefulguro
praefulgurat 3. 119.
praelabor
praelabitur 2. 580.
praemitto
praemissa (nom. f.) 1. 794.
praemium
praemia 2. 310; 4. 231; 8. 253,
praemia 2. 114; 4. 629.
praenosco
praenosceret 1. 732,
praenoscere 1. 231.
praepes
praepete (m.) 1. 578,
subst. f. praepetis 8. 33.
praeripio
praereptum (m.) 3. 543,
praerepta (acc.) 4. 751 (BGL; K praecepta).
praerumpo
praerupti (n.) 2. 88.
praesagus
praesaga 1. 694,
praesaga 5. 433,
praesaga (nom.) 3. 354.
praescius
praescia (nom. f.) 5. 53, 528.
praesens
praesens (m.) 5. 406; 6. 3; 8. 464,
praesentis (f.) 6. 659,
praesentis 4. 446; 5. 598,
praesens 5. 563,
praesenti (n.) 7. 453,
praesentia (nom.) 5. 251.
praesepe
praesepibus (abl.) 3. 56.
praestans
praestantior (f.) 4. 111.
praetempto
praetemptant 1. 314.

praetendo
praetendens (m.) 6. 75 (B; KGL praetentans),
praetentus 5. 166.
praetento
praetentans (m.) 6. 75 (KGL; B praetendens).
praeterea
5. 238.
praetereo
praeterit 5. 74.
praetexo
praetexere 3. 436.
praevenio
praeveniat 1. 768.
praevideo
praeviderat 2. 442.
precor
precor 1. 333, 811; 2. 489, 600; 3. 143,
201; 4. 335, 460, 475, 624; 5. 17, 53, 195,
292, 355, 387, 492; 6. 465, 588; 7. 162,
163 (KG; B patris; L procax), 240,
268, 275, 288, 397, 415, 437; 8. 14,
precatur 4. 64; 5. 244; 6. 212, 315; 7. 352,
precantur 2. 172; 5. 23, 117,
precari 2. 334; 6. 469; 7. 139; 8. 244,
precanti (dat. m.) 7. 387,
precantes (acc. m.) 5. 405,
precatus 2. 512; 5. 213,
subst. f. precantum 2. 240.
prehendo (prendo)
prendit 7. 587 (L; KG mittit; B mulcet),
prendere 7. 246,
prensus 7. 85 (L; KBG praeceps),
prensa 5. 136; 7. 298,
prensum (m.) 2. 26; 3. 145,
prehensum (n.) 6. 648,
prensa (abl.) 3. 534,
prensos 2. 230,
prensa 5. 159,
prensis (f.) 6. 210.
premo
premis 1. 513; 4. 474,
premit 1. 617, 711; 2. 214, 522; 3. 215;
4. 305, 681; 5. 334; 6. 523; 7. 594, 621
(KBG; L metit),
premunt 4. 564; 5. 216; 8. 465,
premebant 6. 428,
premet 4. 524,
pressit 1. 758; 2. 411,
pressere 2. 227, 454; 6. 684,
presserat 3. 417; 8. 256,
preme 1. 334; 4. 130,
premens (m.) 2. 30; 4. 649; 8. 263,
prementem 1. 733,
prementem 2. 614,
premente (m.) 5. 73,
premi 7. 298,
premenda (nom. n.) 3. 370,
pressus 2. 24; 5. 554,
pressam 1. 203,
presso (m.) 7. 63.

prenso
prensat 3. 278 (BG; KL prensant), 640,
prensant 3. 245, 278 (KL; BG prensat).
pretium
pretium (nom.) 3. 627; 4. 230.
prex
preces 1. 341,
preces 2. 326, 336; 4. 218, 372, 471, 547,
581; 5. 321, 662; 8. 442,
precibus 4. 11; 5. 509; 6. 312; 8. 386.
Priamus
Priami 2. 571.
pridem (7)
pridem 5. 313 (L; KBG primum),
iam pridem 1. 537; 3. 397; 4. 214; 6. 43,
467; 7. 224.
primaevus
primaevus 6. 570,
primaeva 2. 480,
primaevum (m.) 7. 341 (B; KL quicumque est; G qui nunc est),
primaeva (acc.) 2. 652.
primitiae
primitiae 3. 516.
primordius
subst. n. primordia (nom.) 8. 402.
primo, primum, primus vid. prior.
princeps
princeps (m.) 3. 80; 8. 298,
principe (m.) 1. 532.
principium
principio (abl.) 2. 475; 4. 133,
principia (nom.) 2. 133.
Prion
Priona 6. 619.
prior
prior 2. 533; 4. 224, 466; 5. 401; 6. 198,
267, 594; 7. 56, 61, 619; 8. 24, 36, 48,
prior 1. 162; 2. 124; 5. 282, 533; 6. 217,
458, 675, 740; 7. 217, 276, 397; 8. 410,
413,
prioris (n.) 2. 81,
priorem 7. 409,
priorem 5. 444,
priores (nom. f.) 6. 464,
subst. m. priores (nom.) 4. 351,
adv. prius 1. 9; 2. 143, 182; 3. 187; 4.
255; 5. 110, 560, 606; 6. 77, 431; 7. 29,
69, 542; 8. 132,
primus 1. 339; 2. 75, 201; 3. 172, 496;
4. 277; 5. 249; 6. 55, 214; 7. 378, 642;
8. 278, 279, 308,
prima 1. 235; 2. 176, 207, 213, 348, 423;
3. 71, 98, 490, 501; 4. 670; 5. 133, 143,
351, 388; 6. 686; 7. 37, 78, 343 (KG;
BL primam), 364, 430; 8. 396,
primi 4. 329; 5. 331; 8. 81,
primae 1. 101; 4. 233, 361, 574 (vid.
nom.),
primi 1. 760; 4. 628; 5. 357,
primo (m.) 4. 310,
primum 6. 18,
primam 2. 85, 136; 3. 81; 4. 237; 6. 714;
7. 343 (BL; KG prima), 494,
primum 7. 605,

primo 4. 394, 730; 6. 83,
prima 2. 331, 587; 3. 324; 4. 294, 398;
5. 96, 472; 7. 434,
primo 1. 709, 823; 2. 255, 403; 3. 257
(KB; GL primos), 679; 5. 69; 6. 689;
7. 260, 338,
primi 2. 121; 3. 470,
primae 4. 490, 574 (vid. gen.),
prima 2. 78,
primis (f.) 8. 44 (vid. abl.),
primis 5. 468,
primos 1. 177; 2. 464 (ad primos KBG;
L adsiduo); 3. 257 (GL; KB primo);
7. 172, 496,
primas 1. 181; 2. 177 (G; KBL pruinas), 637; 3. 10; 4. 434, 702 (BL; KG
primis); 6. 177, 641; 7. 193, 621; 8. 130,
prima 1. 1, 765; 2. 599, 655; 3. 355, 436;
4. 166, 216, 529; 5. 117, 184, 190, 274,
418; 6. 376; 7. 90, 435, 615; 8. 370,
primis 1. 22; 3. 316, 612; 5. 457,
primis 1. 784; 3. 305; 4. 702 (KG; BL
primas); 8. 44 (vid. dat.),
primis 5. 655,
subst. prima (acc.) 6. 171,
adv. primum 1. 563 (KBG; L victo);
2. 82, 445; 4. 187, 504; 5. 313 (KBG; L
pridem), 538; 7. 375 (ubi primum B;
KGL supremum), 547, 610; 8. 221,
nunc primum 2. 639,
tum primum 3. 183; 6. 396,
Vid. priusquam, tunc.
priscus
priscum (acc. n.) 1. 684,
prisca (abl.) 4. 391,
prisca (acc.) 6. 93.
prius vid. prior.
priusquam
  1. c. ind.
prius quam 5. 346; 6. 431,
  2. c. subi.
prius . . . quam 4. 696; 5. 144.
pro (praepos.) (14)
3. 646 (pro moribus L; KBG potioribus); 4. 110, 181, 430; 5. 296; 6. 230
(pro fundis B; K profundis; GL profundens), 678; 7. 90, 240, 326, 423, 487;
8. 387, 439.
pro (5)
2. 52, 291 **bis**; 3. 697; 4. 252 (L; KB
per; G post).
probo
probat 1. 500.
procax
procax (f.) 7. 163 (L; KG precor; B
patris).
procedo
procedit 4. 198 (L; KBG praecedit);
8. 458,
processere 6. 196,
processerat 3. 530,
procedere 5. 351; 7. 109, 306.
procella
procellis (abl.) 1. 612.

procellosus
procellosum (acc. n.) 3. 621.
procer
proceres 2. 347; 5. 386,
procerum 2. 329; 3. 492,
proceres 1. 553; 2. 590; 3. 608; 5. 405;
6. 595.
proclamo
proclamat 3. 269; 7. 320.
Procnessos
Procnesson 3. 34.
procul (55)
procul 1. 158, 256, 284, 401, 698, 825;
2. 279, 300, 311, 497, 597, 634, 647, 648;
3. 175, 398, 450, 451, 553, 726; 4. 56, 74,
166, 199, 298, 388, 405, 416, 453, 570 **bis,**
641, 666, 745; 5. 96, 255, 350, 441, 578;
6. 99, 259, 345, 480, 529, 577, 691; 7. 327,
558; 8. 4, 26, 174, 202, 296, 376,
haud procul hinc 8. 185.
procumbo
procumbit 3. 557; 4. 20; 7. 496 (KG;
BL procurrit),
procubuit 6. 385,
procumbere 3. 438,
procubuisse 3. 271; 4. 753.
procurro
procurrit 2. 637; 3. 595; 6. 697; 7. 496
(BL; KG procumbit),
procurrunt 6. 702.
procus
proci (nom.) 7. 235,
procorum 1. 551; 5. 239; 7. 277,
procis 5. 111,
procos 3. 536; 8. 339,
prodigium
prodigia (acc.) 4. 430,
prodigiis 1. 743.
prodo
prodit 8. 17 (BGL; K promit),
prodidit 3. 195, 410,
prodiderat 4. 481,
prodite 3. 216,
prodere 7. 309,
prodita (nom. f.) 4. 491; 5. 233; 7. 486;
8. 165,
prodita (acc.) 5. 523.
produco
producunt 5. 381,
producere 6. 528.
proelium
proelia 2. 662; 3. 320; 5. 221, 283,
proelia 3. 15, 64, 511 (L; K belua; BG
bellave); 4. 132; 5. 274, 286, 464, 635;
6. 31, 80, 92, 387, 406; 7. 545, 638; 8. 336,
346.
profero
profert 6. 752,
proferet 3. 708,
protulit 1. 205; 4. 245, 580; 6. 385 (KB;
GL propulit),
proferat 8. 191 (KG; BL perferat),
prolata (nom. f.) 2. 630.

proficiscor
  profecti (nom.) 4. 204.
proflo
  proflavit 7. 571,
  proflantes (acc. m.) 6. 435.
profor
  profatur 2. 289; 3. 200, 534; 7. 476.
profugio
  profugit (perf.) 7. 537.
profugus
  profugi (m.) 3. 673; 4. 556,
  profugo 1. 520,
  profugae 8. 10, 48,
  profugum 2. 25,
  profugam 7. 398,
  profuga 7. 129,
  profugi 3. 57; 6. 148,
  profugis (dat. m.) 8. 262.
profundo
  profundens (m.) 6. 230 (GL; K profundis; B pro fundis),
  profusi (nom.) 3. 3; 6. 106.
profundus
  profundo (n.) 5. 593,
  profundum (n.) 7. 401,
  profundis (dat. m.) 6. 230 (K; B pro
  fundis; GL profundens),
  subst. n. profundum 4. 730,
  profundi 1. 160; 2. 383, 605; 4. 180; 7.
  478,
  profundo 4. 403,
  profundum 1. 585,
  profundo 1. 574; 3. 151; 4. 642; 5. 337,
  438; 8. 314.
progenies
  progenies 1. 841; 3. 669,
  progeniem 1. 27, 695; 6. 337,
  progenies (voc. s.) 5. 551.
progigno
  progenuit 5. 462; 6. 50.
progredior
  progresso (dat. m.) 4. 567.
prohibeo
  prohibet 2. 224; 4. 559,
  prohibebit 3. 305,
  prohibere 1. 594; 4. 500; 5. 256.
proicio
  proicit 2. 527,
  proiecerat 7. 141,
  proiectus 4. 268; 8. 90,
  proiecta (nom. f.) 7. 321; 8. 93.
proles
  proles 1. 12, 53, 162, 415, 436, 468, 518,
  771; 2. 149, 153; 3. 345, 543, 667, 705;
  4. 141, 150, 213, 256, 462, 501, 542, 549;
  5. 463 (L; KBG tellus), 581, 653; 6.
  542, 636; 8. 15, 112,
  prolis 3. 737; 6. 126,
  prolem 4. 120, 757,
  proles 4. 327; 5. 204,
  prole 1. 612, 721; 3. 358; 5. 235, 383,
  603; 6. 148.
Prometheus
  Promethei 5. 154.

Prometheus
  Prometheae (gen.) 7. 356.
promineo
  prominet 7. 30.
promissum vid. promitto.
promitto
  promittis 5. 212,
  promisi 5. 494; 7. 288,
  promisere 6. 731,
  promittere 7. 317,
  promittitur 1. 272,
  fuit promissa 8. 153,
  promissam 7. 426 (KGL; B promissum); 8. 222, 249,
  promissum 7. 426 (B; KGL promissam),
  promisse 2. 486,
  promisso (n.) 1. 305,
  promissa (acc.) 5. 621; 8. 420,
  subst. n. promissa 4. 649,
  promissa 1. 182; 2. 577; 4. 59; 6. 22,
  675; 7. 503, 518, 650.
promo
  promit 2. 409; 7. 357; 8. 17 (K; BGL
  prodit),
  promite 6 41,
  promere 4. 144, 624,
  promptus 5. 470 (L; KG propius; B
  prosperus); 6. 344 (G; KB propius;
  L sospes).
promoveo
  promovet 2. 519; 8. 130.
promptus vid. promo.
pronus
  prona 1. 624; 8. 340,
  pronum (acc. n.) 6. 707,
  prono (abl.) 2. 35,
  prono 3. 564,
  proni 1. 185,
  pronae 2. 520 (KG; BL pronas),
  prona 1. 691; 3. 33,
  pronas 2. 520 (BL; KG pronae).
propago
  propago 5. 125,
  propago 6. 547.
propello
  propulit 4. 311; 6. 385 (GL; KB protulit),
  propulsa (nom. f.) 1. 494.
propendeo
  propendens (m.) 7. 588.
propere
  2. 237; 5. 407.
propero
  properantia (acc.) 5. 196,
  properanda (nom. f.) 4. 573 (GL; K
  speranda; B rapienda).
properus
  properus 5. 470 (B; KG propius; L
  promptus),
  properos 4. 176.
propinquo
  propinquat 1. 741, 763; 2. 147; 4. 544;
  5. 359; 6. 29; 8. 364,
  propinquanti (dat. m.) 7. 598.

propinquus
propinquae (gen.) 3. 549; 5. 532,
propinqua (abl.) 1. 569; 3. 214,
propinquas 6. 557,
propinquis (n.) 3. 626.
propior
propior 1. 58, 547; 4. 443, 638,
propior 2. 229; 7. 156 (L; KBG levior),
462,
propioris (m.) 3. 205,
propioris (n.) 4. 514,
propiore (m.) 5. 168,
adv. propius 3. 139; 4. 567, 635; 5. 177,
470 (KG; B properus; L promptus);
6. 344 (KB; G promptus; L sospes),
proximus 1. 394; 5. 266, 579,
proxima (nom.) 2. 531; 3. 72, 392; 5.
327; 6. 48; 7. 618,
proxima (nom.) 2. 136; 4. 99, 589,
proxima 3. 483; 4. 601,
subst. n. proxima (acc.) 4. 440.
Propontis
Propontis 2. 645.
proprius
proprio (abl. m.) 5. 476.
propter
4. 560; 7. 315, 351; 8. 46.
prora
prora 5. 71,
prorae (dat.) 2. 443,
proram 5. 211 (KG; BL puppim),
prora 1. 314, 404; 8. 463.
proripio
proripit 5. 268.
prorumpo
prorumpit 7. 102,
proruptus 6. 632,
prorupti (gen. m.) 4. 507.
proruo
proruit (prs.) 7. 600.
proseco
prosecta (nom. n.) 3. 439.
prosequor
prosequitur 1. 135; 2. 199, 504; 4. 629;
7. 557.
Proserpina
Proserpina (nom.) 5. 345.
prosilio
prosilit 6. 456; 7. 34; 8. 21 **bis**, 309, 357;
prosiliunt 2. 170; 4. 466; 5. 558,
prosiluit 1. 310, 705; 7. 216.
prospecto
prospectat 8. 299.
prospectus
prospectus (nom. s.) 2. 628.
prosper
prospera (nom. f.) 3. 184.
prospicio
prospicio 1. 330,
prospicis 1. 795,
prospicit 3. 559; 7. 311,
prospiciunt 2. 188; 4. 108,
prospexit 3. 130; 4. 115; 7. 575,
prospexerat 7. 193,

prospice 5. 610,
prospiciens (m.) 3. 551.
prosterno
prostravit 3. 185,
prosternitur 6. 508.
prosubigo
prosubigit 4. 288.
prosum
prodes 7. 248,
proderit 8. 355,
profuit 3. 173; 5. 51,
profuerit (ind.) 8. 340.
protero
proterit 6. 522.
Proteus
Protea 2. 318.
protinus (30)
1. 107, 572, 637; 2. 249, 329, 538; 3. 457,
516; 4. 222, 366; 5. 94, 211, 399, 555,
636; 6. 8, 388, 481, 666; 7. 73, 189, 266,
346, 470, 488, 523, 634, 644; 8. 200, 325.
Protis (?)
Protin 3. 158.
protono
protonat 4. 205.
proturbo
proturbat 1. 597.
proveho
provehat 4. 421.
providus
providus 4. 271.
proximus vid. propior.
prudentia
prudentia (nom.) 4. 622.
pruina
pruinae (gen.) 5. 158,
pruinas 2. 177 (KBL; G primas); 7.
358; 8. 210,
pruinis 2. 287; 4. 70; 6. 338.
Psamathe
Psamathen 1. 364.
pubes
pubes 1. 354; 5. 40, 385, 560; 6. 38; 8.
310, 415,
pubis 4. 528 (KB; GL puppis),
pubi 5. 621 (L; KBG puppi),
pubem 6. 5 (BGL; K puppem),
pube 2. 291; 7. 77.
pubesco
pubescere 7. 340.
pudeo
pudet 4. 57; 7. 43,
pudebit 8. 350,
pudeat 7. 482,
pudendum (acc. n.) 3. 26; 7. 331,
pudendo (m.) 6. 502.
pudibundus
pudibunda (acc.) 1. 809; 7. 303.
pudor
pudor 1. 44, 172; 2. 526; 4. 284; 5. 324;
6. 374, 472, 674; 7. 79, 177, 294, 324,
435, 462, 514; 8. 313, 441, 464,
pudoris 2. 148; 5. 356; 7. 386,
pudori 7. 156,
pudorem 7. 411,

pudor 3. 520; 8. 269,
pudore 2. 470; 4. 655.
puella
puellae (nom.) 8. 142.
puer
puer 1. 109, 167, 257, 409; 3. 183, 536;
4. 22, 240; 6. 83, 707,
pueri 2. 415; 3. 555,
puero 6. 642,
puerum 3. 552,
puer 1. 718, 824; 4. 53,
pueros 5. 339.
puerilis
puerilia (acc.) 1. 269.
pugna
pugna 4. 455; 6. 352, 357,
pugnae 2. 419, 509; 3. 210, 689; 4. 259
(KGL; B poenae); 5. 532; 6. 23, 65,
142, 228, 659, 749; 8. 381,
pugnae 2. 197; 6. 298,
pugnam 2. 21; 3. 81; 4. 227, 442; 5. 580,
pugna 4. 193; 5. 663, 675; 6. 180; 8. 319,
pugnae 1. 141; 4. 147; 6. 617 (KGL; B
turmae),
pugnas 3. 250, 518, 710; 4. 609; 5. 129,
692; 6. 32, 108, 177, 558, 601, 720, 728;
8. 344.
pugno
pugnat 8. 373,
pugnent 1. 472,
pugnata (acc.) 1. 770.
pulcher
pulcher 1. 218; 3. 184; 8. 226,
pulchrae 4. 240,
pulchrum (n.) 5. 363,
pulchro 3. 513 (KGL; B pulso),
pulchro 3. 522,
pulchrior 7. 107, 263,
pulchrior 1. 40; 6. 313,
pulcherrima (acc.) 1. 498; 5. 485.
pulsator
pulsator 5. 693.
pulso
pulsat 1. 139; 3. 93; 7. 312,
pulsant 3. 390; 8. 305,
pulset 4. 149,
pulsent 2. 511,
pulsans (f.) 3. 62,
pulsantem (f.) 5. 611,
pulsante (n.) 2. 617,
pulsatur 6. 685.
pulsus
pulsus (nom.) 6. 142,
pulsu 3. 473 (vid. abl.),
pulsu 3. 473 (vid. dat.); 4. 285; 5. 184;
6. 168.
pulvereus
pulvereis (abl. m.) 4. 608.
pulvis
pulvere 1. 13, 452; 2. 419; 4. 267; 6. 188,
415; 7. 645.
puniceus
puniceo (m.) 1. 384,
puniceo (m.) 7. 539,
puniceas 3. 411,

puppis
puppis 1. 181, 422, 479, 619, 638; 2. 322,
445; 3. 41; 4. 220, 615, 733; 5. 557; 8.
139, 357, 378,
puppis 1. 128, 380, 603, 672; 4. 528 (GL;
KB pubis),
puppi 2. 292; 5. 621 (KBG; L pubi),
puppem 1. 94, 185, 215, 370, 628; 2. 71,
541; 3. 459, 474, 487; 4. 114, 542, 606,
666; 5. 116, 220, 294; 6. 5 (K; BGL
pubem); 8. 5, 132, 144, 292, 297, 308,
puppim 5. 211 (BL; KG proram),
puppe 1. 569; 4. 85; 5. 45, 72, 214; 7. 60;
8. 202, 267,
puppi 2. 622; 8. 177,
puppes 3. 132,
puppibus 1. 719; 8. 363,
puppes 2. 108; 6. 412,
puppibus 1. 339; 8. 320.
purpura
purpura (nom.) 1. 428.
purpureus
purpuream 3. 107,
purpureum 1. 573,
purpureo (m.) 3. 422,
purpureos 3. 179.
purus
pura (nom. f.) 2. 56.
puto
putas 8. 467,
putat 6. 175 (B; KGL pater); 7. 204,
215, 639; 8. 443,
putant 1. 625; 2. 10; 3. 367; 4. 694,
putasti 6. 323,
putem 7. 51,
putes 2. 520 (BL; KG rates),
putet 1. 800; 7. 81,
putent 1. 645; 4. 639.
Pylius
Pyliam 6. 202.
pyra
pyras 3. 333.
Pyragmon
Pyragmon 1. 583.
Pyrnus
Pyrno (abl.) 3. 112.
Pyrois
Pyroenta 5. 432.
Pyrrha
Pyrrhae (gen.) 6. 390.
qua (21)
1. interrog.
1. 701, 715,
2. rel.
2. 136 (K; BGL ad), 201, 614; 3. 148,
189, 200, 670 (KB; GL sequar); 4. 310,
345; 5. 327; 6. 328, 375, 514, 670; 7. 229,
270, 618; 8. 268,
qua . . . ibi 6. 584.
quadrifidus
quadrifida (abl.) 1. 663.
quadripes
subst. m. quadripes 3. 552.
quaeat
quaeat 7. 543 (K; BG meat; L parat).

quaero
quaero 8. 270, 440 (K; BGL quaere),
quaerit 2. 124; 3. 609; 6. 450, 578, 682;
7. 119,
quaeritis 2. 595,
quaeret 7. 447,
quaerent 4. 525,
quaererent 1. 425,
quaere 2. 251; 5. 355; 7. 245; 8. 440
(BGL; K quaero),
quaerere 1. 66; 3. 517; 8. 361, 466 (G;
K om.; B lenit; L iras),
quaesivisse 3. 627,
quaesisse 8. 40,
quaerens (f.) 6. 585; 7. 115, 326,
quaerenti (m.) 8. 109,
quaerentem 5. 234; 8. 359,
quaerentem 1. 126; 3. 507,
quaeritur 7. 379,
quaesitam 5. 505,
quaesita (nom.) 8. 253,
quaesita 2. 11,
quaerenda (nom. f.) 2. 284.
quaeso
quaeso 7. 478; 8. 280.
qualis
  1. interrog.
qualis (nom. f.) 4. 398,
qualem (m.) 3. 177,
  2. rel.
qualis 1. 602; 2. 515, 546; 3. 65, 67; 5.
565; 6. 613, 527 (KL; B quali in; G
quale in); 7. 645; 8. 228,
qualis (nom.) 2. 128, 192; 4. 268, 604;
7. 111, 375, 635; 8. 21,
qualem 5. 22, 506,
qualem 6. 260, 711; 7. 261,
quale 2. 495; 6. 527 (quale in G; KL
qualis; B quali in),
quali (f.) 6. 527 (quali in B; KL qualis; G quale in),
quales 4. 104, 700,
quales (nom. f.) 6. 505; 7. 401,
qualis (f.) 7. 274,
qualibus (n.) 5. 566,
qualis (nom. m.) . . . talis . . . talem
8. 27,
qualis (nom. f.) . . . talis 5. 343,
qualem (f.) . . . talis 5. 89,
qualis (nom. f.) . . . cum 8. 461,
qualem (f.) . . . cum . . . talis . . .
talem 8. 446,
subst. m. qualem 5. 80,
Vid. aliter, haud, sic, ubi.
qualiter (6)
qualiter 1. 690; 3. 359; 4. 195; 6. 390,
qualiter . . . cum 2. 458,
qualiter . . . cum . . . ubi . . . sic 5.
304,
Vid. talis.
quam (36)
  1. exclam.
quam 1. 173 (KG; BL quas), 329; 2.
546; 3. 241, 544; 4. 469; 7. 336; 8. 98 **bis**,
  2. interrog.

quam 6. 583,
  3. rel.
a) c. posit.
quam 5. 208,
b) in comparat.
quam 2. 386; 4. 368, 715 (quam vix L;
K quavis; BG quamvis); 5. 408, 493,
569, 686 (quam tum licet B; K quam-
tumlibet; G quantum licet; L quantum
luet); 7. 428; 8. 192, 193, 304,
alter . . . quam . . . ubi 6. 420,
magis quam 2. 522,
magis . . . quam 1. 177; 4. 753,
magis . . . quam cum 7. 623,
magis . . . quam . . . quam 6. 719,
nec minus . . . quam cum 7. 24,
non aliud quam 8. 316,
non secus . . . quam 5. 368; 7. 604,
prius quam 6. 431,
prius . . . quam 5. 144,
quam . . . sic 1. 757,
Vid. aliter, antequam, haud, postquam,
priusquam, secus.
quamlibet
8. 410.
quamquam (15)
  1. c. ind.
2. 562; 7. 94 (G; KBL numquam);
8. 401,
  2. c. subi.
3. 506; 5. 373; 6. 38; 8. 205,
  3. sine verb.
1. 149, 309; 3. 369, 599, 642; 4. 520, 610;
5. 480,
Vid. tamen.
quamvis (5)
  1. c. subi.
4. 715 (BG; K quavis; L quam vix);
6. 447; 8. 80,
  2. c. abl. absol.
1. 360,
  3. c. adi.
8. 113.
quando (23)
  1. adv.
quando 4. 170 (B; KGL fando),
siquando 1. 835; 5. 473; 7. 205, 567;
8. 213, 226,
  2. coni.
a) interrog.
quando 2. 298, 299, 395; 4. 638; 5. 200
bis; 6. 487; 7. 16, 478 (BGL; K quantum),
b) rel.
quando 1. 241; 2. 263; 4. 122; 5. 363;
7. 156, 241; 8. 41.
quantus
  1. exclam.
quantum (acc. n.) 1. 168 **bis,**
quanto 1. 629; 3. 543,
quanta (abl.) 2. 53; 4. 10,
quantis (m.) 2. 52,
quantis (n.) 1. 242 (K; BGL tantis),
quantos 1. 169,
quantas 2. 290,

quanta 2. 563,
quantis (n.) 3. 261,
  2. interrog.
quantus 1. 221; 5. 138, 639,
quanta 1. 847; 3. 499,
quantum 6. 677,
quanti (n.) 6. 45,
quantum (n.) 7. 478 (K; BGL quando),
quanto (n.) 6. 34,
quantis (m.) 6. 596,
quantos 4. 720,
quantis (f.) 7. 540,
  3. rel.
quantus 1. 337; 3. 130; 5. 209; 6. 165, 611,
quanta 4. 604,
quantum (acc. n.) 1. 234,
quanto (m.) 6. 112,
quantum (acc. n.) . . . tantum 2. 528,
adv. quantum 1. 741; 4. 398, 440, 544; 5. 51 bis, 518, 613, 686 (quantum licet G; K quantumlibet; B quam tum licet; L quantum luet); 8. 364 (G; KBL aut),
tantum . . . quantum 1. 319, 406,
Vid. ubi.
quantuslibet
adv. quantumlibet 5. 686 (K; B quam tum licet; G quantum licet; L quantum luet).
quare
5. 538.
quartus
quarto (abl. m.) 2. 367.
quasso
quasso 8. 276,
quassat 1. 528; 5. 526; 7. 578,
quassare 8. 84,
quassans 3. 124,
quassans (f.) 1. 840; 2. 196.
quater
1. 400.
quatio 8. 278,
quatis 1. 195,
quatit 1. 694; 2. 22, 122, 269, 501; 3. 21; 5. 272, 310, 564; 6. 169, 293; 7. 149,
quatiunt 1. 743,
quateret 1. 82; 5. 93,
quaterent 8. 456,
quatiens (m.) 3. 338,
quati 7. 612.
quavis
quavis 4. 715 (K; BG quamvis; L quam vix).
que (1916)
que 1. 2, 3, 7, 11, 14, 20, 30, 31, 32, 37, 41, 43, 46, 49 (meque BGL; K namque), 54, 58, 60, 62, 71, 76, 77, 78, 79, 80, 85, 87 bis, 90, 91, 96, 98, 99, 99 (que vehat L; KBG revehat), 100, 103, 104 bis, 106, 109, 111, 112, 114, 115, 124 bis, 125, 134 bis, 137 bis, 138, 139, 140, 142 bis, 143, 147, 153, 159, 161, 163, 167, 178 (K; BGL om.), 180, 182, 184, 186,

190 bis, 195, 197, 201, 207, 215, 216, 219, 222, 227, 230, 234, 235, 237, 242, 243, 248, 249, 251, 253, 254, 256, 259, 262, 265, 266, 283, 284, 290, 293 bis, 294 bis, 299, 303, 306 (dumque KG; BL nunc), 322, 333, 340, 341, 343, 347, 349, 358, 364, 365, 374, 383, 385, 388, 389 (felixque BL; K felevis; G et levis), 395, 398, 409, 410 (L; KBG om.), 420 (caelataque BL; KG celer aspera), 424, 429, 434 bis, 443, 455, 466, 469, 473, 476, 479, 485, 487, 489, 490, 495 bis, 497, 499, 506, 507 bis, 513, 522, 525, 528, 529, 532, 534, 539, 540, 542, 544 bis, 546, 547, 550, 553, 555, 556 bis, 557, 558, 560, 562, 564, 570, 572, 576, 578, 579, 583, 584, 585, 592, 593, 596, 603, 605, 611, 612, 614, 617, 618, 622, 623, 625, 632, 636, 644, 645, 646, 650, 652, 653, 655, 660, 661, 663, 667, 669 bis, 671, 676, 678, 681, 688, 689, 699, 700, 703 bis, 705, 708, 709, 711, 714, 720, 722, 724, 730, 736, 737, 739, 741, 743, 745, 747, 751, 753, 755 bis, 756, 758, 761, 762, 764, 770, 778 bis, 781, 786, 791, 793, 796 bis, 800, 802, 803, 805, 807, 808, 810, 813, 821, 823, 825, 826, 827, 831, 833, 836, 839, 843 bis, 844 bis, 845, 846, 847, 849; 2. 1, 5, 7, 11, 16, 17, 19 bis, 21 bis, 27 bis, 28, 29, 33, 36, 39, 40, 41, 42, 45, 56, 57, 61 (arsque B; KGL atque), 65, 67, 73, 74, 76, 77, 81, 86, 92 bis, 101, 105, 106, 110, 111, 116, 118, 120, 129, 131, 132, 134, 137, 138, 145, 147, 150, 152, 153, 155 bis, 159, 161, 162, 163, 165 bis, 169 bis, 170, 171, 176, 177, 178 (que quin L; KBG sequi), 179, 181, 182, 183 bis, 186, 188 bis, 189, 190, 191, 194, 197, 202, 205, 208, 210, 211, 212, 213, 221, 222, 224, 226, 229 bis, 230, 234, 236, 239, 240, 241, 246 bis, 248, 250, 254 bis, 255, 258, 260, 264, 265 bis, 266, 267, 268, 269, 273, 281 bis, 286, 299, 301, 301 (BGL; K om.), 308 bis, 309, 310, 313, 318, 320, 325, 326, 327, 328, 333, 335, 336 bis, 340 bis, 343, 351, 356, 359, 360, 363, 366, 370, 371, 372, 376 bis, 379, 382, 388, 390 bis, 392, 393, 398, 401, 407, 408, 409, 411, 412, 415, 418, 419, 426, 431, 437, 439 (diemque BGL; K dicam), 440, 441, 443, 451, 454, 455, 456, 462, 463, 470, 472, 475, 481, 483, 485, 489 bis, 492, 494, 498, 501, 502, 504, 507, 510 bis, 511, 512 bis, 513, 518, 519, 520 bis, 521, 525, 527, 531, 532, 533, 536, 539, 541, 542, 543, 544, 551, 560, 561, 567 bis, 568, 569 (ereptaque BG; KL et rapta), 576, 580, 581, 585, 588, 589, 593, 598, 600, 605, 612, 613 bis, 614, 616, 619 bis, 621, 622 bis, 626, 631, 638 bis, 642, 642 (G; KBL om.), 645, 646, 649, 650, 651 bis, 652, 661, 663; 3. 2, 5, 9 (BGL; K om.), 14, 15, 17, 19, 21, 25, 26, 28, 30, 34, 36, 37, 38, 41 bis, 42, 48, 52, 53, 54, 59, 61, 66, 68 bis, 76, 79, 82, 84 bis, 89 bis, 92, 96, 97, 100, 102, 104, 106, 115, 117,

577, 582, 584, 585, 587 (adque KG; BL atque), 594 **bis**, 595 **bis**, 597 **bis**, 599, 600, 602 **bis**, 603, 605, 609, 612, 613 **bis**, 627 **bis**, 629 **bis**, 640, 646, 647, 649, 652; 8. 7 **ter**, 11, 15, 18 **bis**, 31, 36, 38, 40, 42, 46, 47, 50, 52, 62 (que pavens BGL; K patiens), 64, 68, 69, 71, 73, 74, 75 (que o L; KBG quoque), 84, 88, 96, 102, 117, 118, 120, 122, 126, 135 **ter**, 143, 147, 149, 152 **bis**, 159, 163, 164, 171, 173, 175, 181 **bis**, 191, 201, 215, 222 **bis**, 223, 226, 232, 238, 240 **bis**, 244 **bis**, 245, 258, 260, 263, 264, 274, 278, 284 (que coire BG; KL coiisse), 285 (itque BG; KL atque), 286, 288, 291, 293, 294, 295, 297, 306, 310, 313, 321, 322, 323, 325, 326, 328, 331, 338, 343, 352, 358 **bis**, 362 (KBG; L **om**.), 364, 366, 367, 372, 373 **bis**, 374, 376, 378, 381, 386, 392, 397, 402, 403 (que mora B; KG mortem; L Martem), 403 **bis**, 405, 407, 409, 411, 414, 416, 418, 420, 422, 425, 427, 428, 433, 434, 444, 448, 454 **bis**, 456, 459, 462,

que . . . que 1. 15, 26, 28, 55, 150, 297, 308, 325, 331, 345, 350, 501, 586, 673, 693, 695, 729, 733, 739, 769; 2. 14, 39, 59, 89, 121, 123, 166, 230, 247, 468, 590; 3. 354, 375, 547, 640; 4. 45, 412, 654, 673; 5. 388, 493, 650; 6. 21, 86, 123, 127, 195, 211, 695, 758; 7. 101, 192, 350; 8. 2, 86, 94, 200, 281, 285, 331, 339, 389, 431,

que . . . que . . . que 1. 208, 725; 4. 349; 8. 141,

que . . . que . . . que . . . que 1. 691.

queo
quivi 1. 84,
queat 1. 67, 76, 831; 2. 572; 6. 5; 7. 507.

quercus
quercus 5. 66; 7. 551 (quercus et L; KB velleris; G vellera et),
quercus 1. 448,
quercum 1. 70, 302; 5. 230,
quercu 1. 146; 5. 250; 6. 243,
quercus 1. 544,
quercus 3. 299, 445.

querella
querellas 2. 160,
querellis 6. 433; 8. 158, 453.

queribundus
queribunda (nom. f.) 7. 126.

queror
queror 4. 752; 5. 628; 7. 487,
queritur 4. 46,
queri 1. 519; 7. 225,
querens (f.) 5. 648,
questa (nom. f.) 3. 328.

questus
questu (abl.) 2. 364, 402; 3. 291, 385, 543, 639; 5. 623; 7. 311 **bis**; 8. 171, 454,
questus (acc.) 1. 112, 165, 508, 530; 3. 650; 4. 25, 42, 117; 7. 6, 510,
questibus 1. 50; 2. 167; 6. 726; 7. 195.

qui (adv.)
qui 8. 242 (vid. interrog. adi.).

qui
1. pron.
qui 1. 44, 69, 194, 364, 373, 374, 381, 416 **bis**, 440, 463, 476, 482, 550, 662 (KL; BG cum); 2. 44, 218, 636; 3. 39 (at qui BL; KG atque), 159, 204, 323, 619; 4. 148, 149, 202, 559, 684; 5. 19, 87, 233, 384, 459, 547, 626, 659, 660; 6. 100, 130, 215, 268, 323, 358, 593, 734 (BL; KG quo), 760; 7. 84, 129, 130, 167 **bis**, 263, 316, 341 (qui nunc est G; KL quicumque est; B primaevum), 342, 343, 343 (L; KG quem; B quam), 652 (KGL; B quae); 8. 280,
quae 1. 2, 40, 100, 537, 569, 766, 795; 2. 295, 422; 3. 27, 71, 683, 708; 4. 179 **bis**, 474; 5. 110, 657; 6. 10, 366, 384, 452; 7. 366, 498; 8. 33, 72 **bis**, 189,
quod 1. 830; 2. 494; 4. 88 (KBG; L quo), 457; 6. 40 **bis**; 8. 304,
cuius 1. 108; 2. 12; 6. 267, 434, 518, 524,
cuius (f.) 2. 332, 499; 8. 114,
cui 1. 7, 55, 231, 384, 418 **bis**, 505, 776, 837; 2. 487, 550; 4. 127, 368, 758; 5. 67, 123, 250, 588, 597; 6. 61, 223, 262, 296, 676; 8. 59,
cui (f.) 4. 611; 5. 286, 357,
quem 1. 61, 355, 379, 388, 411, 414, 451, 453, 463, 474, 592, 773; 2. 145, 386, 523, 557; 3. 6, 48, 103, 104, 131, 252 **bis**, 535, 587, 688; 4. 16, 200, 426, 554; 5. 14, 187, 458, 471, 493, 578, 582; 6. 49, 66, 309, 369, 528, 535, 589 **bis**, 641, 673, 742; 7. 28, 267, 315, 343 (KG; B quam; L qui), 520 (quem tanta KBG; L temptanti), 561, 562; 8. 13, 23, 184, 186, 342, quam 1. 81, 657, 660; 2. 117, 154, 286, 623; 3. 88, 109,; 4. 269, 623; 5. 294; 6. 174, 398; 7. 112, 273, 343 (B; KG quem; L qui), 410, 468; 8. 153,
quod 2. 601; 4. 456; 5. 313, 314, 321; 6. 275, 650; 7. 525,
quo 1. 345; 3. 121 (in quo omen K; BG inque omen; L insomnes); 6. 734 (KG; BL qui), 735; 7. 162,
qua 3. 51, 52; 6. 440; 7. 333 (qua non KGL; B cistam), 355; 8. 109, 354,
quo 2. 82; 4. 88 (L; KBG quod); 5. 535; 7. 39, 165; 8. 161,
qui 1. 819; 2. 396 **bis**; 4. 108, 462; 5. 325; 6. 68; 7. 18, 20; 8. 127, 390,
quae 2. 139,
quae 3. 461 **bis**; 4. 711; 7. 15,
quorum 4. 761; 6. 403, 404, 627,
quarum 1. 832,
quorum 1. 845,
quibus (m.) 1. 103, 667, 788; 3. 391, 505 **bis**, 679; 4. 184, 614, 742, 744; 5. 651,
quis (m.) 6. 90, 107,
quibus (n.) 6. 471,
quis (n.) 6. 493; 7. 207,
quos 1. 99, 101, 111, 359, 367, 652; 2. 19, 231, 369 (B; KG qui; L dum); 3. 396; 4. 251; 5. 86 **bis**, 461, 558, 559; 6. 12, 25, 67, 97, 102, 204, 414 **bis**; 7. 12, 51, 52;

quis 2. 251, 571; 3. 355; 4. 215; 5. 48,
171, 578; 6. 219, 515 **bis**, 588; 7. 40 **bis;**
8. 241, 437, 438,
quae 5. 133, 135, 453; 7. 40,
quid 4. 477 (KBG; L haud); 6. 25; 7.
60; 8. 270, 406,
cuius (m.) 5. 63,
cui (m.) 4. 216; 5. 47 **bis**, 481, 482; 6.
200, 201,
quem 1. 417; 2. 456; 4. 466; 6. 355 **ter,**
quam 5. 134,
quid 1. 71, 517 **bis**, 519 (KGL; B quo),
757; 2. 377; 3. 18, 586 **bis**, 660; 4. 25, 55,
142, 599, 600, 688 **bis;** 5. 37, 467, 468,
527, 584 **bis**, 631, 635, 636, 673; 6. 454,
727, 730; 7. 13, 131, 200, 309, 421, 437;
8. 147, 158, 290, 370, 387, 388, 415 (L;
KBG vir), 441, 459,
quo (n.) 7. 434,
quae (n.) 4. 144,
quibus (m.) 5. 608,
quos 1. 225; 3. 270; 5. 282,
quibus (n.) 7. 433,
b) indef.
quis 5. 503, 689,
nequis 8. 51,
si quis 6. 261, 711,
si quid 7. 71; 8. 157,
si quem 4. 591,
quid 7. 507,
si quid 1. 732,
si qua (acc.) 5. 665,
    2. adi.
a) interrog.
quis 1. 172, 291, 387 (L; KBG quin);
3. 574, 697; 5. 453; 7. 36, 37, 493, 517,
529; 8. 58, 148, 259, 313,
qui 1. 744; 2. 66; 4. 704; 5. 139, 283;
6. 46,
quae 2. 218, 352, 469; 3. 75, 304, 305,
373, 542; 4. 439; 5. 353, 605, 609 **bis**,
624; 6. 283; 7. 218, 219; 8. 179 **bis**, 312,
quod 2. 468; 8. 58,
cui (m.) 7. 235,
cui (n.) 3. 293,
quem 1. 223; 3. 177; 4. 62; 5. 517; 8. 77,
quam 2. 290; 3. 511,
quod 1. 598; 5. 658; 7. 479,
quo 1. 768; 4. 396; 7. 9 **bis**, 433,
qua 1. 66, 551 (BGL; K quae); 2. 68;
3. 206, 735; 4. 364, 396, 638; 5. 323;
7. 427; 8. 370, 371,
quo 1. 848 (KG; B quot; L quae);
2. 67; 5. 139, 658; 7. 7, 323,
qui 8. 242 (vid. adv.),
quae (n.) 1. 848 (L; KG quo; B quot);
2. 352; 3. 409; 5. 283, 605; 7. 516, 522,
quibus (f.) 6. 181,
quibus 2. 217; 3. 94 **bis**, 292; 5. 285; 6.
678,
quos 1. 329; 4. 365, 379; 6. 33; 7. 91,
quas 1. 173 (BL; KG quam); 4. 55,
600, 630, 718, 719; 5. 38; 6. 2,
quae 1. 551 (K; BGL qua), 553, 768
(K; BGL quo); 2. 242; 3. 511, 698, 733,

735; 4. 62, 379, 441; 6. 2; 7. 87, 426,
quibus 4. 438,
quis (m.) 6. 35,
quibus 1. 715; 3. 573; 5. 612,
quibus 1. 744; 4. 9, 569,
b) indef.
si quis 5. 509; 7. 266; 8. 264,
nequa 1. 179, 509; 3. 490,
si qua 1. 75; 4. 541, 572, 710; 7. 199,
si quod (nom.) 1. 807,
nequa (abl.) 1. 478,
si quos 5. 474,
Vid. enim.

quisnam
    1. pron.
quisnam 1. 155 (L; KBG quisquam);
3. 475,
quaenam 1. 224,
quaenam (acc.) 1. 211,
    2. adi.
quinam 3. 304; 6. 17,
quaenam 3. 373; 4. 156,
quemnam 3. 376,
quodnam 7. 41,
quinam 7. 234,
quaenam (f.) 7. 529,
quaenam (acc.) 1. 559; 4. 629.

quisquam
quisquam 4. 155 (KBG; L quisnam);
5. 562; 6. 594; 7. 642; 8. 272,
quemquam 7. 203; 8. 158,
quidquam 7. 331,
quicquam 7. 490,
Vid. non.

quisque
    1. pron.
quisque 2. 21; 3. 389; 5. 616; 6. 351;
7. 557,
quaeque 2. 166,
cuique (m.) 2. 191; 3. 336,
quemque 1. 431; 4. 649; 5. 605; 6. 628;
8. 395,
quaeque (acc.) 3. 583,
    2. adi.
quisque 1. 352; 3. 72,
quaeque (s.) 6. 31,
quaeque (acc.) 4. 440.

quisquis
subst. quisquis 4. 240,
quidquid 3. 671,
quicquid (nom.) 8. 73,
quidquid 7. 324; 8. 314.

quo (adv.) (15)
    1. interrog.
1. 519 (B; KGL quid), 768 (BGL; K
quae); 3. 734; 4. 204, 387; 6. 581 **bis**; 7.
91, 297 **bis;** 8. 145,
    2. rel.
2. 107 (L; KBG qui), 306; 3. 400; 4. 26.

quocirca
2. 101.

quocumque
3. 670; 4. 47.

quod (27)
    1. c. ind.
quod 1. 239, 446, 604, 628; 2. 59, 157;
4. 431, 445, 753, 754; 5. 492; 7. 284, 422,
423, 443 (quod iam L; KBG quoniam);
8. 162,
quod si 3. 296,
quod sin 5. 667,
    2. c. subi.
quod 1. 694; 5. 527, 628,
quod si 3. 246,
    3. sine verb.
quod 2. 398; 4. 444; 5. 630, 642; 6. 44.
quondam (15)
1. 51; 2. 18, 220, 473, 586, 617; 3. 380,
609, 737; 4. 116, 118, 432, 464; 5. 231;
8. 441.
quoniam (6)
    1. c. ind.
quoniam 2. 144; 5. 676; 7. 443 (KBG;
L quod iam); 8. 62 (B; KGL contra),
    2. sine verb.
quoniam 5. 532; 8. 320.
quoque (49)
quoque 1. 117, 243, 360, 380, 391, 444,
712, 763; 2. 158, 400, 592; 3. 686; 4. 522,
538, 598, 717, 745; 5. 52, 150, 198, 250,
544, 589; 6. 103, 138, 234, 317, 539, 589;
7. 1, 20, 63, 64, 205, 248, 281, 341, 479,
487; 8. 53, 75 (KBG; L que o), 104,
129, 211, 415,
nunc quoque 8. 440,
tum quoque 8. 26,
tunc quoque 6. 564; 8. 359.
quot (11)
    1. interrog.
quot 1. 217, 552, 553, 848 (B; KG quo;
L quae); 2. 563; 6. 582 bis,
    2. rel.
quot 5. 496; 6. 167 bis,
quot . . . totidem 1. 580.
quotiens (8)
    1. exclam.
quotiens 1. 330, 447, 645; 2. 53; 4. 378,
380,
    2. rel.
quotiens 8. 364,
quotiens . . . totiens 6. 683.
rabidus
rabidam 5. 626,
rabidum 4. 270 (KBG; L rapidum),
rabido (n.) 4. 239,
rabidi 4. 104, 583 (KBG; L rapidi),
rabidas 2. 133.
Rabies
Rabies (s.) 2. 206.
rabies
rabies 6. 355,
rabiem 7. 65,
rabie 3. 216; 7. 125.
radio
radiantis (m.) 5. 408,
radiante (f.) 8. 257,
radiantia (acc.) 8. 461.

rado
raditur 5. 108.
radius
radii (nom.) 6. 414,
radios 6. 55,
radiis 6. 517.
Rambelus
Rambelus 6. 529.
ramus
rami 6. 261; 8. 84,
ramo (abl.) 3. 433; 6. 297,
ramis 6. 506,
ramos 6. 264,
ramis 4. 333.
rapax
rapax (m.) 4. 262, 606,
rapacibus (abl. n.) 5. 2.
rapidus
rapidus 7. 406,
rapidi (m.) 4. 616,
rapidum 1. 484,
rapidum 4. 270 (L; KBG rabidum),
rapido (m.) 1. 291; 4. 510; 8. 54,
rapidi 4. 583 (L; KBG rabidi),
rapidae 5. 33,
rapidis (abl.) 6. 239, 489,
rapidis (f.) 1. 577; 3. 443.
rapina
rapina (abl.) 6. 332,
rapinae 4. 503,
rapinis 6. 538 (KBG; L que Panis),
rapinis 7. 51.
rapio
rapis 1. 749,
rapit 1. 264, 380, 621; 2. 187, 255, 289,
502, 649; 4. 27, 45, 291; 5. 41, 101 (que
rapit B; KGL recipit), 244, 271, 303,
412; 6. 191, 280, 364, 369; 7. 33 (ante
rapit B; K ante petit; G ante aperit;
L antevenit); 8. 309,
rapuit 1. 492; 3. 341,
rapuerunt 4. 31,
rapuere 2. 429; 3. 321, 458; 6. 408, 756;
7. 120,
raperet 6. 581,
rape 2. 252,
rapere 3. 79,
rapiens (m.) 6. 395,
rapientem (m.) 6. 318,
rapientia (acc.) 7. 513,
rapturus 6. 389,
rapitur 2. 273, 312,
rapta fuerint (ind.) 5. 237,
rapi 3. 692,
rapienda (nom. f.) 4. 573 (B; K speranda; GL properanda),
raptus 3. 717; 6. 425,
rapta 2. 664; 5. 216, 331; 6. 119,
raptum 3. 196,
raptum 3. 689,
raptam 1. 86,
rapta (voc.) 4. 118,
rapto 1. 695; 2. 182; 5. 5,
rapta 1. 547; 2. 569 (et rapta KL; BG
ereptaque); 8. 133,

rapto 1. 346,
rapti 4. 646,
rapta 4. 182,
raptis (n.) 8. 392,
raptos 2. 39,
rapta 1. 254, 645; 4. 695,
raptis (m.) 3. 462 (K; B summis; GL
celsis),
raptis (n.) 8. 105.
raptim
8. 288.
rapto
raptat 2. 575, 625,
raptet 1. 798,
raptaverit (subi.) 3. 55,
raptatur 4. 402,
raptatus 6. 748,
raptata (nom.) 7. 146,
raptata (nom.) 6. 361.
raptor
raptor 1. 160; 6. 121; 8. 265, 399.
raptus
raptu (abl.) 6. 502,
raptus (acc.) 2. 414.
raresco
rarescunt 6. 617.
rarus
rara (nom. f.) 1. 835,
raras 2. 74,
raris (m.) 4. 214,
raris (n.) 6. 696 (Phari raris B; K
Euphrataeis; GL pharetratis),
rarior (f.) 2. 627.
ratio
rationis 4. 303.
ratis
ratis 1. 171, 236, 494, 508, 657; 2. 60,
285, 405; 4. 106, 269, 583, 668, 710; 5. 34,
101, 211, 438; 7. 45, 51; 8. 130, 275, 292,
331, 375 (vid. gen.),
ratis 1. 418, 477; 2. 353; 3. 469; 5. 54;
7. 573; 8. 286, 362, 375 (vid. nom.),
rati 1. 466; 2. 374,
ratem 1. 2, 98, 104, 216, 340, 350, 497,
525, 605, 623, 800; 2. 429, 588, 613;
3. 28, 38, 79, 653; 4. 129, 335, 421, 435,
644, 678, 681, 690, 712; 5. 47, 63, 182,
206, 504, 530; 7. 260; 8. 152,
rate 1. 151; 5. 9; 6. 10; 8. 426,
rates 2. 520 (KG; BL putes),
rates 1. 20; 2. 111; 3. 110; 4. 563; 5.
496; 8. 284, 306, 321, 429,
rates 8. 355,
ratibus 2. 658, 661.
raucus
rauco (abl.) 1. 614; 2. 307,
rauco 6. 92,
raucos 1. 330.
reboo
reboat 3. 634.
recedo
recedit 8. 374 (BGL; K resedit),
recedunt 4. 523, 639; 7. 582,
recessit 2. 8; 5. 51,
recedere 7. 616,

recedens 7. 591 (KGL; B residens),
recedens (f.) 7. 118.
recens
recens (m.) 5. 27,
recentis (m.) 7. 605,
recentis (n.) 2. 327,
recentem (f.) 6. 609,
recenti (m.) 3. 433,
recenti (n.) 2. 212; 4. 749,
recentia 6. 455.
recepto
receptat 1. 833.
recessus
recessu (abl.) 5. 556.
recingo
recincta (abl.) 8. 115.
recipio
recipit 2. 14, 532; 5. 101 (KGL; B que
rapit),
recepi 3. 329; 5. 492,
recepit 1. 349,
recipe 7. 492,
receptus 2. 258,
receptum (m.) 5. 524; 6. 369,
receptum 7. 285,
recepti 6. 109.
reciprocus
reciproca (nom. f.) 8. 331.
reclamo
reclamat 3. 596,
reclamant 8. 173.
reclinis
reclinem (m.) 4. 535.
recludo
reclusa (nom. f.) 4. 231,
reclusis (abl. f.) 3. 60.
recolligo
recolligit 5. 431,
recollectam 6. 254,
recollectis (abl. n.) 6. 423.
recolo
recolit 6. 444 (KG; BL recoquit),
recolant 2. 396,
recole 7. 68.
recoquo
recoquit 6. 444 (BL; KG recolit).
rector
rector 1. 588; 4. 679; 5. 69,
rectorem 5. 54,
rector 1. 188, 674; 5. 666; 8. 197.
recordor
recordor 7. 12.
rectus vid. rego.
recubo
recubantem (m.) 7. 523.
recurro
recurrit 4. 395,
recurret 1. 170.
recursus
recursu (abl.) 4. 573.
recuso
recuso 5. 489; 8. 198,
recusat 6. 123 (L; KBG refutat),
recusans (m.) 7. 589.

recutio
  recusso (abl. n.) 5. 166.
reddo
  reddit 1. 440; 2. 331; 5. 534, 589; 6. 591, 671; 8. 59,
  reddunt 2. 259; 6. 520 (B; KGL redeunt),
  reddidit 7. 465; 8. 119, 197,
  reddet 1. 171,
  reddat 7. 427; 8. 191,
  redde 1. 57; 2. 380; 7. 246, 491,
  reddite 2. 600; 6. 213,
  reddere 1. 675; 4. 557; 5. 293, 692; 6. 19; 7. 209; 8. 423, 434, 445,
  redditur 7. 515,
  reddi 5. 261,
  redditus 7. 649,
  reddita 1. 209; 4. 20; 8. 238,
  reddita (voc.) 7. 217,
  reddita (nom.) 6. 570,
  reddita 3. 366; 5. 503.
redeo
  redit 1. 708, 725; 2. 16, 502; 3. 67, 729; 4. 247, 268, 290, 577, 732; 5. 124; 7. 151, 229; 8. 194, 331,
  redeunt 2. 310, 485; 4. 566, 586; 6. 513, 520 (KGL; B reddunt); 8. 160,
  rediit 5. 211,
  redierunt 1. 656,
  rediere 2. 609; 3. 45, 468; 4. 187, 673 (KL; BG cecidere); 5. 66; 6. 77,
  redeat 7. 139,
  redire 7. 379,
  redeuntem (m.) 3. 24, 687; 8. 199,
  redeunte (m.) 1. 437,
  redeuntibus (m.) 8. 175,
  redeuntia 2. 12; 7. 499,
  reditura (nom. f.) 1. 273, 441; 6. 73,
  reditura (acc.) 3. 382.
redimio
  redimitus 1. 278.
reditus
  reditus 3. 304,
  reditus (gen.) 7. 59,
  reditus (acc.) 6. 430; 7. 89.
redoleo
  redolentem (m.) 4. 15.
reduco
  reducit 3. 633; 5. 690,
  reducunt 1. 323,
  reducebat 5. 107,
  reducat 5. 420,
  reducitur 3. 467,
  reducta (abl.) 4. 266; 5. 328,
  reductis (abl. m.) 5. 374.
redux
  reduci (m.) 2. 94,
  reducem (m.) 1. 379; 7. 100,
  reduces (acc. m.) 1. 805.
refello
  refellat 3. 355.
refero
  refert 1. 47, 561; 2. 110, 657; 3. 346; 4. 349; 6. 308, 580; 7. 112; 8. 124,
  referunt 2. 467,

referebat 3. 532; 6. 496,
  referam 1. 173,
  referes 4. 314,
  referet 7. 130,
  referent 5. 683,
  rettulit 6. 215; 7. 79, 538, 614,
  rettulerat 5. 279,
  referam 2. 276,
  referas 7. 268,
  referat 2. 272; 3. 735; 8. 52,
  referemus 5. 323,
  referret 1. 514,
  refer 2. 423; 3. 503; 4. 336; 5. 587; 8. 144,
  referre 8. 43,
  referens 6. 275,
  referens (f.) 2. 321; 5. 84 (L; KBG repetens),
  referentem 3. 563, 610,
  referentem 4. 361,
  referentibus (abl. m.) 3. 347,
  refertur 3. 42,
  referri 7. 100.
reficio
  reficit 1. 506; 2. 62,
  refecit 7. 23,
  refecta (nom. f.) 4. 391.
refingo
  refingi 6. 237(L; KBG relinqui).
reflecto
  reflectunt 5. 454.
refluo
  refluens (m.) 8. 90.
refoveo
  refovet 4. 281,
  refove 5. 18.
refringo
  refringit 1. 595; 8. 322.
refugio
  refugit 2. 413; 4. 294; 7. 117,
  refugit 8. 445.
refugus
  refugi (m.) 1. 579; 3. 587,
  refuga (abl.) 4. 41.
refulgeo
  refulget 4. 405,
  refulsit 3. 195; 8. 58.
refundo
  refusis (abl. f.) 5. 254.
refuto
  refutat 6. 123 (KBG; L recusat).
regalis
  regali (abl. m.) 5. 444,
  regalibus (abl. n.) 1. 820.
regificus
  regifico (abl. m.) 2. 652.
regina
  regina 2. 261, 312, 334, 346; 5. 373, 441; 6. 378, 430, 657; 7. 444; 8. 47,
  regina (voc.) 1. 81; 5. 385.
regio
  regio 1. 517, 537; 3. 75; 4. 100,
  regione 2. 43,
  regionibus (abl.) 2. 118.

regius
 regius 6. 690,
 regia (nom. f.) 1. 162, 668; 5. 400; 6.
 650; 7. 232; 8. 282,
 regia (acc.) 4. 738; 6. 434,
 subst. f. regia (nom.) 1. 563; 5. 67.
regnator
 regnator 2. 620.
regno
 regnare 5. 317.
regnum
 regni 1. 500, 761; 2. 83, 246; 3. 346, 539;
 4. 99, 411, 469,
 regna 1. 702; 2. 593, 642 (L; KBG
 longa); 3. 304; 4. 589; 7. 485,
 regnorum 5. 236,
 regnis 1. 176; 6. 625 (vid. abl.),
 regna 1. 195, 418, 560, 616; 2. 297, 607;
 3. 658; 4. 236, 352; 5. 524, 607, 687; 6.
 138, 608; 7. 35, 371; 8. 211, 215,
 regnis 2. 571; 5. 240; 6. 625 (vid. dat.);
 7. 425.
rego
 regunt 2. 71,
 rexere 3. 109,
 regas 5. 195,
 regat 5. 64,
 regant 2. 165,
 rexisse 2. 319,
 regens (m.) 3. 134,
 regentem (f.) 3. 489,
 recto (abl. m.) 4. 614,
 subst. n. rectorum 3. 649.
relego
 relegit 4. 54,
 relegunt 8, 121,
 relegi 6. 237.
relevo
 relevans (m.) 4. 70.
religio (relligio)
 religio 8. 402,
 relligio 1. 80.
religo
 religant 3. 34.
relinquo
 relinquo 5. 41,
 relinquit 2. 161; 3. 152; 5. 100; 6. 191;
 7. 108,
 relinquunt 7. 2,
 relinquam 2. 181 (vid. subi.); 6. 335,
 499; 7. 487,
 relinquet 1. 442; 6. 597,
 reliqui 3. 295, 685,
 reliquit 6. 679; 7. 161; 8. 269,
 relinquam 2. 181 (vid. ind.),
 relinquas 7. 508,
 relinque 1. 333,
 relinqui 4. 57; 5. 223; 6. 237 (KBG; L
 refingi),
 relictum (m.) 5. 574,
 relicto 4. 6,
 relicta (abl.) 7. 490,
 relictas 5. 167,
 relictis 1. 492,

 relictis 2. 363,
 relictis 8. 47.
reliquiae (relliquiae)
 reliquias 1. 459; 5. 60,
 relliquias 7. 368.
relligio vid. religio.
reluceo
 reluxit 3. 115.
remeo
 remeat 4. 589; 6. 757; 8. 268,
 remeant 4. 212; 8. 434,
 remeavit 1. 567; 6. 344,
 remeent 6. 22,
 remeare 3. 387; 4. 142,
 remeasse 3. 127.
remergo
 remersum (m.) 3. 227 (B; KGL remensa).
remetior
 remensa (abl.) 3. 227 (KGL; B remersum),
 remenso 2. 501.
remex
 remigis 8. 286 (et remigis KB; G regis;
 L et remos).
reminiscor
 reminiscere 5. 197; 6. 516.
remitto
 remittunt 4. 658,
 remittet 5. 681,
 remittens (m.) 3. 407,
 remitti 5. 665; 7. 418,
 remissum (m.) 6. 252,
 remisso 5. 276,
 remissa (abl.) 3. 334,
 remissis (abl. n.) 5. 133.
removeo
 remoti (m.) 3. 306,
 remotum (m.) 2. 279,
 remoti 4. 745,
 remota (nom.) 3. 120.
remurmuro
 remurmurat 2. 453.
remus
 remo 1. 352,
 remum 1. 443; 4. 654,
 remo 1. 340, 359, 391, 450, 460, 471; 3.
 474,
 remi 1. 618; 2. 429; 3. 675; 4. 646; 8.
 161 (B; KG reges; L om.),
 remorum 3. 464,
 remis 2. 13; 3. 469; 6. 326; 7. 25; 8. 296,
 remos 2. 392; 5. 119, 436; 8. 286 (et
 remos L; KB et remigis; G regis), 361,
 remis 1. 98, 125; 2. 77, 311; 4. 680, 689;
 8. 356.
renideo
 renidenti (abl. m.) 4. 359,
 renidenti (n.) 4. 234.
renodo
 renodatam 5. 380.
reor
 reor 2. 617; 4. 633, 741; 5. 320 6. 590,
 reris 1. 164, 170; 6. 309,
 rere 2. 601; 3. 663; 6. 536,

rebar 4. 439 (rebar sic KGL; B sectabar),

ratus 3. 127, 250; 4. 291; 6. 246, 386; 7. 265,

rata (nom. f.) 3. 488.

reparabilis
reparabile (acc.) 6. 562.

repello
reppulit 3. 228,
repellat 7. 273.

rependo
rependo 6. 549,
rependit (prs.) 6. 560,
rependerat 1. 661,
rependat 6. 744,
rependere 6. 4.

repens
repens (f.) 2. 91, 478.

repente (6)
3. 466; 4. 565, 644; 5. 37, 226; 6. 683.

reperio
repperit 1. 201,
reperta (voc.) 8. 39,
reperto (m.) 3. 280; 5. 267, 298,
repertis (abl. n.) 3. 116.

repeto
repetis 3. 493,
repetit 5. 95; 6. 593,
repetunt 2. 238; 4. 574,
repetam 1. 536,
repetet 7. 56,
repetens 4. 59,
repetens (f.) 5. 84 (KBG; L referens),
repetentibus (m.) 2. 15,
repetentes (m.) 6. 11,
repetuntur 3. 719,
repetentur 7. 226 (KBG; L reputentur).

repono
repono 5. 390,
reponit 1. 651; 2. 33; 3. 339,
reponunt 4. 279, 530,
reponat 5. 687,
repone 7. 245 (KGL; B reponens),
reponens (f.) 7. 245 (B; KGL repone),
repostam 2. 286,
repostae 4. 713.

reporto
reportat 8. 267,
reportet 7. 45.

reposco
reposcit 6. 368,
reposcunt 3. 245,
reposcere 3. 601; 7. 650; 8. 152,
reposcor 8. 425,
reposci 1. 85; 7. 432.

reprimo
repressa 6. 278,
represso (abl. m.) 7. 531.

repulsa
repulsae (dat.) 5. 322.

reputo
reputant 2. 139,
reputantes (nom. m.) 8. 385,

reputentur 7. 226 (L; KBG repetentur).

requies
requies 5. 601,
requiem 7. 245.

requiro
requiro 8. 39,
requiris 2. 145,
requirit 2. 351,
requirunt 5. 422,
requiret 3. 396,
requirat 3. 733,
requirens 3. 127,
requirens (f.) 6. 467.

res
rerum 1. 102, 217, 515, 532, 725, 823; 2. 41, 381; 3. 17, 350, 369, 680, 712; 4. 12, 558; 5. 270, 301, 643, 680,
rebus 1. 54,
res 4. 53,
rebus 1. 99, 248, 827; 5. 324.

resero
reserans (m.) 2. 438,
reserantem (m.) 3. 513,
reserata (nom. f.) 1. 655.

reses
resides (m.) 3. 394; 4. 214,
resides (m.) 2. 373; 4. 626; 5. 78,
resides 8. 220.

resideo
residet 8. 28,
resedit 7. 190, 210,
residens 6. 696,
residens (f.) 6. 82, 495, 575; 8. 204.

resido
resedit 8. 374 (K; BGL recedit),
residens (m.) 7. 591 (B; KGL recedens).

resisto
resistunt 6. 755,
restitit 3. 100,
restitimus 2. 53,
resistens (m.) 3. 547.

resolvo
resolvit (perf.) 1. 655,
resolvere 4. 703,
resolvitur 4. 43,
resoluta (nom. f.) 2. 536.

resono
resonat 3. 207 (K; B denset; G donat; L duplicat),
resonare 1. 122,
resonantia (acc.) 4. 18.

resonus
resonos 1. 619.

respecto
respectat 4. 297.

respicio
respicit 2. 528; 3. 522; 5. 562, 589; 6. 200, 562; 7. 593, 624,
respiciet 7. 472,
respexit 4. 696; 5. 255; 6. 514; 7. 106, 384,
respicias 4. 184,
respiceres 1. 292,

respiceret 8. 389,
respice 4. 387; 7. 167, 497; 8. 435,
respiciens 4. 335,
respiciens (f.) 2. 270; 4. 75; 6. 661; 7.
278.
respiro
respirat 7. 648,
respirant 4. 279.
respondeo
respondet 6. 164,
respondent 2. 583,
subst. n. responsa (acc.) 2. 569; 4. 625;
5. 547; 7. 87.
responso
responsant 3. 597; 4. 286.
respuo
respuerit (ind.) 5. 322.
restis
resti (abl.) 2. 387 (L; KG brevis; B
bovis).
restituo
restituunt 2. 70.
resto
restat 1. 458; 5. 57; 6. 677; 7. 519; 8.
458 (restat imago K; BG gloria magni;
L om.),
restet 8. 406.
resumo
resumit 7. 155,
resume 7. 467.
resurgo
resurgunt 2. 538,
resurgere 2. 520,
resurgentem (m.) 2. 28.
rete
reti (abl.) 2. 103 (B; BGL tereti).
retego
retexit 3. 410; 4. 423.
retempto
retemptet 5. 172.
retento
retentet 5. 678,
retentant 3. 97.
retinaculum
retinacula (acc.) 1. 488.
retineo
retinet 3. 344,
retinere 2. 293,
retenta (abl.) 4. 498.
retorqueo
retorquent 6. 399.
retracto
retracta 7. 70.
retro
1. 782 (KBG; L rite); 4. 400; 5. 681;
7. 583.
retrorsus
3. 268.
reus
rei (nom.) 2. 227 (B; KGL manu).
reveho
revehemur 2. 575; 5. 213,
revexit 3. 293,
revehat 1. 99 (KBG; L que vehat),
revecto (dat. m.) 1. 457,

revectos 3. 654,
revectis (f.) 3. 360.
revello
revellit (prs.) 5. 8,
revulsam 3. 566 (K; BGL revulsas),
revulsas 3. 566 (BGL; K revulsam),
revulsis (f.) 5. 168.
reverbero
reverberat 1. 516; 6. 170 (BGL; K
verberat).
reverentia
reverentia (nom.) 5. 598.
revereor
reverentia (nom.) 4. 146,
reverenda (nom. f.) 5. 207.
revertor
revertor 2. 213,
reverti 7. 53, 652; 8. 272,
reversus 2. 14,
reversae (dat.) 2. 355,
reversum (m.) 3. 568,
reverso (m.) 8. 357.
revincio
revinctos 4. 708; 6. 417 (in peste revinctos L; KB om.; G cura cavere),
418.
reviso
revisit 2. 548,
revisunt 2. 170,
reviset 7. 16,
revisat 3. 735.
revocabilis
revocabilis (nom. m.) 7. 461.
revoco
revocat 1. 136,
revocaverat 3. 482,
revocet 7. 115,
revocate 3. 625,
revocare 4. 305; 7. 641,
revocans (f.) 4. 375,
revocantem (m) 6. 257,
revocantibus (abl. m.) 6. 409.
revolvo
revolutus 8. 330.
revomo
revomentem (m.) 2. 25,
revomentes (acc. m.) 1. 822.
rex
rex 1. 174, 595, 748; 2. 556, 635; 3. 337;
4. 101, 219, 463, 467; 5. 405, 419, 487;
6. 432; 7. 53,
regis 1. 52, 61, 345, 694, 797; 2. 4, 352;
3. 205; 4. 101, 316; 5. 7, 289, 300, 516,
662; 6. 5; 8. 286 (G; KB et remigis;
L et remos),
regi 1. 27; 2. 305; 3. 342; 4. 108, 157;
5. 265,
regem 1. 592, 753; 2. 545; 3. 58, 201; 4.
278, 734; 5. 328; 7. 27, 539, 650,
rex 4. 63; 5. 471, 624,
rege 1. 414, 604, 814; 3. 231, 249, 280,
655; 4. 249; 7. 45, 326,
reges 4. 212, 613, 713; 5. 464, 497; 6.
172; 8. 161 (KG; B remi; L om.),

regum 3. 28, 514; 5. 273, 488; 6. 415; 7.
40,
reges 1. 342, 397, 535, 801, 833; 2. 343
bis; 3. 173, 496, 504; 4. 130, 543; 5. 501,
577; 6. 403, 487, 577; 8. 200, 339,
regibus 1. 203; 8. 205.

Rhadalus
Rhadalo (abl.) 6. 69.

Rhebas
Rhebae (gen.) 4. 698.

Rhoas
Rhoas 4. 719 (L; KBG Novas).

Rhodope
Rhodopes 1. 728,
Rhodopen 1. 664.

Rhoetus
Rhoetus 1. 141; 3. 65.

Rhundacus
Rhundace 3. 35.

Rhyndacus
Rhyndace 6. 220.

rictus
rictu (abl.) 1. 758.

rideo
ridet 5. 526,
risit 6. 209,
ridens (f.) 7. 531.

rigeo
riget 4. 726; 6. 233, 328,
rigens (f.) 1. 515,
rigentem 1. 43,
rigentem 3. 92,
rigentia (acc.) 5. 29.

rigesco
riguerunt 2. 203.

rigidus
rigido (abl. m.) 3. 157,
rigidos 4. 345.

rigo
rigat 4. 51,
rigant 4. 498.

rigor
rigor 3. 263, 577; 4. 724.

ripa
ripae 2. 601; 6. 149,
ripae 4. 373,
ripam 5. 341,
ripa 1. 78; 6. 101; 8. 218,
ripas 3. 594; 5. 216; 6. 567; 8. 130,
ripis 4. 402.

Riphaeus
Riphaea 5. 558,
Riphaeo (abl.) 6. 33, 119,
Riphaea (abl.) 5. 602,
Riphaeas 7. 562,
Riphaea 2. 516.

Ripheus
Riphea 6. 558.

rite (5)
1. 782 (L; KBG retro); 3. 445; 5. 99,
193; 6. 93.

ritus
ritu (abl.) 4. 384,
ritus 2. 646,
ritus 4. 146.

robur ·
robur 3. 164, 681,
roboris 2. 534; 8. 298,
robur 1. 561, 634; 5. 364; 7. 555,
robore 4. 591, 684; 7. 72,
robora (acc.) 1. 95, 553; 2. 643; 5. 9,
569.

rogito
rogitas 5. 582,
rogitant 5. 467.

rogo
rogat 4. 205; 7. 343, 385,
rogant 7. 379,
rogari 7. 289.

rogus
rogo (dat.) 5. 30,
rogi 3. 348,
rogos 3. 312,
rogis 2. 476; 5. 36.

Romanus
Romane 6. 55,
Romanas 6. 402.

roro
rorat 6. 259,
rorantes (m.) 5. 415,
rorantes (acc.) 5. 76,
rorantes 5. 176.

ros
rorem 4. 15,
roribus (abl.) 5. 372 (BG; KL fontibus).

roscidus
roscida (acc.) 7. 302.

roseus
roseae (gen.) 5. 365,
roseo (abl.) 8. 30,
rosea 8. 257,
roseo 6. 674,
roseis (abl. f.) 2. 261; 3. 538; 4. 77; 6.
527.

rostrum
rostro (abl.) 7. 360,
rostra (nom.) 2. 77; 8. 297.

rota
rota 3. 559,
rota 5. 414,
rotae 6. 90,
rotis (abl.) 1. 678, 836; 3. 52; 6. 168,
425.

roto
rotat 1. 209; 4. 235, 656,
rotantis (m.) 6. 551,
rotatis (dat. m.) 4. 181.

rubeo
rubens (m.) 3. 131,
rubentes (acc. f.) 3. 176.

ruber
rubri (n.) 5. 77.

rubor
rubor 2. 57; 6. 27; 8. 58.

rudens
rudentibus (abl.) 1. 627.

rudimentum
rudimenta (nom.) 3. 600.

rudis
rudis (m.) 5. 642,
rude 3. 680,
rudis (n.) 1. 771,
rudem (m.) 1. 823,
rudes (acc. m.) 6. 337.
ruina
ruina (nom.) 8. 334,
ruinae (nom.) 6. 185; 7. 529,
ruinas 3. 207; 6. 633,
ruinis 4. 695.
rumor
rumor 2. 318 (G; K fingit; BL **om.**),
rumoribus (abl.) 5. 272.
rumpia
rumpia (nom.) 6. 98.
rumpo
rumpit 3. 241, 509· 4. 627; 6. 645; 7.
33, 144, 222,
rumpunt 6. 127,
rupit 8. 260,
ruperunt 7. 569,
rupere 5. 32,
rumperet 1. 588; 5. 650; 6. 139,
rumpe 1. 306,
rumpere 1. 4, 463, 508, 746; 3. 614; 4.
42, 458; 5. 340,
rupta 3. 46,
rupta 3. 147; 7. 298,
rupto 2. 37,
rupta (acc.) 3. 671 (L; KG plura; B
dura); 5. 174,
ruptis (f.) 4. 661.
ruo
ruit 1. 616; 3. 58, 67, 120, 133, 136, 706;
5. 180, 623; 6. 111, 741; 7. 3, 642 (KG;
B fuit; L fugit), 648 (L; KBG furit);
8. 185,
ruunt 2. 359; 3. 165, 275; 4. 282, 663;
5. 117; 6. 86, 198, 242; 7. 582; 8. 326,
ruont 4. 575,
ruebat 7. 287,
ruebant 7. 456,
ruit 1. 274; 2. 89; 4. 676; 6. 383, 652,
ruat 1. 698; 2. 5,
rueret 1. 113; 4. 377,
ruens (m.) 3. 478, 583,
ruentis (f.) 2. 243,
ruenti (m.) 1. 663, 828,
ruentem 3. 102, 153; 6. 348 (KGL; B
ruentes),
ruentem 1. 849; 2. 504, 532, 604,
ruentes (acc. m.) 6. 348 (B; KGL
ruentem),
subst. m. ruentum 3. 255.
rupes
rupes 1. 580; 3. 108,
rupem 2. 332; 5. 147,
rupe 2. 21, 463, 544; 4. 110, 181, 599; 5.
344,
rupes 4. 71, 637, 657,
rupes 8. 195,
rupibus 5. 169; 6. 393; 7. 191.
ruricola
ruricolae (nom.) 5. 142.

rursum
3. 645.
rursus (25)
2. 257, 389, 526, 628; 3. 307, 532, 540,
596 **bis**, 626; 4. 344, 395, 631; 5. 200;
6. 254, 390, 662; 7. 118, 322, 350, 426,
515, 562 (KGL; B sursus); 8. 329,
365.
rus
rura (acc.) 6. 405, 599; 7. 72, 616.
rutilo
rutilant 5. 250.
rutilus
rutili (n.) 7. 647,
rutilum 7. 620,
rutilam 8. 114,
rutilas 6. 56,
rutilís (n.) 5. 450.
Sabaei
Sabaeos 6. 138.
Sabaeus
Sabaeo (abl. m.) 6. 709.
sacer
sacer 1. 207, 798; 2. 37, 187, 272; 5. 122;
6. 114, 141; 7. 358; 8. 239,
sacri 5. 192,
sacrae 4. 230; 6. 19,
sacri 2. 648; 8. 401,
sacro (n.) 7. 165,
sacram 3. 428,
sacro 1. 659; 4. 338; 6. 64,
sacra 2. 259; 5. 203; 6. 10; 8. 25,
sacra 4. 186,
sacros 1. 632; 2. 650,
sacras 2. 25; 7. 180,
sacra 1. 730, 774; 5. 629,
sacris (m.) 2. 582,
sacris (n.) 2. 347,
subst. n. sacri 1. 785 (BGL; K sacris);
3. 419,
sacra 2. 624,
sacris 1. 785 (K; BGL sacri); 2. 440;
3. 412,
sacra 2. 410; 3. 118, 540; 4. 530; 5. 398;
6. 304, 755; 8. 96, 252, 260, 279,
sacris 2. 432; 3. 232.
sacerdos
sacerdos 1. 685, 755, 839; 2. 437; 3. 233,
432; 4. 85; 5. 261; 6. 294.
sacrificus
sacrifici (n.) 4. 110,
sacrificas 8. 243.
sacro
sacrasse 3. 175,
sacratus 6. 294,
sacrata 5. 238,
sacrata 5. 250,
sacrata 1. 790,
sacrata 7. 48.
saeculum (saeclum)
saecula 2. 245,
saeclis 6. 103,
saecula 1. 99, 535; 4. 560,
saeclis 4. 711.

saepe (12)
saepe 2. 50, 320 (saepe imis KG; B saepimis; L haec imis); 3. 128, 712 **bis**; 4. 158, 352, 622; 7. 317; 8. 72, 408,
saepimis 2. 320 (B; KG saepe imis; L haec imis).

saepio
saeptus 5. 400; 6. 346,
subst. n. saeptis (abl.) 3. 582.

saeptum vid. saepio.

saeta
saetis (abl.) 6. 71.

saetiger
saetigerum (nom.) 3. 50.

saevio
saevit 1. 700; 3. 229; 4. 296, 455, 499; 6. 613; 7. 367,
saeviet 1. 152,
saevire 2. 157; 4. 520.

saevitia
saevitiae (gen.) 4. 478.

saevus
saevus 1. 574, 647; 4. 200 (B; KGL saevos); 6. 28, 152, 454, 586; 7. 207, 301, 307; 8. 134,
saevos (nom.) 4. 200 (KGL; B saevus),
saeva 1. 492, 593; 2. 230; 3. 392; 5. 548; 6. 733; 7. 52; 8. 373,
saevum 5. 154,
saevi 8. 170, 438,
saevae 2. 285; 3. 580; 4. 27; 5. 188; 6. 73, 148, 663; 7. 148,
saevi 4. 411; 5. 495,
saevo 7. 236,
saevae 1. 287; 4. 34; 7. 216,
saevum 1. 115; 6. 703; 8. 19, 100,
saevam 4. 431; 6. 510,
saevo 1. 512, 736; 4. 579; 6. 336, 616,
saeva 1. 370; 2. 279; 4. 596, 637, 743; 6. 646; 7. 285, 603; 8. 57,
saevo 5. 369; 6. 169,
saevi 3. 698,
saevae 3. 655; 4. 147, 586; 5. 531; 7. 328,
saeva 2. 398, 404, 411; 6. 605; 7. 441,
saevos 1. 68 (KG; BL et quos), 748; 8. 219, 241,
saevas 1. 798; 2. 194, 315, 644; 6. 432; 7. 86, 98,
saeva 1. 329, 726, 819; 2. 301; 5. 121; 6. 388; 8. 192, 343,
saevis 2. 175; 3. 31; 4. 105; 7. 558,
saevis 4. 70, 746; 6. 397,
saevis 3. 638,
adv. saeva 1. 47,
saevior 2. 361; 4. 301; 7. 142, 519,
saevior 6. 231,
saevius (acc.) 7. 507,
saevissima (nom. f.) 4. 610; 6. 402; 7. 315,
saevissima (acc.) 3. 47.

Sages
Sagen 3. 182.

sagitta
sagittae (gen.) 5. 136,
sagitta 3. 322,
sagittae 6. 77,
sagittas 1. 393, 437; 6. 698.

sal
salis 4. 722,
sale 3. 422; 5. 121.

salio
salientia (acc.) 1. 206.

Salmoneus
Salmoneus 1. 662.

Salmonis
Salmonide 5. 478.

saltem (6)
1. 421; 3. 326; 7. 133; 8. 99, 421, 435.

saltus
saltus (acc.) 4. 381.

saltus
saltus (acc.) 1. 489; 2. 283; 3. 537; 5. 355,
saltibus 3. 633.

salum
salum 1. 703,
salum 1. 688,
salo 1. 195.

salus
salus 3. 255, 674; 5. 265,
salutis 2. 488; 7. 272.

saluto
salutant 2. 13.

salveo
salve 4. 327, 436.

salvus
salvus 7. 363 (L; KBG sanguis).

Samothraca
Samothraca (nom.) 2. 439 (BGL; K Samothracia).

Samothracia
Samothracia (voc.) 2. 439 (K; BGL Samothraca).

sanctus
sancti (n.) 5. 498,
sanctum (n.) 2. 345,
sancte 1. 11; 6. 288.

sanguineus
sanguineus 3. 588,
sanguinei (n.) 5. 307,
sanguineo (abl.) 4. 132; 8. 228,
sanguinea 7. 330 (BG; KL sanguineo),
sanguineo 7. 330 (KL; BG sanguinea),
sanguineae 3. 85; 4. 309,
sanguineos 4. 235; 6. 187,
sanguineis (m.) 3. 20,
sanguineis (n.) 6. 134.

sanguis
sanguis 1. 336, 533, 814; 3. 234, 345; 4. 192, 226, 256; 6. 49; 7. 363 (KBG; L salvus),
sanguinis 3. 447; 5. 126; 6. 555, 573,
sanguine 1. 41, 524, 740; 2. 541; 3. 286, 391, 672, 689; 4. 126, 331, 348, 754; 5. 76, 134 (KBG; L in aequor), 266, 476, 495, 512; 6. 23, 137, 558, 594, 708 **bis**; 7. 136, 356.

sanies,
  saniem 7. 368,
  sanie 4. 749.
Sarmata
  Sarmata (nom.) 6. 162.
Sarmaticus
  Sarmatici 8. 207,
  Sarmaticae (gen.) 8. 217,
  Sarmaticae (nom.) 6. 232,
  Sarmaticas 2. 176,
  Sarmaticis (f.) 5. 424.
sat vid. satis.
Satarchae
  Satarchae 6. 144.
Satarches
  Satarchen 6. 145.
satis (25)
  adv. satis 1. 674, 769; 3. 682; 4. 519; 5.
  219, 674, 678; 6. 549, 721; 7. 70, 176, 201
  (KG; BL om.); 8. 40, 270,
  sat 1. 174, 526, 765; 3. 688, 703 (satque
  G; KB atque; L aeque); 4. 66, 546; 6.
  548; 7. 291; 8. 194, 393.
sator
  sator 2. 561,
  sator 1. 505.
satum vid. sero.
Saturnia
  Saturnia (nom.) 1. 112, 305, 530; 4.
  543; 6. 458, 477; 8. 324.
Saturnius
  Saturnia (acc.) 2. 364.
Saturnus
  Saturnus 5. 153,
  Saturnum 3. 226.
satus vid. sero.
saturo
  saturare 6. 647.
saucius
  saucius 6. 272, 638,
  saucia (nom. f.) 6. 706.
Sauromatae
  Sauromatae 7. 235.
saxifer
  saxiferae (gen.) 5. 608.
saxum
  saxi 2. 542; 4. 44,
  saxum 6. 648,
  saxo 2. 448, 533; 4. 378,
  saxa 1. 594; 2. 333; 4. 585, 641, 642, 691,
  saxis 4. 659; 8. 196,
  saxa 1. 371; 2. 527; 3. 96; 4. 513, 564,
  660, 672; 5. 174; 6. 335; 8. 182, 193,
  saxis 3. 594; 5. 159; 6. 685.
scando
  scande 8. 111,
  scandere 8. 5.
scelus
  sceleris 2. 123, 327; 7. 332; 8. 444,
  sceleri 2. 256,
  scelus 2. 294; 3. 172; 5. 568,
  scelerum 2. 216; 4. 478; 7. 310; 8. 312.
sceptrum
  sceptri 5. 536,
  sceptra 8. 147,

sceptra 2. 396, 590; 3. 344; 5. 483, 684;
  7. 502; 8. 14,
  sceptris 2. 309; 3. 658; 8. 47.
scilicet (5)
  3. 352, 673; 6. 732; 7. 54; 8. 274.
scindo
  scinditur 8. 377 (KGL; B cingitur).
scio
  scio 1. 196; 5. 289,
  scis 2. 156; 6. 484; 8. 49, 422,
  sciat 5. 516; 7. 286,
  sciret 6. 448,
  scire 7. 7.
Sciathos
  Sciathos 2. 8.
scopulosus
  scopulosa (acc.) 2. 518.
scopulus
  scopuli 4. 202,
  scopulo (dat.) 2. 92, 513,
  scopuli 3. 467; 4. 681,
  scopulis 2. 19, 484; 4. 572, 668,
  scopulos 1. 582; 2. 383, 472, 527, 542;
  4. 370, 683, 688; 6. 633; 7. 582,
  scopulis 2. 23, 538, 603; 3. 621; 4. 68,
  696; 5. 170; 6. 384; 7. 360, 365.
scrobis
  scrobibus (abl.) 1. 735.
scrutor
  scrutaris 2. 602.
scutum
  scuta (acc.) 1. 487, 496; 3. 29,
  scutis 6. 56.
Scylaceon
  Scylaceon (acc.) 3. 36.
scyphus
  scyphus 2. 272.
Scythia
  Scythiae (gen.) 1. 745; 4. 617; 5. 525;
  6. 7, 115, 350, 647 bis; 7. 424; 8. 209,
  Scythiam 1. 43, 87; 6. 34, 428, 728.
Scythicus
  Scythici 1. 2, 345, 503; 2. 379, 574; 8.
  185,
  Scythicae 4. 9,
  Scythici 2. 648,
  Scythicum 1. 331; 2. 595; 4. 728,
  Scythicam 5. 325,
  Scythico 1. 59,
  Scythica (abl.) 1. 442; 5. 224,
  Scythicos 3. 496; 6. 319,
  Scythicas 1. 716; 3. 307; 5. 516; 7. 42,
  Scythicis (f.) 3. 617, 653 (KBL; G
  Scythici); 6. 49,
  Scythici (?) 3. 653 (G; KBL Scythi-
  cis).
Scythis,
  Scythidum 5. 342.
secerno
  secreta (acc.) 3. 372,
  secretis (n.) 1. 751,
  subst. n. secreta 3. 200,
  secreta 2. 438.

seco
secat 1. 224, 453; 2. 2; 4. 271, 601; 6. 414
(L; KBG secant), 424,
secant 6. 414 (KBG; L secat),
secet 5. 453; 7. 608.
secretum vid. secerno.
sector
sectatur 1. 66 (L; KB sed tandem; G
sectantem); 5. 425,
sectabar 4. 439 (B; KGL rebar sic),
sectantem 1. 66 (G; KB sed tandem;
L sectatur).
secundus
secundo (abl. m.) 1. 507; 2. 612; 6. 602,
secundos 4. 130,
secundis (m.) 3. 598.
securiger
securigerum (acc. m.) 3. 191,
securigeras 5. 137.
securis
securem 6. 378,
securi 3. 140, 163; 5. 435, 613; 6. 100,
secures (acc.) 5. 123.
securus
securus 1. 414,
secura 3. 329; 4. 201; 6. 680; 8. 206,
securum (m.) 3. 479,
securum 4. 87,
securo (m.) 1. 423,
securas 5. 48.
secus (10)
haud secus 2. 385; 6. 717,
haut secus 1. 704; 7. 403; 8. 34,
sic ubi . . . haud secus 4. 665,
non secus . . . quam cum 5. 368,
non secus . . . quam si 7. 604,
non secus ac 7. 459,
qualis ubi . . . haud secus 7. 637.
sed (117)
sed 1. 19 (K; BGL si), 19 (KL; BG
seu), 66 (KB; G sectantem; L sectatur), 110, 170, 202 (L; KB **om.**; G tu),
236, 289, 335, 341, 361, 475, 515, 542,
626, 747, 805; 2. 23, 47, 64, 158, 224,
237, 242, 280, 317, 571; 3. 194, 355, 392
(KBG; L et), 396, 642, 650, 655; 4. 166,
169, 172, 225, 460, 544, 604, 614, 621, 691,
715 (L; KBG nec); 5. 36, 385, 460, 498,
592, 652; 6. 126, 217, 418, 421, 653, 673
bis, 687; 7. 20, 160, 174 (L; KBG quin),
176, 241, 435, 446, 479, 641; 8. 73, 104,
158, 348 (B; KGL et), 367, 408,
sed enim 1. 228,
sed neque 8. 247,
sed neque . . . nec 3. 570; 4. 679,
sed neque . . . neque 1. 33,
sed non 1. 26, 198, 441; 6. 241, 718; 7.
584,
sed non et 1. 503,
nec . . . sed 1. 65, 322, 471, 522, 548,
717; 2. 150; 3. 6, 162; 4. 205, 231, 251,
300, 484, 492, 500, 604, 704, 732; 5. 59,
554, 563, 663; 6. 93, 156, 520; 8. 391,
nec . . . sed . . . sed 8. 348,
neque . . . sed 4. 642,

nec . . . neque . . . sed 2. 625,
haut ita sed 8. 318.
sedeo
sedes 6. 486,
sedet 1. 132, 555, 828; 2. 383; 3. 738; 7.
428; 8. 318,
sedent 1. 689; 2. 370,
sedit 1. 282; 2. 446,
sedere 2. 307; 3. 720,
sedeat 1. 178 (K; BGL si des),
sedens 3. 406,
sedens (f.) 5. 72.
sedes
sedis 1. 793; 3. 450; 6. 478,
sedem 5. 8; 7. 208,
sede 2. 257, 522, 530,
sedes (acc.) 1. 846; 2. 606; 5. 538,
sedibus 2. 513; 5. 235, 333; 6. 727.
seges
seges 7. 96, 283, 366.
segnis
segnis 8. 98,
segnis 5. 146; 8. 318,
segne 1. 788,
segni (n.) 1. 633 (vid. abl.) ,
segni (m.) 3. 368,
segni (n.) 1. 633 (vid. dat.); 2. 376,
segnibus (f.) 1. 482,
segnes 1. 175; 4. 152,
segnes 6. 310,
segnia 6. 125,
segnior (m.) 1. 357; 5. 586,
adv. segnius 3. 85; 6. 107, 290; 8. 311.
segnities
segnitiem 3. 396.
semel
2. 282; 3. 212 (KB; GL simul), 709; 4.
572.
semen
semine 3. 665,
semina 7. 68,
semina 3. 382; 7. 75, 555, 608.
semianimis
semianimem (f.) 5. 134.
semidea
semidea (abl.) 6. 223.
semifer
semifero (abl. n.) 6. 51,
semiferi 6. 233,
semiferum (m.) 1. 455.
seminecis
seminecem (m.) 6. 252,
semineces (m.) 6. 509,
semineces (m.) 3. 153; 6. 176.
semita
semita (nom.) 2. 430.
semivir
semivir 6. 695,
semiviri (gen.) 8. 347.
semoveo
semota (nom. f.) 2. 641.
semper (25)
1. 364, 802, 833; 2. 98; 3. 170, 647; 4. 18,
36, 266, 267, 450, 612, 729; 5. 260, 324,

583 **bis;** 6. 455, 557, 759; 7. 230, 319,
510; 8. 165, 218.
senecta
senectae 1. 77, 718; 3. 302; 5. 685; 8.
137,
senectae 1. 809; 4. 475, 551; 8. 280,
senecta 6. 308; 8. 14.
senectus
senectus 4. 470; 6. 283; 7. 65.
senex
subst. m. senis 4. 491; 5. 412,
seni 4. 431,
senem 1. 349, 813; 2. 279; 4. 63; 5. 621,
senex 4. 538,
senes 6. 282,
senes 1. 821,
senior (m.) 1. 760; 5. 224.
senium
senium (acc.) 8. 102.
sensus
sensus (acc.) 6. 580; 7. 172, 196.
sententia
sententia (nom.) 1. 548; 3. 373, 686; 8.
340.
sentio
sentit 1. 357; 4. 303, 354, 434; 5. 377; 6.
610; 7. 111, 324,
sentiet 6. 502,
sensi 4. 121, 442,
sensit 2. 83; 4. 115; 6. 467; 8. 410,
sensimus 4. 746,
sensere 5. 504; 6. 666,
senserat 5. 330,
senseris 7. 503,
sentiat 3. 507.
sentus
senta (acc.) 3. 584.
separ
separe (f.) 5. 58.
Sepias
Sepias 2. 9.
sepono
seponite 1. 632.
septem
1. 283; 8. 90, 187 **bis.**
septemgeminus
septemgemini (gen. m.) 4. 718.
septemplex
septemplicis (m.) 6. 367.
septenus
septeno (abl. n.) 6. 349; 7. 464,
septenos 2. 65.
septimus
septimus 3. 652.
sepulchrum (sepulcrum)
sepulchro (abl.) 1. 813; 4. 314; 6. 314,
sepulcris (dat.) 7. 392.
sequax
sequaci (abl. m.) 7. 619,
sequaci (n.) 6. 263 (KBG; L tenaci),
sequaces (acc. f.) 1. 124.
sequor
sequor 4. 674; 5. 481; 7. 348; 8. 48, 418,
sequitur 3. 63, 86, 153; 4. 596, 695; 5.
267; 6. 368, 682; 7. 394; 8. 291, 342,

sequimur 8. 13, 266,
secuntur 1. 495; 2. 454; 5. 600,
sequuntur 1. 158, 681 (KB; GL sequentum); 4. 506; 5. 414; 6. 190,
sequar 3. 670 (B; KG voces; L vocas),
670 (GL; KB qua),
sequeris 7. 331,
sequemur 8. 189,
sequatur 6. 2. 355,
sequantur 5. 561, 605; 6. 21; 8. 391,
sequi 1. 3, 344; 2. 61, 178 (KBG; L que
quin); 3. 213, 256; 4. 42, 47, 176; 5. 338,
663; 7. 300, 377, 528,
sequenti (dat. m.) 7. 620 (KGL; B
sequentum),
sequentum (m.) 1. 681 (GL; KB sequuntur); 7. 620 (B; KGL sequenti),
sequentia (acc.) 4. 389,
secutus 1. 653; 4. 161, 304; 5. 656; 6. 42,
secutam 7. 225,
secuti 4. 650; 5. 496; 6. 143; 7. 19,
secutae 5. 161,
secutos 5. 114.
serenus
serenus 1. 20,
sereno (abl.) 3. 251, 370,
serena 7. 84,
sereno 2. 475,
subst. n. sereno (abl.) 2. 403,
serenis (dat.) 1. 332.
series
series (s.) 2. 218.
sermo
sermonis 1. 298,
sermone 6. 679; 7. 257,
sermonibus (abl.) 2. 350.
sero
serens (m.) 3. 638 (K; BGL furens),
serentem (m.) 5. 270,
satum (m.) 3. 6,
satis (abl. m.) 6. 437,
subst. satus 3. 646; 4. 249; 5. 263, 456,
473, 488, 567,
satum (m.) 3. 202,
satae 3. 252,
satis (n.) 3. 453,
satos 7. 35,
sata 8. 343.
sero
subst. n. serta (acc.) 2. 265,
sertis 6. 455.
sero vid. serus.
serpens
serpens 2. 65; 6. 59,
serpentibus (abl.) 7. 218.
sertum vid. sero.
serum vid. serus.
serus
serus 1. 48; 2. 564; 3. 713; 6. 750; 7. 1,
sera 1. 803; 4. 247; 6. 723 (K; BGL
foeda),
serum 4. 449,
seri (n.) 5. 260,
serum (n.) 2. 294 (KBG; L miserum);
7. 21 (L; KBG totum),

sera (abl.) 3. 279; 7. 400; 8. 95,
seros 1. 780; 3. 246, 650; 8. 398,
seras 2. 350; 8. 213,
sera 3. 562; 4. 252,
seris (f.) 3. 603; 6. 433,
adv. serum 4. 705,
adv. sero 7. 24 (B; KGL levis).
servio
servire 7. 387.
servitium
servitiis (dat.) 2. 181.
servo
servat 1. 584; 2. 22; 4. 272,
servant 4. 105, 450, 488; 8. 407,
servabant 8. 114,
servabo 8. 77,
servavit 4. 383,
servaverat 1. 780,
servet 7. 275,
servemus 2. 440,
servent 7. 552,
serva 8. 48, 420,
servate 1. 267; 4. 460,
servare 7. 104,
servantem 4. 318,
servantem 2. 138,
servantibus (dat. m.) 4. 640,
servatur 1. 462,
servanda (nom. f.) 1. 18,
servari 7. 574,
servati (m.) 2. 410,
servatum (m.) 7. 482,
servato (m.) 1. 378; 2. 298.
Sesostris
Sesostris 5. 418.
Sestos
Sestos 1. 285,
Seston 5. 201.
seu (sive) (24)
seu 1. 19 (BG; KL sed), 20 (BG; KL
et), 101, 839; 3. 392 (L; KBG si); 8.
230 (KBG; L ceu),
seu . . . seu 3. 624; 5. 502; 7. 96; 8. 316,
seu . . . seu . . . seu 1. 232, 670,
seu . . . sive 5. 248; 7. 351.
severus
severi (gen. m.) 3. 446.
si (111)
    1. c. ind.
a) prs. 1. 5, 6. 265, 323, 807, 829; 2. 383,
485; 3. 378; 4. 472 bis, 735; 5. 19, 52,
378 bis, 631, 642, 665; 6. 305, 711; 7. 58,
71, 199, 452, 454, 494; 8. 417,
b) imperf. 5. 473, 474; 7. 133,
c) fut. 1. 19 (BGL; K sed); 4. 587; 7.
273, 447, 448,
d) perf. 3. 392 (KBG; L seu); 4. 170;
5. 659; 6. 289; 7. 276, 279, 604 (KG;
BL qui), 567,
e) fut. perf. 4. 591; 6. 454; 7. 205, 502
bis,
    2. c. subi.
a) prs. 1. 75, 177, 178 (si des BGL; K
sedeat), 460; 2. 388; 3. 184, 232; 4. 321;
5. 394, 561, 584, 606, 645 (suus at si B;

K lucis; G suus ast; L suus atque),
646; 6. 4, 261, 391, 624; 7. 30, 142, 501
(BGL; K et), 501, 651,
b) imperf. 1. 719, 732; 3. 296, 656; 4.
572; 5. 408; 7. 198 (KBG; L o), 198;
8. 10, 451,
c) perf. 1. 307; 4. 368,
d) pluperf. 2. 405; 3. 246; 4. 710; 5. 495;
6. 311 bis; 7. 99, 440,
    3. sine verb.
1. 51, 324, 336, 835; 2. 559; 3. 184; 4.
461, 541, 572; 5. 382, 509; 6. 51, 306
(si tibi KBL; G sicubi); 7. 266, 507;
8. 157, 213, 226, 264,
Vid. aliter, forte, quando, quis, quod,
secus, tum, veluti.
sibilus
sibila (nom. f.) 3. 50,
subst. n. sibila 8. 103,
sibila 6. 201; 7. 526.
Sibotes
Sibotes 6. 249.
sic (116)
sic 1. 194, 204, 214 bis, 234, 348, 541 bis,
566 bis, 671; 2. 66, 145, 160, 277, 289,
405, 425, 617, 649, 663; 3. 90, 110, 165,
492, 534, 545, 590, 616; 4. 7, 8, 61, 121,
175, 210, 239, 291, 314, 439 (rebar sic
KGL; B sectabar), 485, 507 (sic ubi K;
BGL sicut), 585, 598, 687, 721; 5. 69,
131, 193, 213, 309, 362 (KGL; B sunt),
363, 392, 536, 552, 590, 591, 630, 664 bis,
670 (nequeat sic KBG; L cedam tibi),
672; 6. 163, 212, 281, 307, 338, 356, 407,
408, 430, 540, 629, 646, 735; 7. 8, 9, 20,
44, 124, 127, 131, 171, 214 (K; BGL
hic), 418, 472, 537, 570, 581, 608, 628;
8. 36, 44, 171, 177, 444,
sic cum 1. 682,
sic demum 4. 616,
sic ubi 4. 661; 8. 239,
sic ubi . . . cum . . . sic 4. 507 (vid.
sic 4. 507),
sic . . . ubi 3. 558 (KBG; L ceu . . .
ubi),
ceu . . . sic 3. 468; 5. 522; 6. 347,
ceu . . . sic . . . sic 3. 281,
ceu . . . cum . . . sic 3. 579,
qualis . . . sic 4. 271; 6. 615,
quales . . . sic 4. 107,
quam . . . sic 1. 759,
ut . . . sic 4. 725,
ut . . . ut . . . cum . . . sic 3. 210,
Vid. qualiter, secus, veluti.
Sicanius
Sicanium (acc. n.) 2. 29.
sicco
siccabat 4. 332.
sicubi
4. 105; 6. 306 (G; KBL si tibi).
Siculus
Siculum (acc. n.) 2. 619,
Sicula 2. 24; 5. 344,
Siculo 1. 136; 7. 648,
Siculos 1. 589.

singulto
singultantia (acc.) 2. 211.
singultus
singultibus (abl.) 3. 107, 218, 338; 6.
511, 738; 8. 45.
singulus
singula (acc.) 6. 576,
subst. n. singula (nom.) 8. 160.
sinister
sinistrum (acc. n.) 3. 121 (B; KGL
ministri); 8. 375,
sinistra (abl.) 1. 847,
sinistris (abl. m.) 3. 303,
subst. f. sinistrae (dat.) 8. 124,
sinistra 4. 291.
sino
sinit 2. 3; 3. 140; 6. 177; 7. 585; 8. 319,
409,
sinunt 8. 407,
sinat 8. 395,
sinant 3. 184,
sine 2. 275; 4. 624 (sine me L; K
sileam; B sileo; G sileo et); 7. 455,
sinite 4. 635.
Sinope
Sinope 5. 109,
Sinopes 5. 108.
sinuo
sinuatus 4. 728.
sinuosus
sinuosa (acc.) 2. 452; 3. 277.
sinus
sinus (nom.) 2. 607; 5. 154,
sinu (abl.) 1. 653; 2. 423, 629; 7. 450,
sinus 2. 498,
sinus 2. 36, 104, 212, 268, 502; 4. 720;
5. 109; 6. 319, 274; 7. 252, 355; 8. 18.
Sirius
Sirius 1. 683; 5. 369.
sisto
sistit 5. 183; 6. 7,
sistat 2. 219; 4. 396,
sisteret 6. 583,
siste 8. 144,
sistere 2. 381; 5. 190; 7. 188.
sistrum
sistro (abl.) 4. 418.
sitis
siti (abl.) 4. 379.
situs
situ (abl.) 3. 400; 4. 183.
sive vid. seu.
socer
socer 1. 658,
socerum (acc.) 5. 232,
soceros 6. 274,
soceris 1. 403.
sociatrix
sociatrix 5. 499.
socio
sociabant 5. 281,
sociare 5. 289, 516.
socius
socius 3. 380,
sociae (gen.) 4. 528,

socio (abl.) 8. 356,
socia (abl.) 1. 73; 3. 162,
socios 3. 312; 4. 543,
socias 3. 30, 268 (KBG; L caesas),
663; 5. 666; 6. 218, 484, 747; 7. 625,
subst. socius 1. 408,
socium 1. 117, 165; 3. 619,
sociam 6. 450; 8. 403,
socio 3. 642,
socii 3. 261, 720; 4. 31, 292; 5. 25, 60,
173,
socium 3. 4; 6. 369, 388,
sociis (m.) 1. 234; 3. 598; 4. 85, 144,
697; 5. 275, 547; 6. 192; 8. 127, 404,
socios 2. 540, 565; 3. 146, 245, 412, 570,
616, 715, 735; 4. 8, 56, 626; 5. 41, 118,
190, 214, 465; 6. 400; 7. 593, 614, 649; 8.
43, 221, 336, 423,
socias 5. 376,
socii 1. 242, 250; 2. 55; 8. 183,
sociis (m.) 4. 242, 554; 8. 377.
Sol
Sol 1. 504; 3. 401; 4. 92,
Solis 1. 44; 3. 730; 5. 224, 581; 6. 442,
518; 8. 282, 460,
Sol 8. 350,
Sole 5. 263, 456, 567.
sol
sol 1. 274, 843; 2. 444; 5. 92, 177,
solis 3. 37,
sole 1. 495; 2. 441; 4. 730,
soles (acc.) 4. 632,
solibus 2. 287; 3. 612.
solamen
solamen (nom.) 5. 56,
solamine 3. 319; 4. 443.
soleo
soles 2. 129,
solet 8. 63, 354,
solebat 5. 473,
solita est 7. 180,
soliti (nom.) 1. 586; 3. 45,
solitos 1. 112,
solitis (n.) 2. 660,
subst. n. solito (abl.) 7. 66.
Soligena
Soligenae (gen.) 5. 223,
Soligenam 5. 317.
solium
solio 6. 742,
solium 1. 690; 3. 385,
solio 1. 597; 2. 309; 5. 268.
sollemnis
subst. sollemnia (acc.) 2. 599.
sollers
sollers (m.) 5. 64.
sollicito
sollicitat 3. 548; 6. 156,
sollicitant 1. 261.
sollicitus
sollicito (dat. m.) 5. 389.
solo
solata (nom. f.) 3. 41.

solor
solantur 3. 285,
solabor 4. 578,
solabere 2. 151,
solatus est 7. 412,
solans (m.) 4. 86.
solum
solum 4. 100, 713,
solum 2. 296; 4. 565,
solo 5. 312; 6. 366; 7. 104,
sola (acc.) 4. 497.
solus
solus 1. 295, 467; 2. 380; 3. 324, 736
(L; KBG solis); 4. 52, 203, 479; 5. 112
bis, 668; 6. 586; 7. 69, 559,
sola 1. 76; 3. 255; 4. 269; 5. 638; 6. 332,
439, 483, 486; 7. 51, 224, 249, 272, 443;
8. 143, 206, 425, 455,
soli 2. 305; 7. 3,
soli (f.) 7. 174,
solum 1. 152; 4. 499; 7. 351,
solam 8. 62, 147,
solum 8. 349,
sola (voc.) 8. 38,
solo 5. 375; 7. 13,
sola 5. 642; 8. 391,
solo 7. 116,
soli 6. 398,
solis 3. 681,
solis (f.) 4. 621,
solos 5. 625,
solas 3. 247; 6. 41,
sola 1. 615, 799; 5. 55, 541; 7. 15,
solis 6. 751,
solis 3. 736 (KBG; L solus); 4. 5, 621,
solis 3. 673.
solvo
solvit 1. 433; 3. 363; 4. 311,
solvimus 2. 294,
solvit 4. 758,
solvimus 1. 629,
solverat 1. 351; 3. 1,
solvat 7. 169 (solvat et G; KL fallat;
B insomnem), 169 (KBL; G volvat),
solverit 5. 606,
solvere 2. 88; 3. 435; 6. 154; 8. 220,
solvitur 1. 638; 3. 351; 4. 731; 8. 358,
solvimur 3. 383,
solutus 3. 357,
solutae (gen.) 8. 361,
soluto (abl.) 5. 149,
soluta 3. 180,
soluti 7. 383.
Solymus
Solymo (abl. m.) 1. 13.
somnifer
somniferas 7. 247.
somnium
somnia 3. 418,
somnia 3. 59.
Somnus
Somne 8. 70 **bis.**
somnus
somnus 3. 179,

somni 1. 296; 4. 16, 50, 367, 531; 7. 213;
8. 8,
somno 2. 71,
somno 1. 300; 2. 568; 3. 260; 4. 41; 8. 65,
somnos 2. 183; 3. 33; 4. 389; 5. 695; 7.
144, 169; 8. 82.
sonipes
subst. m. sonipes 1. 431; 3. 334; 4. 230;
6. 214, 218, 258.
sonitus
sonitum 2. 339; 6. 180,
sonitu 1. 819 (BGL; K foribus); 4. 180,
453,
sonitus 4. 641,
sonitus 3. 97, 207, 244.
sono
sonat 2. 112, 226, 455; 4. 228, 307; 5.
142; 6. 112,
sonant 3. 166; 4. 92, 283,
sonuit 2. 37; 3. 197; 4. 384,
sonuerunt 7. 322, 611,
sonuere 5. 33,
sonent 5. 252,
sonaret 8. 455,
sonantem 3. 198,
sonantem 2. 105; 5. 99,
sonantes (acc. m.) 1. 262.
sonor
sonor 6. 152 (K; BGL honor),
sonoribus (abl.) 5. 305.
sonorus
sonorae (gen.) 1. 667,
sonoro (abl. m.) 3. 61.
sons
sontes (f.) 5. 658,
sontibus (dat. f.) 5. 42,
subst. m. sontum 1. 794,
sontes 3. 389.
sonus
sonus 3. 464, 561,
sonum 2. 260; 3. 106,
sono 6. 479; 7. 390.
sopor
sopor 1. 48; 3. 39, 417; 4. 43; 6. 8, 444;
7. 143, 244; 8. 87,
soporis 8. 81,
sopore 5. 49.
soporifer
soporiferas 2. 295.
soporo
soporato (abl. m.) 5. 237,
soporatos 5. 333.
soporus
subst. soporos 2. 221.
sorbeo
sorbet 1. 638.
sordidus
sordidus 1. 775,
sordida (nom. f.) 3. 740.
soror
soror 1. 134, 286, 447, 643; 2. 229, 589;
3. 514; 5. 188, 414; 6. 224, 661; 7. 39; 8.
141, 171,
sororis 4. 465; 7. 117, 152,
sorori 6. 491; 7. 202,

spirantis (m.) 6. 523,
spirantes (m.) 6. 129,
spirantia (nom.) 7. 327.
splendeo
splendet 1. 404.
spolio
spoliare 2. 382,
spolientur 5. 632.
spolium
spolium (acc.) 3. 26, 707; 7. 45,
spolia (nom.) 6. 703,
spoliis (abl.) 1. 745; 5. 122, 593.
spondeo
sponde 3. 504,
spondentibus (abl. n.) 6. 117,
subst. sponsae (gen.) 8. 300.
sponsa vid. spondeo.
sponte (10)
1. 198, 835; 2. 435; 4. 207, 358; 5. 481;
6. 28, 400, 467, 498.
spretus vid. sperno.
spuma
spumas 1. 688.
spumeus
spumeus 4. 666,
spumea (nom. f.) 2. 430.
spumo
spumare 6. 447; 8. 83,
spumantem (m.) 3. 102; 4. 195,
spumanti (n.) 4. 268; 5. 179,
spumantia 1. 260,
spumantia 1. 194.
spumosus
spumosum (acc. n.) 3. 36.
squaleo
squalentem (f.) 6. 397; 7. 535,
squalentes (acc. m.) 6. 525.
stabilis
stabilem (m.) 2. 263.
stabulum
stabula 7. 566,
stabulis 1. 682; 7. 392,
stabula 2. 548; 6. 531,
stabulis 1. 158; 2. 205, 478, 566; 5. 151;
6. 613.
stagno
stagnat 1. 736.
stagnum
stagna 3. 558,
stagna 6. 568.
stamen
stamine 1. 431; 6. 699.
statio
statio 3. 361,
statione 8. 379.
statuo
statuunt 1. 188; 8. 327,
statui 7. 57,
statuit 1. 786; 6. 743,
statuere 5. 472,
statuissem 5. 495,
statuisset 3. 653.
status
status (nom. s.) 5. 284.
status (adi.) vid. sto.

stella
stellis (dat.) 1. 482; 3. 38.
stello
stellantia 2. 499,
stellantia 3. 98; 5. 622,
stellatus 2. 42.
sterilis
sterilem (f.) 6. 695.
sterno
sternit 2. 590; 3. 139; 6. 523,
sternunt 3. 57,
sternere 2. 231; 6. 4,
sternitur 7. 143,
sternuntur 4. 339; 8. 258,
sterni 5. 174; 7. 639,
strata 1. 578,
stratam 3. 248,
strata (acc.) 3. 605,
subst. n. strato (dat.) 7. 141,
stratis (abl.) 1. 310; 4. 535.
Sterope
Steropen 1. 446.
Sthenelus
Sthenelus 5. 89,
Sthenelo (abl.) 5. 488.
stimulo
stimulant 1. 104,
stimulaverit (subi.) 5. 137.
stimulus
stimulis (abl.) 6. 591.
stipo
stipat 7. 557,
stipant 5. 467.
stirps
stirpis 2. 562,
stirpe 1. 523; 3. 668; 5. 500.
sto
stas 1. 679,
stat 1. 6, 401, 516, 580; 2. 98, 343, 532;
3. 88, 121, 434, 606; 4. 203; 5. 109, 188,
288, 410, 579; 7. 362; 8. 217,
stant 1. 494, 784; 2. 411, 599, 651; 3.
284, 402; 4. 505, 639, 729,
stabat 1. 776; 7. 82, 354, 560,
stabo 1. 806,
stetit 3. 256, 673; 4. 61, 165; 5. 336, 391,
560; 7. 337, 525; 8. 463,
stetimus 4. 652,
steterunt 2. 360 (KB; GL steterant),
steterat 4. 225,
steterant 2. 360 (GL; KB steterunt);
4. 282,
steteris 3. 105,
steterint 4. 583,
stet 5. 324; 6. 452,
steterit 1. 278,
stare 1. 98, 671 (stare et BG; K claret;
L stare); 2. 84; 4. 632; 5. 338; 7. 545;
8. 196, 249,
stans (m.) 4. 24; 7. 530,
stantem (f.) 1. 78,
stante (f.) 8. 77 (hic stante L; KB
adstante; G instante),
stantia (acc.) 8. 269,
stata (acc.) 2. 488.

stolidus
stolidum (acc. n.) 6. 537.
stomachus
stomachi (gen.) 3. 200.
strages
stragem 2. 179,
strage 3. 270, 276; 5. 158; 6. 508; 7. 151.
stramen
stramina (acc.) 4. 497.
stratum vid. sterno.
strepito
strepitant 4. 288.
strepitus
strepitus (nom.) 7. 392,
strepitum 5. 650,
strepitus (acc.) 1. 849.
strepo
strepit 6. 302,
strepuere 6. 28.
strideo (strido)
stridet 2. 63,
stridunt 4. 498,
stridens (m.) 1. 640; 6. 556 (K; BGL
  frendens),
stridente (m.) 1. 373,
stridentes (f.) 2. 585,
stridentes (f.) 6. 746,
stridentia 3. 278.
stridor
stridore 2. 273; 3. 239, 566.
stringo
stringunt 7. 483 (KBG; L spargunt),
stricto (m.) 4. 182,
strictum (m.) 7. 287; 8. 360,
stricto 3. 119; 5. 579; 6. 281; 7. 530,
stricta 3. 524,
stricto 3. 425,
strictis (m.) 3. 111,
strictis (n.) 2. 449,
strictos 1. 513, 820.
Strophades
Strophadas 4. 513.
struo
struit 2. 101,
struximus 5. 294,
struxerat 1. 430; 5. 452,
struat 3. 586,
struerem 1. 535; 3. 617; 6. 728,
structae (gen.) 1. 603,
structas 3. 570.
Strymon
Strymona 6. 193.
studium
studium (nom.) 1. 103, 837,
studiis 5. 624,
studiis 3. 628.
stupefacio
stupefactus 5. 620,
stupefacta (nom. f.) 5. 337,
stupefacta (acc.) 6. 228.
stupeo
stupet 1. 149, 262, 742; 2. 510; 4. 72,
549; 5. 96, 596; 6. 149, 442; 7. 83, 393,
640,

stupuit 2. 619; 5. 375,
stupuerunt 5. 602,
stupuere 4. 712.
Stygius
Stygiae (gen.) 2. 601; 3. 398, 450,
Stygiam 8. 87,
Stygia (abl.) 6. 155,
Stygiis 1. 730,
Stygiis (f.) 2. 106,
Stygias 1. 781; 2. 173; 3. 446,
Stygiis (m.) 7. 364.
Styrus
Styrus 3. 497; 5. 459; 6. 266; 8. 299,
329,
Styri 8. 335,
Styre 6. 275.
Styx
Styga 1. 464; 4. 401.
suadeo
suadet 3. 548; 6. 600.
sub (58)
  1. c. acc.
1. 581; 2. 72, 608; 4. 118, 217, 685; 6.
603; 7. 394, 596; 8. 347,
  2. c. abl.
1. 269, 578, 604, 774, 823, 826, 827; 2.
119, 171, 192, 258, 329, 359, 587, 657; 3.
132, 165, 240, 589, 600, 655; 4. 105, 184,
637; 5. 140, 220, 226, 317, 344, 483
(KGL; B sua), 521; 6. 82, 140, 604; 7.
230, 336, 338, 367, 370, 400, 418, 538,
539; 8. 95, 101, 288, 367, 454.
subduco
subducere 6. 624.
subeo
subit 2. 519, 556; 3. 105; 4. 198, 299,
357; 5. 184, 437; 6. 251, 439; 7. 460; 8.
229, 322,
subeunt 1. 185, 713; 3. 72; 7. 554,
subibat 5. 660,
subibant 2. 585; 7. 404,
subibit 3. 230,
subiit 4. 188; 6. 322; 8. 67,
subierunt 8. 161,
subiere 1. 128, 759; 2. 604,
subeat 7. 182,
subiret 3. 702,
subire 7. 428; 8. 192,
subiisse 4. 736; 5. 569,
subeuntibus (abl. n.) 4. 90,
subitus 1. 180, 620, 641, 693; 2. 51, 477;
3. 115, 188; 4. 490,
subiti 6. 573, 694,
subitae (gen.) 1. 672,
subitum 3. 101,
subitam 4. 712; 6. 154,
subito 2. 312, 541,
subita 1. 86, 218; 4. 626; 8. 261,
subito 3. 477,
subitae 1. 141; 3. 405,
subitos 2. 400; 6. 705,
subitas 1. 437; 4. 292; 8. 306,
subitis (f.) 8. 413,
subitis 8. 136,

subst. n. subitis (abl.) 1. 756,
adv. subito 4. 384, 480, 501; 6. 283, 715;
7. 85, 122, 304, 396, 524, 564, 581, 637,
643; 8. 56, 177.
subicio
  subicit 2. 659.
subigo
  subigit 1. 471.
subito, subitus vid. **subeo.**
sublabor
  sublabitur 6. 556.
subligo
  subligat 3. 445; 5. 579; 6. 700.
sublimis
  sublimis (nom. f.) 7. 157,
  sublimem (m.) 3. 546.
sublustris
  sublustri (abl. f.) 3. 142.
subnecto
  subnectitur 2. 103.
suboles
  suboles 3. 317.
subsequor
  subsequitur 2. 430.
subsido
  subsedit 2. 8,
  subsederat 3. 167.
subsisto
  substitit 2. 334; 5. 352; 7. 383.
subsum
  subest 7. 386.
subtegmen
  subtegmine 6. 227; 8. 234.
subter (adv.)
  3. 404.
subter (praepos.)
  4. 594.
subtexo
  subtexit 5. 413.
succedo
  succedunt 6. 506,
  succedet 8. 338,
  succede 7. 67,
  succedite 1. 797,
  succedere 3. 139,
  succedens (f.) 2. 453.
succendo
  succensus 3. 585.
succurro
  succurrere 2. 457; 7. 199, 280, 313, 506;
  8. 363.
sucus
  sucos 6. 441.
sudo
  sudantem (m.) 1. 374.
sudor
  sudor 3. 556; 5. 287, 288,
  sudore 3. 577,
  sudoribus 5. 668,
  sudoribus 4. 276; 7. 646.
sudus
  subst. n. sudum (acc.) 2. 115.
suesco
  suetus 1. 343.

Suetes
  Sueten 6. 550.
sufficio
  sufficit 2. 325; 6. 381; 7. 623,
  sufficiet 8. 275,
  suffecerat 7. 457 (K; BL se flexerat; G
  suffixerat),
  suffecta (nom. f.) 2. 105,
  suffecta (acc.) 1. 821.
suffigo
  suffixerat 7. 457 (G; K suffecerat; BL
  se flexerat).
suggero
  suggerit 1. 299; 3. 7,
  suggere 6. 289.
sui
  sui 3. 665; 8. 412,
  sibi 1. 239, 524, 529, 779; 2. 123; 3.
  128, 221, 242, 356; 4. 238, 521; 5. 3. 119,
  270, 384, 490, 524, 529, 572; 6. 351; 7. 8,
  354, 355, 615, 651; 8. 118, 401,
  se 1. 487, 629, 701; 2. 38, 115, 218, 318
  (KL; B **om.**; G est), 320, 346, 661; 3.
  265, 423, 500, 583, 641; 4. 22, 49, 396,
  676; 5. 268, 325, 339, 404, 456; 6. 18,
  96, 543, 581, 610; 7. 81, 138, 150, 297,
  309, 323, 398, 400, 457 (se flexerat BL;
  K suffecerat; G suffixerat), 526, 538,
  583, 614; 8. 25, 35, 94, 109, 129, 136
  (G; KBL **om.**), 247, 448,
  semet 7. 127,
  sese 1. 65, 514; 3. 100, 635, 694; 4. 199,
  296, 501; 6. 181, 678; 7. 337, 470, 576;
  8. 315, 391,
  se 7. 475,
  secum 1. 150; 5. 448; 6. 741,
  sibi 1. 502; 2. 394; 3. 374,
  se 1. 222, 610; 2. 234; 4. 4, 189; 5. 117,
  695; 7. 18; 8. 387,
  sese 2. 171; 3. 187; 6. 353; 8. 383,
  sese (abl.) 3. 630,
  secum 5. 280.
sulcus
  sulco (abl.) 1. 568; 3. 32; 7. 611,
  sulcis (abl.) 1. 222.
sulphur
  sulphure 2. 450; 8. 348.
sum
  sum 7. 159; 8. 417,
  es 1. 750; 4. 140, 191, 240; 7. 291,
  est 1. 166, 174 (L; KBG **om.**), 327, 508
  KL; BG et), 586, 771; 2. 318 (G; KL
  se; B **om.**); 3. 309, 599; 4. 113, 127, 449,
  471, 735, 741; 5. 125, 126, 387, 643, 645;
  6. 82 (K; BGL et), 724 (K; BGL it);
  7. 71, 176, 199, 341 (quicumque est KL;
  B primaevum; G qui nunc est); 8. 12,
  40, 170,
  sumus 3. 272 **bis,**
  sunt 1. 723, 724; 5. 362 (B; KGL sic),
  688,
  eram 1. 602,
  erat 1. 337, 350, 534, 588, 627; 3. 32; 4.
  185, 652 (nuper erat B; KG perculerat;

L caecus erat); 5. 349, 442; 6. 642; 7.
11, 211, 334 (pestis erat KGL; B pestiferam), 407, 640; 8. 160, 443, 448, 461,
erant 2. 221; 8. 165,
eris 8. 345,
erit 3. 672; 4. 130; 8. 272,
fui 7. 249,
fuit 1. 670; 3. 337, 684; 7. 219, 642 (B;
KG ruit; L fugit),
fueras 3. 324,
fuerant 4. 711,
fuerit 4. 572 (L; KB fieret; G fiet);
7. 205,
sim 2. 420; 7. 159 (mihi sim B; KGL
mecum), 501,
sis 4. 37; 7. 159 (sis hunc L; KB
tecum; G tantum), 477,
sit 1. 118; 3. 450, 682; 4. 476; 5. 265,
492, 678; 7. 280, 521; 8. 15, 273,
simus 2. 156.
sint 3. 449; 4. 144, 192; 5. 292; 8. 191,
essem 2. 142,
foret 1. 509; 6. 316,
essent 1. 719; 3. 297,
forent 1. 115,
fuerint 1. 675,
fuisset 6. 311; 7. 99; 8. 167, 433,
este 3. 451,
esto 5. 249,
esto 1. 557,
esse 1. 65, 118; 2. 560; 3. 631, 684; 6. 23,
430; 7. 51, 215, 265, 286,
fore 1. 27; 4. 476,
futuri (n.) 6. 490; 8. 206,
future 6. 313,
futura (abl.) 7. 125,
subst. n. futuri 4. 404; 7. 192,
futuris 4. 593,
futura 1. 361,
futuris 1. 699.
summa
summa (abl.) 5. 301.
summitto
summittit 3. 528,
summissa 7. 476,
summisso (abl. m.) 6. 245.
summus vid. superus.
sumo
sumit 2. 466,
sumat 1. 815,
sumptis (abl. m.) 4. 112,
sumptis (n.) 5. 637.
super (adv.) (23)
1. 29, 345, 516; 2. 228, 596; 3. 203, 427;
4. 46 (vid. praepos.), 178, 312, 680, 717;
5. 544; 6. 195, 263, 342; 7. 335, 642; 8.
19, 33, 120, 157, 435.
super (praep.) (30)
  1. c. acc.
1. 160, 317 (super eminet KBG; L supereminet), 620; 2. 319, 459; 3. 51, 109,
150, 274, 314, 567; 4. 24, 96, 631, 688;
6. 7, 88, 525, 610, 747; 7. 56, 473,
  2. c. abl.

1. 731; 2. 626; 3. 60, 641, 704; 4. 46 (vid.
adv.), 84; 7. 196.
superabilis
superabilis (nom. m.) 3. 648.
superaddo
superaddit 1. 129.
superbia
superbia (nom.) 3. 699.
superbus
superbus 1. 395, 745; 5. 321,
superbi 1. 161,
superbi 1. 434,
superbo (m.) 1. 119; 5. 599,
superbum 6. 735,
superbam 1. 98,
superbo (m.) 4. 607,
superba (nom.) 4. 649,
superbis (dat. m.) 2. 544; 3. 634,
superbis (abl. n.) 3. 9 (BGL; K om.),
superbior (m.) 7. 66.
superemineo
supereminet 1. 317 (L; KBG super
eminet); 5. 367.
superfugio
superfugit 3. 554.
superincendo
superincendit 2. 126.
superne
3. 168.
supernus
supernis (abl. f.) 1. 827.
supero
superat 2. 431 (L; KBG transit); 7.
595,
superant 5. 52,
superabat 2. 545,
superet 1. 74 (KBG; L speret); 6. 599;
7. 131; 8. 179,
superare 4. 19; 5. 617,
superati (nom.) 3. 516.
supersum
superest 1. 631, 809; 6. 760; 8. 303,
supersunt 5. 236; 8. 253,
supersint 7. 522,
superesse 1. 785; 5. 26.
superus
superi (gen. m.) 3. 380,
superas 2. 94; 4. 73; 6. 113,
superis 7. 498,
superis (f.) 7. 259 (a superis KG; BL
Hesperiis),
subst. m. superi (nom.) 1. 501; 4. 218;
5. 296; 6. 729,
superum 1. 241, 671, 792; 2. 456; 3. 16;
4. 152, 541; 5. 598,
superis 1. 308; 3. 297, 399; 5. 657,
superos 4. 761; 6. 152, 212; 7. 311; 8. 53,
superi 1. 267,
superis 7. 452,
supremum (m.) 7. 375 (KGL; B ubi
primum),
supremam 3. 251; 4. 442,
supremo 1. 752, 781; 3. 349; 8. 172,
supremo 5. 25,
suprema 7. 133,

supremos 5. 32; 6. 629; 7. 201a; 8. 10,
supremas 6. 644,
suprema 1. 635; 2. 471; 4. 751,
subst. n. suprema (acc.) 1. 786,
summus 1. 189; 4. 203, 545,
summa 1. 542,
summi 1. 690; 2. 560; 4. 260, 267; 5. 280,
622; 6. 261,
ısummi 5. 243,
summe 1. 505,
summo 1. 199, 255, 386, 472; 3. 487;
4. 377; 5. 19, 161; 8. 318,
summa 4. 22, 85, 406; 5. 45; 7. 606;
8. 202, 309,
ısummo 1. 313; 3. 525; 4. 426,
summos 1. 656; 4. 275 (KBG; L summis),
summas 2. 6; 3. 456, 481; 6. 612,
ısumma 3. 334, 465; 4. 647; 6. 490, 664;
8. 122,
summis 2. 537; 3. 462 (B; K raptis;
GL celsis),
summis (f.) 2. 78; 4. 275 (L; KBG summos); 7. 616,
subst. n. summa (acc.) 1. 558,
summis 4. 517.
supplex
supplex 3. 640; 4. 61, 537, 648; 6. 74;
7. 143, 446; 8. 44, 286 (KBG; L iit),
397,
supplex (f.) 5. 398; 6. 458,
supplicis (m.) 7. 431,
supplice (f.) 3. 424; 4. 11,
subst. supplicis (f.) 8. 442,
supplice (m.) 7. 290.
supprimo
suppressum (acc. n.) 5. 469,
supra (praepos.) (5)
3. 137; 4. 110; 5. 185; 6. 687; 8. 152.
supremus vid. superus.
surgo
surgis 1. 456,
surgit 1. 580; 2. 78, 165, 321, 634; 3. 690
(B; KGL urget); 4. 455, 617; 6. 419;
8. 129,
ısurgunt 4. 224, 254, 283; 5. 39 (KGL;
B surgent), 221; 8. 307,
surgent 5. 39 (B; KGL surgunt),
surrexit 2. 56,
surgat 5. 608,
surge 4. 35,
surgere 2. 261; 4. 632; 7. 250; 8. 216,
surgentis 3. 437,
surgentis (f.) 3. 561,
surgentem 2. 510,
surgentem 1. 209; 4. 599,
surgentes (acc. m.) 5. 245,
surgentia 2. 533,
surgitur 5. 695.
sursus
7. 562 (B; KGL rursus).
sus
suum 6. 91.
suscito
suscitat 2. 125; 3. 209, 546; 7. 603; 8. 233.

suspendo
suspendit (perf.) 2. 85.
suspicio
suspiciens (m.) 1. 265,
suspectae (gen.) 6. 149,
suspecti (nom.) 1. 245,
subst. n. suspecta (acc.) 3. 244.
suspirium
suspiria 1. 713,
suspiria 1. 173; 4. 359; 8. 457.
suspiro
suspirat 1. 133; 4. 532.
sustineo
sustinet 4. 406; 6. 249 (KBL; G sustulit); 8. 81, 231,
sustinuit 1. 349; 3. 101; 4. 2,
ısustineat 5. 560; 6. 276.
sutilis
sutilis (nom. f.) 6. 81.
suus
suus 1. 431; 2. 625; 5. 12, 487, 645 (suus
at si B; K lucis; G suus ast; L suus
atque); 6. 443; 7. 53,
sua 2. 191, 505; 3. 6; 4. 200; 5. 265; 6.
609, 628, 713; 7. 26, 556; 8. 237,
sui 1. 359; 5. 659; 6. 11,
sui 5. 229; 8. 226, 258,
suum 8. 94,
suam 3. 343; 6. 21; 7. 286; 8. 235,
suum 7. 167, 408,
suo 1. 246, 532; 7. 261,
sua 4. 754; 6. 28; 7. 203,
suo 1. 348,
sui 7. 466,
sua 2. 71, 310; 3. 393; 4. 278 **bis;** 6. 145,
suarum 5. 643; 7. 121,
suorum 7. 310,
suis (m.) 5. 616,
suos 3. 389; 6. 509,
ısuas 2. 21; 4. 564; 6. 143; 7. 317; 8. 234,
395,
ısua 1. 352, 461, 543; 2. 436, 512; 3. 276
bis; 4. 421, 559, 563, 597, 732; 5. 381,
483 (B; KGL sub), 503, 523, 676, 695;
6. 13, 21, 143, 172, 386, 408, 509, 621,
671; 7. 35, 371, 432, 526, 638; 7. 643;
8. 1, 89, 221,
suis 7. 391, 601; 8. 289,
suis 5. 559; 7. 96; 8. 61,
\suis 5. 90; 6. 31, 737; 7. 425,
subst. m. suorum 1. 812; 2. 220; 3. 336;
4. 127, 162; 5. 419; 6. 93, 725; 8. 464.
Syenes
Syenen 6. 74 (KBL; G Syrenen), 703.
Symplegas
Symplegas 4. 221,
Symplegados 5. 299.
Syrenes
Syrenen 6. 74 (G; KBL Syenen).
Syrtis
Syrtibus 4. 716,
ıSyrtes 7. 86.
tabulatus ،
subst. n. tabulata (acc.) 3. 463; 8. 305.

tabum
tabo (abl.) 1. 816; 2. 212; 3. 150; 4. 749.
taceo
tacet 3. 732,
taceat 2. 337,
tacitus 2. 526, 567; 3. 636,
taciti 4. 201,
tacitae (gen.) 5. 231,
tacitum 4. 57,
tacitam 1. 464,
tacitum 1. 479,
tacito 3. 418; 5. 351; 6. 584,
tacita 2. 257, 267; 5. 567; 6. 262,
tacito 4. 4,
taciti 1. 64, 689,
tacitae 2. 100; 3. 402,
tacitis (f.) 4. 625; 5. 638; 7. 405,
tacitos 3. 441,
tacitis 7. 488,
tacitis (f.) 2. 60, 279; 5. 333,
subst. m. tacitum 2. 254.
tacitus vid. taceo.
taeda
taedae (gen.) 5. 348; 8. 402,
taedae (nom.) 5. 443; 8. 240,
taedas 2. 173, 235; 7. 180; 8. 284.
taedium
taedia (acc.) 6. 325.
Taenarius
Taenarii (n.) 5. 512,
Taenario (abl. m.) 1. 427.
Taenaros
Taenaron 1. 365.
taetae
taetae (?) 2. 317 (K; BG cete; L taete).
taete
taete (?) 2. 317 (L; K taetae; BG cete).
taeter
taetro (abl. n.) 1. 63 (ex taetro L; K ex
terno; BG externo),
taetra (nom.) 4. 183.
Tages
Tages 6. 223.
Talaus
Talaus 1. 358,
Talai 3. 471,
Talaum 3. 478; 5. 366; 6. 720.
talis
1. adi.
talis 3. 295; 5. 680; 7. 20; 8. 125,
talis 4. 150; 6. 316, 411, 636, 667; 7. 640,
tale 5. 410,
tali (f.) 2. 292,
talem 1. 728; 3. 329; 7. 19; 8. 95,
talem 2. 123; 6. 339; 8. 167, 448,
tale 1. 626; 3. 560; 5. 657,
tali 2. 402; 3. 631, 683,
tali 3. 583; 4. 205; 6. 589; 7. 34,
tali 2. 144; 5. 534,
tales (acc.) 1. 733; 2. 151 (B; KGL
aliis), 492, 643; 3. 53, 223, 300; 4. 117;
6. 487, 515; 7. 108, 416,
tales 1. 504; 2. 399; 3. 300, 518, 574;
4. 430; 7. 421,
talis (f.) 4. 24,

talia 1. 182; 3. 17, 243; 4. 222, 430; 5.
470, 568; 6. 427, 515; 7. 251,
talibus 3. 715,
talibus 6. 623,
talibus 4. 38; 5. 269; 7. 101, 371,
qualis . . . talis (nom. m.) 8. 30,
qualem . . . talis (nom. m.) 5. 91,
qualis . . . talis (nom. f.) 5. 348,
qualem . . . talis (nom. f.) . . . **talem**
(f.) 8. 448,
qualis . . . talem (f.) 8. 31,
qualiter . . . tali (abl. n.) 6. 394,
cum . . . talem (m.) 1. 728,
ut . . . talis (nom. m.) 6. 361,
    2. subst.
talis 3. 120,
talis (nom. f.) 8. 96,
talem (m.) 4. 156,
tales (acc. m.) 1. 343 **bis,**
talia 1. 156, 240, 740, 767; 2. 57, 274;
4. 249, 707, 740; 5. 37, 296, 648; 7. 197;
8. 59, 467,
talibus (n.) 1. 58, 111, 335, 666; 2. 610;
3. 235, 690; 4. 537; 5. 519; 8. 414,
Vid. ceu, quam, velut.
tam (19)
1. 47, 649 (BG; KL iam); 2. 490, 642
(G; KBL iam); 3. 694; 4. 551 **bis;** 5.
541 (L; KBG tum), 659; 6. 128 (miseri
tam KBG; L miserandi), 283, 336, 410;
7. 13, 319; 8. 58, 241 (KBG; L iam),
273, 399.
tamen (44)
tamen 1. 199 (KBG; L avet), 317, 734;
2. 151 (ac tamen KB; GL attamen),
388, 465, 641; 3. 290, 309, 696; 4. 170,
191, 330, 524, 652, 691; 5. 56, 222, 338,
454, 488, 658, 677; 6. 385 (B; KGL tandem), 499, 733; 7. 58, 87, 205, 452, 511,
627; 8. 335, 365, 412, 420, 465,
at tamen 7. 285,
nec tamen 5. 501, 586,
quamquam . . . tamen 3. 506; 5. 374;
6. 39; 8. 206.
Tanais
Tanais 4. 719,
Tanain 1. 538 (KB; GL Tanai),
Tanai 1. 538 (GL; KB Tanain).
tandem (45)
    1. in declarat. sentent.
tandem 1. 4, 79, 209; 2. 90, 262; 3. 509,
358; 4. 20, 153 (KBG; L tantum), 259,
317, 732; 5. 29, 295, 311, 330; 6. 3, 385
(KGL; B tamen), 561; 7. 7, 88, 163,
278, 412, 427, 531, 591, 649; 8. 76, 220,
368, 374, 416,
iam tandem 4. 483; 6. 749,
tandem etiam 7. 127,
vix tandem 5. 505; 7. 436,
    2. in interrog. sentent.
tandem 1. 66 (KB; G sectantem; L
sectatur); 7. 217,
vix tandem 7. 217,
    3. in optationib.

tandem 7. 135, 282, 313,
    4. c. impy.
tandem 4. 475.
tango
tangit 5. 86; 8. 43,
tangunt 1. 605,
tetigit 6. 426,
tetigere 8. 198,
tangat 7. 479,
tetigissent 8. 432,
tangere 2. 436; 4. 634,
tetigisse 2. 345,
tangens (m.) 1. 787; 3. 441,
tactus 3. 581.
tantus
tantus 1. 680; 2. 62, 507; 5. 641 (B;
KGL tantum); 7. 37; 8. 67,
tanta 3. 246; 4. 481; 6. 338; 7. 424, 520
(quem tanta KBG; L temptanti); 8.
165,
tanti 3. 290, 329,
tantae 3. 27, 479,
tanti 1. 75; 2. 246; 3. 721; 6. 20, 24;
7. 332; 8. 191, 385,
tantum 1. 766; 5. 315; 7. 159 (G; KB tecum; L sis hunc),
tantam 1. 499,
tantum 2. 375; 3. 301; 4. 541; 5. 37,
tanto 1. 60, 444, 731; 3. 629; 4. 745;
5. 297; 7. 132; 8. 159,
tanta 3. 363, 586; 7. 294, 316; 8. 375,
tanto 3. 39, 619; 5. 371 (KG; BL tantum); 6. 592; 7. 631,
tantae 4. 715 (L; KBG tantas); 5. 635;
7. 529,
tantarum 8. 38,
tantis (f.) 8. 400,
tantis 1. 242 (BGL; K quantis); 7. 420;
8. 41,
tantos 1. 247, 849; 6. 736; 7. 438; 8. 363,
tantas 4. 715 (KBG; L tantae); 6. 732;
7. 19,
tanta 3. 644; 5. 471,
tantis 5. 576; 7. 443,
tantis 3. 55,
tantis 1. 57; 2. 293; 7. 533,
subst. n. tantum (acc.) 1. 119; 6. 600,
adv. tantum 1. 46, 202, 546, 606; 2. 49,
103 (K; B iam tum; G iam tumet; L
tunc avet); 4. 153 (L; KBG tandem),
427; 5. 173, 371 (BL; KG tanto), 641
(KGL; B tantus); 8. 186, 289,
subst. n. quantum . . . tantum (acc.)
2. 529,
adv. tantum . . . quantum 1. 318, 405,
tantum . . . velut 2. 227,
Vid. non.
tapete
tapetis (abl.) 1. 147; 6. 696,
tapetibus (abl.) 4. 487.
Taras
Taras 6. 102.
tardus
tardus 3. 547,
tardi (n.) 2. 139,

tardum (n.) 3. 229,
tarda (acc.) 6. 290,
tardior (f.) 3. 483; 6. 238 (BL; KG
altior); 7. 393.
Tartara
Tartara (acc.) 7. 312.
Tartareus
Tartarei 1. 828,
Tartareae 3. 212,
Tartareo (m.) 1. 730,
Tartaream 6. 435,
Tartareo 4. 393,
Tartareo 3. 665; 7. 632,
Tartareas 4. 579,
Tartareis (n.) 8. 83.
Tartarus
Tartarus 4. 258.
Taulas
Taulantis 6. 222.
taureus
taurea (acc.) 1. 420; 6. 360.
Taurus
Taurus 1. 647.
Taurus
Taurorum 2. 301.
taurus
taurus 1. 775; 2. 458, 548; 3. 582; 4.
230; 5. 67; 7. 571,
tauri 1. 206, 787; 3. 266; 4. 250 (L;
KBG tauris); 8. 266,
taurum 2 329,
tauro 4. 732,
tauri 7. 64, 207, 283,
taurorum 1. 221,
tauris 4. 100; 6. 451; 7. 466, 553,
tauros 4. 152, 684; 6. 434; 7. 185, 504,
545; 8. 106, 342, 437, 450,
tauri 7. 547,
tauris 4. 250 (KBG; L tauri); 7. 233,
516.
taxus
taxi (gen.) 1. 777.
Taxes
Taxes 6. 252.
Taygeta
Taygeta (voc.) 4. 329.
Taygetos
Taygeti 4. 229,
Taygeton 1. 429.
tectum
tecti 2. 397; 5. 243,
tecta 5. 318; 7. 327,
tectis 1. 797; 5. 534,
tecta 1. 162; 2. 170, 650; 4. 504, 566,
739; 5. 386, 410, 623; 6. 456; 8. 269,
tectis 2. 341; 3. 3; 4. 522, 760; 7. 163,
306, 440, 505.
Tegeaeus
Tegeaeo (abl. n.) 1. 375.
tegmen
tegmen (nom.) 6. 234,
tegmine 6. 349,
tegmina 6. 702,
tegmina 1. 454; 3. 99, 670 (KB; GL
agmina); 5. 361; 6. 54; 7. 303.

tenebrosus
tenebrosa (nom. f.) 3. 400.
teneo
tenet 1. 353, 364, 680; 2. 517, 632; 3. 132, 155, 263; 4. 270, 324; 6. 348, 364, 485, 674; 7. 30, 110, 129, 214, 257, 303; 8. 23,
tenent 1. 102, 262, 297; 3. 49; 4. 7; 6. 171,
tenebant 8. 127,
tenebis 4. 52,
tenebit 2. 159; 5. 647, 684,
tenui 4. 129,
tenuit 7. 468,
tenuere 2. 100, 584; 4. 189; 6. 693,
teneat 2. 270,
teneant 1. 511,
tenerem 3. 658,
tenuisset 2. 406; 4. 365 (BL; K finxisset; G timuisset),
tene 1. 215; 2. 253; 5. 251,
tenens 1. 698; 5. 484; 6. 331 (KBG; L vehens),
tenens (f.) 2. 590; 7. 192, 293; 8. 211,
tenenti (dat. f.) 7. 399,
tenentibus (f.) 2. 407,
tenentibus 2. 543,
tenentia 4. 103,
tenetur 4. 575,
teneri 3. 620.
tener
tenero (abl. m.) 6. 714,
tenerae 6. 247,
teneris (f.) 3. 528,
teneros 6. 670; 7. 375,
teneras 1. 491,
subst. m. tenero (dat.) 3. 516.
tenor
tenor 6. 141.
tentorium
tentoria (acc.) 6. 7; 8. 380.
tenuis
tenuis (nom. f.) 2. 431,
tenuis (m.) 2. 634,
tenuem (f.) 4. 436,
tenui 7. 22; 8. 452,
tenui 2. 108; 3. 525; 4. 672; 5. 52,
tenui 3. 319, 712; 4. 689,
tenues (f.) 1. 128,
tenuia 6. 225,
tenues 1. 738; 4. 330,
tenuis (m.) 3. 278,
tenues 7. 157.
tenus
1. c. acc.
1. 538,
2. c. abl.
3. 141; 7. 434.
tepidus
tepidae (gen.) 5. 422,
tepidi (nom.) 3. 218.
ter (8)
1. 193, 400 (BGL; K te); 3. 347, 348, 441 **bis**; 6. 397; 7. 610.
teres
tereti (dat. f.) 6. 59,
tereti (abl. n.) 2. 103 (KGL; B reti).

tergeminus
tergeminam 1. 781.
tergum
tergo 1. 400,
tergo 1. 145; 2. 109; 6. 369, 520,
terga 4. 283; 7. 552,
terga 1. 359, 410, 421; 2. 460, 511, 518, 658; 3. 150, 254, 255, 260, 478, 567, 607, 738 (KBG; L aegra); 4. 176, 340; 5. 148, 242, 412, 554; 6. 100, 135, 216, 347, 360, 399, 726; 7. 108, 605, 651; 8. 43, 132, 202.
tergus
tergore 1. 130,
tergora (nom.) 3. 440 (L; KBG pectora).
ternus
terno (abl. n.) 1. 63 (ex terno K; L ex taetro; BG externo).
tero
terit 8. 23 (B; KGL ferit),
tereres 6. 312,
trito (abl. n.) 2. 448 (L; KBG tracto).
terra
terra 2. 81, 387, 629; 4. 146; 8. 4,
terrae 1. 168; 2. 422; 5. 474 (vid. nom.) 575; 6. 711,
terrae 1. 10; 3. 460,
terra 2. 297; 3. 660; 4. 408, 511; 6. 466,
terrae 1. 607; 4. 574 (vid. gen.); 8. 176,
terris 1. 675; 2. 639; 3. 697; 4. 480, 559; 5. 262, 279, 293, 323, 508, 683; 6. 18; 8. 147, 199,
terras 1. 69, 195, 276, 322, 463, 465, 524, 567, 585, 746, 795; 2. 120, 616; 3. 388, 410; 4. 96, 132, 217, 352, 553, 734; 5. 72, 143, 164, 197; 7. 437, 617; 8. 322,
terrae 1. 631,
terris 1. 533; 2. 303, 363, 437, 592; 3. 617; 4. 636; 5. 247, 382, 480, 644; 6. 31 (G; KBL telis), 410, 693; 7. 58.
terrenus
terrena (acc.) 1. 558.
terreo
terret 4. 239,
terrent 2. 41,
terruit 2. 588,
territus 3. 471; 4. 295, 332; 5. 420, 682,
territa (nom. f.) 5. 329.
terribilis
terribilis (nom. m.) 1. 230, 723,
terribiles (acc. f.) 6. 111.
terrifico
terrificat 1. 228,
terrificant 8. 428.
terrificus
terrifici (n.) 1. 785 (BGL; K terrificis),
terrificae 5. 398,
terrifica 6. 174,
terrifici 1. 29; 4. 663,
terrificis (n.) 1. 785 (K; BGL terrifici),
terrificis (m.) 6. 446, 618.
terrigena
terrigenae (nom.) 7. 629,

terrigenum 2. 18,
subst. terrigenas 7. 505; 8. 107, 450.
territo
territat 2. 656; 5. 260; 6. 323.
Terror
Terror 3. 89.
terror
terror 2. 362; 5. 138; 6. 46; 8. 333,
terrore 6. 151, 533, 744; 7. 508,
terroribus (abl.) 3. 715.
tertius
tertius 6. 60,
tertia (nom. f.) 1. 351; 3. 1; 6. 115.
testis
teste 7. 418.
testor
testor 3. 711; 7. 347,
testatur 5. 623,
testantem (m.) 3. 291.
testudo
testudine 1. 187, 277; 3. 147.
Tethys
Tethys 2. 36; 5. 431.
Teucer
Teucer 1. 511.
Teucri
Teucros 4. 58.
Teutagnonus
Teutagnono (abl.) 6. 97.
texo
texitur 5. 435,
textam 4. 93,
textos 2. 409,
subst. n. texta 5. 514,
texta 3. 276.
thalamus
thalami (gen.) 7. 325; 8. 222,
thalamis 2. 147, 371; 5. 258; 6. 267, 464;
8. 392,
thalamos 1. 131, 226; 2. 170, 215, 398;
6. 45, 455; 7. 239, 249; 8. 283,
thalamis 1. 709; 2. 152, 233, 568; 3. 328,
495; 5. 446; 6. 486; 8. 1.
Thamyris
Thamyrim 3. 128.
Thapsus
Thapsum 3. 191.
Thaumantias
Thaumantias 7. 398; 8. 116.
Thebae
Thebae 3. 69.
Thebae
Thebae 5. 420.
Thebe
Thebes 6. 118.
Thermodon
Thermodon 4. 601; 5. 121.
Theseus
Theseus 4. 701,
Thesea 2. 193; 3. 65.
Thespiacus
Thespiaca (acc.) 1. 93 (BGL; K Thespia et).
Thespiades
Thespiades 2. 368.

Thespiades
Thespiaden 1. 124,
Thespiade (voc.) 5. 44.
Thespius
Thespia (nom. n.) 1. 478,
Thespia 1. 93 (Thespia et K; BGL Thespiaca).
Thessalia
Thessaliae (gen.) 6. 598,
Thessaliam 5. 474; 8. 170.
Thessalicus
Thessalici 1. 244; 5. 218,
Thessalicae 1. 380,
Thessalicae 5. 622,
Thessalicam 5. 530,
Thessalico 7. 1,
Thessalico 1. 424,
Thessalici 8. 161,
Thessalicae 7. 220,
Thessalicis (f.) 5. 683,
Thessalicos 3. 173; 8. 421,
Thessalicas 7. 146,
Thessalicis (f.) 5. 480,
Thessalicis 7. 198.
Thessalis
Thessalis 1. 737, 780.
Thessalus
1. subst.
Thessalus 7. 40,
Thessale 7. 437,
2. adi.
Thessalus 5. 277,
Thessala (nom.) 2. 445,
Thessala (nom.) 1. 607,
Thessala 3. 13; 8. 380.
Thetis
Thetis 1. 131, 658,
Thetidis 2. 589,
Thetidi 1. 190; 2. 286.
thiasus
thiasi (nom.) 1. 844,
thiasos 3. 540; 5. 78.
Thoanteus
Thoanteae (dat.) 8. 208.
Thoas
Thoantis 2. 418.
Thoe
Thoen 6. 375.
tholus
tholus 2. 259 (L; KBG chorus),
tholo (dat.) 1. 57.
thorax
thorax 6. 186,
thoraca 7. 620,
thoracibus 6. 248 (vid. abl.),
thoracibus 3. 87; 6. 248 (vid. dat.).
Thrace
Thraces 2. 406.
Thraces
Thraces 2. 251; 5. 664,
Thracas 2. 107.
Thracius
Thracius 1. 277; 4. 85,
Thracia (nom. f.) 3. 705.

Thracus
Thraca (nom. f.) 2. 202.
Thrax
Thraces (nom. m.) 1. 611.
Threicius
Threiciis (abl. n.) 2. 432.
Threissa
Threissa (nom.) 2. 147.
Thressa
1. subst.
Thressae (nom.) 2. 165,
Thressas 2. 132, 239,
2. adi.
Thressa (nom. f.) 2. 344.
Thybris
Thybris 6. 406.
Thydrus
Thydrum 6. 639.
Thyias
Thyias 3. 265; 5. 81,
Thyada 8. 447,
Thyiades (nom.) 6. 757.
Thyneus
Thynea (acc.) 4. 424.
Thyoneus
Thyoneus 1. 726.
Thyotes
Thyotes 2. 438.
Thyrsagetes
Thyrsageten 6. 135,
Thyrsagetas 6. 140.
thyrsus
thyrsos 5. 76.
tiaras
tiaran 6. 700.
Tibareni
Tibarenum 5. 147.
Tiberinus
Tiberine 7. 84.
tibia
tibia (nom.) 6. 142.
Tibisenus
Tibisena (acc.) 6. 50.
tigris
tigris 3. 635; 6. 706,
tigridis 5. 593; 6. 148,
tigrin 6. 704,
tigres 2. 260 (BGL; K lynces),
tigres 1. 491.
timeo
timet 1. 413; 6. 438,
timebam 1. 322,
timuere 1. 628; 5. 167; 7. 19,
timuissem 1. 328; 7. 440,
timuisset 4. 365 (G; K finxisset; BL tenuisset),
time 7. 183,
timuisse 1. 361; 2. 344,
timens (f.) 5. 189,
timenti (f.) 7. 435,
timentem (m.) 1. 490,
timendus 1. 38,
timendi 4. 627.
timide
7. 597.

timidus
timido (abl. m.) 4. 515.
timor
timor 4. 651; 8. 3, 259,
timori 8. 436,
timorem 1. 325; 2. 328; 6. 754; 7. 240,
timore 5. 352; 8. 35,
timores (acc.) 5. 525; 6. 459; 8. 408.
tingo
tinguntur 6. 247 (B; KGL liquuntur).
Tiphys
Tiphys 1. 419, 481, 689; 3. 37, 259, 483, 614; 4. 695; 5. 42,
Tiphyn 2. 390; 3. 2; 5. 15, 25,
Tiphy 1. 649; 5. 102; 8. 181.
Tirynthius
Tirynthius 1. 107, 253; 2. 373, 574; 3. 133, 161, 485, 565, 590; 4. 5; 6. 462; 7. 623; 8. 125.
Tisaeus
Tisaeae (gen.) 2. 7.
Tisiphone
Tisiphone 2. 194; 6. 179, 403,
Tisiphonen 3. 214; 4. 394, 410.
Titan
Titan 2. 37, 57.
Titan
Titan 5. 169,
Titana 4. 79.
Titanis
Titanida 7. 212.
Titanius
Titanius 6. 79,
Titania 5. 463,
Titania (voc.) 7. 347,
Titania (nom.) 4. 91.
Titanius
Titania (acc.) 5. 156; 7. 449.
Tithonia
Tithonia (nom.) 1. 311; 3. 1.
Tityus
Tityum 3. 226.
tolero
tolerare 3. 626, 657.
tollo
tollit 2. 328, 508; 4. 555; 6. 610; 8. 446 (cum tollit KBG; L contollit),
tollunt 1. 222; 3. 472; 4. 4; 8. 295,
sustulit 1. 624, 629; 2. 37; 3. 731; 4. 49, 473; 6. 249 (G; KBL sustinet), 397; 7. 399, 527,
tollat 1. 99; 3. 500,
tolleret 5. 93,
tollere 1. 340, 539, 601; 4. 22, 148, 209, 262,
tollens (f.) 6. 179,
tollitur 2. 516; 3. 133; 5. 306; 6. 244; 7. 158, 360; 8. 55, 328,
tolli 1. 671.
Tonans
Tonantis 2. 560; 3. 299; 4. 428, 474,
Tonanti (dat.) 4. 119, 529.
tondeo
tondebit 1. 379,
tondentes (acc. m.) 2. 9,

subst. f. tonsa (abl.) 1. 369,
tonsas 1. 313, 471; 3. 34; 5. 66.
tonitrus
tonitru (abl.) 1. 85, 617; 2. 199,
tonitrus (nom.) 1. 692; 4. 663.
tono
tonat 4. 612,
tonuit 4. 507,
Vid. Tonans.
tonsa vid. tondeo.
tormentum
tormenti 2. 195,
tormenta (acc.) 1. 718.
torqueo
torquet 2. 22; 4. 111, 594,
torsit 1. 727; 4. 509; 7. 525, 568, 634,
torserat 3. 193; 7. 292,
torqueat 4. 600,
torsissem 1. 116,
torquens 1. 639; 6. 83,
torquens (f.) 2. 184,
torquentem (m.) 2. 28,
torta 3. 119,
tortae (gen.) 3. 96,
tortum (n.) 1. 372,
torto (n.) 8. 20,
tortas 1. 362.
torques
torques 2. 112.
torreo
torrens (m.) 4. 409,
torrenti (dat. m.) 4. 263.
torris
torre 3. 116.
torus
torus 1. 137; 2. 342; 3. 121,
torum 2. 140,
toro 5. 444; 7. 21, 145, 210, 296, 321,
tori 2. 651,
toris 2. 132, 168, 355; 4. 530 (vid. abl.);
7. 124,
toros 2. 159, 214; 4. 29, 487; 5. 460; 7. 5,
596; 8. 7, 260,
toris 1. 253, 295; 2. 168, 202, 230, 234,
510; 3. 59, 463; 4. 245, 530 (vid. dat.);
5. 244, 331; 6. 457; 8. 255.
torvus
torvus 8. 218,
torvae (gen.) 3. 50,
torva (acc.) 8. 60,
adv. torva 2. 555.
Toryni
Toryni 6. 144,
Torynis (dat.) 6. 145.
tot (32)
1. 342, 506; 2. 216 **bis**, 643; 3. 303, 511,
535; 4. 716 (B; KGL et); 5. 196 **bis**,
376, 475 **bis**, 481, 484, 485, 669; 6. 163,
220; 7. 36, 168 **bis**, 221, 274, 277, 332;
8. 211, 284 **bis**, 339, 390.
totidem
totidem 1. 283; 6. 221,
quot . . . totidem 1. 581 (totidem KL;
BG totiens).

totiens (6)
totiens 1. 581 (BG; KL totidem); 2.
75; 5. 49; 7. 513; 8. 215,
quotiens . . . totiens 6. 685.
totus
totus 1. 207; 3. 133 (G; KBL tento);
4. 322; 6. 493; 7. 600; 8. 373,
tota 2. 248; 5. 559; 6. 119; 8. 137, 453,
totum 7. 542 (KGL; B tutum),
toti (n.) 7. 627,
totum 1. 274, 843; 7. 464,
totam 2. 163; 3. 325,
totum 7. 21 (KBG; L serum),
toto 4. 368, 409; 6. 588; 8. 73,
tota 2. 401, 521; 3. 682; 4. 264; 6. 101;
7. 590,
toto 1. 306 (KG; BL tuto); 2. 530; 3.
277, 726; 4. 341, 590, 657 (KBG; L
moto); 5. 39 (B; KGL tuto), 247, 438,
483 (KGL; B tutor); 6. 673; 7. 334,
559; 8. 103, 332,
toti 1. 637,
totos 3. 438 (GL; KB totis); 7. 126,
369, 463, 548 (K; BGL totas); 8. 123,
totas 7. 548 (BGL; K totas),
totis 3. 438 (KB; GL totos); 7. 613;
8. 194,
totis 2. 579; 3. 193; 6. 257; 7. 166, 588,
totis 2. 536.
trabalis
trabalia (acc.) 8. 301.
trabs
trabe 1. 663; 3. 484,
trabes 5. 162; 7. 565,
trabibus 2. 19,
trabes 1. 125; 5. 640; 6. 77; 7. 395,
trabibus 6. 384.
tractus
tractu (abl.) 1. 614; 2. 664; 6. 359.
trado
tradis 5. 47,
tradit 2. 166,
tradimus 8. 66,
tradidit 2. 606,
tradat 1. 475,
tradiderim 6. 104,
tradere 1. 418; 5. 242.
traho
trahis 2. 295; 3. 317,
trahit 1. 290, 370; 2. 230; 4. 655, 739;
5. 222, 540; 6. 96, 253, 414; 7. 374, 531,
594; 8. 414,
trahunt 1. 200 (B; KGL trahant); 3.
717,
trahebat 5. 548,
traham 1. 764; 8. 425,
traxi 7. 271,
traxit 2. 381; 3. 651; 4. 97 (KBG; L
sparsit),
traxere 6. 81,
trahat 1. 479; 4. 179,
trahant 1. 200 (KGL; B trahunt); 2.
352; 4. 109,
traherent 8. 457,
traxerit 4. 441; 6. 13,

trahens 2. 551; 3. 221, 225, 372; 5. 619;
8. 400,
trahens (f.) 5. 125,
trahentem 3. 609; 4. 135,
trahentem 3. 331,
trahor 7. 10,
trahitur 4. 459; 6. 414, 663; 7. 594,
tracto (abl. n.) 2. 448 (KBG; L trito).
tranquillus
tranquilla (acc.) 2. 608,
adv. tranquilla 1. 38.
trans
7. 113.
transabeo
transabeunt 4. 511.
transcendo
transcendere 4. 220.
transcurro
transcurrat 4. 615,
transcurrere 4. 598; 8. 176,
transcurrens (m.) 3. 157.
transeo
transit 2. 162, 431 (KBG; L superat);
3. 559; 5. 69, 120; 8. 208,
transibit 1. 467; 7. 184,
transierat 4. 347,
transierit (ind.) 3. 502,
transire 3. 446; 8. 214.
transfero
transferet 8. 337,
transferre 4. 690.
transfodio
transfosso (abl. n.) 6. 222.
transigo
transigit 3. 192,
transigitur 6. 247.
transmitto
transmittens (m.) 3. 434,
transmissa 2. 622,
transmisso (abl. m.) 1. 464.
transtrum
transtri 3. 721,
transtro (abl.) 3. 480,
transtris 1. 352, 450,
transtra 1. 461; 8. 361,
transtris 1. 312, 470; 2. 442; 3. 78, 459.
transverto
adv. transversa 2. 154.
tremefacio
tremefacta (nom. f.) 6. 526 (KGL; B
tumefacta).
tremendus vid. tremo.
tremibundus
tremibunda (nom. f.) 4. 180; 6. 168.
tremo
tremit 1. 427; 2. 413; 8. 303,
tremunt 2. 78, 500; 7. 370,
tremuit 5. 108,
tremuerunt 4. 356,
tremuere 3. 348,
tremerent 4. 376,
tremere 4. 565 **bis,**
tremens 5. 244,
tremens (f.) 2. 470; 7. 372, 394, 431;
8. 34,

trementem (f.) 2. 197,
trementum (m.) 3. 463; 5. 339,
trementes (m.) 7. 595,
tremendi (m.) 3. 384,
tremendum 4. 232,
tremendam 6. 175, 449,
tremendum 2. 209.
tremor
tremor 4. 490.
tremulus
tremulum (m.) 1. 620,
tremulos 1. 469, 749 (L; KBG famulos).
trepido
trepidat 1. 699,
trepidant 3. 132; 4. 515,
trepident 6. 335,
trepidare 2. 47,
trepidans (m.) 6. 304,
trepidantibus (m.) 1. 621,
trepidantia 7. 525.
trepidus
trepidus 6. 342; 8. 397,
trepida 4. 357; 7. 103,
trepidi (m.) 4. 269,
trepido (m.) 3. 149; 8. 59,
trepidum 5. 430,
trepidam 3. 213; 4. 3, 10; 5. 220, 358,
391; 8. 1,
trepidi 1. 158; 5. 23, 440,
trepidae 4. 399; 6. 520,
trepidis (f.) 1. 324,
trepidis 2. 504; 6. 154,
trepidos 6. 401,
trepidas 7. 296,
trepidis (f.) 3. 52.
tribuo
tribuit (perf.) 1. 231.
tridens
tridenti (abl. n.) 1. 688,
subst. m. tridentis 1. 615,
tridentem 1. 115.
trietericus
trieterica (nom. n.) 2. 259, 623.
trifidus
trifida (abl.) 1. 641,
trifidis (abl. m.) 6. 54.
triformis
triformis (gen. f.) 7. 395.
trilinguis
trilingui (abl. m.) 7. 184.
trilix
trilicem (f.) 3. 199.
Trinacria
Trinacria (nom.) 2. 32.
Trinacrius
Trinacrio (abl. n.) 1. 579.
triplex
triplici (abl.) 6. 63,
triplici (f.) 3. 62.
tripus
tripodes 1. 544.

tristis
tristis (f.) 2. 426; 3. 54, 544,
triste 2. 396,
tristi (f.) 2. 302,
triste 1. 747,
tristi (m.) 2. 470; 3. 281,
tristi (n.) 1. 351,
tristes (f.) 8. 120,
tristis 4. 121,
tristibus (n.) 3. 694,
tristes 7. 249,
tristes 2. 177; 5. 73; 7. 358,
tristia 3. 264, 441; 4. 131; 8. 407,
tristior (f.) 5. 297,
tristius (nom.) 1. 631,
subst. n. tristissima (nom.) 3. 369.
trisulcus
trisulco (abl. m.) 2. 500.
Triton
Triton 1. 679.
Tritonia
Tritonia (nom.) 1. 93; 2. 49; 7. 442.
triumphus
triumpho (abl.) 5. 124; 6. 119,
triumphi 4. 743,
triumphos 3. 300.
Trivia
Triviae 3. 321,
Triviae 5. 103,
Triviam 3. 68.
trivium
triviis (abl.) 3. 453.
Troia
Troiae (gen.) 2. 558, 573, 578; 4. 58, 78,
Troiam 1. 552.
tropaeum
tropaeo (abl.) 4. 739.
trunco
truncantem (m.) 6. 568.
truncus
trunca (abl.) 2. 300,
trunco 6. 251,
truncae 6. 91,
trunca 4. 181,
truncas 3. 444,
subst. m. trunco (abl.) 8. 461,
trunci 2. 234,
truncos 7. 620,
truncis 8. 287, 447.
trux
trux (m.) 2. 30; 4. 109,
trucis (m.) 1. 564; 4. 299; 7. 78; 8. 180,
trucis (n.) 1. 714; 3. 253,
trucem (m.) 4. 232,
truces (m.) 2. 73; 7. 653; 8. 456,
truces (m.) 1. 743; 4. 618; 6. 43,
truces 1. 673; 2. 207, 463.
tu
tu 1. 7, 16 (KB; GL iam), 19, 55, 76,
87, 202 (G; KB om.; L sed), 215, 267,
391, 438, 648, 669, 791, 794; 2. 145, 152,
253, 479, 485; 3. 15, 323, 412, 662, 663;
4. 36 (KGL; B tum), 242, 243, 467, 468,
603; 5. 195, 198, 250, 388, 507, 511, 638;
6. 323, 486 **bis,** 516; 7. 37, 38, 61, 179,

223, 248, 269, 290 **bis,** 331, 339, 430, 490,
507 (BGL; K tum), 550; 8. 14, 78, 104,
435,
tui 7. 478,
tibi 1. 15, 172, 177, 188, 189, 220, 291,
322, 433, 457, 477, 478, 546, 649, 677,
747; 2. 79, 114, 133, 142, 144, 149, 242,
303, 468, 560, 662; 3. 16, 173, 535, 541,
663, 667, 671 **bis,** 689, 711; 4. 66, 106,
124, 192, 240, 471, 538, 557, 567, 599,
606, 610, 629, 757; 5. 102, 204, 236, 246,
287, 359, 382, 475, 491, 500, 644, 651,
654, 670 (cedam tibi L; KBG nequeat
sic); 6. 219, 290, 305, 306 (si tibi KBL;
G sicubi), 311, 487, 538, 605, 606; 7. 76,
170, 172, 175, 198, 231, 234, 250, 266,
332, 344, 438, 443, 518, 521 (BL; KG
mihi), 532; 8. 15, 66, 96, 142, 148, 154,
163, 251, 277, 312, 424,
te 1. 77, 85, 165, 200 (KGL; B me), 268,
324, 343, 345, 380, 400 (K; BGL ter),
442, 444, 477, 672, 712, 715, 718, 750,
824; 2. 80, 244, 275, 292, 304, 405, 592;
3. 35, 177, 290, 295, 326, 328, 670 (ego te
B; K ego et; GL egomet); 4. 36, 64,
65, 121, 191, 469, 474, 560, 621; 5. 19,
106, 200, 208, 380, 384, 390, 493, 506,
517, 626, 647, 677 **bis;** 6. 103, 297, 305,
317, 346, 499, 536, 589, 688, 719; 7. 1, 2,
38, 59, 73, 84, 128, 182, 218, 222, 259,
281, 289, 342, 343 (L; KG et; B heu),
415, 447, 453 (K; BGL om.), 454, 479,
481, 485, 486, 494, 495, 498, 502 **bis,** 517,
534, 589; 8. 40, 46, 50, 53, 69, 70, 75, 95,
99, 147, 156, 162, 174, 197, 270, 275, 350,
422, 425, 427, 434 (BL; KG et), 437,
temet 1. 57,
te 1. 19, 177, 269, 332, 507, 765; 3. 317;
5. 44, 390; 7. 348, 418, 487, 490, 491;
8. 433, 439,
tecum 1. 303; 2. 380; 3. 309; 5. 194; 7.
70, 159 (KB; G tantum; L sis hunc);
8. 50 **bis,** 154, 415,
vos 1. 243, 788; 3. 82, 216, 311, 679; 4.
460, 461; 5. 129, 150, 151, 202 **bis;** 6. 647,
729 **bis;** 7. 547; 8. 178, 349,
vobis 1. 565, 807; 3. 449; 4. 145, 524,
585; 5. 217; 7. 50 **bis;** 8. 264,
vos 2. 422; 3. 452, 624; 4. 484, 742, 748;
5. 534, 673; 6. 283; 7. 37.
tuba
tuba 1. 319, 351,
tuba 3. 349,
tubae 3. 19, 44, 84; 5. 252; 6. 28; 7. 629,
tubas 2. 129; 3. 51.
tueor
tueor 6. 589,
tueri 3. 647; 6. 3 (KGL; B videri),
tuens 1. 38, 499, 562, 739; 2. 555; 3. 378;
5. 418; 6. 726; 7. 84, 369,
tuens (f.) 5. 212,
tuenti (m.) 5. 207 (L; KBG fluentia),
tuentem 7. 503,
tuentem 2. 154,
tuentes (acc. m.) 2. 223,

tutus 3. 659,
tuta 5. 265, 556; 8. 314,
tutum (nom.) 7. 542 (B; KGL totum),
tuto (abl. n.) 1. 306 (BL; KG toto);
5. 39 (KGL; B toto); 6. 159,
tutae 4. 634,
tutos 5. 355,
tuta 1. 154; 2. 546; 8. 15,
subst. n. tuta (acc.) 1. 84, 698; 2. 74,
tuendo (abl.) 4. 200.

tum (116)
tum 1. 38, 88 (BL; KG tunc), 162, 188,
210, 369, 402 (BGL; K tunc), 531, 609,
626, 677, 730, 746, 781 (BGL; K cum),
807, 847; 2. 103 (iam tum B; K tantum; G iam tumet; L tunc avet), 110,
167, 167 (BGL; K et), 214, 273, 340, 477
(BG; KL cum), 517 (nox tum L; KBG
necdum), 547 **bis,** 590 (BGL; K dum),
610, 636; 3. 12, 189, 249, 274, 350, 372,
424, 492, 622 (nec tum K; BGL necdum), 714; 4. 11 **bis,** 36 (B; KGL tu),
119, 226, 248 (lustrant tum L; KBG
lustrarunt), 298 (G; K tunc; BL **om.**),
348, 357 (KL; BG cum), 373, 497, 530,
553, 626 (KBL; G cum), 711; 5. 3 (tum
non KBG; L dudum), 6 (BGL; K
tunc), 61, 157, 190, 242, 309, 358, 451,
459, 460, 540, 541 (KBG; L tam), 546,
616, 686 (quam tum licet B; K quantumlibet; G quantum licet; L quantum luet); 6. 31 (B; KGL tunc), 206,
270, 693; 7. 21, 87, 121, 171, 215, 222,
263, 325, 503 (KG; BL iam), 557; 8. 26,
67 (K; BGL vi), 163, 237, 247, 251
(KG; BL iam), 296,
tum demum 3. 633,
tum primum 3. 183; 6. 396,
tum vero 2. 525, 576; 3. 576; 6. 469; 7.
475, 631; 8. 295,
iam tum 3. 515,
tum . . . cum 3. 634, 699,
tum . . . tum . . . tum . . . cum 4. 42,
tum . . . cum . . . cum 1. 533, 621,
tum . . . dum 5. 168,
si . . . tum 7. 507 (K; BGL tu),
si . . . si . . . si . . . tum . . . tum 7.
504,
sin . . . tum 4. 112,
ubi . . . tum 2. 69.

tumefacio
tumefacta (nom. f.) 6. 526 (B; KGL
tremefacta).

tumeo
tumet 2. 103 (iam tumet G; K tantum;
B iam tum; L tunc avet); 5. 521; 6. 2,
tumeant 2. 271,
tumens 2. 547; 3. 677,
tumens (f.) 5. 411,
tumentibus (f.) 4. 46 (vid. abl.),
tumentes (m.) 2. 83,
tumentibus (f.) 4. 46 (vid. dat.).

tumidus
tumidum (m.) 1. 83,
tumido 4. 726,

tumida 6. 329,
tumido 2. 645; 7. 112,
tumida (nom.) 3. 714,
tumidis (abl.) 4. 128,
tumidis (f.) 1. 221; 8. 13.

tumor
tumor 2. 54; 5. 654.

tumultus
tumultu (abl.) 1. 736; 2. 312; 6. 757.

tumulus
tumulo 7. 209,
tumulum 2. 580 (B; KGL tumulos);
5. 96, 185,
tumulo 3. 434; 5. 58, 198,
tumuli 2. 494,
tumulos 2. 580 (KGL; B tumulum),
tumulis 2. 599; 6. 109.

tunc (77)
tunc 1. 88 (KG; BL tum), 402 (K;
BGL tum), 498, 561; 2. 103 (tunc avet
L; K tantum; B iam tum; G iam
tumet), 184, 253, 257, 362 **bis,** 390, 418,
431; 3. 25 (BL; KG nunc), 173, 233,
239, 253, 308, 439; 4. 249, 398 (K; G
tum; BL **om.**), 339, 436, 573 (KG; BL
nunc), 699 **bis;** 5. 6 (K; BGL tum),
204, 265, 291, 296, 312, 692; 6. 31 (KGL;
B tum), 166, 292, 383, 400, 534, 587,
618, 708; 7. 6, 107, 186 (KL; BG Iuno),
208, 345, 346, 369, 570, 589, 612; 8. 6,
109, 127, 365, 437, 453,
tunc etiam 2. 316; 4. 73,
tunc primum 2. 445,
tunc quoque 6. 564; 8. 359,
tunc vero 6. 613,
tunc . . . cum 1. 181; 2. 435; 4. 606,
748; 5. 236,
tunc . . . cum . . . cum 1. 587,
cum . . . tunc 1. 595; 4. 584; 5. 674,
cum . . . cum . . . tunc 1. 172,
tunc . . . dum 2. 31,
ubi . . . tunc 5. 684,
ut . . . tunc 5. 33,
Vid. velut.

turba
turba 1. 101, 750; 2. 327, 551; 3. 272,
335; 4. 200; 5. 267; 6. 107, 485, 627; 8.
145,
turbae (gen.) 5. 88,
turbam 1. 849; 4. 738.

turbidus
turbidus 1. 81, 747; 3. 252, 676; 5. 664;
6. 293, 616; 7. 147,
turbida (nom. f.) 2. 115; 3. 113; 7. 596;
8. 323.

turbo
turbat 2. 281; 4. 305; 7. 143, 524,
turbant 4. 454,
turbavit 3. 561; 8. 260,
turbet 7. 505,
turbantem (m.) 3. 182; 5. 595,
turbetur 7. 132,
turbata 4. 503; 5. 341, 427, 446; 6. 672;
8. 413,
turbatum (m.) 4. 293; 6. 255,

turbatum 3. 531,
turbata 3. 125,
turbati 6. 9,
turbatos 3. 408,
turbata 1. 299, 651.
turbo
turbo 1. 621; 4. 262,
turbinis 2. 90,
turbine 1. 609; 2. 196, 262; 3. 42, 78,
243; 4. 452, 510; 6. 280, 353, 747; 7. 571;
8. 368.
turgeo
turgentia (acc.) 2. 464.
turica (?)
turica 2. 572 (K; BGL Dorica).
turifer
turiferos 6. 138.
turma
turma (nom.) 4. 607,
turmae (nom.) 6. 195, 617 (B; KGL
pugnae),
turmis 6. 722,
turmas 3. 146; 6. 87, 120, 133,
turmis 5. 612.
turpis
turpe 1. 361; 7. 387,
turpi (dat. n.) 7. 319,
turpi (abl. f.) 2. 131; 6. 308,
turpes (acc. f.) 6. 290.
turris
turre 1. 14,
turres 2. 520 (KGL; B turris); 3. 258,
turres 3. 238,
turris 2. 520 (B; KGL turres).
tus
tura (acc.) 8. 248.
Tuscus
Tusci (n.) 7. 234.
tutela
tutela 1. 301; 5. 643,
tutela (voc.) 5. 246.
tutor
tutor 5. 483 (B; KGL toto),
tuteris 5. 195,
tutata (nom. f.) 5. 630.
tutus vid. tueor.
tuus
tuus 3. 298, 650; 4. 755; 5. 636; 7. 420;
8. 441,
tua 1. 12, 404, 506; 2. 153; 4. 192; 5. 252,
292; 7. 198, 453, 505; 8. 146,
tuum 7. 419 (KBG; L tuas),
tui 5. 483; 7. 429,
tuae 1. 477; 5. 54, 494; 7. 485,
tui 6. 317,
tuae 1. 347; 4. 130; 7. 224, 449,
tuum 1. 443 (L; KBG tuo); 7. 240 (atque tuum G; KL atque illum; B ac
vanum), 550,
tuam 8. 431,
tuo 1. 443 (KBG; L tuum); 7. 499,
tua 2. 426; 3. 504; 7. 342, 439; 8. 101,
422,
tuo 3. 480; 7. 495; 8. 72,
tui 5. 142,

tuae 7. 506,
tua 1. 674, 723; 4. 34; 6. 730; 7. 2, 348;
8. 103, 174,
tuorum 8. 181, 431,
tuarum 7. 265,
tuorum 8. 312,
tuis 2. 147; 3. 519,
tuis 4. 346,
tuis 2. 378, 421, 564; 8. 42, 276,
tuos 1. 398; 3. 308, 318, 537; 6. 466; 7.
11, 200; 8. 423,
tuas 4. 756; 7. 347, 419 (L; KBG tuum),
tua 1. 8, 173, 371; 3. 177; 4. 160, 569;
5. 247 bis, 386, 480, 655; 6. 130, 288;
7. 483,
tuis 1. 441; 7. 71,
tuis 5. 518; 6. 460,
tuis 1. 445; 2. 242; 7. 90, 446,
subst. m. tuorum 5. 199; 8. 145,
tuis 1. 825; 3. 170; 7. 218,
tuos 2. 612,
Tydeus
Tydeus 1. 387; 3. 103.
tympanum
tympana (acc.) 2. 267; 6. 134; 7. 304.
Tyndareus
Tyndareus 1. 167,
Tyndareos 1. 571.
Tyndarides
Tyndarides 4. 247, 290,
Tyndariden 6. 207, 212,
Tyndaridae 3. 187,
Tyndaridas 5. 367.
Typhoeus
Typhoeus 2. 24; 4. 236,
Typhoea 6. 170 (KG; BL Typhona).
Typhois
Typhoides (nom.) 4. 428.
Typhon
Typhon 3. 130,
Typhona 4. 516; 6. 170 (BL; KG Ty-
phoea).
Tyra
Tyra (nom.) 6. 84.
tyrannus
tyranni 1. 244; 2. 577; 4. 59, 751; 5. 258,
319, 387, 547, 659; 6. 16; 7. 78,
tyranno (dat.) 1. 30, 71; 5. 264, 470;
6. 44; 7. 87, 491; 8. 153,
tyranni 7. 93,
tyrannos 7. 134.
Tyres
Tyres 4. 719 (KB; GL Lycus).
Tyres
Tyres 6. 201.
Tyrius
Tyrio (abl. n.) 2. 342,
Tyriae 1. 644,
Tyriis (dat. f.) 1. 17.
Tyrrhenus
Tyrrhenus 4. 715; 7. 83,
Tyrrheni (gen. m.) 1. 130,
Tyrrhena (acc.) 1. 576.

Tyrus
Tyro (abl.) 4. 632.
uber
ubere 2. 185, 203; 6. 39, 711.
uber
subst. **n.** uberrima (acc.) 1. 511.
ubi (75)
I. interrog.
1. c. ind. a) prs. 1. 560,
b) imperf. 7. 615,
2. sine verb. 4. 469 **bis,** 649; 5. 42 **bis,**
43; 7. 41, 442 **bis,**
II. rel.
A. locat.
1. c. ind. a) prs. 1. 843; 4. 229; 5. 148,
179; 6. 750; 8. 218,
b) perf. 6. 336; 7. 180,
2. c. subi. prs. 5. 203,
3. sine verb. 5. 443; 6. 95, 337,
B. tempor.
1. c. ind. a) prs. 1. 357; 3. 487, 558; 4.
174, 303 (L; KBG enim), 433, 535, 661;
5. 306; 6. 123, 420; 7. 153, 323, 635; 8.
321,
qualis ubi 2. 515; 7. 111,
qualis . . . ubi 2. 548,
b) fut. 5. 318, 683,
c) perf. 1. 300, 487, 785; 2. 69; 3. 84,
265, 286; 4. 68, 114, 507 (sic ubi K;
BGL sicut); 5. 602; 6. 182, 322, 546;
7. 4, 375 (ubi primum B; KGL supremum), 461; 8. 239, 243,
quantus ubi 3. 130; 6. 611,
d) prs. et perf. 2. 584,
e) fut. perf. 3. 411,
2. c. subi. imperf. 1. 448; 4. 376,
3. sine verb. 2. 384; 4. 378, 653; 5. 54;
7. 349, 511; 8. 405.
Vid. aliter, ceu, illinc, qualiter, quam,
secus, sic, tum, tunc.
ubicumque
1. 678.

udus
uda (acc.) 5. 79.
ulciscor
ultus 2. 549; 4. 753; 7. 510,
ulta (nom. f.) 2. 214.
ullus
ullus 3. 515; 4. 590; 7. 642; 8. 163,
ulla 1. 26, 540, 650; 4. 130, 221, 573, 582;
5. 18, 297, 359, 551; 6. 37; 7. 100, 205,
333, 386, 438; 8. 4, 271, 364 (BL; KG
ille), 381, 435,
ullo 1. 229,
ulla 4. 174,
ulla 3. 318; 8. 162,
ullis (m.) 1. 276, 517,
ullos 4. 146,
ullas 4. 563; 6. 76; 8. 156,
ulla 1. 34; 2. 296; 3. 327, 685; 4. 103;
5. 44, 663; 7. 339, 491; 8. 39,
ullis 2. 479; 3. 656; 6. 146,
ullis 1. 533,
ullis 3. 648,

subst. ulli (f.) 2. 166,
ullum (m.) 7. 204,
ulla (nom.) 2. 244,
Vid. haud, nec (neque), necdum, non,
nondum.
ulna
ulna (abl.) 3. 234,
ulnis (abl.) 1. 658.
ulterior
ultimus 5. 154; 7. 206,
ultima (nom. f.) 5. 614; 6. 259,
ultima (acc.) 3. 155, 383; 4. 373, 623;
8. 6, 294,
subst. **n.** ultima (acc.) 6. 249; 8. 385.
ulterius vid. ultra.
ultimus vid. ulterior.
ultor
ultor 1. 521 (BGL; K ultro); 3. 308;
4. 747.
ultra (17)
ultra 2. 662; 3. 161, 530, 663; 4. 53, 125
(KB; GL ultro), 241, 519; 5. 44; 7. 274,
622; 8. 3, 196, 404,
ulterius 1. 515; 5. 653; 6. 470.
ultrix
ultrices 5. 445,
ultrices (voc.) 1. 796.
ultro (20)
1. 107, 521 (K; BGL ultor), 720; 2. 124,
637; 3. 512, 613 (L; KBG ausus); 4. 39,
125 (GL; KB ultra), 299, 555; 6. 242,
254, 310; 7. 216, 546, 640, 651; 8. 62, 223.
ululatus
ululatu (abl.) 4. 393,
ululatibus 1. 318,
ululatibus 8. 143.
ululo
ulularunt 2. 537,
ululare 3. 453,
ululantia (nom.) 3. 232,
ululata (nom. f.) 4. 608.
Umber
Umbro (abl.) 6. 420.
umbo
umbonibus (abl.) 3. 90.
umbra
mubra 1. 49; 3. 215, 560, 579; 4. 681
(KG; BL unda); 5. 53, 108,
umbrae (gen.) 6. 260,
umbram 1. 826; 3. 99, 239; 5. 175, 193,
606; 6. 235; 7. 395, 524,
umbra 1. 466, 778; 2. 116, 519; 3. 142,
525 (K; BGL unda); 4. 41; 5. 94, 228,
642; 7. 55, 393; 8. 28, 33, 101,
umbrae 7. 402,
umbrarum 3. 403, 458,
umbris 2. 413; 3. 172; 4. 313,
umbras 1. 95, 283, 783; 2. 350; 3. 1, 482,
595, 708; 4. 258; 5. 57; 6. 287, 448, 752;
8. 128,
umbris 1. 732, 791; 2. 46; 3. 55 (KBG;
L undis); 7. 538.
umbro
umbrata (acc.) 4. 137.

umbrosus
umbrosae (nom.) 4. 729,
umbrosis (abl. f.) 3. 565.
umeo
umentem (f.) 5. 606.
umerus
umero (abl.) 3. 68,
umeri 1. 223; 7. 619,
umeris 2. 545; 8. 126,
umeros 1. 346, 434, 659; 2. 492; 4. 244;
5. 135; 7. 108, 599,
umeris 1. 109, 185, 219.
umidus
umida (acc.) 1. 288.
umquam (13)
umquam 1. 118, 811; 2. 434; 3. 452, 648;
4. 710, 735; 6. 219; 7. 461, 501,
haud umquam 5. 354,
haut umquam 4. 35,
haut . . . umquam 8. 412,
Vid. non.
una (6)
1. 501; 2. 497; 3. 728; 6. 221; 8. 244, 412.
unanimis
unanimis (nom. f.) 8. 232 (KBL; G unanimes),
unanimes (nom. m.) 6. 128 (L; KBG
ambo animis); 8. 232 (G; KBL unanimis).
unanimus
unanimi (m.) 4. 162,
unanimum (m.) 3. 571,
unanimi 1. 615,
unanimis (abl. n.) 6. 60.
uncus
uncus 2. 428,
uncum 8. 298.
uncus
uncis (dat. f.) 7. 312,
uncis (m.) 6. 400; 8. 150.
unda
unda 1. 290, 653; 2. 143, 453, 506, 582,
588; 4. 656, 677, 681 (BL; KG umbra),
725; 5. 411, 522; 7. 564,
undae (gen.) 2. 54, 285,
undam 1. 624; 4. 533, 628; 6. 147, 573;
8. 188, 245, 287, 355,
unda 3. 36, 525 (BGL; K umbra); 4.
22, 406; 5. 104, 428; 6. 67, 164; 8. 299,
undae 1. 274, 590; 4. 374, 716; 5. 92,
undarum 1. 667; 2. 611; 3. 523,
undis 1. 281; 2. 407, 607; 3. 476; 4. 46
(vid. abl.),
undas 1. 120, 155, 362, 373, 545, 581,
627, 646, 802; 2. 28, 76, 435, 637; 3. 411,
421, 554; 4. 118, 397, 434, 640; 6. 641;
7. 138; 8. 4,
undis 1. 202, 507; 2. 3, 64, 358; 3. 55 (L;
KBG umbris); 4. 46 (vid. dat.), 97,
198, 710, 714; 5. 75, 299, 350; 7. 540;
8. 13.
unde (13)
1. interrog.
1. 219, 220, 328; 2. 216, 353; 3. 19; 4.
707; 7. 438,

2. rel.
4. 172, 347, 570 **bis**; 7. 242.
undique (12)
1. 121, 640; 2. 133, 627; 4. 107, 263, 327;
5. 158; 6. 105, 424; 7. 628; 8. 333.
undisonus
undisoni (n.) 4. 44,
undisonam 1. 364.
undo
undat 1. 539,
undantem 4. 95; 5. 303; 6. 618,
undantem 2. 196,
undanti (f.) 1. 822,
undanti 8. 254,
undantes (acc. f.) 3. 117.
unguen
unguine 6. 360; 8. 302.
unguis
ungue 8. 8 (L; KBG ante),
unguibus (abl.) 1. 157; 4. 457; 8. 150.
unus
unus 2. 561; 6. 582; 7. 263,
una 3. 51, 324, 387; 4. 431; 5. 438, 536;
7. 15, 44, 45, 70, 539 (B; KGL vana),
540; 8. 274,
unum 5. 56,
unum 1. 196; 5. 68; 6. 371, 684, 734;
8. 71, 413,
unam 7. 265, 342; 8. 297,
unum 8. 325,
una (voc.) 2. 243,
uno 2. 359; 4. 598; 8. 288,
una 6. 439, 615; 7. 59, 318 (KBG; L
cruda), 567; 8. 267, 307 (KGL; B ima),
uno 2. 58; 7. 230; 8. 186,
unis (abl. f.) 5. 20,
non una (nom. f.) 7. 236,
subst. unus 8. 392,
unum 3. 294,
unius (m.) 2. 353; 6. 719,
unum 3. 282, 629; 4. 494 **bis**; 5. 87,
unum 6. 380; 7. 96,
una (abl.) 5. 376,
Vid. una.
urbs
urbs 2. 635; 3. 114; 5. 442; 8. 137,
urbis 2. 308, 374; 5. 319; 6. 285 (BL;
KG urbem); 7. 380,
urbi 2. 494; 3. 202, 502; 5. 273, 402,
urbem 1. 458; 2. 91, 135, 163, 165, 181,
249, 273, 298, 539; 3. 31, 46, 325, 343; 5.
259, 300, 325; 6. 285 (KG; BL urbis),
385, 717; 7. 62; 8. 170,
urbe 2. 279, 370, 393, 626; 3. 3, 125; 5.
224, 557, 620; 7. 135,
urbes 4. 288,
urbes 1. 21, 33, 96, 680; 2. 442, 613;
3. 23, 209, 452; 4. 171, 401, 509; 5. 562;
6. 46, 498; 7. 17, 130, 146, 448,
urbibus 2. 29.
urgeo
urget 1. 358, 491; 2. 34, 362, 550, 624,
666, 690 (KGL; B surgit); 4. 472, 727;
5. 27, 399, 486, 537; 6. 281, 350, 394, 591;
7. 308, 601,

urgent 3. 90, 332; 4. 325; 8. 304, 386,
urgebat 4. 426,
urgete 7. 93,
urgens (m.) 3. 715,
urgentis (n.) 4. 252,
urgentem (f.) 3. 465,
urgenti (n.) 1. 289,
urgentes (acc. f.) 4. 273,
urgentibus (f.) 4. 92 (BL; KG cingentibus); 8. 24,
urgeris (prs.) 8. 428.
urna
urna 1. 219; 2. 484,
urna 5. 58.
uro
urit 3. 736; 5. 528; 7. 646,
urebat 2. 287,
urat 1. 476,
ureret 1. 665,
usto (abl. n.) 2. 150.
ursa
ursa 3. 635,
ursae (gen. 4. 724.
ursus
ursi (nom.) 2. 73.
usquam (5)
usquam 3. 592,
haud usquam 6. 417,
haut usquam 6. 76,
nec usquam 6. 500,
non usquam 6. 300.
usque (5)
    1. adv.
usque 7. 9,
usque ad 8. 421,
usque . . . ad 2. 369,
usque adeo 4. 120,
    2. c. acc.
usque 2. 29.
usus
usum 1. 482,
usu 1. 439,
usus (acc.) 1. 169, 462, 780.
ut (133)
    I. interrog.
1. c. ind. a) prs. 1. 671; 4. 4,
b) perf. 1. 281, 282; 3. 260,
2. c. subi. a) prs. 2. 156, 164, 271 **bis,**
272, 511, 568; 3. 30 **bis;** 5. 419; 6. 595,
b) perf. 1. 42, 278; 5. 137, 418,
    II. rel.
1. c. ind. a) prs. 1. 164; 2. 26, 321
(KBG; L et), 637; 3. 151, 208 **bis,** 633;
4. 724; 5. 212, 213, 487; 6. 300 (utque
KL; BG atque), 358, 373, 462, 755;
7. 147, 270, 400, 431,
ut cum 4. 286,
ut . . . cum 6. 169,
ut . . . ita 8. 408,
b) imperf. 2. 221; 7. 407,
c) fut. 5. 689,
d) perf. 1. 127, 128, 205, 257; 2. 39, 91,
207, 261, 401, 609; 3. 72, 268, 428, 709,
720; 4. 137, 273, 674; 5. 32, 59, 90, 116,

350, 549; 7. 120, 327, 394, 602, 616; 8.
127,
e) pluperf. 3. 556; 5. 330,
2. c. subi. a) prs. 1. 21, 408, 421, 469,
475, 811; 2. 419; 4. 153, 705; 5. 24, 215,
293, 632; 6. 17, 498; 7. 45, 52, 163, 226
(ut iam L; KBG etiam), 239, 285 (GL;
K at; B ac), 522, 534 (BG; KL **om.**); 8.
392,
b) mperf. 1. 791; 5. 92; 6. 320, 691, 728;
7. 39, 54; 8. 151, 166 (KGL; B aut),
398,
c) perf. 7. 119,
3. sine verb. 1. 68 (G; KBL om.), 69
(ardet ut K; GL creditus; B creditur),
494 (G; KBL it); 2. 310, 619; 3. 43, 516
(BL; K **om.**; G et); 4. 19, 181 (BG;
KL at), 684; 5. 269 (que ut K; BGL
quin), 553; 6. 383 **bis,** 607; 7. 159, 542,
560; 8. 296,
Vid. haud, sic, talis, tunc, vero.
utcumque
8. 465.
uterque
uterque 7. 570,
utrumque (m.) 6. 553,
utroque 4. 298,
utraque (abl.) 8. 218,
utraque (acc.) 4. 693,
subst. m. uterque 3. 551; 4. 527; 7. 407,
511,
utrumque 6. 197; 8. 250 **bis,**
utrisque (dat.) 3. 271.
uterus
utero 2. 325,
utero 2. 424.
utilis
utilis (nom. m.) 2. 524.
utinam (11)
    1. c. prs.
2. 659; 6. 599; 7. 520, 534; 8. 13,
    2. c. imperf.
1. 113; 8. 439,
    3. c. imperf. et prs.
2. 142,
    4. c. perf.
3. 617,
    5. c. pluperf.
2. 176; 7. 135.
utrimque (8)
1. 679; 2. 45; 3. 93; 4. 499; 5. 275; 6. 58,
361, 404.
utrum
utrum . . . an 8. 64.
vacca
vaccae (nom.) 8. 457.
vaco
vacat 1. 468; 6. 14, 375; 8. 231,
vacant 3. 721 (BGL; K vocant),
vacantes (nom. m.) 2. 370.
vacuus
vacui 2. 602,
vacuae (gen.) 2. 308,
vacuum (n.) 2. 454; 4. 588,
vacua 1. 399 (B; KGL patula),

vacuo 1. 148; 4. 248 (B; K vocuo; GL
vacuos); 7. 528,
vacuis (m.) 4. 39,
vacuos 1. 421; 3. 222, 661; 4. 248 (GL;
K vocuo; B vacuo); 8. 173,
vacuas 4. 302,
vacuis (m.) 3. 589; 4. 21.

vado
vadis 7. 235,
vadit 3. 334; 6. 229, 236, 237,
vade 2. 127,
vadite 5. 689.

vadum
vada 3. 359,
vadis 2. 27, 631; 3. 43,
vada 6. 140; 7. 221,
vadis 2. 536, 622; 4. 725.

vae
5. 670 (que vae L; K aliqua et; B aliquae; G aliqua).

vagor
vageris 6. 498.

vagus
vagus 3. 525; 5. 115,
vaga 3. 597; 7. 111,
vagum (m.) 4. 17,
vagam 2. 116,
vaga 3. 558,
vagi 3. 122; 5. 152,
vaga (acc.) 6. 132, 584,
vagis (f.) 6. 135.

valeo
valet 2. 230; 5. 631,
valuere 1. 341,
valeat 5. 613,
vale 2. 440 (BL; KG mane).

validus
valido (n.) 7. 602,
validam 1. 609; 6. 349,
valido 1. 260,
valida 1. 369; 4. 337,
valido 4. 684,
validas 2. 273; 7. 365,
validis (m.) 1. 157; 2. 311; 4. 689.

vallis
valle 2. 538; 4. 135, 396,
vallibus 2. 523,
valles 4. 382,
vallibus 4. 54.

vallo
vallaverit (subi.) 1. 697.

vanesco
vanescunt 3. 266.

Vanus
Vanus 6. 115.

vanus
vana 1. 383; 2. 167; 5. 75, 678; 7. 539
(KGL; B una),
vani (n.) 2. 525,
vanum (m.) 7. 240 (ac vanum B; KL
atque illum; G atque tuum),
vano 3. 128; 4. 43,
vana 3. 632; 8. 374,
vano 4. 540,
vani 8. 198,

vanos 4. 25; 8. 408,
vanas 4. 581,
vana 5. 31,
vanis (m.) 3. 220,
vanis (n.) 4. 173,
subst. n. vana (acc.) 1. 699; 3. 198.

vapor
vaporibus (abl.) 2. 333.

vario
variat 4. 95,
variant 3. 623,
variaverat 3. 11.

varius
vario (abl.) 3. 686,
varia 3. 390; 5. 416,
varii 4. 181,
varios 1. 129, 535; 2. 79; 3. 572; 5. 302,
487; 7. 6, 196,
varias 5. 281; 6. 438,
variis 3. 393,
variis 2. 113; 7. 256,
variis 1. 742; 2. 663; 3. 430; 5. 329, 564.

vasto
vastata (acc.) 1. 489.

vastus
vasta 2. 596,
vasti (m.) 1. 37,
vasto (abl.) 1. 616, 638; 4. 149, 595;
8. 329,
vasta 5. 232,
vasto 3. 588; 8. 314,
vasta 3. 405,
vastos 2. 534; 4. 717,
vastis 8. 382,
vastis (f.) 6. 620.

vates
vates 1. 227 (hac vates B; K om.; G
nimia; L longa), 277, 383; 2. 316, 439
(KG; BL vati); 4. 348, 445; 6. 114,
vatis 1. 5; 4. 342,
vati 1. 210; 2. 439 (BL; KG vates);
3. 217, 397 (KBG; L menti),
vatem 2. 217,
vates 1. 28; 4. 546,
vatum 3. 301.

-ve (38)
-ve 1. 117, 176, 245, 368; 2. 228, 529;
3. 6, 67, 295, 455, 511 (bellave BG; K
belua; L proelia), 574 **bis**, 578, 649,
664; 4. 129, 204, 218, 241, 478, 752; 5.
172, 297, 306, 468, 508, 679; 6. 464, 682;
7. 37, 200 (KB; GL ne), 219, 401, 434;
8. 313, 388,
-ve . . . aut 2. 466.

vecto
vectare 3. 23.

vector
vector 1. 282,
vectorem 1. 425.

veho
vehit 2. 29 (L; KBG dedit); 3. 34; 6.
252,
vexit 1. 8; 8. 462,
vehat 1. 99 (que vehat L; KBG revehat),

vexerit 5. 134, 628,
vehens (m.) 6. 331 (L; KBG tenens),
vehitur 1. 131; 6. 72,
vehar (ind.) 5. 200,
vectae (nom.) 5. 669,
vectos 4. 741,
vecta 5. 511.
vel (31)
vel 1. 51 (vel pendere KBG; L expendere); 2. 178 (vel iam KBG; L et iam);
3. 541, 689; 4. 322, 472, 675 (KBG; L
nec); 5. 86, 638 (KG; B quin; L iam);
6. 37, 113, 213; 7. 9, 201a (L; KB ne;
G **om.**), 236, 636; 8. 349, 451, 457,
vel . . . vel 1. 480; 3. 604, 676; 4. 376,
724; 6. 328.
velamen
velamina (acc.) 2. 626 (KGL; B caelamina); 5. 7.
velifer
velifero (dat. n.) 1. 126.
vello
vellitur 5. 170,
velli 6. 357 (GL; KB pelli).
vellus
vellus 1. 273,
velleris 6. 150; 7. 551 (KB; G vellera
et; L quercus et); 8. 258,
vellus 1. 377; 5. 262; 8. 157,
vellere 1. 167, 346, 519; 6. 82; 7. 429,
495, 517; 8. 178,
vellera 1. 546; 5. 201, 237, 250; 7. 551
(vellera et G; KB velleris; L quercus
et),
vellera 1. 56, 61, 64, 88, 223, 289, 328,
528; 4. 556, 706; 5. 228, 323, 434, 527,
531, 540, 621, 629, 666; 6. 11, 18, 321,
429, 593, 734 (K; BGL fallat); 7. 14,
168, 526; 8. 40, 89, 101, 268, 270, 393,
462,
velleribus 2. 139 (BL; KG litoribus);
8. 106.
velo
velat 1. 219,
velatur 1. 659,
velatus 2. 270; 6. 564,
velatis (abl. n.) 8. 29.
velociter
velocius 7. 333 (B; KGL velocior).
velox
velocem (f.) 4. 77,
velocior (f.) 7. 333 (KGL; B velocius).
velum
velo 2. 59,
velum 2. 14,
velo 1. 600; 3. 34,
vela 4. 749,
vela 1. 495, 620, 646, 701, 766; 2. 13,
403, 424; 3. 364, 700; 4. 680; 5. 150; 6.
116, 597; 7. 474; 8. 328,
velis 1. 381; 2. 447.
velut (15)
velut 4. 261; 6. 492; 8. 20, 455 (G; KBL
veluti),

ac velut . . . cum pariter . . . sic tunc
7. 567,
ac velut . . . haud aliter 2. 43,
ac velut . . . sic 3. 108; 5. 67,
ac velut . . . talis 6. 664,
velut . . . sic 3. 587; 4. 686; 7. 213, 607,
velut . . . talis 6. 632,
tantum . . . velut 2. 227.
veluti (8)
veluti 8. 455 (KBL; G velut),
veluti cum 3. 224,
veluti . . . cum 2. 465,
ac veluti . . . cum . . . sic 3. 163,
veluti cum . . . sic 6. 353,
veluti . . . cum . . . sic . . . sic 6. 402,
veluti si 4. 321,
sic . . . veluti cum 3. 91.
venalis
venali (abl. m.) 6. 558.
venator
venator 1. 270, 490; 6. 420; 8. 28,
venatori 3. 194.
venatrix
venatrix 3. 335.
venatus
venatus (nom.) 6. 146,
venatu (abl.) 8. 253,
venatibus 3. 242,
venatibus 3. 67.
venenum
veneno 7. 165,
veneno 1. 63, 108; 6. 447; 7. 586, 632,
venenis (abl.) 5. 450; 6. 85, 157, 276,
477; 7. 198, 291, 327, 354, 371; 8. 18, 83,
97.
veneror
veneranda (voc.) 8. 182,
veneranda (acc.) 1. 11.
venia
veniam 1. 196; 4. 584; 8. 280.
venio
venio 7. 224,
venis 2. 561; 4. 157; 7. 414,
venit 1. 839; 2. 506; 3. 240, 374; 6. 155,
216, 478, 656; 7. 117, 543; 8. 30, 134,
venitis 5. 674,
venies 4. 616; 7. 72,
veniet 1. 549; 2. 158; 4. 148,
venisti 7. 437,
venit 1. 521; 3. 292; 6. 716; 7. 42, 221;
8. 243,
venimus 1. 165,
venistis 5. 59; 6. 648,
venere 3. 385,
venerat 6. 691; 8. 25,
venias 1. 460,
veniat 7. 142,
veniamus 4. 705,
veniant 1. 644; 5. 300, 544,
venerit 5. 610,
venisse 6. 20, 24,
veniens 5. 618; 6. 60; 8. 91,
veniens (f.) 6. 159; 7. 3,
venientem 4. 137,
venientem 1. 250; 4. 408.

vestris (n.) 1. 88, 793,
vestros 3. 413; 4. 163,
vestras 2. 575; 5. 130,
vestra 8. 418,
vestris (n.) 7. 423.
vestigium
vestigia 3. 721 (KBG; L fastigia),
vestigia 1. 711; 4. 394; 8. 8, 266.
vestigo
vestigat 2. 116; 4. 435; 7. 158.
vestio
vestit 4. 666; 5. 565.
vestis
vestis (nom.) 2. 111,
vestem 1. 755,
veste 1. 822 (KBG; L peste), 839; 2.
141, 259; 3. 406, 432; 8. 115,
vestes 1. 220,
vestes 1. 289, 433; 2. 265; 3. 10, 340,
442; 7. 246; 8. 234,
vestibus 7. 212.
Vesvius
Vesvius 3. 209.
veto
veto 4. 12,
vetat 2. 436,
vetui 8. 431 (L; KBG merui),
vetuit 7. 53,
vetet 8. 304,
vetitis (abl. f.) 2. 64.
vetus
veteris 1. 526; 2. 580,
veteris (f.) 1. 774; 5. 158,
veteri (m.) 1. 71,
veterem (f.) 2. 632,
veteri (n.) 1. 261,
vetera 1. 531,
veterum (m.) 1. 11; 3. 344; 8. 290,
veteres (f.) 2. 340,
subst. m. veteres 4. 419,
veterum 1. 40, 143; 5. 314; 6. 94, 141
vid. subst. n.),
subst. n. veterum 6. 141 (vid. subst. m.).
vetustas
vetustas 2. 528.
vexillum
vexilla (acc.) 6. 89; 8. 286 (KB; G vox
illa; L vox alta).
via
via 1. 545, 841; 3. 624; 4. 204, 438; 5.
564; 7. 272; 8. 179, 184,
viae 4. 208,
viae 1. 271 (B; KG mero; L animis),
viam 1. 803; 2. 612; 3. 397; 4. 405, 674;
5. 327, 397; 6. 205, 430; 8. 109, 265,
via 5. 323,
viae 5. 316,
viarum 2. 43; 7. 26, 223; 8. 38,
vias 1. 32, 92, 104, 197, 283, 502; 2. 319,
372, 603; 3. 17, 119, 501, 629; 4. 54, 108,
350, 371, 558; 6. 443; 7. 19; 8. 51, 169,
viis 3. 738.
vibro
vibrat 2. 342, 583; 8. 61,

vibret 2. 67,
vibrantem 1. 62,
vibrantem 6. 518,
vibrantes (acc. f.) 7. 617; 8. 57,
vibrantia 3. 142,
vibrantibus (f.) 8. 449,
vibrata (acc.) 8. 306.
vicinus
vicina (nom. f.) 4. 592,
vicina (acc.) 2. 527.
vicis
vices (acc.) 1. 506; 2. 664.
vicissim
1. 671; 3. 473; 5. 382; 6. 359.
victor
victor 2. 546; 3. 141; 4. 229, 323, 528,
589; 5. 540, 684; 6. 209, 268, 307, 332,
344, 645; 8. 133, 228,
victoris 8. 345,
victori 4. 343,
victorem 1. 145, 346,
victores (nom.) 6. 512.
victrix
victrix 4. 392,
victricia (acc.) 5. 129.
victus
victu (abl.) 4. 459.
video
video 1. 342,
vides 1. 303, 715; 2. 472, 658; 3. 396; 4.
566; 6. 589; 7. 234, 427,
viden 3. 499,
videt 1. 33, 77, 125, 523, 529, 701; 2. 124,
367, 637; 3. 29, 156, 238, 488, 571, 605,
735; 4. 175 (KL; BG dolet), 227, 394;
5. 186, 469; 6. 273, 300, 373, 434, 451,
714, 720; 7. 22, 86, 154, 298, 309, 433,
577; 8. 62, 248, 372,
videmus 5. 506,
videtis 1. 241; 2. 335; 8. 179,
vident 1. 604; 2. 17, 541, 582, 626; 4.
331, 424, 645; 8. 50, 293,
videbam 2. 490; 8. 95,
videbat 7. 474,
videbant 6. 721,
videbo 1. 645, 764; 2. 299; 5. 45,
videbis 2. 661; 5. 607; 7. 430; 8. 100,
345,
videbit 3. 177,
vidi 1. 86, 598; 3. 326; 4. 756; 7. 137,
343 (KG; BL vidit),
vidisti 3. 538 (BGL; K vidistis),
vidit 1. 258; 2. 262, 401, 496; 4. 137, 277;
5. 55, 89, 351; 6. 536, 546, 574; 7. 343
(BL; KG vidi), 397, 411, 617; 8. 93,
vidimus 3. 514; 4. 750,
vidistis 3. 538 (K; BGL vidisti); 6. 398,
viderunt 1. 390, 607; 5. 549,
videre 2. 40; 3. 268; 4. 351, 492, 563,
674; 5. 116; 7. 619, 630 (KBG; L audiere); 8. 306, 325,
viderat 5. 339; 6. 115, 203,
videris 7. 339,
viderit 7. 274,

virga
virgae (gen.) 4. 139,
virgam 8. 68 (B; KG crimen; L vimen),
virga 7. 212, 247.

virgatus
virgata (nom. f.) 2. 159.

virgineus
virginei 5. 356,
virgineae 6. 478,
virginei 5. 133,
virgineam 2. 483,
virgineo (m.) 5. 392, 427,
virgineis (f.) 8. 6,
virgineos 8. 18,
virgineas 2. 544; 5. 646,
virgineis (m.) 7. 574.

virginitas
virginitate 6. 449.

virgo
virgo 2. 456, 526; 3. 88, 506; 4. 14, 407,
670; 5. 123, 240, 258, 280, 282; 6. 267,
396, 491, 671, 682, 754; 7. 104, 200, 279,
306, 397, 442, 515; 8. 32, 45, 59, 282, 426,
448, 463,
virginis 1. 292, 537; 2. 463; 4. 122, 238,
353; 5. 379; 6. 157, 370, 372, 718; 7. 173,
194, 268, 482; 8. 67, 136, 355, 409,
virgo 1. 795; 2. 127, 468, 611; 3. 16; 6.
606; 7. 2, 415, 419, 499, 529; 8. 38,
virgine 1. 141, 547; 3. 495; 5. 220, 334;
6. 440; 8. 132, 236, 268, 308, 368, 387,
394,
virginibus (dat.) 2. 106.

viridis
viridem 6. 50, 699,
viridem 1. 77; 8. 293,
viridi (f.) 1. 137; 2. 412; 4. 334,
virides (nom. f.) 3. 524,
virides 5. 148,
virides 2. 270; 3. 708; 5. 216.

virido
viridantem (m.) 6. 136.

virilis
viriles (nom. m.) 1. 55.

virtus
virtus 1. 30; 2. 647; 3. 230 (virtusque
KL; BG virtute), 256, 679; 4. 124; 5.
86; 6. 200; 7. 453; 8. 341,
virtutis 1. 177, 850; 4. 151,
virtute 3. 230 (BG; KL virtusque); 5.
682; 6. 590, 735; 7. 439; 8. 391.

vis
vis 2. 352; 3. 86; 4. 283, 426 (BGL; K
sors); 5. 359; 6. 683; 7. 165 (K; BGL
quin), 355,
vim 4. 318, 722; 6. 609; 7. 460; 8. 87,
vi 1. 520; 3. 492; 6. 236; 7. 599; 8. 67
(BGL; K tum), 370,
vires 1. 51; 2. 325, 564; 4. 126; 6. 123,
viribus 4. 621,
vires 1. 243, 357; 2. 70, 340; 6. 603, 732;
7. 320, 353, 450,
viribus 3. 103, 193; 5. 284; 6. 257; 7. 588.

viscum
visco (abl.) 6. 263.

viscus
viscere 7. 359,
viscera 6. 416,
viscera 1. 206; 6. 555.

viso
visit (prs.) 4. 211.

visus
visum 3. 460,
visu 1. 464, 707; 2. 169, 462; 4. 38, 141,
246, 394, 496; 6. 211, 549; 7. 121; 8. 369,
453,
visus (acc.) 3. 661; 5. 454; 6. 453; 7. 513.

vita
vita 6. 493,
vitae (gen.) 4. 86; 6. 325,
vitam 6. 706,
vita 3. 180,
vitae 6. 188.

vitalis
vitalia (acc.) 4. 309.

vitta
vittam 1. 208,
vitta 5. 79,
vittae 1. 776,
vittis 8. 6,
vittas 4. 361, 548; 6. 64, 302,
vittis 1. 189, 278, 839; 3. 424; 5. 11, 348;
7. 57, 302.

vittatus
vittata (nom. f.) 1. 385; 2. 588.

vivo
vivere 7. 351.

vivus
vivo (abl.) 3. 115; 5. 61; 7. 45,
viva (abl.) 3. 422,
vivos 5. 394.

vix (21)
vix 1. 593 (K; BGL in), 628; 3. 330;
4. 262 **bis**, 282, 574, 702, 715 (quam vix
L; K quavis; BG quamvis); 5. 29, 253,
431; 7. 193, 293, 537 (G; KB **bis**, L
mihi); 8. 119, 212,
vix tandem 5. 505; 7. 217, 436,
vix . . . cum 1. 240.

vixdum (6)
4. 166, 233, 508, 671; 5. 93; 6. 376.

vocatus
vocatu (abl.) 2. 207.

vociferor
vociferans 3. 81, 685; 5. 170; 6. 301,
vociferans (f.) 8. 446.

voco
voco 8. 71,
vocas 1. 175; 3. 670 (L; KG voces; B
sequar); 5. 213,
vocat 1. 212, 524, 736; 2. 313, 390, 540;
3. 226, 315, 433, 448, 475, 534, 724; 4.
513; 5. 65, 193, 437; 8. 62 (ac vocat
KGL; B advocat), 181,
vocant 3. 364, 721 (K; BGL vacant);
4. 344, 761; 7. 113,
vocabat 1. 62; 2. 456,
vocabant 3. 2,

vocabis 3. 713,
vocavit 6. 566,
voces 3. 670 (KG; B sequar; L vocas),
vocet 3. 232,
vocato (2. pers.) 7. 228,
vocantem (f.) 1. 78,
vocantes (acc. m.) 2. 372,
vocantibus (m.) 3. 341,
vocor 7. 546,
vocer 5. 653,
vocari 5. 421; 7. 321,
vocato (dat. m.) 5. 97,
vocati 4. 218; 6. 607,
vocatis (dat. m.) 2. 576,
subst. m. vocatis (dat.) 1. 754.
vocuus
vocuo (abl. n.) 4. 248 (K; B vacuo; GL vacuos).
volatus
volatu (abl.) 4. 515.
volito
volitabant 3. 418,
volitet 4. 221,
volitans 1. 751,
volitans (f.) 4. 607,
volitantia (acc.) 1. 620.
volnus vid. vulnus.
volo
volat 1. 432, 687, 741; 3. 593; 4. 80, 407; 5. 82; 6. 631; 8. 137,
volant 1. 142; 5. 600; 7. 631 (B'GL; K micant); 8. 175,
volans 4. 647,
volans (f.) 3. 78; 4. 672,
volantem 6. 567,
volantem 8. 291.
volo
vultis 1. 266,
volunt 1. 272; 5. 26; 8. 212,
volebam 7. 346,
volet 1. 650; 5. 689; 8. 337,
voluit 1. 246, 368; 7. 421,
velim 1. 118, 560; 3. 453; 7. 74,
velis 7. 481; 8. 65,
velit 1. 110, 773; 2. 388; 7. 352, 652; 8. 364,
velint 2. 523; 5. 679; 7. 314,
vellem 3. 270; 8. 150, 432,
vellet 1. 67; 3. 241; 5. 372; 7. 262,
vellent 5. 372,
velle 2. 372; 7. 490; 8. 467,
volens 1. 596; 3. 410, 505; 4. 484,
volens (f.) 2. 324; 7. 10.
volucer
volucer 1. 704,
volucris (nom. f.) 7. 398 (K; BGL volucri); 8. 151,
volucri (n.) 2. 524,
volucrem (f.) 2. 587; 7. 186,
volucri 2. 85; 3. 21, 581,
volucri (f.) 5. 428; 7. 398 (BGL; K volucris),
volucrum (m.) 6. 457; 8. 323,
volucres (f.) 2. 516,
subst. f. volucri (dat.) 4. 79,

volucres 4. 570, 633; 6. 506,
volucrum 3. 354; 6. 165,
volucres 4. 492, 579; 6. 647.
volumen
volumina 2. 514 (vid. acc.),
volumina 2. 503, 514 (vid. nom.); 4. 250; 7. 536 (L; KBG lumina).
voluntas
voluntas 1. 506; 4. 158, 471, 476; 6. 463.
voluptas
voluptas 4. 156; 5. 481.
voluto
volutat 2. 567,
volutant 7. 91,
volutans (m.) 5. 263.
volvo
volvit 3. 29, 408; 4. 759; 6. 186; 7. 463,
volvunt 4. 84,
volvet 1. 451,
volvat 4. 716; 7. 169 (G; KBL solvat),
volvite 3. 311; 7. 548,
volvere 1. 829,
volvens 2. 358; 5. 121; 7. 572,
volvens (f.) 7. 196,
volventibus (abl. m.) 1. 505,
volvitur 1. 670,
volvendum (acc. n.) 6. 620.
vomer
vomere 1. 25, 69; 7. 63, 610.
vomo
vomit 1. 688.
Voraptes
Vorapte (voc.) 6. 288.
voro
vorat 8. 332.
votivus
votivo (abl. n.) 2. 487.
votum vid. voveo.
voveo
votas 5. 123,
subst. n. vota 1. 200, 323, 342; 8. 149,
votis 2. 294; 4. 257 (vid. abl.),
vota 1. 685; 2. 377; 3. 415; 4. 538; 5. 172, 616; 7. 29, 273; 8. 48,
votis 2. 145; 3. 601; 4. 257 (vid. dat.), 437, 762; 5. 505.
vox
vox 1. 21, 209, 210, 317; 2. 91, 226, 452; 3. 44, 51, 618; 4. 518, 580; 5. 233, 252, 528; 6. 32, 278; 8. 286 (vox illa G; KB vexilla; L vox alta),
vocis 2. 455; 3. 464,
vocem 2. 200; 3. 245; 4. 49; 5. 600; 7. 78, 155, 373 (vocemque . . . paventem BGL; K pavens . . . oscula miscet),
voce 2. 167, 274; 4. 32, 42, 70; 5. 37, 672; 6. 212, 646; 7. 434,
voces 2. 241; 3. 405; 7. 308,
vocibus 7. 419; 8. 49, 400,
voces 1. 257, 504; 2. 210, 259, 321; 3. 602; 4. 24, 292; 5. 16; 6. 496; 7. 32, 237, 269, 299, 347, 388, 412, 497; 8. 362,
vocibus 1. 302; 2. 126; 7. 256, 384, 402; 8. 304.

Vulcanius
 Vulcanius 4. 686,
 Vulcania (nom. f.) 2. 78; 4. 440.
Vulcanus
 Vulcani 2. 336,
 Vulcanum 2. 88; 6. 433.
vulgo
 vulgat 3. 703 (B; KG vulgi; L fulgit),
 vulgabat 6. 10,
 vulgavere 4. 420,
 vulgatum (m.) 5. 74,
 vulgata (acc.) 7. 277.
vulgus
 vulgus 3. 267,
 vulgi 3. 703 (KG; B vulgat; L fulgit);
 4. 158; 5. 264, 270,
 vulgus 1. 761.
vulnificus
 vulnifico (abl. n.) 1. 420.
vulnus (volnus)
 vulnus 3. 197; 6. 653,
 vulnus 3. 154; 6. 275,
 vulnere 1. 525; 3. 192; 4. 184, 307; 5.
 136; 6. 65, 199, 247,
 vulnera 1. 220, 723; 2. 234; 6. 541,
 vulnera 1. 480, 836; 4. 332; 6. 59, 193,
 520,
 volnera (acc.) 3. 279; 6. 75.
vultur
 vultur 7. 359,
 vulturis 4. 69.

vultus
 vultus (nom.) 2. 66; 3. 578; 6. 708, 760
 (BGL; K vultum); 7. 541,
 vultum 1. 39, 419; 6. 760 (K; BGL vul-
 tus); 7. 155,
 vultu 3. 370; 4. 60, 359; 5. 519, 570
 (BGL; K cultu); 6. 175, 584, 622; 7.
 292, 407, 575; 8. 164,
 vultus (acc.) 1. 368, 390, 738; 2. 608;
 3. 150, 288, 343, 507, 532; 4. 634; 5. 85;
 6. 662; 7. 11, 32, 105, 191, 390, 416, 514;
 8. 237, 333.
Zacorus
 Zacorum 6. 554.
Zelys
 Zelyn 3. 152.
Zephyrus
 Zephyrus 1. 611,
 Zephyrum 1. 350,
 Zephyris 1. 190,
 Zephyros 1. 686,
 Zephyris 1. 640.
zephyrus
 zephyri (nom.) 3. 92. 364,
 zephyros 2. 372.
Zetes
 Zetes 1. 469; 4. 465, 466,
 Zetem 6. 572.
zona
 zona (nom.) 1. 516.